ISBN 978-1-330-06705-5
PIBN 10017393

This book is a reproduction of an important historical work. Forgotten Books uses
state-of-the-art technology to digitally reconstruct the work, preserving the original format
whilst repairing imperfections present in the aged copy. In rare cases, an imperfection in
the original, such as a blemish or missing page, may be replicated in our edition. We do,
however, repair the vast majority of imperfections successfully; any imperfections that
remain are intentionally left to preserve the state of such historical works.

1 MONTH OF
FREE
READING

at
www.ForgottenBooks.com

By purchasing this book you are eligible for one month membership to ForgottenBooks.com, giving you unlimited access to our entire collection of over 1,000,000 titles via our web site and mobile apps.

To claim your free month visit:
www.forgottenbooks.com/free17393

PENOLOGICAL

. AND

PREVENTIVE PRINCIPLES.

PENOLOGICAL

AND

REVENTIVE PRINCIPLES,

WITH SPECIAL REFERENCE TO

EUROPE AND AMERICA,

AND TO

CRIME, PAUPERISM, AND THEIR PREVENTION;
PRISONS AND THEIR SUBSTITUTES;
HABITUAL OFFENDERS;
CONDITIONAL LIBERATION;
SENTENCES;
CAPITAL PUNISHMENT·
INTEMPERANCE;
PROSTITUTION;
NEGLECTED YOUTH;
EDUCATION;
POLICE.

BY

WILLIAM TALLACK,

SECRETARY OF THE HOWARD ASSOCIATION, LONDON.

Second and Enlarged Edition.

"The lessening of the crime of a country is an object worthy of the best thoughts and the best efforts of our best men."—GENERAL BRINKERHOFF (U.S.A.).

LONDON:
PUBLISHED BY WERTHEIMER, LEA & CO.,
CIRCUS PLACE. LONDON WALL, E.C.
1896.

Price 8s.

LONDON:
PRINTED BY WERTHEIMER, LEA AND CO.,
CIRCUS PLACE, LONDON WALL.

INSCRIBED, WITH ESTEEM,

TO

FRANCIS PEEK,

CHAIRMAN OF THE COMMITTEE OF
THE HOWARD ASSOCIATION.

PREFACE TO THE FIRST EDITION.

THE familiar proverb "Who shall decide, when doctors disagree?" applies, with much force, to the complex questions involved in the treatment and prevention of Crime, and to the kindred difficulties in the diminution of Vice and Pauperism. The writer of the following pages has often had occasion to remember that proverb, when listening to the varying experiences and divergent opinions of practical men, whose prolonged official careers entitled the views of each of them to respectful consideration. And in many visits to Prisons, Reformatories, Workhouses, and other public Institutions, at home and abroad, he has observed a corresponding diversity in the modes of management. But notwithstanding such differences, both of opinion and of practice, there may be noticed a preponderance of experience in certain directions; and it is the special design of this book to render aid in the recognition of these converging lines and approximating conclusions.

Through the writer's position, as Secretary of the Howard Association,* for thirty years, he has been brought into connection, either personally or by correspondence, not only with the officers of penal and reformatory insti-

---

* The HOWARD ASSOCIATION was instituted, in London, in 1866, for the Promotion of the best Methods of the Treatment and Prevention of Crime.

tutions, but also with many other authorities, in regard to the questions here considered. The numerous references which he has made to the opinions of such persons, may be expected to possess an interest for thoughtful and practical minds.

This book relates more to present and prospective requirements, and to principles of permanent validity, than to the history of systems and conditions now out of date. The author hopes that it will commend itself to the approval of persons who are practically engaged in efforts to diminish Crime, Vice, and Pauperism, for whose help and service it is chiefly designed. He is not acquainted with any other similar work which is so specially devoted to the exposition of *comprehensive and preventive principles*, as illustrated and supported by recent general experiences, on both sides of the Atlantic. The writer may further remark that he has earnestly endeavoured to exercise *impartiality*, in his treatment of the various vexed questions upon which he has entered.

He is quite aware that, on several points, he has ventured to differ from the views entertained by some persons of sincerely philanthropic intentions; but in these matters, the practical testimony of facts must constitute the final ground of decision.

Perhaps the frequent reference made, in this book, to the influence of Christianity, may be deemed irrelevant, by certain readers. The validity, or otherwise, of such an objection, depends upon the authority which, in matters of Penology and general Philanthropy, is to be attributed to the Gospel of Christ. This, in the opinion of the most successful leaders of beneficent effort, including John

Howard and innumerable others, is not an incidental, or secondary, but a primary one. To that fundamental principle, in particular, the writer has sought to render humble homage.

The Committee of the Howard Association have encouraged the preparation and issue of this work; but they must not be considered responsible for all its conclusions. Even these gentlemen have not always been able to arrive at absolute unanimity, in reference to some subjects treated of in its pages. But the Author believes that the work, in general, will meet with the approval of these, his esteemed friends and colleagues.

PREFACE TO THE SECOND EDITION.

Seven years having passed, since the publication of the First Edition, which has been exhausted, the Publishers wrote to the Author as follows:—"We have had repeated inquiries, of late, for copies of your 'Penological Principles,' which seems to be generally regarded as the standard work on the subject. Do you not think it would be well to consider the desirability of preparing a Second Edition?" The Committee of the Howard Association having also encouraged a fresh issue of the book, the Author has now revised and enlarged it. New chapters have been added on SENTENCES, CAPITAL PUNISHMENT, PAUPERISM, INTEMPERANCE, PROSTITUTION, SOCIAL CRIMES, etc., whilst some omissions have also been made. The Author has **again** gratefully to acknowledge the aid he has received, in the final revision of both Editions, from his Wife, to whom also, he is indebted for various useful suggestions.

It has been very gratifying to him that the book has met with such decided welcome and approval, from influential and official persons in all parts of the world, and from the conductors of the Press.

September, 1895.

CONTENTS.

PENOLOGICAL AND PREVENTIVE PRINCIPLES.

CHAPTER I.

PRINCIPLES ESSENTIAL FOR DIMINISHING CRIME AND PAUPERISM.

The Importance of Principle in General.

PRINCIPLES are the sources of rivers of influence, the seeds and roots of growth, the causes of effects, the determining forces of development. They are, or should be, the *first* things to be attended to, whether in religion, politics or social progress. But how often and extensively they are neglected, both by administrators and communities!

If a child tries to destroy the weeds in his garden, merely by cutting off their tops, instead of pulling up their roots, he is not more unwise than the legislator who seeks to get rid of crime and pauperism, by modes of action which do not diminish their causes.

Thus Crime chiefly arises from ignorance and the absence of virtuous education. Yet, for ages, the almost sole reliance of Governments, for its repression, was punishment for the effects of these privations, instead of preventing the results, by supplying or facilitating a good training.

And now, when people are more awakened to the

B

value of such reformatory influences, they are still too generally unobservant of the practical principle, that criminals detained in association must, of necessity, further corrupt each other. For, in the majority of modern prisons, both in America and Europe, the inmates are grouped in gangs or companies, instead of being carefully and continuously separated, whilst, at the same time, they are too often as unwisely debarred from visitation likely to benefit them. In ordinary life in the community, and under natural conditions, bad persons are at least controlled in considerable degree by the influence of the virtuous; whereas the collected criminality in a jail concentrates and intensifies evil influences and powerfully neutralizes good ones. Hence it is not to be wondered at, that in certain countries, notwithstanding the establishment of so-called "reformatory" prisons or kindred institutions, in which a chief essential for reform is thus neglected, there has been observed a serious collateral increase of crime. It is just as sensible to attempt to cleanse linen by washing it in muddy water, as to expect to reform criminals in daily association with each other.

The great Swedish statesman who exclaimed "With how little wisdom the world is governed!" had his chief justification for such a conclusion, in the very frequent neglect of principles, on the part of rulers. And still, how numerous are the legislators, councillors and editors, who, from the same cause, and in various places, hinder instead of aiding social progress.

First.—The Adaptation of Means to the Desired Object.

In connection with efforts for the prevention, or diminution of Crime and Pauperism, it is especially observable that the claims and counsels which beset the path of the reformer are so various that, in the *first* place, constant vigilance is needful THAT THE PROPOSED MEANS OF

RESTRICTING SOCIAL MALADIES DO NOT BECOME ENCOURAGE-
MENTS OF THE VERY EVILS TO BE REPRESSED.

That special condition of philanthropic success, the combination of a hard head with a warm heart, is essential
for the discriminating selection of the right means for the
attainment of requisite objects, and for the continual
application of the rigid TEST OF PROVED RESULTS. It is a
condition habitually lacking amongst the mischievous class
of indolently sentimental persons, whilst it characterises
true philanthropists, such as JOHN HOWARD and GEORGE
PEABODY, both of whom combined with their benevolent
feelings a business-like hard-headedness and a constant
regard to the logic of facts and results.

PAUPERISM AND THIS PRINCIPLE.

In reference to Pauperism, general experience still justifies
a persevering reiteration of the simple but wholesome
truism that if money, or other relief, be given, unconditionally, to mendicants or the needy, in such a way as to
obviate motives to self-help, or to prevent exertion, more
harm than good ensues, and the very spirit of pauperism is
further developed and strengthened. It has often happened that benevolently intentioned persons have rendered
themselves absolute nuisances to the parishes in which they
reside, by their profuse bestowment of alms upon all the
beggars who apply at their houses. They become attractive centres for laziness and imposture. Thus their neighbours suffer greatly from the vice and drunkenness produced by these unwise almoners. Not such was the true
charity of St. Peter, who with strengthening help, and
with the animating words, " Rise up and walk," enabled
the lame man, at the gate of the Temple, thenceforth to
exert himself. He infused real power into him, and removed the source of his impotence and inactivity. St.
Peter's miraculous gifts are no longer available; but the
principle and the lesson inculcated, remain. With few

exceptions, habitual mendicants are vicious or criminal impostors. Investigation proves this in nineteen cases out of every twenty. But the public in general will not, or cannot, take the trouble of such investigation.

Vagrants often impudently proclaim their detestation of self-supporting industry. One of this tribe begged money of a lady, "to save him from something he very much dreaded." She gave him half-a-crown, and inquired, "Now, my poor fellow, what have I saved you from?" The answer was scoffingly returned, "From being obliged to go and work to-day." Another mendicant made reply to an offer of occupation, "No; not so long as I can get twelve shillings a day and a skinful, by begging; it's only fools and horses that work."

Excessive Resort to Institutions.

Not only is there a danger of frustrating the desired object by an unwise treatment of individual cases of mendicancy or distress, but a greater peril consists in the wholesale discouragement of self-exertion on the part of the destitute or indolent, as classes, by such mere impulsive relief, and by the relaxation of their natural responsibilities, as parents, in regard to their offspring, by similar spurious charity, producing really cruel injury on a larger scale.

There are many well-meaning persons and Societies, especially in London, New York, and other cities, who are continually exclaiming, by their practice, "Look at these thousands and myriads of neglected children and destitute adults. Fellow Christians, build institutions for all these; pour out your money upon them more abundantly; offer them food, clothing, shelter, training, more willingly; invite and welcome them to share your generosity!" To a certain extent, this liberality may be beneficial; but if carried out generally, it may become an influence working incalculable mischief, both to its objects and to the community. Even under the guise of "Christianity" it may foster a dishonest selfishness. It weakens, at its very source, the sense of parental responsibility. It tends to remove the God-imposed duty of self-help and self-development from the poor. It actually impoverishes them by the very "gifts" thrust upon them; and, like the widening circles upon a pond, into which a stone has been thrown, it extends its influence to surrounding myriads. The numerous improvident and intemperate persons, who will never do anything for themselves what others can be induced to do for them, are thus increased in manifold degree. If professing Christians exclaim, "Bring your children in thousands to us, and we will place them in institutions at our expense, and relieve you of all responsibility," of course the thousands are forthcoming, and tens of thousands more soon follow. Hence, we see some of the rapidly increasing burdens upon the tax-payers of Christendom, with a very disproportionate benefit as to. the objects desired. The moral strengthening, or the development of personal ability, is the primary essential of genuine charity; which being neglected, or weakened, certain failure results. As an able writer remarks, "The help which makes people helpless, is worse than no help at all."

For example, in 1875, a "Children's Law" was enacted in NEW YORK, which authorised the magistrates to commit destitute children to the various private and public institutions of the district, and to order the payment of two dollars a-week, for each child, out of the taxes; and what has been the actual result of this measure? It has been followed by a vast and continuous increase of such dependent children, far out of proportion to the increase of population. So much for the mischievous effects of spurious "charity," the "institution craze," and the foolish undertaking to remove from parents their natural responsibilities, instead of enforcing their better fulfilment. Even in Great

Britain, it is a fact not to be necessarily assumed as satisfactory, that the number of children in certified INDUSTRIAL
SCHOOLS and " REFORMATORIES " have greatly increased of
late years.   Their parents or friends, meanwhile, have only
paid about one shilling in the pound per annum, on the
average, towards their support.

It is surprising that the great young Republic of the
New World has failed to profit by the social experience
in this respect, of the old Continent.   In a well-written
exposition of the abuse of public Institutions, especially
in California, by Mr. EDMOND T. DOOLEY, Superintendent
of a Boys' and Girls' Aid Society, he remarked : " The
great cities of our Continent are under the control
of political ' bosses ' and their grog-shop following.   If
we are not absolutely ruled by the criminal classes, the
character of our political and social life is certainly
very much modified by the baser elements of our
people.   Has not New York City alone suffered infinitely
more from its ' boodle aldermen ' than all that the old
Colonies ever endured from English oppression ? "   This
impartial American testimony is very noteworthy.
Mr. Dooley also complained that, in California, the criminal
and corrupt element had hitherto successfully checked the
efforts put forth by the wiser minority of the people to
obtain legislative reforms designed to bring about an effective and economical mode of dealing with the pauperism
and crime which had so rapidly increased in that State.   It
was shown that out of every 1,000 children supported in
Californian institutions, at the public expense, at least 600
could be cared for by their own parents and relatives, and
further, that most of these establishments and also the
prisons, were still increasing and perpetuating the evils
they were ostensibly presumed to check.   The consequence
had ensued that the ratio of State-supported " dependent "
children was more than twelve times greater in California
than in Michigan, in proportion to the respective popu-

lations of the two States. The criminality of the former was also vastly greater than that of the latter.

For Michigan is a wiser State, in reference to its treatment of pauperism. It aims primarily at prevention, and especially in regard to the young. It has taken under State control the really destitute children, in limited number, if free from crime and disease, in order to undergo two educational processes; firstly, a preparatory training in a public school, at Coldwater, for rather less than one year on the average; and, secondly, in a subsequent distribution amongst the farmers and cottagers all over the State. This is, in fact, a general process of boarding-out, or of systematically providing family instead of institutional life for actually destitute children. The State retains its sole and absolute control over such young persons until twenty-one years of age, and also provides for the oversight and visitation of each one placed out. The result is that, during a recent period of years, the paupers in the poor-houses of Michigan only increased 20 per cent., whilst the general population increased 40 per cent.

Minnesota, Wisconsin, and Rhode Island have adopted a similar system, with great advantage. Whereas, in Indiana, with a population just the same as that of Michigan. the pauper and dependent children of the State are nearly ten times as many as in the latter State, owing to a comparative absence of arrangements to prevent or check the increase of this class.

It may be remarked, in this connection, that there is occasionally to be noticed in Refuges and Asylums for destitute children, a well-meant abundance of comforts, as in the dietary, furniture, pictures, and carpets. But even these apparently reasonable indulgences are not without their dangers. If too freely lavished, they tend to encourage parental improvidence and neglect. Because it is not real beneficence to render the condition of the children of idle, dishonest, and profligate parents more

enviable than that of the offspring of the hard-working
and virtuous poor of the vicinity. The privileges of the
honest toilers should not be less than those of vicious
people. It is not benevolence, but wasteful mischief, which
so administers individual or public gifts, or institutions, as
to discourage industry and perpetuate indolence amongst
surrounding multitudes. The more that is given in such
a way, the more there will have to be given, as the evil is
increased.

And further, it is possible to inflict real injury upon the
poor children themselves, who may be crowded into the
artificial and dependent conditions of institutional, as
distinguished from healthy family life, or training in ordinary separate self-exertion, with a more limited but a
more judicious measure of assistance from without, when
necessary. An American journal recently mentioned an
incident not unsuggestive on this point. A little girl
from a city home was invited to visit some friends in
the country. In their garden she was delighted with a
tame robin, that was a great favourite with the family.
But the child's interest in the bird made her exclaim,
"Poor little robin! it has got no cage." She had no idea
of thoroughly happy bird-life, apart from a cage. Similarly
many good people appear to limit their views of juvenile
training to mere institutional "cages."

The most liberally supported gratuitous Homes, Reformatories, Industrial Schools, Aid Societies, and Foundling
Hospitals, if too extensively provided, for the purpose of
taking neglected children off the hands of drunken, or
vicious, or improvident parents, may become the very
means of doing more harm than good, both to the children
and parents. For, by the process of virtually rewarding
parental neglect, that vice is of course encouraged and
increased. Wherever practicable, the authorities should
rather punish such parents, by fining or imprisoning
them, or at least deprive them of all further control

over their offspring, so as to prevent any future injury to the latter.

This Principle in Regard to the Essential Element of Non-attractiveness.

One of the most insidious, and at the same time, one of the most unwise modes of dealing with Poverty and Vagrancy, consists in the offer of relief, especially "outdoor relief," under any such terms as to render the condition of the publicly-supported pauper an easier and more enviable one than that of the honest toiler. The argument is often raised, by ignorant speakers and writers, "Inasmuch as a pauper, inside a workhouse, costs, on the average, including the expense of the officers, and the outlay on buildings, from ten to fifteen shillings a week, or more, how much less burdensome to the community it would be to allow such persons a payment of eight or ten shillings at their own homes." This specious plea overlooks the important fact that if relief could be generally obtained, on too easy terms, without the needful checks, the number of applicants would speedily increase in a manifold proportion. Or, for every thousand pounds now devoted to the maintenance of the public poor, five or ten times as much would be required from the ratepayers, in consequence of extended and easy outdoor relief. It is, however, to be noted that in some instances, especially in America, even workhouses themselves have been rendered mischievously attractive to the lazy and improvident.

It is a primary principle, for the diminution of Paupers and Vagrants, that the board and lodging supplied to them by the community shall not be more comfortable on the whole, than that of the ordinary labourer; and also that any work which may be done by them shall be paid for at a decidedly lower rate than the average wages given by employers in the neighbourhood. Such a course is a simple practical essential. Any other plan is eventually found to be a costly mistake.

It has repeatedly occurred that when, in some season of special industrial depression, multitudes of persons have clamoured for relief, or for occupation on public works, and have been responded to by the offer of help, under wise conditions, and with due checks against laziness, the number of applicants has at once wonderfully diminished. In some of the largest towns in England, on such occasions, the local authorities have strictly confined their relief to offers of reception into the workhouse, with its discipline of classification, restraint, cleanliness, temperance and early rising. This condition, whilst furnishing a universally accessible refuge from starvation, has promptly sufficed to reduce the thousands of claimants to as many hundreds, or even scores. Again, in other cases, the demands for employment on public works have been granted, by finding occupation at road-making, stone-breaking, and other such industry, at a rate of wages sufficient to provide absolutely necessary sustenance, but with decidedly less than the average local pay for similar labour in the open market. This prudent course has also been found very efficacious in speedily reducing the ranks of the ostensible seekers for work.

True "Giving" is not Taking Away.

The Scriptural injunction, "Give to him that asketh thee," should always be interpreted and acted upon in connection with common sense and with other Biblical precepts, such as "Blessed is he that *considereth* the poor," and, "If any will not labour, neither should he eat." For the indolence of mere inconsiderate alms, especially when bestowed on an habitual applicant, does not really "give." On the contrary, it *takes away* his incentives to industry and self-help. It is worse than useless; it inflicts cruel injury, whereas true charity ever seeks to impart some moral aid, some encouragement to exertion and elevation, Private benevolence can always find abundant objects for its exercise in the relief of the sick, the maimed, the blind, and orphans. But the unknown, or the apparently professional mendicants, are best dealt with by official organisation in each locality. And it is a material aid to both the private and the official dealing with destitution, to adopt, as far as possible, the principle also of the *subdivision of districts,* as strongly recommended by Dr. Chalmers and others.

The Christian Church and Christian work are, after all, the greatest instruments of real charity, and comparatively little can be done without them. The moral restraints, the abiding and grateful love to the Redeemer, which are afforded by Christianity, are the highest aids to beneficence. When the Apostle, himself destitute of silver or gold, said to the beggar, " In the name of Jesus Christ, of Nazareth, rise up and walk," he manifested the best combination of assistance, namely, Divine help, fellow-help, and stimulus to self-help. It is always the largest charity which unites the three. Our Saviour, who went about doing good, mainly manifested His beneficence by such modes, and especially by removing the hindrances to self-help, as by giving sight to the blind, by healing the diseased, and by restoring the cripples and the paralytic. Similarly, the best modern charity enables the poor to " rise up," by removing the degrading influences of insanitary conditions, overcrowded dwellings, bad drainage, ignorance, and extreme temptations to intemperance and other vices.

Efficient help to a poor person consists in such modes of benevolence as may be comparable to placing a staff in his hand, rather than a crutch under his arm, to cause him to lean idly on for external support. The Dutch people, in various ways, exemplify a willingness to hand a temporary staff to the poor ; but none are more judiciously jealous of providing permanent " crutches " for this class. Hence, in Holland, where the benevolence of the Churches is specially facilitated by the State, pauperism has been more effec-

tually kept within bounds than perhaps in any other
country.

But there is *no panacea* for diminishing Pauperism. It
must be dealt with in a variety of ways, and with many
modes of patient adaptation of means to end. The Scriptural motto, " Here a little and there a little," is eminently
characteristic of the process and its modes. Apparently
indirect means of diminishing pauperism are often incomparably more effectual than other forms of assistance.
They tend to relieve present necessities, and also to obviate
their recurrence. And this latter point is of immense
importance. For if it is desired to empty a cistern, where
there is a steady inflow, the cessation of that supply must
somehow be first effected.

Most instructive are the following words by a North-
amptonshire Rector, the Rev. W. BURY :—" The parson who
establishes a co-operative store in a country village, has
done more for his parish than if he had spent all his living
in ' charity ' so-called. Good and pleasant cottages, at fair
and not fictitiously low rents, are more improving and
really helpful, than miles of flannel and rivers of soup and
wine. Sanitary and Education Acts, properly administered,
advance the interests of the poor a thousandfold more than
the good intentions of ' pious founders,' however piously
carried out. There can be no manner of doubt that the
better administration of Poor Law relief, in the Union to
which I belong, by means of which the proportion of
paupers to population has been reduced from 1 in 12 to
1 in 60, has done more for the labourer in ten years' time
than all the charities, coal-clubs, doles and almsgiving
which have flowed for centuries from all the Halls and
Rectories within the district."

PRISONS AND THE OPERATION OF THIS PRINCIPLE.

The same general principle of removing inducements to
evil, from agencies ostensibly meant to prevent it, is also

eminently necessary in regard to Prisons. If their discipline is rendered lax and indulgent, then the objects proposed are missed. Violence and fraud are encouraged, evil-doers are not intimidated, and cruel injuries to the weak and unprotected are abundantly occasioned through a neglect of the severity necessary for repression.

Hence there is a certain sense in which some of those prisons which are sometimes styled the "best," may be really inferior, in so far as the main objects of imprisonment are concerned. For instance, it was remarked by an officer of great observation, that the now abandoned prison-farm of Lusk, near Dublin, was rendered so agreeable to the inmates that, on the expiration of their terms, "they almost had to be kicked out." The writer of this book was once at Lusk, when a resident in the neighbourhood spoke to him of the total absence of walls and high hedges, and said, "The convicts are better off in there than they would be outside; so they do not care to escape." Again, some of the inmates of a greatly praised Refuge for criminal women were found to be very unwilling to leave it; and this was made a matter for boasting by the Superintendent. Also at a female convict establishment near London, and at an American State prison for women (considered to be a model establishment of the kind), such remarks as these have often been heard from the prisoners —"Yes, ma'am, I'm very comfortable here; very comfortable indeed. Quite contented here." But ought it ever to be the case that any criminal should feel perfectly contented with prison life?

Failure especially ensues, if prisoners are associated in pleasant but corrupting companionship, in their workshops, or in mutually contaminating gangs in the open air. Prison life being thus divested of most of its rigour, evil is increased and perpetuated. Temptation is intensified. Reformation is prevented.

A Second Essential.

A second important principle for diminishing Pauperism and Crime is THE NECESSITY OF AVOIDING THE DIVORCE OF ELEMENTS WHICH SHOULD ALWAYS BE HELD IN UNION.

Especially in relation to Criminals, the threefold combination of Prevention, Repression and Reformation, needs to be maintained in unintermitting activity.

So far as the treatment of Crime is concerned, there is probably no country in the world which has so successfully sought to secure this tri-unity as Great Britain, especially of late years; although it is not for a moment to be assumed that she has attained perfection. But she has set an honourable example of efforts to prevent crime, by greatly-increased popular Evangelisation on the part of all the Churches, and especially by such extremely valuable organisations as the London City Mission and many other similar bodies; also by elaborate systems of Education, both denominational and secular, together with various arrangements designed for the rescue and training of neglected or vicious youth; whilst, for Repression, she has done much to infuse a moderate but merciful severity into her prison system. And for Reformation, she has, both by State and private benevolence, encouraged the supplementary, or rather complementary, operations of Discharged Prisoners' Aid Societies and of a vigilant and wisely administered Supervision of conditionally-released convicts. As a consequence, there has been, of late years, a marked diminution of various crimes in Great Britain.

But in most countries, one or another element of the triad in question has been practically neglected. For example, in the northern United States, considerable and partially-successful efforts, at least in certain localities, have been made to prevent crime by extensive efforts at popular evangelisation. Much good has thus resulted, but the benefit would have been greatly increased if these labours had had the collateral assistance of a more rigorous repression of wilful and brutal offenders. But the latter essential has, for the most part, been absent. In the Southern States the crime of murder has been exceedingly prevalent. The gallows and lynch-law have both been called into requisition with frequency, but the main and obvious element of prevention has been practically ignored, inasmuch as the frequent carrying of arms, such as the pistol and bowie-knife, by private persons, has been. permitted, or approved by popular custom. Italy and Spain have had the same failure, as to the non-prevention of murders, and from a similar cause.

In Belgium a uniform and largely efficient system of cellular prison discipline has been established. Yet the prevention of crime *before* imprisonment, and the oversight of discharged prisoners, have both been in too considerable degree neglected. Hence, an undue proportion of relapses and re-convictions has resulted. Drunkenness also and vice have been increased, until very recently, by their excessive encouragement in that Kingdom. But it. is gratifying to find that some efforts at reform are being made by the Belgian people.

Holland, Switzerland, and Scandinavia have, like Great Britain, though in less degree, devoted much attention to the above triad, and with considerable success. Few other nations have consistently cultivated these three elements in active collateral development. Their systems rather resemble unfinished and unroofed edifices.

Not only each of the above-named three essentials, but especially the first in order, Prevention, needs to be increasingly regarded. Attempts at Repression by deterrence only, by mere penalty or imprisonment, have often received an exaggerated amount of reliance. An efficient and vigilant Police establishment, together with like agencies, has done more, in Great Britain for example, to check the horse-stealings, highway robberies, and other numerous crimes formerly punished with death, than all the gibbets and gallows of those times.

Similarly, as to Red Republicanism, Nihilism, and other forms of Anarchy, the wise freedom of Great Britain, America, Holland and Scandinavia, has been much more efficacious and preventive than the guillotine, or the dungeons, of other lands.

Prevention, Repression, Reformation—these have ever to be simultaneously maintained, and especially the first, in active vigour and with comprehensive application.

As to PREVENTION, it has various departments, all requiring equal vigilance. Such are the diminution of Intemperance, of Over-crowding, of Ignorance, of Idleness, and of Ungodliness. How very limited must be the efficacy of mere repression, or punishment, amongst the squalid multitudes of over-crowded Naples, or the uneducated masses and infidel or superstitious populations of large districts in various countries? The axe must be laid to the *roots* of the tree of evil. The streams of vice must be cleansed at their *sources*. The outbreaks of violence, or the external manifestations of crime and sin, need to be checked at the centres of vitality, and in the very inmost motives of their activity. Otherwise failure is certain to ensue.

In proportion as any of these essential elements of safety and progress are neglected, the whole social system suffers. The strength of a chain is measured by that of each separate link, or even of the weakest one. In like manner, the absence of any one important reform or precaution, mischievously restricts the good efforts already put forth in other departments. The activity of each has to be maintained, and the divorce of one from the other avoided.

Whilst the element of Repression, or Deterrence, is, in its due place and proportion, an indispensable condition for safety, it is of great importance to remember, in practice,

that it is a minor influence in comparison with PREVEN-
TION. Not only is the latter proverbially better than
cure, but it is also greatly superior to forcible repression.
And whilst it would be both untrue and unwise to assert
that "Force is no remedy" for social evils, it should only
be regarded as a minor and altogether subordinate auxi-
liary for their diminution. Yet one of the greatest hindrances to the deliverance of modern communities from
two of the most pernicious maladies with which they are
plagued—namely, PROSTITUTION and INTEMPERANCE—consists in the greatly exaggerated estimate of the power of
mere force, as a means of prevention, which is entertained
by many philanthropic leaders of opinion.

PROSTITUTION AND PREVENTION.

It would appear that more than a few of the professed
advocates of public morality have the least faith in the
power of Moral Suasion, if one may judge by their clamour
for the enforcement of social virtue, mainly by the help of
Police, Penalties, and Prisons. As to Prostitution, for
example, many persons seek to deal with it chiefly by
driving the unfortunate women "from pillar to post," and
by urging the police to keep them moving on, and to shut
up their lodgings. In Berlin this kind of policy has been
carried out with special rigour. Thousands of wretched
girls have been locked up; many of them have been
repeatedly arrested, and brothels have been suppressed by
the score. And with what result? With this: that Berlin
remains one of the most immoral cities in Europe—a place
where prostitution is, perhaps, more generally diffused
amongst the households, and scattered over the whole town
and suburbs, than almost anywhere else. And for the very
simple and sufficient reason that the causes and sources of
this vice have there been left comparatively untouched.
The more effectual work of dealing with these deep roots
of the evil, however, requires much patience and distri-

butive individual labour—exertions which some denouncers
of vice find it easy and agreeable to shrink from or neglect.
It is as impossible for any police to suppress or extinguish
vice, by mere force, as it is for a quack doctor to cure
leprosy by covering the diseased limbs with sticking
plaister.

Even the good work of ASYLUMS and REFUGES does not
materially affect the roots and sources of Prostitution.
These institutions may be multiplied indefinitely, whilst at
the same time the vast evil itself may be developing in a
greater ratio than ever.   Again, it does not appear that any
diminution of sexual immorality has resulted in consequence of the great expenditure of money and effort
devoted by some benevolent persons in recent years, in
England, in order to abolish the "CONTAGIOUS DISEASES
ACT." The movement in question was a superficial and
not a radically preventive one.

The effectual means for the diminution of Prostitution
must be looked for only in the *restriction of its chief
causes;* namely in the discouragement of Intemperance,
which is in itself so fruitful a source of vice; in the improvement of the dwellings of the poor—because over-
crowded tenements foster the grossest impurity and even
incest; in the extension of industrial training amongst
girls; and in the reduction of the vast European standing
armies of mostly unmarried men, whose presence in towns
and barracks neccessarily involves a fearful stimulus to
female ruin and degradation; whilst, at the same time,
these armed hosts withdraw from millions of women their
natural protectors and bread-winners.   In their turn, these
great armies can only be dispensed with, in proportion as
statesmen and the peoples are willing to devise means for
the more systematic application of International Law and
Arbitration to the settlement of disputes, rather than by
the sword or brute force.   And yet further, Prostitution
needs for its prevention every possible extension of Reli-

gion, and of the inducements to purity and godliness furnished by the hopes and fears of the Gospel of Christ as preached in its reasonableness and attractiveness. To render men and women indisposed to this and other forms of evil, their *hearts* must be reached, by the love and reverence of God, and by the " powers of the world to come." And, in short, the work of promoting social purity· must always, and chiefly, be based upon a practical recognition of the fundamental truth of that admirable motto of the American theologian, Dr. HORACE BUSHNELL :— " The soul of all improvement is the improvement of the *soul.*"

INTEMPERANCE AND FORCE.

Similarly, as to the huge evil of Intemperance, mere force is, and always must be, but a partial and subordinate means for its prevention. Both in Great Britain and in the United States, drunkenness is an offence which is punishable by imprisonment, and very many thousands of poor inebriates are annually sent to jail. And not only so ; but a large proportion of these have to be re-imprisoned, over and over again. Almost every city can point to unfortunate men and women who have been committed to jail, for drunkenness, more than thirty, sixty, or even a hundred times, in succession, and who still remain undeterred and unreformed by this application of force. Though, even force, if more systematically applied, would have a certain minor proportion of utility in such cases. But far more efficacious, incomparably more successful, are preventive endeavours, by means of the early education of youth in temperate habits and by the exercise of good personal example and moral suasion, together with wisely devised measures for the removal of temptations to inebriety.

When, either in America or Europe. the aid of law and of force has been sought for the diminution of these temptations, some advantage has, however, been gained. In

Maine, Kansas, Iowa, and other States, and also in Canada
and other British Colonies, where either by Prohibitory
Legislation or by the operation of Local Option, the
sale of intoxicants has been more or less limited,
good results have ensued, even although these may
have fallen far short of what had been expected by too
enthusiastic, or too hasty advocates of reform.   It is
the testimony of a multitude of impartial observers that
through the operation of law, in diminishing facilities
for drunkenness in such States, the number of crimes has
greatly decreased, and pauperism and misery have also
been invariably lessened. Fewer jails, fewer police, fewer
accidents, less taxation, and more general happiness
and prosperity, have been the fruits, in many districts,
of these efforts to use law for the removal of the
causes, more than for the punishment of the effects, of
drunkenness.

But it is also to be observed that where the aid of the
legal force has been usefully secured for a time, or in part,
for the prevention of drunkenness, this always depends for
its first success, and wholly for its subsequent maintenance,
upon the amount of Moral Suasion exerted for bringing
about the object in view.

The efficiency of Law and of Force in relation to
drunkenness may probably be best secured by *limiting*,
as far as may be *popularly* possible, the *number* of public-
houses in proportion to the population; in imposing a
heavy taxation upon them; in making *all debts for retailed
liquor irrecoverable* by law; in restricting licenses to the
actual vendors resident upon the premises, and not granting
them to the premises practically in perpetuity; and in
making it an offence severely punishable to sell liquors to
very young persons, or to known habitual drunkards.   The
principle should be secured of "*one man, one license*;" that is
to say, no person should be permitted to own, or hold, more
than one house where alcohol may be sold.   It is through

such reasonable and practical means as these that the powers of compulsion may be safely applied to restrain, *as far as can be popularly done*, the excessive supply of intoxicating drinks.

The liquor traffic mainly depends upon the public, rather than upon the publicans. Until the former are persuaded and willing to restrict their own use, or abuse, of alcohol, they will certainly secure publicans to serve them. The latter are then sure to be found; if not in one way, in another. It is a truism that the demand must be primarily influenced. Then the supply will be also modified. But it is radically unwise to direct attention to the secondary agents, rather than to their masters, the sovereign public. NORWAY, which was formerly one of the most drunken countries in Europe, has of late years become a temperate . nation, or at least comparatively so. The reason is that the sale of alcohol, and the proportion of its vendors, have been placed under the control of the actual general wish of the population in each district.

In Great Britain, of late years, much progress in promoting Temperance has been made by the happy combination of personal example, moral suasion, and an increasing provision (especially upon a profitable and self-supporting basis) of establishments for the sale of non-alcoholic refreshments of good and attractive quality, as distinguished from the slops and rubbish which used to characterise the commissariat department of many, if not most, of the " Temperance Hotels."

But it is needful to notice that even in England, so far as Prohibitory Law has been approximately called into action, it has already developed a pernicious form of evasion. For just in proportion as legislation has attempted the intrinsically excellent object of the prevention of the sale of alcohol during Sundays and after certain hours at night, there have simultaneously started into existence thousands of PRIVATE DRINKING CLUBS, where, without the regulations

and police supervision imposed upon ordinary inns, intoxicating liquors may be indulged in without stint all day
and all night throughout the week. Some of these
" clubs " are quiet and orderly; but unquestionably many,
of them are pests to the neighbourhood. A Middlesex
magistrate described one as a " den of thieves." At
Cardiff, for example, their numbers and their influence
render them a flagrant nuisance. There is nothing
to prevent many of them from becoming the haunts
of the vilest men and women. For instance, at a
certain Midland town, a policeman in plain clothes,
as a private visitor to one of these houses, witnessed in
the back premises, a series of acts of the grossest immorality. On the other hand, clubs where (as in the case
of a very successful and useful one for working Jews and
Jewesses, in East London) the sale of alcoholic liquors
has been prohibited by the managers, have become very
helpful institutions to the happiness and prosperity of the
classes for whom they were established.

It has happened again and again in America, that certain
parties have bargained with the Prohibitionists, " If you
will vote for our men, or for our place-hunters, we will
vote in turn for Prohibition." When such agreements
have been accepted, and some sort of Prohibition measure
carried, in consequence, by nominal " Law," the thousands
who voted, merely on party grounds, have, either willingly
or from sheer indifference, supported the wholesale evasion
and virtual nullification of the legislation in which they had
previously acquiesced. But what is likely to be the popular
respect for, or obedience to " Prohibition " Law, when the
very constables or police appointed to enforce it, are known
freely to indulge in alcohol, and to carry about bottles of
spirits with them ? Yet this appears to be the case in
various places in America. A prohibition advocate mentioned in the British Parliament, as an illustration of
innumerable American " Prohibitionists," a certain New

Englander, who, in answer to a question, replied " Yes, I'm in favour of the Maine Liquor Law; but I'm against its enforcement !"

The danger of gross inconsistency, results from a tendency of Prohibitionists, on both sides of the Atlantic, to enlist in their ranks, as adherents, individuals who, without being abstainers themselves from alcohol, clamour for legal powers and penalties to compel others to become such. Even the " United Kingdom Alliance for the Total Suppression of the Liquor Traffic," receives into its membership people who are not teetotallers, but who demand to be, by law, permitted to prohibit others from drinking liquors which they themselves enjoy and refuse to relinquish ! What can be said for the consistency of such persons ?

In regard to all great moral Reforms, it needs to be repeated :—Force is but a very subordinate remedy, at the best. The law is weak in comparison with the power of the Churches, and the personal example and work of their individual labourers, and a chief reliance on preventive rather than repressive influences. The conditions of advancement in all good movements must still, for the most part, be characterised by the heart-reaching, and often gradual action of the " Kingdom and patience of Jesus Christ." Empirics may point to other modes, but this grand ancient basis of true progress must again and again be returned to. To " overcome evil with good " must always involve, for its chief lines of operation, a recourse to moral and spiritual, rather than to physical, constraints and restraints.

HOPE AND FEAR.

A sacred precept ordains, "What God hath joined together, let not man put asunder." This may be accepted in its relation to the necessity of arrangements, in social and penal systems, for the simultaneous double influence of HOPE and FEAR, of REWARD and PUNISHMENT.

But how often, and how generally, have the elements of hope and reward been neglected, whilst the powers of fear and punishment, valuable as they are, have been too exclusively relied on. Here, again, the avoidance of such divorce needs strict practical regard. The penal systems of Bentham, Maconochie, Barwick Baker, Crofton, Obermaier, Rumford, Ducpetiaux, Suringar, Petersen, Brinkerhof and others, were by no means perfect, but they attained a certain measure of special success, in so far as they gave prominence to the animating forces of reward and hope. In the old fable of the contending wind and sunshine, the warm and genial glow of the latter was found to be much more powerful than the chill violence of the former. Yet, in their respective provinces, both sunshine and wind, as also rewards and punishments, are each necessary.

State and Individual Action.

Another pair of co-ordinate activities which should not be divorced, are those of central and local, of State and individual energy. There is a work for each, which neither, alone, can perform, but which is essential for the community. The main function of the State is to protect and facilitate individual well-doing. Beyond this, its interference is often mischievous. In view of the terrible wars, persecutions, murders, jobbery and waste, which, in almost every age, have characterised Governments, it is obvious that State-action may be as potent for evil as for good. Whereas the influences of religion and morality have at all periods, mainly flowed upon the world through individual action; through the Prophet, the Preacher, the Philanthropist, the Author, the Philosopher, acting either one by one, or in voluntary union, and more often effecting their reforms in spite of the opposition of the State, than by its encouragement. For example, in regard to improvements in Prison Discipline in particular, the chief impulses have originated, in noteworthy degree, with private individuals, such as John Howard, Sarah Martin, Elizabeth Fry, Sir Fowell Buxton, Dr. Wichern, Thomas Eddy, and many other good men and women, whose influence has stimulated official and legislative activity.

There is a peculiar and *almost inevitable tendency to indolence and inertia in State functionaries as such*, unless quickened by the constant vigilance and criticism of the public, and by private rivalry. The temptation is extreme, on the part of Government officials, in every land, just to enjoy their honours and draw their salaries, with as little exertion as possible, outside the easy beaten tracks and the grooves of precedent.

On the other hand, the best intentioned efforts of individual and merely local reformers, are apt to remain imperfect, or unsystematic, for want of that regulating assistance and encouragement, which it is in the special power of the State, or central Government, to furnish.

Individual efforts must necessarily be slow and gradual in their operation. Hence they are apt to be unduly despised and under-estimated by the public, who, in their impatience, cry out for the more hasty action of Governments. But it has been repeatedly observed that as the Lord Jesus Christ sent out His disciples, two and two, on foot, to discharge their mission in humble perseverance, so, in all subsequent ages, the great bulk and mass of philanthropic, or religious work, has had to be wrought out, in similarly patient detail, and as at a footpace. Nevertheless, great results have followed the aggregate of such efforts; works often comparable, in magnitude, to the vast coral reefs, wrought, grain by grain, by the insects of the deep. The powers of States and Governments are but weak for the accomplishment of those universally essential moral reforms, which require, for their success, the persistent labour of individual effort and personal virtues.

Physical force can check, or temporarily restrain, various

forms of evil ; but sometimes at the cost of rendering them still more intense and permanent. It is the force of gentleness, of patience, of persuasion, and of religion, which can radically destroy wicked dispositions and feelings. But this is by far the more arduous work.

A Third Great Principle.

Thirdly AN EVER VIGILANT HESITATION AS TO THE ACCEPTANCE OF FASHIONABLE DOGMAS OR POPULAR CONCLUSIONS, IS REQUISITE.

The *Vox populi* is by no means necessarily the *Vox Dei*, in philanthropic and penal matters, any more than in general politics. Sometimes it is the very reverse. Neither are the ideas in favour amongst fashionable and influential circles, therefore infallible. Nor does truth necessarily dwell amongst majorities ; on the contrary, it is often to be found on the side of unpopular minorities.

As Dante says :—

> " Full often bends,
> Current opinion in the false direction,
> And then the feelings bind the intellect."

Modern experience has proved that republics and democratic majorities are just as ready as arbitrary kings, to rush into foolish wars, or to insist upon unwise legislation, to the detriment of the community.

The jocular monarch, Charles II., of England, is said to have propounded, with apparent seriousness, before the philosophers of the " Royal Society," the question, " Why is it that a dead fish is heavier than a living one ? " Some of these sages, hastily assuming that a monarch's dictum, even on science, must be true, adduced various reasons which appeared to them to afford a solution of the difficulty. At length a shrewder thinker quietly asked, " But is it actually the case, your Majesty, that a dead fish is the heavier ? " "Ah, my friend," replied the king, " now you are on the right track." Similarly, both current popular assumptions, and also Ministerial or Parliamentary Statements, and even the statistical reports emanating from Government and State Departments, should always be critically examined, if the attainment of truth is desired; for even these are often apt to mislead.

There are various widely accepted conclusions which only need real investigation, in order to prove their un-wisdom; as, for instance, the too generally supported axiom that mere secular instruction mainly constitutes Education. There is no doubt but that Education, in its true meaning, as including especially the patient training to habits, not only of study, but also of industry, of morality, and of godliness, is a most essential and efficient means of promoting the happiness of the people, and preventing vice, crime, and pauperism. But instruc-tion in reading, writing, arithmetic and so forth, if unaccompanied by due attention to the other constituent parts of education, may develop the ignorant and com-paratively harmless idler into the cunning and dangerous thief, or defrauder. It has been made a matter of com-plaint, by some of the highest police authorities in Great Britain, that since the establishment of public compulsory "Board School" teaching, there has been created a more dangerous and unmanageable type of juvenile criminals than formerly. It is at the same time, admitted that inasmuch as, in many of these schools, the religious and moral elements have not been lost sight of, a large measure of good has resulted. The statistics of German and American prisons prove that a very general diffusion of secular instruction amongst the populations, is found in connection with a great increase in the number of offences and imprisonments. "Knowledge is power" — for evil, as well as for good. The Devil and his instruments are characterised by intelligence; though it is utterly perverted in its objects.

CURRENT POPULAR ERRORS AS TO IMPRISONMENT, AND PRISON LABOUR.

The subject of Prisons, also, is a matter on which prevalent official and popular conclusions require critical examination. The special efficacy of prolonged imprisonments, as a means of repressing crime, has been enormously over-estimated, in most countries, and not least in England. Yet it can be shown that more efficient means of diminishing offences are to be found, in a combination of magisterial and philanthropic activity, with a vigilant but merciful Police Supervision. By such a course, the county of Gloucester was able, in a period of forty years, to abolish six out of its seven jails, and to reduce its daily average of prisoners by a very large percentage. Like results would follow similar modes of action, if adopted in other localities.

Also, in connection with prisons, the question of the Remunerative Labour of their inmates is a subject of two widely diffused popular fallacies, in opposite directions.

On the one hand, many persons object to teaching prisoners trades and useful occupations, or to employing them in profitable industry, on the ground that they are thus placed in unfair competition with the honest workers outside. But it is precisely because they have not already competed, in the ranks of honest industry, that they have become criminals. And until they are induced, or compelled thus to earn their livelihood, by labour, they will remain a far heavier tax upon the public, than the very worst forms of industrial competition could involve. The respectable tax-payers have to support prisoners, like a dead weight upon their shoulders, unless the latter are obliged to earn their own living, as far as possible. And further, unless they are discharged from incarceration under circumstances which admit of a reasonable prospect of their finding employment, they will again inflict injury and expense upon the virtuous portion of the community, An idle prisoner, or criminal, is a very costly nuisance. An English convict lately remarked to a fellow-prisoner, " I have been convicted seven times ; but I won't work. By the last robbery I gained £450 ; and when I am discharged, I will have another go at it." Hence the public cannot afford to encourage such lazy villains in their idleness and crime. And in any case, the competition of prison with free labour is almost infinitesimal. For the proportion of prisoners to the free population is, happily, small in all nations. In Great Britain there is not, on the average, so much as one prisoner to every thousand of the outside population. In a very few instances, where a majority of the prisoners have been concentrated upon a single industry, such as mat-making or shoemaking, some small (though for the most part imaginary) inconvenience may have been caused to a few free workers. But generally speaking, the objection to a profitable prison industry is either unfounded, or " penny wise and pound foolish."

Of a similar nature, and in opposition to real economy, is the other popular extreme of making the immediate profits of prison labour the primary or exclusive object to be aimed at. This has been especially observable in some of the American States, where, in certain instances, their prisons have been rendered entirely self-supporting. Such a result is secured by leasing the criminals to contractors and working them, either in out-door gangs, as usually in the Southern States, or in crowded workshops, as in the North. In both cases, the corruption and evil, which are thus fostered, tend to perpetuate vice, and to render the jails themselves the very nurseries of further crime. It has been remarked that, both in the United States and in France, the jail workshops, with their cheerful associated labour, tend to keep the prison population permanently numerous, and, on the whole, decidedly on the increase. Whereas, the more deterrent, more reformatory, but more immediately costly conditions of cellular separation, though less favourable to rapid profits from labour, are far cheaper in the end, for they tend to keep down the *ultimate* number of prisoners. It has been well remarked that the main object of a prison is to be *empty.* And the most certain test of the efficiency of any penal system is the ultimate continued diminution of offences throughout the community. This is a far more reliable criterion than either the amount of prison earnings, or even the percentage of prisoners known to be reclaimed.

The Principle of Justice—Divine and Human.

A further great essential principle is JUSTICE—Justice with the level scales ; the fair weighing of both sides of every matter, and of the claims of each party. How often is the sacred name of Justice applied to a one-sided severity, or to a partial regard to one class of persons, whilst the eyes are kept blind to the rights or circumstances of another class ! For example, how disproportionately favourable is the Legislation of most countries to the assumed Rights of Property, as compared with the laws in regard to the collateral, and greater Moral Rights of the community, including the very poorest. Whilst much poverty is self-created, a large proportion of it is the inevitable result of social or hereditary causes, uncontrollable by the sufferer. Sharp deterrence is just and necessary for wilful offenders and for the lazy and improvident. But discriminating mercy and help are due to our fellow-creatures under privation, and even under transgression, *in so far* as their circumstances are occasioned by the faults or misfortunes of others. In avoiding one extreme, we must also seek to keep clear of the other.

Justice may briefly be defined as the "Golden Rule" in practice, and as exercised, not only as regards individuals, but also nations. It is even a duty towards dumb Animals, which have been created by God, and which have their many claims upon human mercy. But how much more important are the claims of men themselves, however degraded, ·upon the consideration of their fellows, inasmuch as they are all members of that world of humanity so loved by God, that He gave Himself for it, through the Incarnation, in His only begotten Son.

In reference to offenders against the laws and rights of the community, it is a primary matter of justice that these shall be restrained and discouraged from continuing in crime, by means of a merciful severity, and by a gradual cumulation of penalties certain, but not too heavy. On the other hand, the general circumstances and antecedents of the offender are, in fairness to him, deserving of practical consideration ; as, for example, whether he has been driven to crime by powerful hereditary impulses and passions, in combination with ignorance and privation, and especially parental and social neglect. If the Law has also permitted such persons to be subjected to excessive temptations, as, for example, from a disproportionate abundance of licensed facilities for drunkenness or other vice, the lawmakers and the community are themselves partially responsible for the effects thus produced. The writer, in visiting an English prison, was struck with the remark of a veteran warder who spoke of the heartless inconsiderateness of a large section of the public towards the more unfortunate class of offenders. He said, " People are apt to exclaim, on seeing, for instance, a lad in jail, ' The young rascal ! he has wickedness imprinted on his face ; it is a good thing to punish him sharply.' " " Well, perhaps so," the warder would remark, in reply to such an observation ; " but let us remember that the lad (like many of his class) is the son of parents, both of whom were thieves and drunkards ; both of whom deserted him ; that he had no home ; no early training in virtue ; that he usually found a bed under arches, or on doorsteps, in holes and corners of the city, until the police-cell, or the work-house, or the prison, received him into comparative luxury, though accompanied by restraints hateful to his wild habits." For such an one, justice demands a prolonged training to self-supporting industry, if possible, at some expense to his parents, if otherwise, at the cost of the State, which also has, in some measure probably, neglected him or his progenitors.

To how many criminals, in our own day, are applicable the words recorded of the wretched Judæan king, Ahaziah, son of the cruel idolatress Athaliah,—" For his mother was his counsellor to do wickedly." By natural constitution, a mother's influence is pre-eminently powerful, whether for good or for ill. Hence those who have had bad maternal training are thereby entitled to a specially merciful regard in the retribution, or correction, of their consequent misdeeds.

Again, as to the Pauper; he, too, may have fought the battle of life against a heavy over-weight of disadvantage, from miserable parentage, hereditary incapacity or disease, or both; and perhaps in a wretched home, with a bad example on the part of those around him, as to intemperance and vice. If, having the offer of labour, he refuses it, then it is just to let him suffer either punishment, or sharp privation.

How much of the vice and crime of Glasgow and other crowded cities arises, almost by sheer irresistible necessity, from the shocking crowding of whole families into *single rooms*,—each the sole scene of birth, wedlock and death, of feeding, living, and sleeping. Yet near some of these cities, thousands of fair acres are permanently kept waste, for the enjoyment of a few sportsmen. Is not this a grave injustice towards men and towards God? When will Scotland, in particular, rouse herself and deliver her poorest population from the terrible evils of criminal over-crowding and cruelly locked land?

The severity of penalty and the rigour of· discipline should be everywhere qualified by just consideration; and also by the fact that honour is due to all men, by reason of the intrinsic worth of each soul gifted with a capacity for immortal life, and endless moral development. The basest of men, the most degraded of women, for all of whom Christ has lived, died and risen, may, through the power of His Spirit, be purified into saintly excellence. Even the once diabolical King Manasseh of Judah, ultimately became prayerfully and practically repentant. From Mary Magdalen, her seven possessing devils were effectually expelled by the Holy Christ. So, through Divine Grace and patient human effort, sinners of any guilt and dye may be led to virtue. Even these can never be justly divested of a certain claim to honour, on account of God's relation to them and their potential immortal restoration. As Dr. W. ELLERY CHANNING has well remarked, "Christianity indeed gives us a deeper, keener feeling of the guilt of mankind than any other religion. But it does not speak of this as indissolubly bound up with the soul, but as a temporary stain, which it calls us to wash away. Its greatest doctrine is that the lost are recoverable; that the most fallen may rise; and that there is no height of purity, power, felicity, in the universe, to which the guiltiest mind, may not, through penitence, attain."

GODLINESS THE CHIEF PRINCIPLE.

Beyond all other fundamental principles, for the diminution or restoration of criminals, TRUE GODLINESS IS THE STRONGEST.

The mighty powers of evil passions and the immense inertia of indifference can only be effectually combated by forces which are still more potent; those of the love of God in Christ, and the hopes and fears of Eternity. The experience of the general history of humanity, shows that the

D

greatest success in the reclamation of lives from evil has been achieved by this power of Divine love.

Yet much has been authoritatively promulgated in Christ's name, which has been singularly opposed to His example and precepts. He Himself laid down, for all time, the simple but decisive test of true Christianity—" By this shall all men know that ye are My disciples, if ye have love one to another." And His Apostle showed the real fruits of His Holy Spirit to be " Love, joy, peace ; long suffering, gentleness, goodness ; faith, meekness, temperance."

Further, it is of essential importance to all communities and individuals, that the Divine declarations of what is a truly just retribution, or reward, in a future state, should be earnestly regarded. For these furnish a sustaining encouragement to right doers, however unknown amongst their fellow-men, arising from the well grounded hope, that there awaits them an eternity of joy and congenial activity in the Heaven of Christ's personal presence ; in association with the beloved relations and friends of a former life, and with the good and wise of all ages ; in grand missions of Divine beneficence, and in vast extensions of knowledge and power. Such justly founded hopes of unending bless-ings convey a powerful stimulus to patient obedience, and to loyal service to God, by promoting the best interests of His human and brute creation.

On the other hand, strong restraints from wrong-doing, from cruelty, from indifference, from impurity, are to be found in a sense of the necessity of having hereafter to meet the judgment of a God of awful purity and power, irresistibly hostile to deliberate transgression, though ready to forgive all past sins, on sincere repentance, through the law-honouring justification and affection-winning power of Christ's most precious Blood. For through His own Incarnation and voluntary Sacrifice, " He tasted death for *every* man," and thus for evermore rendered it cousis-tent even with immaculate Divine sanctity, to pardon the sinner, on returning to God, who is at once a Being of unfathomable mercy and of irreconcilable hatred of evil.

Pre-eminently, God is Love. Love is the disposition, both in the Deity and in man, which regards and encourages the favourable features and the good capacities of others. Hence love is true charity. For the word *charity* (*caritas*) is akin to *carus*, dear, and implies that there is a genuine sense in which man is, or should be, intrinsically dear, or precious, to his fellow man, in view of the grandeur of his future capabilities and the possibilities which may be wrought in him by ages of eternal education. For it must be remembered that God has all Eternity to work in, whether that work be the perfecting of an individual, or of a race. And when millions of years have been occupied in such development of the immortal beauty of moral grandeur, no time has been lost or wasted. And God's processes are usually very slow indeed, being chiefly based on the principle of moral suasion, acting upon wills free to choose the evil, or the good, for the present at least. He is so very patient, *because* Eternal. Hence God loves mankind so much, for He beholds, in His poor human family—even in the lowest and weakest of them—*capacities of infinite growth*, and the possibility of immortal life in Christ. He knows thoroughly and sympathisingly, that the hereditary tendencies of mankind to evil, and the accumulated power of habit, operating through hundreds of generations of frailty and ignorance, from the first Adam's days to our own, impart a peculiar and vastly *additional* value and interest to the faintest efforts of resistance to such mighty antagonism. The struggles of a sin-burdened soul after righteousness, even if only partially successful at the time, may be more honourable and more fruitful for the development of eternal goodness, than the perfect but easier obedience of possibly untempted angels. And if the noblest feelings on earth are the self-sacrificing love of a mother, and the pitying compassion of a father, it was naturally and reasonably to be expected that God, the great archetypal Father and Mother in one, would at some time, and in some manner, show forth to the very uttermost, even in infinite degree, His own perfections, also, of parental love. This necessarily involved a miracle of condescension, which chose for its channel the vast descent of the Incarnation—the measureless self-denial of God's own Spirit in Christ and upon the Cross—resulting in the triumphs of His Resurrection and Ascension, to be followed by His second Advent, as the visible King and glory of His redeemed Church. But He declares the certainty of irresistible chastisements upon those beings, who, after really fair opportunities of knowing His love and goodness, shall have wilfully disobeyed, or deliberately disregarded, His sovereign grace.

The temporary existence of evil is probably, and even evidently, an essential condition for the final victories of Divine Love, and for God's grand purposes of the moral education of the human race, throughout time and eternity. If there was no evil to combat, where would be the scope for moral growth, and where would be the possibility of the development of righteous strength and overcoming power? Adam and Eve, in a Paradise continuously free from temptation, must have remained mere adult babes, as to the real might and worth of goodness.

The Supreme declares Himself to be absolutely holy—a Being of spotless and crystalline purity. He is irreconcilably opposed to sin, whether in the smallest or greatest degree. And He is eternally destructive of it. For "our God is a consuming fire," and, as such, declares that He will ultimately overcome every contrary influence. Christ is promised to come again, in loving majesty, to rule His people. But His advent was also prophesied to be as " with refiner's fire and fuller's soap,"—that is to say, most searchingly and unsparingly corrective.

These motives of hope and fear towards God have a potency over the Philanthropist, the Missionary, the Editor, the Prison-Officer (whether principal òr subordinate), over the managers of the Poor-house, the Orphanage, the Hospital, which no commands of mere earthly Monarchs or Governments can possess. All mortal powers and rulers will soon, as shadows, pass away; and meanwhile they can be easily disobeyed and deceived. But the eternal God sees every action, however secret; knows every motive and thought, even the inmost; appreciates every humble kindness to man or beast, and will finally reward and judge the whole, with unerring justice and irresistible power.

The smallest services of grateful love, and even the apparently or temporarily unsuccessful efforts of His children, will secure His ultimate recognition and reward. And, on the other hand, every act of cruelty and of deliberate wickedness, will as surely come up for remembrance hereafter, before the just judgment seat of Christ. For God is indeed most mercifully just, to the Christian, to the Jew, to the Pagan. And through the infinite merits, and representative or substitutionary sufferings of His own glorious Incarnation, whereby the majesty of the moral law, of the Sovereign of the Universe, is adequately upheld, He offers pardon for all repented sin, and abundantly bestows the visitations of His Holy Spirit in the hearts of men, and promises reward and final acceptance to the virtuous of all ages, even amongst those who have not enjoyed the superior advantages of a preached Gospel, or of the Bible revelations of His love.

Such certain first principles of the Divine claims—such eternal grounds for hope, reverent affection, and fear—are the truest foundations of civil society. They are mighty, where the transitory rulers of the world are weak; and they are infinitely more penetrating in their application, and more far-reaching in their issues, than anything that human legislation can devise. They are the great motives furnished by the Gospel, which is the power of God unto salvation, both for individuals and communities; inasmuch as it places men's souls in contact with the influences of Eternity, and of the Supreme goodness.

All the best Prison Reform, for example, has been, and ever must be, based on these religious principles and on the relations and possibilities of the soul, in regard to God and Eternity. Just as an acorn, lying in a muddy woodland path, becomes interesting, when it is regarded in view of its possible growth to a huge century-living oak tree, so the soul of even the most degraded of human beings becomes precious, in view of its capacities for future endless development. And as is the difference between a dry fir-cone and its ultimate change into a magnificent tree, the glory of a mountain side, so is the possible transmutation of any degraded man or woman into a being of celestial brightness and beneficence, under the æonian training of Christ's Heavenly Kingdom.

Meanwhile, too, even in this little space of preliminary mortal existence, the grandeurs of future soul-development give a real interest and importance to the material influences of Sanitary and Physical Reforms, as connected immediately with the corporeal environments of men whose souls are of such infinite value and preciousness.

It was the characteristic contribution of ELIZABETH FRY, and her colleagues the BUXTONS, GURNEYS, and others, to modern prison reform, that they perseveringly urged the extensive introduction of *Scriptural knowledge* amongst the inmates and officers of penal and reformatory establishments. There still remains, not only in many such institutions, but amongst large sections of the populations throughout the world, an urgent need for more habitual regard to the Inspired Message of God's redeeming love to man—a gift equally indispensable for the help of the virtuous and of the offending elements of all human society.

M. TSCHUDI, the Director of a Swiss Reformatory, has

well remarked, that, " It is for want of the fear of the Lord that criminals are what they are. And for this very reason it is our bounden duty to instruct them in those religious principles which have too often been withheld from them ; for it is only in the sunshine of religion that good feelings glow and that the flowers of the Christian virtues unfold themselves. ' Mere phrases !' exclaims the man of the world. Very well. But let any one attempt the reform of depraved persons, *without* having recourse to religious influence, and it will be practically proved that the results will be very unsatisfactory."

There is a striking passage in the life of the Rev. JOHN CLAY, where he describes his own observations of the impression sometimes produced by preaching the Gospel judiciously to criminals. He says: " The preacher may speak of heaven ; but those men cannot understand him. They know of no happiness beyond gross, foul, animal indulgence. The preacher may speak of hell ; and they will wince. It would be terrible, if true. But is it true ? They harden themselves and won't believe it. But now let him preach Christ crucified ; and mark the effect of his preaching, as, in vivid, strong words, he tells the story of that Life and that Death, the story of that Friday morning at Calvary. Watch those men's faces, brutalised by years of selfishness and lust and gross ignorance. Gleams of intelligence and better feeling pass athwart their features. That strange, novel idea of *God having actually suffered, to save them from suffering*, astounds and bewilders them. Vaguely and dimly they begin to feel that they ought, they must, they will, love this Jesus, who has so loved them. They feel that they should like to do, to suffer, something to prove their love. The old self-love is shaken ; the new life from God is stirring within them ; and when those men go back to their cells, they kneel down, and in their half-dumb, inarticulate fashion, gasp out a prayer."

Scriptural religion is a chief principle of all social progress, both for the worse and the better elements of the
community, because it is most potent in producing the best
forms of citizenship.   Yet some persons who profess a
regard for Science, at the same time manifest the strange
inconsistency of indifference to the claims of Christianity.
This neglect is radically unphilosophical and unscientific;
because there is no department of Science which is more
verifiable by its outward and visible results than the
Christian System, in so far at least as its adherents prae-
tise, as well as profess, obedience to its precepts.   It remains
to be the chief and surest basis of administrative wisdom
and of the safety and happiness of nations.

This is no mere dogmatic assertion.   It is confirmed by
all historical experience.   In proportion as the simple principles of primitive and Scriptural religion have been prae-
tically exemplified by any communities, they have enjoyed
special, or at least, comparative exemption from Crime and
Pauperism.   For example, in New England, under the
later and milder Puritan *regime*; in Pennsylvania, under
William Penn; in Scotland, in so far as godly Presby-
terianism has regulated its parishes and its schools; in the
Ban de la Roche, during Oberlin's pastorate; in and around
the establishments of the Catholic " Christian Brothers,"
and of the mediæval "Brotherhoods of the Common Life"
of Holland; in the elder Mennonite bodies in Holland,
Germany, and Russia; in the Society of Friends, or
Quakers, the "Plymouth Brethren," the "Bible Christians,"
the Baptists, and other sects of Great Britain and America;
in the local influence of very many of the clergy and
faithful members of the grand Anglican Church, especially
in recent times; amongst evangelical Unitarians of the
Channing school; and in certain districts or counties of
peculiar religious earnestness, as for instance, Cornwall:—
all these and such as these, have afforded genuinely
scientific verifications of the special efficacy of Christian
principle amongst communities.

And, on the other hand, other abundant historic proofs demonstrate that principles contrary to those of true Christianity bring failure and ruin to nations and peoples. The Atheistic basis of the French Revolution of 1789, and of the Paris Commune of 1871 were ever-memorable illustrations of this. Similarly, all political, social and even ostensibly philanthropic movements which disregard, or ignore, the primary element of godliness, are manifestly doomed to disappoint the hopes they may have raised. For the only true liberty and advancement amongst nations, must be ever and continuously based upon the happy freedom resulting from the living service of the one and undivided, but tri-unely manifested God and Father of humanity.

Chapter II.

CRIMES OF SOCIETY.

"The Whole is Greater than its Part."

There are crimes of the individual and crimes of society; but the latter are immensely more important and more disastrous than the former. Yet this has been strangely neglected by legislators and leaders of the people. All manner of punishments have been devised for the erring individual; whilst the social conditions which, in innumerable instances, tempted, if, indeed, they did not almost compel him, to become a criminal, have too extensively been regarded with a wonderful indifference. And this still continues to be the case, in great degree. It may perhaps be one of the achievements of the Twentieth Century to rectify this oversight.

The disregard of the pre-eminent importance of social, as compared with individual crime, is, in fact, the neglect of one of the simplest and most incontestable principles, namely, that "the whole is greater than its part"—a truth which is to some extent involved in one or two of the principles alluded to in the last chapter. But, in connection with both Crime and Pauperism, it is so very important as to claim special consideration.

The Case of Belgium.

Many a State, for example, punishes Drunkenness as a nuisance, whilst it not only tolerates but powerfully encourages and maintains social and legislative systems which necessarily produce a vast development of this vice. This, then, is being blind to the fact that "the whole is greater than its part." The offence of the State is hugely greater and more multitudinous than that of the weak individual. Hence it is with good reason that certain social reformers in BELGIUM have protested against the inconsistency of their own country, in this respect. They draw attention to the enormous sums devoted to the construction of the grand and palatial establishments for the treatment of the individual offender, as compared with the very small expenditure devoted to measures for preventing drunkenness, and the comparatively slight interest manifested in educating popular opinion to a sense of its evils.

The visitor to Brussels sees, in the upper portion of that beautiful city, a sort of artificial mountain of masonry, probably more massive than the famous Tower of Babel, rising with majestic proportions far above surrounding edifices, and compelling admiration for the boldness, the wealth and the skill of a people who can erect such a structure. It is the Palace of Justice, the seat of the administration of Law and Penalty, in regard to individual crime. At a little distance, and standing on a still higher elevation, is one of the most splendid prisons in the world—that of St. Gilles, replete with almost every conceivable arrangement, suggested by the experience not only of Belgium but of Europe. And if the traveller visits other cities in that bright little kingdom, such as Ghent, Bruges, Antwerp, and similar provincial capitals, he will again and again find beautiful Palaces of Justice, and Prisons of the most approved modern style of construction, abounding in architectural and sanitary improvements. So much for the consideration, in Belgium, of the individual offender.

But turning to the Belgian legal and social system as a great whole, although here, too, there are some cheering indications of progress, yet the careful observer can hardly fail to be impressed with the very small comparative amount of money, effort, and ability devoted to the *prevention* of those conditions out of which, in that, as in other countries, individual crime chiefly springs.

The amount of drinking, in that Kingdom, and the vast number of places for the sale of alcohol, in proportion to the population, are very striking. Then, too, the considerable encouragement or practical toleration of Prostitution by the State, and the somewhat special share of Belgium in the traffic in girls, for home and foreign brothels, are features which impress an observing moralist. Not that, unfortunately, Belgium is so much worse than her British, French, or German neighbours, in these matters; for she is not. But being a small country, and having made such unusually splendid and costly provision for dealing with the crime of the individual, she furnishes a particularly visible illustration of the very generally prevalent unwisdom of neglecting that important simple principle—" the whole is greater than its part." For there can be scarcely a doubt, but that if only a moderate fraction of the many millions there devoted to Courts and Prisons, had been directed to the organisation of Moral Instruction and of Child-saving and Girl-rescue institutions, together with an active endeavour to punish purveyors of vice and to check drunkenness at its sources, then there would not be a necessity for the very costly buildings and establishments which are now used for the purpose of individual punishment.

PROSTITUTION AND THE SWEATING SYSTEM.

In regard to PROSTITUTION, also, as arising from the vice of Society more than of the Individual, much might be said, especially in relation to British and American cities. Some earnest and observant Social Reformers in the United

States have been inviting attention to the very serious temptations, the frequent ruin, misery, and even suicide, to which previously virtuous girls in that country are driven by the extension of the SWEATING SYSTEM, especially in connection with those huge shops and trading establishments which are so widely driving the small trader out of the field. It is complained that in such cities as New York and Chicago, thousands of poor girls are almost irresistibly compelled to prostitution, by the utterly inadequate wages they receive—wages on which, in a large proportion of cases, it is impossible for them to exist. But often the shop-girl, or the type-writer, especially if pretty, is insolently told that if she will be "accommodating" she can readily better her condition, and find some young man, or some head of the trading departments, willing to supplement her poor earnings, but only on the condition of her sacrifice of what is most precious in womanhood. This abominable system is a crime, not indeed of society as a whole, but, at any rate, of considerable sections of it. And it is of incomparably more importance to devote State and Social attention to the means of preventing such wrongs, than to confine efforts to the promotion of Penitentiaries and Homes for the fallen. Nor must it be forgotten that Prostitution, besides being itself a vice, is also a fruitful cause of crime, particularly of robbery and murder.

EXCESSIVE MILITARISM.

In connection both with the ruin and degradation of womanhood, and with the extension of violence, there is another social crime which, hitherto, has held its sway mightily over the nations—namely, excessive MILITARISM, leading to the withdrawal of myriads, or rather millions, of vigorous young men, during the years when their passions are strongest, from the shelter of home, the influence of parental guidance and of the Church of their childhood, and away, too, for the present, from the prospects and the

possibilities of virtuous marriage. By this vastly extensive substitution of the barracks for the home, how vicious
are the habits forcibly implanted in innumerable young
men; and what hosts of victims amongst the womanhood
of nations are, in consequence, sacrificed to them. And not
only is there this physical degradation, with its abounding
maladies, present and prospective; not only is there the
ruin of so many brave and fair bodies; but incomparably
worse is the destructive influence on the *souls* of such
myriads—in view of the claims upon them of God's
authority and love—and of the importance of eternal
retribution. Not only does this enormous Militarism constitute a gigantic engine of both vice and crime, but also of
impiety. It takes the *moral manliness* out of the soldier, too
generally, just as it takes the womanly purity out of his
poor victim. The DUKE OF WELLINGTON said : " Men who
have nice notions about religion have no business to be
soldiers." What greater condemnation of the crime of
Militarism can there be, than this declaration from such
an authority ?

But it is, of course, replied that this universal Militarism
is a necessity. Can nations, in the present state of other
nations, dare to dispense wholly with their armies and
navies? Perhaps not. The maintenance of these vastly
demoralising armaments has been, alas! forced upon the
world. But the huge social crime, especially of Christendom, in this matter, consists in its shameful *apathy*, and in
the neglect to put forth even moderate efforts to bring
about a better state of things, or at least to endeavour to
diminish the evil. It is true that, during the Nineteenth
Century, about a hundred international disputes, some of
which might otherwise have led to war, have been settled
by the peaceful modes of ARBITRATION and MEDIATION.
And probably in the Twentieth Century, such settlements
will be much more general and numerous.

But who can doubt that vast relief to the burdened

peoples might be secured, if a series of Congresses, or Conferences, of official representatives of the nations, to consider if any means can be devised for reducing Armaments, were assembled, in good faith and purpose, by the Governments of the world. Eminent jurists have shown the great advantages which would result from the establishment of a High Court of Nations, with well-paid and permanent officials. Such a Court might not prevent all war, but it would doubtless obviate many conflicts, and it would greatly facilitate a disbanding of myriads of youths now compelled to lead idle and vicious lives.

The Christian Nations have expended thousands of millions of pounds upon their Armaments; but which of them has yet spent a single million, or a considerable fraction of a million, upon *any earnest endeavour* to enlist a common consideration even of initiatory steps to check this huge scourge of humanity? Nay, have all the Christian nations *together*, ever yet contributed one million to such an object?

And it is the absence of any such very feeble proof of real national interest in reducing this evil, which constitutes the awful social crime of existing Militarism, with its debasing Conscription. But at the same time, war is a most fruitful source of individual crime. Here, too, how enormously the whole is greater than its part! The official statistics of the UNITED STATES show that one result of the CIVIL WAR of 1861-65 was an exceeding and abiding development of crimes of every description. Similarly, as to the effect of the War of 1870-71 upon victorious GERMANY, it has been well remarked by an English journalist, Mr. W. T. STEAD: — "The citizen, plunged for months into all the license and savagery of war, acquired a taint from which he did not purge himself for years. War is the unloosing of all crimes, the negation of the sanctity of property and of life. To accustom men to war is to accustom them to live in a world where the

ordinary *moral* code is suspended.   The criminal statistics
of Germany, since 1871, show a terrible increase of crime ;
murder, highway robbery, thefts by violence, burglary,
assaults on women and children."   Such is the appalling
testimony, always, of facts, in opposition to the silly
sentimentalities and imaginative poems which ascribe
specially elevating and refining influences to this great
accumulator of lust and savagery.

Let us hope that the Twentieth Century will bring about
at least such an amount of interest in this question of
Armament-diminution, as may be manifested by grants of a
few millions to enlist the best efforts of the ablest men, in
order to devise and bring about some appreciable reform.

Irreligious Education.

There is another social crime of portentous mischief—that
of indifference, or opposition, to Religious Education,
especially as characteristic of France, Holland, some of
the United States and certain British Colonies.   For,
happily, hitherto, the Home Country has been wiser.   But
what can be greater national or governmental folly, than to
train up children in ignorance of the love and power of
God, and in indifference to the possibilities and retributions
of Eternity ?   What can be more suicidal to law, order, and
public security ?   To how many leaders of the peoples, both
aristocratic and democratic, are fairly applicable, in this
respect, the words used by the Prophet Isaiah, in describing
the Government of ancient Egypt : "Surely the Princes of
Zoan are fools ; the counsel of the wise counsellors of
Pharaoh is become brutish."

The Case of France.

For instance, look at the treatment of the youth of
France, for centuries, by the State and by the State Department claiming to be " the Church."   Is it any wonder that
revolution, anarchy, assassination, have been so often

generated amongst that intelligent people, who, if rightly trained and led, are capable of illustrious national and individual life? Has not education there been systematically rendered godless, if not positively immoral?

An eminent French Senator, M. JULES SIMON, writing in the last decade of the Nineteenth Century, of the lately executed anarchists, incendiaries, and assassins, says : " Most of the wretched men upon whom justice has laid her hands for the recent outrages, were young men, grown up whilst the image of God was everywhere veiled from them. A nation cannot, with impunity, thus pass many years, whilst chasing its thoughts of God from the education of the young." He complains that the French Municipalities have sent to " examine even the school libraries, in order to remove from them the books containing the word ' God.' " And then, alluding to the consequent crimes and outrages, M. SIMON adds :—" The lesson is given ; it is terrible."

NAPOLEON I. said :—" Man is not a man, when without God. I saw the man without God, at work in 1793. We don't govern such men ; we mow them down with cannon." But the men of 1793 had had such " education" as a wicked " Church " and Government gave them, under the guise of religion.

In the Nineteenth Century, too, as all along for many centuries past, France has had abundance of artistic education. She has largely led the world in Design, Painting, and Architecture, in the Drama and the Dance. But how little, comparatively, of *real* education — that of training in the love and fear of God, and the practice of Christian brotherhood and liberty—has gone with this ! The superb cathedral, rising side by side with the Inquisition, and both under Church administration ! The splendid castles and mansions of lovely provinces, like Touraine, with exquisite developments of the Renaissance and other Art, but together with *oubliette* and torture chamber ; with the stake, the massacre, the burying alive,

E

the rack, the wheel; and contemporary with such debased monarchs as those of the Valois, and their Jezebels, like Catherine de Medicis!   Later centuries brought little real improvement in the education of French youth.   If anything, the detestable "piety" of those arch-hypocrites, Louis XIV. and Madame de Maintenon, was worse than all the rest, with their Revocation of the Edict of Nantes and its horrors.

But one horror alone, in feudal and Catholic France, down to the outbreak of the Revolution, one thing alone, sufficed to corrupt the nation to its very heart.   And this was the abominable, special "'*droit*' *du seigneur*" which permitted every "nobleman" and great landowner to claim the first night with every newly-married girl on his estate !   This custom was, unfortunately, not exclusively limited to France, but it was far more generally insisted on there than elsewhere.

When we read of the destruction of so many of the beautiful *chateaux* of the *ancien régime;* of the bonfires of priceless antiquities, ornaments, books and pictures, from those castles, made by the at length self-emancipated peasantry, and of the daily harvest of the guillotine, for months, of hundreds of the bravest nobles and most learned priests of France, is it possible for any impartial man to deny that Royalty, Nobility, and the Church, were now only reaping the terrible whirlwind which for generations they themselves had been bringing about, by their neglect and perversion of popular education, as well as by the influence of their own pernicious examples?

It is not consistent for the Roman Catholic Church, at least, to point to modern Anarchism and say, "Behold the fruit of godless education !"   For she, under the name and guise of godly and Christian authority, had the almost sole and absolute training of the youth of France, for centuries before the Revolution.   And what did she ever do to make its "godliness" real, in view of such legalised evils as the devilish *droit du seigneur?* Scores of Papal Bulls were launched for ages against so-called "errors" and "heresies," either the acceptance or rejection of which scarcely made an atom of difference, as to promoting a better service of God or man. Interdict after interdict was laid upon powerful monarchs and peoples, for some real or assumed infractions of the pecuniary interests or claims of the "Church," but when was any "Bull" or "Interdict" levelled against the upholding of the "*droit du seigneur*" and various other atrocious tyrannies upon the people's inalienable and God-given rights? Rome might have done so much, if she had only made half as vigorous efforts for the people's interests, as for her own.

VOLTAIRE alone, to his lasting honour, did more to abolish torture in Europe than all the ecclesiastics and " orthodox" Churchmen on the Continent, who indeed had for ages been such special originators and inflictors of that diabolic practice. It was VOLTAIRE, too, who wrote those ever noteworthy words, " Not to expect from God, either punishment or reward, is to be truly an Atheist. Of what use is the notion of a God, who has no power over you? If you have committed crimes by abusing your liberty, it is impossible for you to prove that God cannot punish you for it; I defy you to it. The belief in God, as the rewarder of good actions, the punisher of the wicked, whilst the pardoner of minor faults, is *the most useful faith* for humanity." (*Jenni,* c. x., xi.)

Our SAVIOUR told the " orthodox" of His day that if they and others held their peace respecting His goodness, " the very stones would cry out." And so, in the Eighteenth Century, when the education of the youth of France was being polluted and perverted, such men as Voltaire raised at least some protest, which happily did not altogether, or ultimately, fall unheeded to the ground.

Modern observation and events, together with the writings of MM. ERCKMANN-CHATRIAN and others, especially Miss

BETHAM EDWARDS, who has so long and lovingly studied
the French people, show conclusively that the French
Revolution, unspeakably awful as it was at the time, was
overruled for vast blessing. It was an exorcism of devils,
both in State and "Church." And no exorcism of such
can be accomplished without tremendous wrenches and
upheavals. It was the cleansing of Augean stables; and
nothing but an overwhelming river could suffice for that
process. The body of the French people have been
gradually gaining in happiness ever since; they have now
many million peasant proprietors of land. Everywhere the
poorest have their own little incomings of fruit, vegetables,
poultry, honey, flowers, and so forth. Everywhere is the
local free museum and picture gallery. But still the youth
of France, for the most part, await their precious birthright
of instruction in the love, fear and reverence of their
Heavenly Father, who, through the manifestation of His
Son and Holy Spirit, can grant them temporal and eternal
blessedness, beyond the power of language to describe.

THE CASE OF THE UNITED STATES.

Great national crimes are sure to bring their own penalty,
ultimately. It was so with SLAVERY in the UNITED
STATES. Generation after generation stored up the deluge of
misery which burst forth so irresistibly and terribly in the
CIVIL WAR of 1861-5. That country may be preparing gradually another deluge, firstly, by a SCHOOL SYSTEM, largely
separated from unsectarian Biblical instruction; secondly,
by the sanction of vast CAPITALIST COMBINATIONS which
are crushing the poor and the toiler, as they were perhaps
never crushed before; and, thirdly, by CITY "RINGS"
of dishonest and unworthy Aldermen, or Committees. And
there is the social crime committed against the great body of
American boyhood, by the action of the TRADES UNIONS in
almost forbidding APPRENTICESHIPS generally. The Reports
of American Prison Managers largely testify to widespread

idleness, crime, vagrancy and ruin, thus forced upon thousands of bright and capable boys, by largely excluding them from handicraft training.

Thus, the PENNSYLVANIA PRISON SOCIETY reports: "The reason why so many boys and young men become criminals, is because they have now no chance to learn a trade. Labour Unions prohibit boys from becoming apprentices." This is not democratic liberty, but gross demagogic tyranny and injustice of a very bad character.

The United States Prisons' Reports also complain of the very one-sided and therefore unjust action taken by the Legislatures of some States, on the compulsion of Trades Unions again, to restrict to an excessive degree the industrial training of prisoners whilst in jail. In some districts the prisoners have thus been obliged to pass their time in most mischievous idleness and vice.

In regard to such social crimes, an American orator remarks:—" There is a strange disposition to condone the crimes which are gigantic, provided they be successful ; we punish the man who steals a loaf, we hail the man who, by monopolies and 'corners' in wheat, makes the loaf smaller and coarser in a hundred thousand homes. If a man steals a bar of iron, we railroad him to prison; if he steals an entire railroad, we say he is a 'financier.'"

So that in America there are still great national crimes which involve little or no restriction to the guilty, whether large capitalists, "cornerers," and "ring-bosses," or whether Trade Unions of comparatively poor men, but equally despotic, to the extent of their power, over those weaker than themselves.

In the last decade of the Nineteenth Century, the American SENATOR INGALLS, declared: — "A financial system under which more than one-half of the enormous wealth of the country, derived from the bounty of nature and the labour of all, is owned by a little more than thirty thousand people, while one million American citizens, able and willing to toil, are homeless tramps, starving for bread, requires readjustment. A social system which offers to tender, virtuous and dependent women, the alternative between prostitution and suicide, as an escape from beggary, is organised crime, for which some day unrelenting justice will demand atonement and expiation. We are accustomed to speak of this as the land of the free and the home of the brave. It will soon be the home of the rich and the land of the slave."

SOCIAL CRIME IN GENERAL.—ANIMALS—GIRL-WIDOWS.

In every nation there are these social crimes. In GREAT BRITAIN and IRELAND, but especially in "orthodoxy"-professing SCOTLAND, there is perhaps the worst Drunkenness in the world. In this Kingdom also, there has too frequently been a most criminal sanction of PESTILENTIAL DWELLINGS for the poor, especially in rural districts.

In SOUTH EUROPE generally, there is the crime of CRUELTY TO ANIMALS. The shocking way in which horses, in particular, are maltreated in many parts of ITALY, FRANCE, and SPAIN, is a disgrace to those countries, especially to their "Churches," who might, if they chose, do so much for the help and comfort of these faithful creatures, which men ought so gratefully to cherish, both for the love of God and out of regard to the value of their own services.

There is à terrible and widespread social crime in INDIA, in the treatment of GIRL-WIDOWS. These are married, or betrothed, often whilst mere infants, or very young children, to child-husbands of similar age. Of course, in myriads of instances, the husband dies whilst still a child; but though his wife may grow up to womanhood and live many years, she is rigorously prohibited from marrying again. The consequence is a vast amount both of suffering and vice. British authority has long ago suppressed the horrors of the Juggernaut Festival; but the condition of these child-widows as loudly calls for interposition. Some efforts are being made to diminish this huge social crime, which, it is to be hoped may not survive far into the Twentieth Century.

Union of Social Forces for Social Reform.

Though the removal, or diminution, of social crimes is evidently a matter of immense and peculiar difficulty, yet doubtless much more might be done in this direction, both by Churches and peoples, than has hitherto been achieved, if still more united and organised efforts were put forth.

In the first place, the Church needs to be further freed from fictitious claimants of its authority and from counterfeit constituents. How continuously has the very term "Church" been misapplied and usurped, all through the centuries. The only true and Catholic Church is "the congregation of *faithful* men and women," who in every age serve God from the *heart*. It is a body largely invisible, as such, to man. It involves "the priesthood of all believers." Again and again, in the Bible, it is declared that its ranks include many, from east and west, north and south, outside the artificial pale of a mere conventional, if authoritative "orthodoxy"—the men and women who have *done* good in God's sight, rather than professed it. Our SAVIOUR, the primary authority, declared that "*Many* will say to Me, in that day, Lord, Lord, have we not prophesied in Thy name," and so forth; "and then will I profess unto them, I never knew you; depart from Me, ye that work iniquity." Again He says, "Many that are first shall be last, and the last first."

Someone has surmised that those who are privileged to enter Heaven will be astonished at two things; firstly, at the presence of so many whom they had not at all expected to see there; and, secondly, at the absence of so many whom they had taken for granted would be sure of admission. The Bible fully confirms this view.

The State has persistently, throughout Europe at least, usurped a share and control in the Universal Church, for which it can show no Divine authority, and which has, on the whole, been deleterious to the world. At present, though since a very recent period merely, the State Churches of ENGLAND and SWEDEN are, perhaps, exceptions to the general rule. They are admirable bodies, in many respects. But even these have less fervour, less spiritual power and purity, probably, than they would have, if not controlled by, and muddled up with, State connection.

The actual history of Christendom shows that just in proportion as the Church, everywhere, has been specially ceremonial, it has been least Christian, in the sense of the example and spirit of the Lord Jesus Christ. By the introduction of non-Apostolic novelties, such as indulgences for sins and the enforced celibacy of the clergy, the great Roman branch of the Church has itself caused much crime. Priestly Celibacy is an evil which has diffused, and still diffuses, incalculable immorality and seduction amongst the women of Roman Catholic countries, whilst sacerdotal pardon tends specially to destroy veracity and honesty.

THE " CHURCH " *versus* SCIENCE AND REASON.

The continuously disastrous effect upon the progress of science and general social welfare, which the professing or usurping, as distinct from the real and Christ-like Church, has exercised, all through the ages, has been most strikingly depicted by Dr. JOHN WM. DRAPER (U.S.A.), in his valuable work, " History of the Conflict between Religion and Science," and by LECKY'S " History of Rationalism." But Dr. DRAPER, like so many others, has made the egregious mistake of confounding fictitious with real Christianity, and its quasi-professors with its genuine exemplars, as tested by the *one great standard*, the personal example of the LORD JESUS CHRIST. There is no conflict whatever, and never can be, between *real* religion and real science, or between true religion and reason. They are allies of each other. And each is a gift of God, and thus is holy and blessed.

As the Church becomes increasingly regarded as only consisting of good *doers*, and in so far as Christ's morality is recognised as the essence and test of "orthodoxy," then the power of the real Church for the diminution of social crime, will immensely increase, and achieve vast blessings for humanity.

POPULAR UNION FOR SOCIAL PURIFICATION.—THE REAL PEOPLE AND DEMAGOGIC USURPERS.

The conception, too widely prevalent, of the true meaning of a people and a State, has often been most partial, and has again tended to substitute a part for the whole. LOUIS XIV. exclaimed, " I am the State "; utterly ignoring the fact that he was a mere gilded clod. And the proclamation issued by the "Three Tailors of Tooley Street," commencing, " We, the people of England," if not actually a historic document in itself, yet admirably serves to illustrate the constant, the almost universal assumption of "popular opinion" and of the names of "THE PEOPLE" and of "THE STATE" by some of the most contemptible, though most audacious, of minorities. Small sections of the community, led and voiced by a few loudly persistent Demagogues and Editors, especially if backed up by cunning "Caucuses" or other electoral organisations, continually usurp the name of "the people," whilst such are often most despotically unjust to the larger sections and main body of the community.

It is these usurping sections who bring upon the real people such undeserved satires from cynics, as that "the masses" are "them-asses," and that the demagogic claims to infallibility are true, in so far as they are "infallibly wrong."

YOU MAY TRUST THE WHOLE PEOPLE; ESPECIALLY IF THE WOMEN ARE NOT IGNORED.

But the best and wisest Statesmen, such as WASHINGTON and LINCOLN, PEEL and BRIGHT, have acted on the conviction—"You can safely trust the people, as a whole." President ABRAHAM LINCOLN, for example, said, "You can fool some of the people all the time; and you can fool all of the people some of the time; but you cannot fool *all* the people all the time." It is one of the most patent facts of history, that it is wonderful how much patience, common-sense, helpfulness and sympathy there is in *all* the people of any one country, when you really include them all in the view — the poor, middle class, and rich, and the women as well as the men. Even in non-democratic ages, this has been recognised in such proverbs as " *Vox populi, vox Dei,*" and " *Securus judicat orbis terrarum,*" statements which, though by no means always literally correct, yet embody a large amount of truth and fact.

, Five frogs croaking in a pool, or six cackling geese, will make more noise than fifty oxen quietly feeding beside them. In like manner, the blatant bark and brag of mob-leaders and partisan legislators, seeking for votes and emoluments, continually usurp the attention and the influence which ought to be shared amongst large masses of the community, whose real work is apt to be too often concealed and eclipsed by modest silence and attention to daily duty.

The SWISS REFERENDUM perhaps approximates more closely to a true democracy, to an actual voicing of "the people " in the proper sense of the word, than the political system of any other nation in the world. And Switzerland, whilst one of the most democratic, is perhaps also one of the least demagogic of nations, for this very reason.

Yet no Referendum even, which excludes WOMEN, can express the voice of a real and complete Democracy. How numerous and varied are the important matters of social welfare, in which woman is often *better* qualified than men to speak with the authority of experimental knowledge, such, for example, as the education of youth, the care of childhood, the succour of the miserable, the bearing of political measures and taxation upon home necessities, and so forth. Then, too, the cause of the poor dumb beasts, the victims of so much social crime in almost every land, would pretty certainly find special consideration amongst women. In so far as, in the Nineteenth Century, women have been tentatively allowed to share in the decision of public questions, their influence has been at least as good as that of men, as for example as Guardians of the Poor, as members of Committees for Boarding-out Pauper Children, as Public Inspectors, as Members of Royal Commissions, and so forth. And in proportion as they have attempted to influence Municipal Life, in the purification of abuses and the promotion of Temperance, they have already achieved remarkable successes on both sides of the Atlantic. But in the grand service of the sick and wounded, whether in home or hospital, and as organised Sisterhoods and Deaconnesscs, the beneficent work of woman is above all praise.

Doubtless she must always be precluded from some activities and offices, by reason of her special function of *maternity*. The caustic remark was not without a certain weight: "Think of a Chief Justice upon Circuit, with twins, or a Commander-in-chief, in the midst of a campaign, who was 'doing as well as could be expected.'" But what added dignity does this very function of maternity confer upon the sex !

Then how self-contradictory must be the claim of any one to be a true democrat, or lover of liberty, who would exclude those who, at least in many departments, are " the better half " of the people ?   And what a fiction is any acceptation of this term, " the people," which excludes its multitudinous women !

In the Twentieth Century, probably, woman will be able to attain a worthier share of popular control ; and experience and precedent fully lead us to hope that, with her accession of power and her alliance with her brethren, the diminution of social crimes will then proceed at a more satisfactory rate than it has done hitherto.

CHAPTER III.

THE SOCIAL CRIME AGAINST PRISONERS.

ONE of the worst crimes of the community, in most countries, has been that perpetrated against its prisoners, by placing them under such demoralising conditions as of necessity to render them more depraved by their punishment itself. The physical evils of prisons which, since John Howard's days, have been so greatly ameliorated, were hardly worse than the cruelties of moral and spiritual degradation, which, in many instances, still exist, even in conjunction with much modern reform, so far as the structural and sanitary arrangements of jails are concerned.

SOME INSTANCES OF SOCIAL CRIMES AGAINST PRISONERS.

Although, happily, decided progress in the treatment of prisoners, and in the prevention of crime, has been achieved during the Nineteenth Century, yet it is surprising how very slowly, in many countries, this advance has been made, and how much still remains to be accomplished during the Twentieth Century.

HOLLAND and BELGIUM were early and foremost in the good work of penal reform. SWEDEN, NORWAY and DENMARK also were honourable pioneers in the same department, owing largely to the influence and labours of the wise King OSCAR I.

GREAT BRITAIN.—TRANSPORTATION.

If, however, we merely glance at the social crimes against prisoners committed by four of the chief nations of the world, namely, GREAT BRITAIN, FRANCE, RUSSIA and the UNITED STATES, and extending down to the end of the Nineteenth Century, we find that GREAT BRITAIN entered upon that century with the incubus of Australian Transportation; and even down to 1850, or later, experienced many powerful obstructive influences to Prison Reform at home. In the central metropolitan prison of Newgate, so lately as 1845, the spectacle (so common in other prisons with association) was constantly witnessed, of groups of men and lads fighting, whilst others were shouting blasphemy and obscenity, or persecuting the weaker, or less vicious prisoners, with kicks, indecencies and brutal outrages.

But it was under the Australian Transportation system that the British criminals were specially sinned against by the action of the State. Nor was it until the middle of the Nineteenth Century that this system was abandoned ; and then only through the determined resistance of the Colonies themselves, and not from any sense of justice, or repentance, on the part of the Home Government and people.

Wherever numbers of criminal men, in the vigour of life, are kept together under conditions which necessarily, and for a long time, separate them from the other sex, and especially if they are allowed to associate, either by day or by night, with each other, all experience shows that scarcely any amount of vigilance will prevent the horrible sin of Sodom and Gomorrah from exercising its dreadful influence.

More particularly is this great evil increased by the location of penal establishments in regions more or less remote from easy and constant oversight by the Government, and from public observation ; as for example, in the secluded districts of AUSTRALIA and TASMANIA formerly, and in the similarly distant settlements, such as NEW CALEDONIA and CAYENNE, where, in the last decade of the Nineteenth Century, this terrible vice is in active operation amongst the French convicts.

The extent to which the sin of Sodom prevailed in the Australian penal establishments was fearful; as is shown by the awful evidence contained in Parliamentary papers and reports. The local authorities found it utterly impossible to suppress this evil, under any system of associated life and labour. And they practically shut their eyes to it. But the debasing effect was immense, especially upon the wretched youths and lads who were its chief victims. Some of these committed suicide ; even boy convicts, who were little more than children, drowned themselves, as the only means of escape from the daily and nightly hell into which the State had plunged them.

· Then also, the cruelties perpetrated upon the Australian and Tasmanian convicts, by many of their officers, were atrocious. These are described in authentic Parliamentary records. And such official brutality of course increased the savagery amongst the convicts.

MACQUARRIE HARBOUR, for example, was a British penal settlement in south-west Tasmania. A missionary of the Society of Friends, Mr. G. W. WALKER, who visited it in 1832, stated that five-eighths of the deaths, there, were caused by murders or accidents, and that even cannibalism was an occasional feature of convict life, at that remote station, almost surrounded by the forests. He writes:—"We went into a fissure of the rock, on the southern side, called ' Murderer's Cave,' in consequence of the number of convicts who have been murdered there. We were also shown the stains of blood that yet remained on the floor of their large apartment, where a poor fellow-creature met his fate very recently." In the convict burial-ground, the inscription " murdered," was conspicuous by its frequency. Mr. Walker adds :—" A considerable proportion of those murdered by their companions are supposed to have been devoured by them ; for it is a horrid, but undoubted fact, that on several occasions, when a party of men were determined on taking to ' the bush,' some unsuspecting simple man has been inveigled into the conspiracy, for the express purpose of furnishing food." The horrors of convict life in NORFOLK ISLAND were similar to those at Macquarrie Harbour. CAPTAIN MACONOCHIE introduced a temporary gleam of reform ; but reaction soon commenced, even under his well-meant efforts.

The life of the convicts during the voyage out to these settlements was also, in general, a fearful time. Innumerable cruelties were committed in the holds of the vessels, by the prisoners. Scaldings, robbings, garottings, and beatings were freely, and with general impunity to the perpetrators, practised upon the weaker convicts.

Murders were deliberately committed by the Norfolk Island convicts, in order that they might be sent to Sydney for trial and execution. For these murders and for revolts against the official ferocity of the convict authorities, prisoners were hung, by the dozen at a time, during the first half of the Nineteenth Century. ARCHBISHOP ULLATHORNE (then Roman Catholic Prison Chaplain), testified, before a Parliamentary Committee, in 1838, respecting one large party of men thus sentenced :—" As I mentioned the names of those men who were to die, one after another dropped on their knees and thanked God that they were to be delivered from that horrible place ; whilst the others remained standing, mute and weeping. It was the most horrible scene I ever witnessed."

In the year 1834, forty-four executions took place in New South Wales, with a population of less than seventy-thousand ! The same year there were only thirty-four executions in England and Wales, with a population, then, of fourteen millions. There would have been more than nine thousand executions in the latter, if the Australian proportion had been followed.

An accurate picture of the transportation system is to be found in a popular novel, written by an Australian, entitled "*For the Term of his Natural Life*," by Marcus Clarke. Although a work of fiction, the statements respecting convict life contained in it are verifiable by the most unimpeachable official reports. In fact, no account could exaggerate the horrors of that system, or of its crimes of cruelty, of lust and injustice.

At length a crusade against these atrocities was aroused, mainly through the labours of the apostolic WILLIAM WILLSON, the first Roman Catholic Bishop of Tasmania; and outraged humanity, both at home and in the colonies, indignantly compelled the British Government, though with culpable slowness and reluctance, to abandon a system where the worst evils were found to be in existence, and which terminated amid lasting infamy.

THE BRITISH CONVICT SYSTEM.

After the forced abolition of Australian transportation, Great Britain had to locate her Convicts in special establishments in the Home Islands, Bermuda, and Gibraltar, where, although an immense comparative advance was made in the treatment of the prisoners, yet, inasmuch as the congregate or "gang system" was still maintained, gross demoralization was found inevitable.

Royal Commissions and Parliamentary Committees proved the recurrence of the sin of Sodom amongst the convicts at Bermuda and Gibraltar. Even during the last quarter of the Nineteenth Century, a Royal Commission elicited testimony as to the existence of the same sin amongst convicts in the United Kingdom. And, human nature being what it is, it is probably impossible, even with the utmost care, wholly to stamp out this abomination from any similar establishments of bad men, associated in gangs, for months and years, apart from natural relationships and home influences.

However, it is not for a moment to be denied that some excellent features, especially much training in varied useful handicraft labour, have collaterally characterized the British convict prisons; and they have had many humane and judicious officers, especially of late years.

BRITISH LOCAL JAILS.

The British local jails for ordinary prisoners, as distinct from "convicts" (that is to say for offenders confined for periods varying in length from one day to the legal maximum of two years), have also been greatly improved during the Nineteenth Century, and are amongst the best of their class in the world; but *only so in that measure* upon which they are conducted on the plan of *separating* their inmates from one another.   Whenever (as is too often the case) this fundamental essential of good prison discipline has been relaxed, then these local jails have also, in such degree, been rendered the means of crime against the prisoners.

BRITISH COURT HOUSE ABUSES, 1887.

During the last quarter of the Nineteenth Century, in 1887, there was issued an official Report of a Committee appointed by the English Secretary of State for the Home Department, to inquire into the condition of the places of brief temporary detention for untried prisoners, in the Court Houses of the various counties and boroughs, where Quarter Sessions and Assizes are held.   This report justly astonished the public, and excited the indignant protests of the press.

For it was shown that after more than a century of active legislation and philanthropic effort for the improvement of criminal treatment, and after a continuously vast expenditure of money on Royal Commissions, Stipendiary Magistrates, Inspectors and Police, a shocking series of abuses still prevailed in many of the principal towns of the Kingdom and under the eyes of presumably vigilant and effective Magistrates and Municipal Corporations, who had been regarded as models of local administrative wisdom. But the too "dark places," around, or beneath them, even within a few yards of their habitual presence, were, meanwhile, literal "habitations of cruelty."

This Government Committee stated that only a few of the 189 Court Houses of England and Wales, were in a really satisfactory state; whilst they added "Many are as bad as they can well be. And it is not too much to say of some of these, that, in them, nearly every requisite of humanity and even of common decency is wanting." The Committee recorded that in some Courts "the worst evils of that promiscuous association, against which it has been a primary object of modern prison discipline to guard, must be encountered for hours and even days together, by children, women and men, who may be, and some of whom are, *innocent.*"

In other places, the persons awaiting trial were kept separate, "but by means which appear to be capable of amounting to positive torture," that is to say, by locking them up in narrow cells, or rather cupboards, less than a yard square! Some of these were dark, damp and cold; others overheated with gas and very deficient in ventilation. Many of them had no seats for the inmates, others only seats of stone, or iron.

The Committee added, in regard to the separation of the sexes, that "even this elementary requisite of decency and good order is not always provided for." They continued: "In some cases, the offices of nature, if performed at all, must be performed in the presence of from two to eight or ten spectators, and the odours of the closet, or pail, must be added to the products of the gas-burner, and to the necessary exhalations of humanity!" Places characterized by this shocking indecency were named. Of one of them it was stated: "At the City Court, where there are sometimes four prisoners, there is an earth-closet for prisoners and warders. There is not so much as a screen, to isolate the person using it. At another place, where five are some-times confined together, an earth closet in the middle of the cell, without any partition or screen, is the accommodation." Elsewhere, in certain localities named, the Committee report that " there is no water-closet, or privy, or other accommodation of any sort."

In such places and under such conditions, for hours or days, children and young women, many of them virtuous and absolutely innocent, have been crowded together with thieves, prostitutes, and all manner of vile characters. In addition to this, during the transit from the jails to the Court houses, or from prison to prison, many of these persons, innocent and guilty alike, have been habitually subjected to the company and insults of the vilest offenders.

The Home Office Committee were informed, by the governor of a large jail, from which the prisoners had to be taken a considerable distance to and from the court in a non-cellular van, " that he thought any decent man would gladly compound for that ride by a month's im-prisonment." The report remarked that the miseries of vile association, in the court-cells and waiting-rooms, and on the way to and from them, " must be, to a respectable man or woman, mental or moral torture." And it was added, " What are we to say, as to its influence upon boys and girls ? "

It is particularly to be remembered that this Committee disclosed abuses which had gone on, for generations, in places where many excellent magistrates and philan-thropists were residing. Seeing that the gross abuses laid bare in this official report, had long continued unin-terruptedly, up to 1887,* in England, with its unsurpassed

---

° Of course, the publication of the Report caused material improve-ments in these English Court Houses. It is specially to be noted that the British LOCAL PRISONS, under the visitation of Government Inspec-tors and regularly appointed Justices, afforded, meanwhile, a very favourable contrast, on the whole, to these Court Houses, which were nominally under efficient municipal or magisterial oversight. For what is *any* one's business, is very apt, in practice, to be attended to by *no* one.

public freedom, private beneficence, and newspaper and official vigilance, what ground is there for surprise at the existence of prison abominations in despotic Russia, Morocco, or Turkey ?

Wherever there are prison walls and wards, there is almost inevitably involved *a dangerous secrecy* of administration, arising either from the absence of adequate inspection, or from the frequent inertia and habitual optimism of the officials concerned.   Whilst the British Inspectors of Local Prisons were regularly visiting those establishments, the Court Houses were exempt from their examination.   But meanwhile, even in the *inspected* Prisons, circumstances have occasionally transpired which have given ground for great public dissatisfaction, and have awakened suspicions as to further possible evils which may have continued to be effectually concealed.

CASE OF GATCLIFFE, IN AN ENGLISH PRISON.

For example, as late in the Nineteenth Century as 1889, the following shocking occurrence took place in one of the largest and best reputed English prisons, that of Manchester, where there was a man named Gatcliffe, undergoing several weeks' imprisonment, for being drunk and disorderly. Before that term expired, he was a dead man.   The last night of his life, he was in a room containing five other prisoners and one officer.   In the morning he was a corpse, and his body was found to be in a most terrible condition, having six of the ribs broken, three of them being fractured in *two* places, also the breast-bone (one of the strongest bones) broken.

An inquest was held, at which the surgeon, who had been called in to examine the corpse, stated :—" All the injuries must have been caused within forty-eight hours before death, or may have been caused nearer death.   It was impossible for the deceased to have received those injuries before his admission, without their effect having been detected by the prison surgeon on examination. The bruises and fractures must have been caused by the fist of some other person. The fracture of the breast-bone might have been caused by the pressure of the knee of some other person."

Three of the other five prisoners who were in the room on the fatal night, were also summoned before the jury as witnesses. They agreed in their testimony as to having heard and seen terrible things that night. They stated that Gatcliff was lying "strapped down, both hands and feet, with towels and handkerchiefs, to the iron cot;" that they heard the sound of blows "the whole night, with five, or ten, or fifteen minutes' interval, in fact many times during the night, until the early morning." It was stated, in the evidence before the jury, that the voice of Gatcliffe was also heard to shout out, "Murder, murder! You are murdering me." He also shouted that his artificial teeth were being broken. Another voice was heard to exclaim, "I'll break your d— head!" "I'll break your ribs!" "Take that, you —!" "I wish you were dead!" Later on, Gatcliffe was heard to cry for water, and a voice replied, "Not a — drop!" One of the prisoners deposed, "I would have shouted 'Murder!' only I was afraid of getting a blow myself." Towards morning "there was a great deal of white froth coming out of his (Gatcliffe's) mouth; he then became quieter." And presently it was the long silence of death, with the poor wretch.

The coroner's jury returned a verdict of "Manslaughter" against an officer, who was subsequently tried, at the Liverpool Assizes, and acquitted. It was especially urged, at the trial, that as the only evidence was that of prisoners, their testimony was not worthy of being entertained.

Beyond the reports of the proceedings of the Coroner's Inquest and Assizes, in reference to this case, it seemed likely to pass off without further attention. But the matter was considered by the HOWARD ASSOCIATION to be one which, in the interests of common humanity, demanded much more notice. And accordingly the COMMITTEE and their SECRETARY enlisted the services of several MEMBERS of PARLIAMENT, who brought the matter forward, in the House of Commons, on *four* successive occasions.

But even the Home Secretary repeatedly pleaded his inability to clear up the matter satisfactorily. He stated that two of the subordinate officers at Manchester prison "would not again be employed," and that sundry minor changes in the administration of that prison had been made. He also added some words which bore indirect official testimony to the value of the labours and vigilance of such efforts as those repeatedly made, in this and other instances, by the HOWARD ASSOCIATION, to bring before Parliament and the Press, cases of cruelty, or abuse, in the penal administration. For the Home Secretary now said that, "*Nothing was more calculated to keep prison officials up to the mark, than the application to them of this constant watchfulness.*"

The extraordinary fact, however, remains, that just a hundred years after John Howard's death, and in one of the principal English prisons, a poor misdemeanant was terribly done to death, as just described; whilst all the Prison Officials, Commissioners, Inspectors, Visiting Justices, Judge, and Home Secretary were unable to bring home the act to any one person !

DR. WINES ON "DARK PLACES."

The late Dr. E. C. WINES, of New York, who had probably visited prisons more extensively than any other man in the United States, and who was by no means a severe critic, has well remarked in his work on "The State of Prisons," " The dark places of the earth are full of cruelty—and prisons are exceedingly dark places—in the sense of being screened from observation. Their walls are as effectual in keeping critics out, as in keeping culprits in. The class of

officials, who look upon the inmates of their institutions as
mere subjects for discipline and severity, have a thousand
ways of evading any real supervision, or any searching
scrutiny." (Page 623.)   There is, and always must be, a
certain extent to which these words are applicable to every
description of jails and places of detention, whether comparatively bad or good.

Only certain approximate remedies can be secured in
reference to the dangers of abuse in prisons, especially in
those which are located in places remote from cities.   It is,
however, of primary necessity that the work of INSPECTION
and the reception of APPEALS, in regard to abuses, should
never be *exclusively* vested in the central authorities, or in
the actual administrators of the Prison Department.   In
some way or other there should be provision for some IN-
DEPENDENT REPRESENTATIVES of the Press and of the local
respectable population to have access, under reasonable
conditions, to the prisoners of every class.   Comparatively
little has, as yet, been permitted effectually, in this dirce-
tion, in any country.   It should be practically recognised, as
a fundamental axiom, that *no* Executive Department, and
least of all a largely secret one, can be safely entrusted with
the chief or sole exercise of inspection *over its own* sphere of
action.   That should be placed, somewhere, clearly *outside*
of its own influence.   But up to the last decade of the
Nineteenth Century, this reasonable precaution has not
been taken, in regard to prisons and their inmates, even in
Great Britain.

FRENCH CRIMES AGAINST PRISONERS.

In France, that eminently intelligent nation, a large
proportion of the prisoners still remain, at the end of
the Nineteenth Century, the victims of social, or State
crime, against their prospects of either reformation or
deterrence, by reason of the persistent maintenance of
corrupting association, both in the Home and Colonial

penal establishments. (Some progress has, however, been secured, especially of late years.)

In 1890 there was published a remarkable work, by a Medical Officer of the Paris prisons, namely "*Les Habitués des Prisons de Paris,*" by DR. EMILE LAURENT (Paris, G. Masson), in which (at pp. 367, 368) the experienced author describes the frightful prevalence, in those prisons, of the sin of Sodom. He says that the degraded votaries of this vice often find, inside the prisons, debauched or effeminate youths, who, for a cigarette, or other trifling gift, " yield themselves to it with a revolting cynicism, almost under the eyes of the warders. Many a time (says Dr. Laurent), in the prison infirmary, I have come upon a couple of wretches in the act, and as little embarrassed by my presence as if they were two dogs in the street."

This single official testimony might almost suffice, so far as France is concerned, to establish the fact of the criminality of the State and of society which could allow, in so many of its prisons, such a state of things, through every decade of the Nineteenth Century !

It is not surprising, then, that the "*Revue Penitentiaire*" the ably edited organ of the French Prison Society, stated, in 1895, that "The *increase* of criminality in France, cannot, and ought not, to be a secret, for any one !

In the distant penal establishments of NEW CALEDONIA and CAYENNE, matters are as bad, or worse.

In 1886 there was issued in Paris a book entitled, " Le Bagne et la Colonisation Pénale de la Nouvelle-Calédonie, par un Témoin Oculaire." (Charles Bayle, publisher.) The author was M. LEON MONCELON, an official delegate from New Caledonia to the Government of the mother country. His book is a vigorous protest against the great abuses which he describes as characterising the system of transportation and penal treatment in that island.

For example, he mentions the case of a convict, there,

sentenced to death three times, for different crimes, but who was thrice pardoned and then liberated. In another instance, a female monster who had killed her two children, was pardoned and permitted to marry ; after which she murdered a third child. Murderers and murderesses, thieves and prostitutes, are paired off, from time to time, with official and priestly blessing. One of these worthies, within forty-eight hours of his marriage, attempted to cut off the head of his bride, but was re-arrested amid his endeavours. He however managed, after all, to escape into the bush, where he set fire to some huts of the natives.

Another witness, an Australian writer, Mr. JULIAN THOMAS, in his work "*Cannibals and Convicts*" (London, 1886), remarks respecting French convicts in New Caledonia and the adjacent Islands: "At the *pénitenciers agricoles*, where plots of land were given to 'good conduct' men, and wives allotted to them, there was, and is, a condition of society as abominable as ever existed in the Cities of the Plain."

As to the *Cayenne* convict establishments a traveller reports that the pestilential prison stations there are named The "Devil's islands." The seas around swarm with sharks—the living sepulchres of the poor wretches, when their miserable lives end. The visitor describes the bare stone cells, small, and dark. Here many maniacs were chained to the walls, fed on bread and water, and left to await death. "In the first cell lay a confirmed idiot, his eyes half closed and besieged with flies, his feet swollen and suppurating with chigoes, a tropic insect pest, which pierces the flesh and breeds under the nails. The attendant gave him a kick to stir him up, the better for us to see, and remarked as he did so, ' The sooner he dies, the better.' "

RUSSIAN CRIME AGAINST PRISONERS.

The vast Empire of Russia maintains the system of transportation to Siberia, at the end of the Nineteenth

Century. Abundant complaints have from time to time appeared in European and American books and journals respecting the treatment of prisoners, both in the Siberian convict prisons and mines, and also in the local jails, or *ostrogs*, scattered over the Empire. Charges of cruelty and vice have been persistently urged by many travellers and inquirers—especially by Mr. GEORGE KENNAN, of America—whilst they have been met by repeated official denials, or qualifications. Probably extreme statements have, as usual, been made on both sides. But even the Russian *Law Messenger* has been quoted as stating that of the thousands of young females sent or taken to Siberia, scarcely any one reaches the end of the journey "without having been subjected to a gross offence."

And in 1893, statistics were submitted to the Czar, showing that in the preceding ten years, *three thousand* persons, mostly guilty merely of agricultural thefts, had died from the effects of the cruel punishment of the *knout*. The Czar is stated to have at once issued orders that this penalty shall no longer be used for that class of offences. But it is a savage treatment, even of the worst criminals.

A decisive, impartial and unimpeachable testimony, may suffice to settle the question as to the management of Russian prisons. It is from PRINCE NICHOLAS GALITZIN, who had been sent out as special Imperial Commissioner, with full powers from the Czar to visit and examine thoroughly the Siberian penal establishments. In 1894, after his return from that journey, he made the following statements :—"The fact is that it is immensely difficult for an inspector to get near the political prisons at all. These are usually off the beaten tracks, and very jealously guarded. Even I, with all my special permits and passports from the Czar himself, found much difficulty in entering them. In the first five or six that I did visit, I was humbugged entirely. The officials presumed on my inexperience, and it was only gradually that I learned how to circumvent their desire for secrecy, and to make my own investigations. For instance, they would at first always be very polite, bowing and scraping, 'Your Excellency' here and there ; but they would always show me the wrong prisoners. Finally I learned to go round alone with a turnkey only, and to find the prisoners by the private papers that I carried with me from head-quarters. And remember that I was sent direct by the Minister of the Interior, with all power to inquire. Now, Mr. Kennan did not even speak Russian ; how then could he do all this ? What he judges from, is simply the ordinary criminal prisons ; he is superficial. Yet I like always to be just to the devil—and Kennan is not the devil, you know. So let me say that he did not exaggerate, in his account of some of these prisons. In my private report to his Majesty, I say that the *only reform* good enough for some of these pest-holes is *a can of petroleum oil and a few matches.*"

This, then, is the verdict of a most competent native authority, and a trusted friend of the Emperor of Russia, respecting the official hindrances even to Imperial efforts at improvement, and the extreme necessity, at any rate in some localities, for not only the reform but the destruction of existing prisons, as being hopelessly bad.

In 1895, in one of the local prisons in Russia, three prisoners, for an attempted escape, were so savagely beaten with the butt ends of rifles, by official order, that one of them died under the blows; his body being little more than a pulp, with four ribs broken.

In connection with the evils of Siberian prisons, mention may also be made of the formidable secret society of the ARTEL, consisting of a combination of prisoners, who systematically murder those of their members who may betray or disobey the officers of the organisation. A similar secret society, the CAMORRA, exists in the prisons of ITALY. And many a murder, both in and out of prison, has been committed by its orders.

OTHER COUNTRIES—GERMANY, ETC.—COMMON DORMITORIES.

Much could be said of the crimes against prisoners committed by other countries. For example, even in Germany, a nation where Prison Discipline has received much praiseworthy attention from Monarchs, Statesmen, and others, there continues (as throughout the European Continent too generally) the adoption in many prisons, down to the last years of the Nineteenth Century, of common dormitories, of a most mischievous character.

The writer has observed, in such Continental prisons, well managed in some other respects, that the narrow beds, or " bunks," in the dormitories, are so close together, that a space of about five feet by five contains the ends of four of them. They are thus so placed that each sleeper is only a few inches apart from his neighbour at his side, and only about eighteen inches below another neighbour lying immediately overhead. About fifty beds may be thus crowded into a comparatively small chamber. Such nocturnal overcrowding may be seen in some of the prisons, even in countries where much attention is devoted by the authorities to certain aspects of the discipline. This is a condition which cannot but be very pernicious to the morals and future conduct of the inmates, whilst also injurious to their health.

And it must have contributed towards the increase of crime which has taken place in Germany. A German authority, M. VON MAYR, former Under Secretary of State in Alsace-Lorraine, shows in an article in the *Revue Penitentiaire* (1895) that during the six years ending 1893, German crime in general increased 21 per cent., whilst the population of the country only increased 7 per cent.

There is a great prison at Santiago, in Chili, in one part
of which the inmates are employed usefully at various
trades and under humane conditions.   And yet in another
portion of the same establishment, the "Solitary" System
appears to be carried out in a manner which renders it
a worse punishment than the prompt infliction of the
death penalty would be.

A traveller in Chili (F. B. WARD) thus describes, in
1893, this portion of the Santiago prison:—" In this
splendid 'model' institution there are noisome, slimy
cells, where daylight never enters, in which human
beings are literally buried alive.   Under the massive
arches of the enormously thick walls, where even in the outside rooms perpetual twilight reigns, are inner cells, two
feet wide by six feet long, and destitute of a single
article of furniture.   Until recently, those confined in
them were walled in, the bricks being cemented in place
over the living tomb.   Now there is a thick iron door,
which is securely nailed up and then fastened all around
with huge clamps, exactly as the vaults are closed in
the Santiago Cemetery, and over all the great red seal of
the Government is placed—not to be removed until the
man is dead, or his sentence has expired.   The tiny
grated window is covered by several thicknesses of closely-
woven wire netting, making dense darkness inside, so
that the prisoners cannot tell night from day.   There is
no ventilation except through this netting, and no opening
whatever to admit outside air into the tomb.   Low down
in the iron door, close to the ground, is a tiny sliding
panel, a foot long by a few inches wide, arranged like a
double drawer, so that food and water may be slipped
in on shallow pans and the refuse removed.   Twice in
every twenty-four hours this panel is operated, and if
the food remains untouched a given number of days, it is
known to a certainty that the man is dead, and only then

can the door be unsealed, unless his time is up. If the food is not touched for two or three days no attention is paid to it, for the prisoner may be shamming ; but beyond a certain length of time he cannot live without eating. Not the faintest sound nor glimmer of light penetrates those awful walls. In the same clothes he wears on entering, unwashed, uncombed, without even a blanket or handful of straw to lie upon, he languishes in sickness, lives or dies with no means of making his condition known to those outside. He may count the lagging hours, sleep, rave, curse, pray, long for death, dash his brains out, go mad if he likes— nobody knows it. He is dead to the world and buried, though living. They told us that only one man has ever survived a year's sentence, there. Those that survive six months are almost invariably driveling idiots or raving maniacs."

THE UNITED STATES CRIMES AGAINST PRISONERS.

Turning from the South to the North of the Western Hemisphere we still find, at the close of the Nineteenth Century, and in spite of many admirable efforts at improvement, that wherever the association of prisoners has been maintained, as is the case too generally throughout the United States, with a few honourable local exceptions, the prisoners have, in so far, been grievously sinned against and injured, by being subjected to this ruinous system.

UNITED STATES LOCAL JAILS.

The Executive Committee of the NATIONAL PRISON ASSOCIATION of the UNITED STATES, in their official Report issued not longer ago than 1874, signed by Dr. E. C. WINES, as Secretary, used these remarkable and emphatic words :—

" If, by some supernatural process, our two thousand

jails could be unroofed, and the scenes they conceal be thus instantly exposed to our view, a shriek would go up from this Congress and this country, that would not only reach every nook and corner of the land, but be heard in Scripture phrase, ' to the very ends of the earth' ! There might, and would, be a few cheering spots, little oases scattered here and there, in the wide desert of obscenity, profanity, wretchedness, filth, enforced idleness, seething corruption, and dreary moral desolation, that would, at all points, meet the gaze and make every nerve quiver with horror."

About ten years later, in the *North American Review,* 1883, Mr. Z. R. BROCKWAY, Governor of Elmira State Penitentiary, New York, declared: "The American jails of to-day are, with here and there an exception, substantially what Howard, in the eighteenth century, found English jails to be."

A similar general condemnation of American jails appeared in the twelfth annual report of the OHIO BOARD of STATE CHARITIES, issued in 1888. That Board included the Governor of that influential and highly advanced State, together with General Brinkerhoff and other gentlemen. They reported, " Of all the public institutions in America, the county jails are the most unsatisfactory ; and our Ohio jails are not an exception to the rule. Compared with other States, we have doubtless made more progress than any other; but we are still so far behind the best experience of the world, that we have but very little to boast of. With less than half-a-dozen exceptions, *every jail* in Ohio is *a moral pest-house and a school of crime."* This in 1888, and in one of the most advanced States !

Let us come down later still, to one of the last years of the Nineteenth Century. The New York *Evening Post* of March 9, 1895, contained the following account of a local jail in " the EMPIRE STATE," at that date, as described by a visitor, Mr. WILLIAM M. F. ROUND, the energetic Secretary of the New York Prison Association :—

"As illustrating the abuses possible under the present system, W. M. F. Round described to-day the condition of the county jail at Carmel, Putnam County, which he inspected a few days ago in the interest of the Association. Mr. Round said : " The jail at Carmel measures 32 by 32 feet inside the walls, and has accommodations for eighteen prisoners. At present there are eighty-six persons confined in it. Its bathing facilities consist of a single bathtub, which I am told is scarcely ever used. When I entered the building, which was at nine o'clock in the morning, the atmosphere was so foul that I almost staggered. At expressing surprise at the large number of prisoners confined there, the Sheriff said, ' Oh, that is nothing ; we have had as many as 160 here at one time ! ' Fortunately, there are no women there now, but under present arrangements six, eight, or ten men sleep in a single cell measuring 7 feet by 8. Besides this, the prisoners sleep on the floor of the corridor, and close to the top of the cells. This is bad enough, but I cannot imagine what they did when they had 160 there. In one of the alcoves between the doors of the cells, a long table had been provided where some eight or ten prisoners were disputing over a pack of greasy cards. The cards were so dirty that I could not discern, in the dim light, the spots they contained. The place was scandalously dirty throughout. The Sheriff receives 2½ dols. per week board for each prisoner, which gives him at present an income of 215 dols. (£43) a week. He has to pay no rent, of course, and light and heat are furnished him by the county.

" The jail at Carmel is certainly bad enough, but such a jail is possible in every county, *as long as the present vicious system lasts.* The present system is simply a part of the political scheme of the State, and every *jail is merely a plum* which the *Sheriff gets out of the political pie !* "

The low, ignorant and self-seeking class amongst the Sheriffs, are some of the greatest pests of American democracy, or rather of its demagogy—for they do not represent the great body of respectable men and women in the country, but merely the blatant wire-pullers and ofhee-seekers. Is it any wonder that murders, robberies and outrages of all kinds so abound in the United States at the close of the Nineteenth Century, when the numerous jails and their administrators are such as have thus been described by the most unimpeachable native authorities.

Thieves, tramps, and other offenders enjoy the dirty, lazy life in many of these jails, because they have fire, good food, cards, tobacco and whisky. Dr. F. H. Wines, of Illinois, mentions that in one of the prisons of that State, " a white man and a black woman, taken up on the charge of adultery were given the liberty of the entire jail ! " But to the more respectable or still unhardened prisoner, such places and the horrible conversation, are means of torture.

The comparatively small number of persons in America practically desirous of remedying the prevalent state of affairs in their jails, are, however, securing considerable improvements. But the unceasing changes of office-bearers, in every department of Government and administration in their country, place immense difficulties in the way of obtaining good influences over the prisoners, as a whole. In a few of the large State Prisons in the North, a comparatively permanent tenure of office has been secured for the chief employés.

Mr. C. E. FELTON, of Chicago, governor, for more than a quarter of a century, of large prisons in America, reports, " The county jails, in all parts of the country continue to be footballs to be kicked from party to party, as political power changes. Office and patronage seem to be the only inspiring motives in securing their control. With few exceptions, county jails are abominations, throughout the land."

Again the WISCONSIN " State Board of Charities and Prisons," remark : " An ordinary jail, with its disorder and idleness and indiscriminate association with low people, is a great punishment to any ordinarily decent man, and no punishment whatever to a dirty loafer. In fact, in *many* counties, where the *officers encourage* it, for the sake of fees, the jails are full of *willing* prisoners."

A well-informed observer in New York State wrote to the English Howard Association as follows :—"Our jails are under full control of the Sheriffs : and the Sheriff, in each county, is always or nearly always, the leader of the domi- nant political faction. He is paid by fees; and in some counties these fees amount to many thousand dollars a year, for each Sheriff. So you will at once see that, in over sixty counties (in New York State alone), the Shrievalty forms a powerful political machine, with places that furnish a sufficient income to make it worth the while of unscrupulous and greedy politicians to spend money to get them."

The popular indifference to this condition of things, in the United States, is amazing. Intelligent as the American people are in some matters, certain sections of them appear to be strikingly ignorant of the immense pecuniary waste and increasing criminality thus so prevalent in their midst. And too often these manifest a great want of appreciation of the labours of the penal reformers in their country.

Until a national change in the appointment and func- tions of American Sheriffs and Justices takes place, there seems to be little prospect of the needful radical improve- ment in the thousands of ordinary Local Jails. It may, however, be admitted that of late years, some of the worst scandals, as to insanitary abuses and the non-separation of the sexes, have been, in certain States, materially diminished. Some of the Prison Associations in America, have already been able to secure some progress in the reform of these institutions.

It was shown, in 1895, that in a Northern local jail, under the charge of an "easy-going, fatherly" Sheriff, the prisoners, male and female, were turned over to the care of two burly prisoners, who, at times, robbed them, beat them with clubs, and thrust them into dark underground holes, without windows, or ventilators, and where the wretched inmates were fastened to iron rings in the floor. This in 1895, within a few miles of New York and Philadelphia!

It is to be particularly observed, that the chief officers of the American *State* Prisons, as distinguished from those of the Local Jails, include many very superior men and women.

A report to the Canadian Minister of Justice (Ottawa) contained the following emphatic and general retrospect of the mischiefs of jail association, by the Inspector of Prisons for CANADA. It applies mainly to American and Colonial experiences, but unfortunately would serve also as a verdict respecting many European and other prisons, more than one hundred years after John Howard's death: " Society has found, by terrible experience, that her jail, or prison, or penitentiary system, has too often turned out to be the largest factor, and the most successful machine, in *the fabrication* of the evil it was seeking to destroy."

AMERICAN IMPRISONMENT OF INNOCENT WITNESSES.

In some American States, and even in Canada, *innocent witnesses* of grave crimes are sometimes imprisoned with the vilest criminals, in order to secure their testimony at the trial of the latter! A Minnesota Prison Report mentions the case of a man who was attacked by foot-pads, robbed and beaten. He identified his assailants, and caused their arrest. The robbers gave bail and went free. But their *victim*, being a stranger, could not give bail, and *therefore* was sent to jail, as being a witness!

Again, in 1894, in Indiana, a carpenter was assaulted and badly injured by a man who was arrested for it, and locked up in jail. But the carpenter was also shut up in the same jail as a witness. Time passed and the criminal was bailed out. At the June term of court, the case was put over until September, but the carpenter was kept locked up, while the criminal roamed the country. Tired of the confinement and knowing no other way to escape, the carpenter committed suicide in his cell and the criminal went scot free.

The *Chicago Record*, commenting on this case, remarked : "If there is anywhere a worse perversion of what is called justice, it certainly does not exist outside of the United States. It is such administration of injustice that makes anarchists, and begets a wholesome contempt for law and precedents. In this case it was the injured man who was punished and driven to suicide, while the real criminal was at liberty and living in comfort."

In one year in the last quarter of the Nineteenth Century, in New York, 317 *innocent witnesses* of crime were imprisoned !

. America sends many missionaries to Asia and Africa. But there is a vast field of labour, inadequately occupied by Christian effort hitherto, in many of her own States, for the removal of these evils. To these jails, in particular, may be applied the words of KING OSCAR I. of Sweden : "In truth, heathenism thrives much better within prisons, than among distant tribes who are still in a state of nature."

UNITED STATES UNDERGROUND DUNGEONS.

At the beginning of the Nineteenth Century, and well on during its course, some of the northern United States (including Puritan Connecticut) confined their prisoners in horrible dungeons, underground. In some cases, unfortunate wretches were kept in darkness, in idleness, and almost starved. They were debarred from useful industry, from reading, from visits, from exercise, and, of course, many of them went mad, or committed suicide. These events tended largely to horrify the American people, from this extreme of the cruel "Solitary" System, and incited them to the opposite extreme of general association of the most mischievous character. Yet down to the last decade of the Nineteenth Century, the New York journals describe the continuing use of some underground dungeons, in New Jersey!

" Leased Out " Convicts of the Southern States.

In some of the Southern United States a system has long been adopted of " farming out " all, or most of the convicts, to contractors, for labour in the open air, chiefly on plantations, or in the construction of railways and canals, or the working of coal mines. These States virtually conclude— " We will not burden ourselves with the outlay of a dollar for the support of our rogues. They shall maintain themselves, at whatever cost to them, whether of life or limb, even if the result ruins them body and soul. And if they are re-committed, they shall be sent for a further long period to re-undergo the same process. If they are worked to death in consequence, let it be so. That is for them to calculate. It is no matter of ours. We are determined to be rid of them; and, whatever the criminals may suffer, they shall not have our shoulders to bear them up, or our purses to pay for their deeds."

Hence some of these States have been able *entirely to dispense with* any regular maintenance of convict prisons. And they have, by leasing out all the convicts, at so much per head, to private speculators and contractors, managed to obtain an absolute profit, or net revenue, from the whole body of criminals. The system has the merit of being cheap, at least in its immediate operation. And in many instances it may have resulted in removing habits of inveterate laziness. For these Southern States have had little scruple as to the competition of their criminals with free labour. One American prison governor wisely remarked, " We put the house-breaker and the robber, the sneak-thief and the pickpocket, into open competition with honest men in the community around them. We do this exactly. For it was their previous trying to live by vice, *without* competing in the fields of productive labour, which was just the *essential cause* of the crimes for which they are sent here. We make a short end of that."

The Southern States generally make a speedy end of this vicious exemption from that competitive productive labour which is the divine ordinance for individual and civil occupation. But then they do this also by means of a most unwarrantable amount of cruelty, and by a neglect of their own duties.

Mr. G. S. GRIFFITH, the President of the Maryland Discharged Prisoners' Aid Society, has sent to the English Howard Association, reports of visits made by him to some of the Southern States, where the convicts are leased out to contractors. He noticed that one pernicious tendency of this system is to encourage a merciless prevalence of terribly long sentences. Even little children, in the South and of both sexes, are committed to this virtual slavery, for protracted terms; often for the most trivial offences. The reports showed that out of 1,243 convicts leased out in GEORGIA, 100 were boys from 10 to 16 years of age; and 400 from 16 to 20 years. In one convict establishment, two little boys were found under sentence of five years for stealing a box of cigars. They were in association with the most atrocious characters. In these establishments, very inadequate attention is paid to the separation even of the sexes. Many wretched infants are born in them. Gross immorality is frequent, both on the part of officers and convicts. At night, the latter are shut up in strong stockades, guarded by bloodhounds and by watchmen parading around with revolvers, which they freely use with deadly effect, in cases of attempts to escape. In the construction of railways, the convicts are also lodged, at night, in stockades, or in waggons, and are guarded by dogs and armed patrols. But the mortality and the attempts to escape are alike excessive. The reports state that at one convict establishment, during two years, out of 1,966 convicts, 237 escaped; 140 died; and 9 were killed while trying to escape.

An official State Report in TEXAS recorded the commitment of "a much larger number of convicts than were ever before received in the same length of time." There were 236 successful escapes from the convict camps and gangs, in that State, during two years. The same report mentioned that out of 221 deaths of prisoners, in two years, "18 were killed outright." These and many similar statements, it must be borne in mind, are made on official authority, and may be regarded as not being specially unfavourable representations of the real condition of American convict camps and gangs. But what tragedies and cruelties, what scenes of despair and misery, do they imply !

A New York journal, describing the horrors of the Southern States convict camps, has remarked, "It is barbarous to confine women in the same prison-pens with a horde of desperate ruffians who respect nothing under heaven."

The same journal contained a Memorial from some of the Ladies of GEORGIA addressed to their State Legislature, in which they plead—"There can be no apology for a system which places the lash and the musket in irresponsible hands [that is, of any negro, or white man, whom the contractors may choose to employ as overseer]; which substitutes vicious criminals for guards; which chains together all grades of convicts; which has neither mercy for childhood, nor protection for the sex of females; where no elevating tendencies are encouraged; where few reformatory influences are allowed; and where brutal instincts are given full play, provided the work of a brute is performed."

Of late years some of the Southern States have either restricted or abandoned this horrible system. But in other of these States it still remains, in the last decade of the Nineteenth Century!

It is to be hoped that the progress of public enlightenment and morality, in America, may not permit it to continue a feature of *any* portion of the great Republic, during many years of the Twentieth Century.

LIMITATION OF THIS SOCIAL CULPABILITY.

It must not for a moment be supposed that these officially verified illustrations of the crimes of States and Communities against prisoners, up to the close of the Nineteenth Century, in the very foremost countries of Europe and America, are to be regarded as universally descriptive of their penal institutions. On the contrary, in all of them, in Great Britain, France, Russia, and the United States, with the other nations, there have been collaterally introduced great and extensive improvements in prison discipline; and, what is of incalculably greater importance, in efforts for the *prevention* of crime.

Many excellent men and admirable administrators have in their various countries, laboured with a large measure of success in these departments of social progress.

Nevertheless, the stern and ugly reality remains, that with all the undoubted progress thus secured, there has continued, right down to the end of the century, a very serious amount of the vilest criminality and most odious vice, produced in prisons by the *radically incurable* evil of *associated* imprisonment—a system which no vigilance, no endeavours, can render anything but a continuous crime and cruelty against those who are its victims.

DIFFICULTIES INVOLVED BY PRISON SYSTEMS GENERALLY.

Apart from the numerous instances in which prison discipline, or penal treatment, has been a disgrace, or crime,

on the part of the State and the Community, it is to be
observed that even the very best conditions of imprisonment
necessarily involve some grave difficulties and dilemmas,
which have hitherto baffled almost every effort to remove.
Thus, for more than a century, the question of what is the
best system of prison discipline, has been energetically
discussed on both sides of the Atlantic. Libraries of
literature upon the subject have been written. Governments and Parliaments have set apart special Commissions
and Committees, times without number, for its investigation, either at home or by foreign travel. Congresses and
Conferences have repeatedly been convened, to arrive at
decisions on the matter. Various alternations and revolutions of opinion have taken place, in regard to the
respective merits and demerits, of separation, or of association; of penal and remunerative industry in prisons;
and of countless details affecting the architecture, the
administration, inspection, and general routine of these
establishments. Millions of pounds have been spent in
building up, altering, or pulling down prisons, in accordance
with these changes of opinion. And although there is
now, at least in Europe, a growing feeling in favour of the
absolute separation of prisoners from one another, yet
experienced observers still remain divided in opinion, as to
the best modes of criminal discipline.

Ultimately, after this century of wordy discussion, costly
construction and destruction, there is an increasing impression, amongst experienced observers, that the efficacy
of even the best systems of imprisonment, has, all along,
been exceedingly over-estimated, and that their disadvantages, both to the State and to the criminal, have been too
much lost sight of.

In several countries, some of the results of wise Police
Supervision and of Conditional Liberty and Liberation, are
pointing to the conclusion that by these there may be
secured a decidedly greater degree of deterrence and refor-

mation amongst offenders, with a minimum of imprisonment, because the longer terms of ordinary confinement
have, by their very nature, tended to habituate prisoners
to their lot, and to destroy, by producing indifference, both
their hopes and fears, as to the future.

The British prisons are more calculated to exercise a
deterrent influence over their inmates than the penal
establishments of most other nations; yet, even in these,
much corrupting association continues, and it is found that
a considerable proportion of the prisoners re-enter their
walls dozens, and even scores of times in succession. It is,
however, very important to observe that these very frequent
recommittals are not so much to be attributed to a failure
of Prison Discipline, as to the absence, hitherto, of any
rational system of *gradual* but *certain* cumulation of SEN-
TENCES. But the longer terms of penal servitude, for
robberies, burglaries and violent crimes, have also been
followed, in many cases, by·further reconvictions.

There are various reasons why prolonged imprisonments
must necessarily be of very limited efficiency. If prisoners
are to be maintained in health, and enabled to work usefully
whilst in confinement, their condition must unavoidably be
rendered in some respects superior to that of the honest
labourer outside, especially as to food. For it is a well
observed fact that prisoners require a better nourishment
to enable them to endure the ordinary restraints of incarceration, at least for a continuance, than would be sufficient
to support the same persons in a state of liberty. If, on
the other hand, they are placed on the same dietary as the
poorest outside workers, they will, in many instances, pine
away and die. Hence the food, and to a considerable
extent, also, the clothing, general lodging and warming of
convicts, place them for months and years, in circumstances
which at any rate appear unjust to the industrious free
labourers. Nevertheless the latter are too apt to overlook
the important matter that the real punishment consists

mainly in the absence of vicious indulgences, amusement and alcohol; together with the enforcement of regular hours and unpaid work.

As to the subject of Prison Dietary, in particular, it gives rise to many difficulties, some of which are almost inseparable from any system of detention. A matter which requires special vigilance in connection with this, is the combination of a low scale of food with hard penal labour, during the first stages of imprisonment. Either the one or the other, separately, may be justifiable. But both in combination are dangerous, and tend to cruel and even occasionally fatal injuries.

Even in prisons of the better description, and where the State maintains an array of religious and moral instructors for the benefit of the inmates, each prisoner knows that, whether comparatively idle or industrious, he will not be able, in general, to earn by his labour more than a small sum of money to help him on his discharge—merely enough to support him for a few days or weeks, and not always even that. On the other hand, he not unfrequently resolves to work as little as possible, when set at liberty, for he knows that by resuming his thievish habits, he can supply himself in a few hours with more money than months of honest hard work would bring him.

Whilst in prison, he is apt to nourish a feeling of resentment against the authorities and the community, a state of mind very unfavourable to growth in virtue and morality. In many cases—and especially if he belong to the less depraved class of offenders—he is worried by anxiety concerning the interests and support of his family, who are probably thrown upon charity for maintenance during his incarceration. If, also, these relatives are—as is sometimes the case—persons of respectable character, he is deprived of their good influence, except through an occasional letter or visit. And whilst he is temporarily placed out of the reach of the temptations of former bad companions, he is also separated from the needful discipline of ordinary life. He listens to the sermons of the Chaplain, in praise of the virtues of honesty and sobriety; but inasmuch as he is no longer in circumstances to exercise any practical self-control against drunkenness or stealing, that which he hears, or resolves, is peculiarly apt to be of an exceedingly superficial and unreliable influence, as to permanent effect.

The adoption of cellular separation from evil (but not from good) association during the shorter terms of confinement, has been attended with marked advantages in prisons in Great Britain, Holland, Belgium, Pennsylvania, and elsewhere. But even in these cases, it has not been in the power of the authorities to obviate some of the grave evils inseparable from *any* form of incarceration. The State, as such, cannot make its officers, in those or any other prisons, religiously and morally competent for their functions. The State often cannot secure the adequate amount of instruction and good influence, either by official or voluntary helpers, for the reformation of prisoners. And further, however useful cellular separation may be, as a preventive of mischievous corruption from other criminals, it does not afford a positive guarantee for improvement in itself. It may prevent prisoners from getting worse (and in most prisons, with association, they do get worse), but it only makes them better, in so far as it is accompanied by religious and secular instruction and industrial occupation. And even with all these, there will, of necessity, be still lacking those tests and developing agencies of reformation which are only afforded by the discipline of everyday life and liberty. A prisoner in an association-jail is like a man thrown amongst a group of lepers or plague-stricken wretches. The inmate of a cellular prison is like a child in leading-strings, or a bird in a cage, with very imperfect or inadequate qualification for free existence. *The chief function of the cell is deterrence, with the least danger of further corruption.*

For these and similar reasons, it is the frequent if not the general testimony of the most experienced prison officers, that the actual reformation of an habitual prisoner, by means of *any* system of discipline, during incarceration, is a rare occurrence. The Governor of a large English convict establishment remarked to the writer: " Our Chaplain is a most painstaking minister, and he labours earnestly amongst the men ; but where are the results ? If we had a Chaplain for every convict, we could not reform these criminals." Such an observation was far too discouraging in its tone ; but, unfortunately, it resembled many utterancs of intelligent and observant custodians of habitual offenders. On the other hand, it is an unquestionable fact that occasionally there have been striking instances of permanent reformation of character effected during imprisonment.

If imprisonment thus fails, in general, to secure reformation, it is only efficacious, in a limited degree, in regard to deterrence. And it must be so from its very nature, and from the necessary operation of the laws of habit upon the human mind and constitution.

Repeatedly has the declaration been made by prison-officers : " We have often noticed that when offenders— especially the younger ones—first enter these walls, they are overpowered by fear and apprehension. For a few days, or even weeks, these feelings continue ; and then gradually a change takes place. They begin to get accustomed to the daily routine ; they are rallied by their companions, and realise that, after all, a jail is not nearly so dreadful a place as they had supposed it to be. On the contrary, they find that it furnishes them with some advantages which they had never before enjoyed. Their fears are dispelled ; and when their time of discharge arrives, they have become not more, but less, in dread, than previously, of breaking the law and meeting its penalties." Then, in such cases, it is fairly a question whether the imprisonment has not done more harm than good. For it is a most undesirable result to remove the fear of law and the dread of penalty.

Where the imprisonment continues for very long periods, a sullen apathy is the frequent if not general effect. Year after year passing by, renders the prisoner less qualified for freedom, and increasingly hardened in his sense of hatred to authority and to mankind. The evil communications of his comrades tend to perpetuate and increase the moral corruption of his heart. Almost the only voluntary effort of any kind which he puts forth is, too often, the cultivation of increasingly cunning endeavours to impose upon the officers, to avoid punishments by a superficial observance of routine regulations, and to practise as much hypocrisy as possible.

The introduction, as in the British and various other prisons, of the " GOOD MARK " system, followed by " CON-DITIONAL LIBERATION " and the extension, as in some American jails, of pardon after continued satisfactory behaviour, are influences which, it must be admitted, have materially modified and counteracted the deadening tendencies of long imprisonment, by introducing some measure of the stimulating effects of hope and reward. But even these influences are of very limited power in connection with the disheartening tendencies of prolonged incarceration. It is continually observed that the worst criminals are apt to become, whilst in confinement, the most plausibly obsequious and the most practically obedient, from motives of self-interest. And, notwithstanding all ameliorations, there is experienced an abundant proportion of re-convictions and of relapses into crime, on the part of offenders who have already undergone these protracted imprisonments, and earned many " good marks." They have become, in fact, thoroughly habituated to the prison, and familiarised with its conditions. They have prae-tically realised the truth of the old saying that "Familiarity breeds contempt." For surely their frequent returns to crime indicate a very genuine contempt, both of the severest laws and of long terms of imprisonment.

Accumulating experiences, everywhere, show that the imprisonments which tend to produce the maximum of good with the minimum of evil, are those which are comparatively "*short and sharp.*"   And the only system which adapts itself to this maximum, both of deterrence and reformation, both of mercy and severity, is that which carefully separates criminals, under detention, from that debasing association with one another, which is at once so welcome to evil-doers and so destructive of all improving influences.

PRISON REVOLTS.

The State-crime of congregating prisoners, eminently fosters another evil which is at once an injury to the State itself and to the inmates of its prisons.   This is the facility for *revolts* and *conspiracies*, afforded by associated imprisonment.

It is not generally realised how frequent and how serious are these outbreaks, even in the penal establishments of the most civilised nations.   The following are but a few examples, out of very many others, which have occurred during the last two decades of the Nineteenth Century.

In 1884, at Mandalay, in Burmah, a revolt of many hundred prisoners took place.   This was suppressed by the stern process of a regular massacre, during which 200 lives were sacrificed.   The same year, a comparatively minor outbreak occurred in Frankfort prison, U.S.A., when three convicts were killed and others injured.

In 1885, at Khokand prison, in Russia, during a revolt, more than ten prisoners and officers were killed.

In 1886, serious assaults occurred in the prisons of Portsmouth and Portland, in England.   The same year, a revolt broke out in Montreal prison, Canada.   In quelling it, seventeen persons were shot, several of them fatally.

In 1886, also, a French convict ship was the scene of a revolt which resulted in many injuries. The same year various serious mutinies took place in French penal establishments.

In 1887, at Revel prison, in Russia, 300 convicts mutinied. Twenty of them were killed, and others wounded. A month later, at Mountjoy prison, Dublin, some convicts desperately assaulted a warder.

In 1888 a revolt of Russian convicts took place in the Caucasus; in the suppression of which many soldiers and prisoners were killed. In the spring of the same year, 500 inmates of Beaulieu prison, in France, mutinied, and two detachments of soldiers were sent to reduce them to submission. The " Bulletin " of the French Prison Society remarks, that within the year ending April, 1888, *eighteen* revolts had occurred in the seventeen central prisons of France! In April, 1888, a body of Mexican convicts, at Calaya, set fire to a building where a bull fight was going on. Such terrible confusion ensued, that eighteen persons were killed, sixty-eight injured, and the prisoners escaped. In March, 1888, in one of the English jails, at Armley, Leeds, three prisoners being left in the same cell, one of them killed another. In April, 1888, nineteen prisoners and police were killed in a revolt at the prison of Damanhour, in Egypt.

In 1891 and 1892 the following revolts occurred :—

At an Italian convict prison, on the Lipari Islands, a rebellion broke out, in the course of which sixty prisoners were wounded by the military. At Valencia, in Spain, 300 prisoners mutinied and the soldiers were called in to suppress the outbreak. At Rampur, in India, thirty prisoners, armed with knives, attacked their officers; six of the former were shot or hanged. At Lisbon ninety prisoners set upon their guards. Several volleys of shot were discharged amongst them. At Vladivostock, in Siberia, sixteen convicts, working together on a railway, killed five men and then escaped. At Gadsden, in Alabama, a gang

H

of prisoners seized the warders and the sheriff. Two were
shot dead, and others wounded. At San Quentin prison,
California, 1,300 convicts working outside the prison
became riotous. Dynamite was found under the beds
of seven of them. At Granada, a revolt of prisoners
had to be quelled by musketry. At Boston, U.S., a
party of 125 prisoners took temporary possession of the
jail. At Akyab, Burmah, in an outbreak, some of the
prisoners were killed. At Montpellier, France, a party
of five prisoners murdered a warder. In August, 1892,
thirty prisoners at Rouen revolted, and were only reduced
to order by soldiers with fixed bayonets. In September,
at Chattanooga, U.S., a gang of eighteen prisoners all broke
away from their custodians and escaped. In various other
instances, disturbances and escapes resulted from the association of criminals in prison.

In 1893 and 1894 were the following outbreaks, amongst
others :—

At Tourah convict prison, Egypt, thirty-nine prisoners
were shot dead (June, 1893). At Sing Sing, U.S.A., three
outbreaks, with fatal results; at Ionia, U.S.; and in
Tennessee; at Bangkok, Siam (eleven prisoners killed); at
Tarragona, Spain (nine killed); at Znaim, Moravia (many
convicts bayonetted); at Oswego, U.S.; at Atlanta, U.S.;
at Laramie, U.S.; at Tomsk (Siberia), many killed; at
Honolulu; at Auburn, U.S.; at Nashville, U.S.; at Jack-
son, U.S.; at Zurich; at Rheims, France; at Charleston,
U.S.; at Folsom, U.S. (three convicts killed). A prisoner's
brains were beaten out by others, in Nuremberg prison,
Germany. Two convicts at Borstal prison, Kent, attacked
a warder with a shovel. A riot in Steyer prison, Austria,
when two prisoners were shot. A riot at Huelva prison,
Spain, when thirteen convicts escaped. At Thorn prison,
in Germany, three convicts escaped together. At Iglau
prison, Bohemia, a riot, in which three prisoners and one
officer were killed. A riot at Troyes prison, France. At
Secoma State prison, U.S.A., several prisoners conspired to

poison the officers, and almost succeeded. Riots amongst Siberian convicts, etc., etc.

In 1894, also, at a Boston prison, U.S.A., there was a mutiny of the inmates, who had to be fired upon before order was restored. Again in the same year, there was an outbreak amongst the French convicts at Cayenne, resulting in twelve prisoners and several of their guards being killed.

It is to be remembered that many disturbances and serious assaults in prisons are carefully hushed up by the authorities of the various countries, who are most anxious to prevent the publicity of such occurrences. Hence it may fairly be inferred that the events of this kind which come to light, are but examples of a much larger number which are successfully concealed; or that, at least, these are but the more flagrant cases, which cannot be hidden.

It is one of the many merits of the Separate System of imprisonment, that it is free from such evils as these.

The governor of an English cellular jail once remarked to the writer—" Our prisoners are always kept apart from each other, and *therefore they are never a power."*

Even in REFORMATORIES and TRAINING SHIPS, the aggregation of young offenders frequently leads to evils of a less tragic nature. The English and Scotch institutions of this description have repeatedly, of recent years, been the scenes of mutinies and incendiarisms.

In 1886, at a French reformatory, a disturbance took place, and thirty-seven boys escaped. They were pursued by armed men, and shot at! Two of the poor young fellows were killed. One of the bodies was found to have received sixty-seven shots, of which five had entered the heart. And at an English Reformatory in 1895, an outbreak occurred which resulted in the destruction of £200 worth of property, in forty-five boys being arrested, and in twelve of them being committed to prison for various periods.

A GENERAL INFERENCE.

On the whole, it is very obvious, even from the limited survey here taken of the recent and present **condition of** penal establishments in all parts of the world, that they are, at best, very unsatisfactory and very incomplete institutions. They possess, when under good administration, a certain amount of efficacy ; but this is so restricted by the inevitable defects of every system of incarceration, that it has become a most important problem for the statesman, the jurist, the tax-payer, and the philanthropist, to consider the practicability of greatly modifying many of the practices and principles which have hitherto been prevalent in this department.

CHAPTER IV.

THE SOCIAL CRIME OF CRUEL LAXITY.

THERE is a social, or State crime, of an opposite, or very different character, from that which imposes corruption and undue suffering upon prisoners. It consists in an excessive laxity towards deliberate and violent offenders. There is scarcely anything which is in itself the source of so much suffering to a community, especially to women, children, and the weak or unprotected, as this pernicious leniency toward the class who may be distinctively termed ruffians.

This form of social crime is almost entirely of modern development. It is a product of the Nineteenth Century, and is one of the mischievous fungoid growths which tend to counterbalance some of the advantages of increasing civilization and general education. It was unknown in Howard's days, or even in the earlier years of the Nineteenth Century. It results from the "swing of the pendulum" of popular feeling, after becoming conscious of the evils of the old system of almost indiscriminate savagery in punishments.

But both extremes are bad, and not least that which attends the carrying out of a well-meant policy, beyond the limits of reason and safety. "*Corruptio optimi pessima.*"

So very serious are the sufferings caused to society itself, and especially to many of its weakest, as also to many of its most virtuous members, by the insufficient restraint of brutality, that it may be well believed that if John Howard was now living, he would feel it specially incumbent upon him, as a wise and judicious philanthropist, to urge upon his countrymen and the world, that it is even a more pressing duty to humanity to guard communities against ruffians and against laxity, both of opinion and retribution, in reference to them, than it is to promote leniency to prisoners in general.

Public sentiment, which is so apt to be both hasty in its expression and undiscerning in its conclusions, having become aroused to the fact that many offenders belong to the pitiable class, who may be rightly regarded as the victims of circumstances beyond their own control, has latterly shown a tendency to rush to the extreme conviction that all criminals may be considered as forming a vast flock of poor strayed sheep, whom it is a duty to gather into a fold where they may be treated with indiscriminate gentleness. But it is widely forgotten that this great flock includes many ravening wolves, who, if so folded and so indulged, will afterwards continue to worry the community, in a still worse degree, because of the comparative impunity which has thus been permitted them.

This crime against society arises largely from ignorance, or heedlessness, on the part of Legislators and others. During the last decade of the Nineteenth Century, it has found influential advocates amongst some weak Members of Parliament and certain Editors, from whom more intelligence might have been expected. In Europe, in America, and in the British Colonies there are widespread proofs of the disastrous effects of this crime of cruel laxity.

An infinite number of illustrations might be adduced in proof of this; but a few only must suffice, and they are exclusively selected from the occurrences of the last decade of the Nineteenth Century.

AMERICAN CRIMINAL LAXITY.

In the first place, there is reason to conclude that the UNITED STATES furnish the most numerous specimens of this form of cruelty. But of late years a certain section of strangely misnamed " humanitarians " have also been urging Englishmen, Frenchmen, Italians, and others to adopt a similarly disastrous course.

An American review (*The Probe*), remarks:—"As things now stand, the whole system of our criminal policy, viewed as a means of suppression, may be said to have degenerated into a farce. The admirable benevolence of BECCARIA, HOWARD and others, in its application to the criminal administration of the UNITED STATES, has become obsolete, irrelevant and wholly inapplicable. In fact, it is not too much to say, that in the United States, to be a prisoner has become a luxury; and that the career of a criminal has been rendered by the Government, safe, profitable and even agreeable to him. If the industrial classes of the world are brought into comparison, we are amazed to find that felons in the United States are better housed, fed, clad and comforted than the labouring poor of any other portion of the globe. Criminals emerge, after the expiration of their sentences, after a sojourn in quarters where every care and want have been abundantly supplied, quite as impenitent, hostile and *implacable public enemies* as before."

This is one native testimony. But many others corroborate it.

A paper by a popular American author, Mr. C. DUDLEY WARNER, in the *New Princeton Review*, characterised many of the United States' prisons as being "still barbarous in management," whilst others which are accounted "model" jails, and as under specially humane management, "soften the rigours of imprisonment by means of entertaining lectures and readings, concerts, holidays, anniversary dinners, flowers and marks for obedience to rules, which shorten the terms of confinement." But the reviewer significantly asks, in regard to the indulgence of the latter class of establishments, "*Do* these reformed prisons *reform ?*" He shows that there is some justification for the views of a minority of the population, who hold " that all this better lodging and better feeding of convicts is nonsense, *because it does not diminish the volume of crime.*" Mr. Warner continues—"The American public mind has not yet come to have any faith in the 'reforming' influence of our 'improved prisons.' *Why should it ?*" He further exposes the unwisdom of the course adopted, both in the United States and Great Britain, of *repeated short sentences* on *habitual* offenders, for whom he says, "We pay immense sums for a police to watch men and women, perfectly well known to be criminals, lying in wait to rob and murder; and other immense sums to catch and try, *over and over again*, these criminals, who are shut up for short terms, well cared for, physically rehabilitated, and then sent out to continue their prowling warfare against society."

At a recent American National Prison Congress, there was so much morbid sentimentality propounded that one of the chief speakers complained that the assembly "had gone off into the region of gush." A number of foolish suggestions were made in favour of continuing and even increasing the practice of pampering criminals in prison. An experienced observer protested against this course, as having been already carried to a pernicious extreme in various States. He remarked, "The fare in some prisons is alarmingly good. At one jail he had found that, for breakfast, the inmates had beefsteaks, hot biscuits, butter, and, in general, a bill of fare that would do credit to an hotel. For dinner they often had pies, after a full list of substantials; and preserves were frequently given to the prisoners with their tea."

A visitor to some of the NEW YORK prisons, reported in an American journal, in 1893, "I was surprised, on a visit to the Tombs Prison, in New York city, when prisoners took matches from their pockets and lighted cigars, while I was preaching, and no one restrained them. It was a surprise to me, too, to learn that if a prisoner had money, he could have any fare he chose to pay for, and friends might bring dainties to the prisoners. I saw one young fellow eating cake and raspberry jam, that his mother had brought him. If a prisoner is poor, however, he has to take what he can get.

"After preaching in Sing Sing Prison, New York, I made a tour of the cells, with the chaplain. In one, we found a prisoner lying in bed, although it was eleven o'clock a.m., reading a newspaper and smoking his pipe. In another cell a convict was making tea over his lamp."

An ILLINOIS newspaper, in 1895, reports that the prisoners in that State had consumed four tons of tobacco ·in five months.

THE ELMIRA SYSTEM.

There have been erected, during the last quarter of the Nineteenth Century, in some of the United States, as in NEW YORK, OHIO, and MASSACHUSETTS, "model" or "reformatory" prisons, which have been held up to the admiration not only of America, but of the civilised world, as examples of what penal institutions ought to be. The most famous of these is that of ELMIRA, in New York State, which unquestionably possesses some excellent features. Special attention is there paid to the classification and education of the inmates, who are exclusively persons undergoing a *first* committal. They include, however, criminals of every grade, murderers, burglars, thieves, and violators of women. The *maximum* sentence is, in general, five years, for each, irrespective of the nature of his crime. But by good behaviour and diligence inside the prison, this term is practically reduced, in most instances, to a detention of two years, the original sentence being thus rendered (but merely in such small degree) "indeterminate," as it is curiously styled.

Great effort is made to improve the inmates of Elmira by study and labour. Much trouble is also taken to secure situations for them, immediately on discharge. And it is claimed that 80 per cent. of them are reformed, so far at least as the subsequent careers of those who remain in the the same State can be traced. Unquestionably, then, there are praiseworthy features in the Elmira system.

But it is fairly open to question whether the many privileges there extended to the prisoners, do not tend to excite the envy of myriads of honest toilers outside. For example, the educational, or rather collegiate training of the inmates, is a most prominent feature. About a dozen of the professors or teachers of colleges and schools in the vicinity are engaged to instruct classes in the prison, and to deliver lectures on various topics. The Governor states that these include Writing, Drawing, Designing, German, English and American History, Business Law, Arithmetic, Physical Geography, Economics, Practical Ethics, Political Science, etc. Very thorough examinations on these and other subjects are periodically held. The amount of proficiency displayed tends to increase the prisoner's "good marks" proportionately. There is, in the prison, an "experimental school of industrial art" for practice in the work of terra-cotta, encaustic tiling, modelling, and designing from nature, embossing in brass, moulding metal pieces ornamentally, executing portraits in hammered copper, and so forth. Some of the convicts are also trained in telegraph-printing and shorthand. A paper written by a prisoner in Elmira, on a cold, snowy day, compassionately alluded to the wretched homes, almost visible from the walls of the establishment, where ill-clad and ill-fed children and wives of unemployed or weary men were crouching in the cold, and contrasted their lot with that of the convicts; adding, "Here, at this prison, 'tis the dinner-hour; up from the great dining-hall below rises the fragrant odour of good food, and the hum of animated voices, with rippling laughter interspersed. The food is hot, and sufficient as to quantity; the apartments are warmed with steam, and, after the short day is past, the electric light brightens things for the long evenings; long but not dreary, for books are abundant." The convict writer complacently inquires whether, with such a contrast of reward, " Is godliness profitable ? " or the contrary ? But he admits that, after all, liberty has charms.

The Directors at Elmira furnish a list of what is termed by them a " Reformatory Library " of the " very best contemporary publications," amongst which they specify the novels of Alexandre Dumas, Eugene Sue, " Ouida," Bulwer, Jules Verne, and others. There is also a liberal supply of newspapers and periodicals.

It has been stated that this system has not rendered Elmira attractive to criminals, but the reverse. Some instructive light was thrown upon the matter, in 1894, when it was proved, before a STATE COMMISSION of INQUIRY, that, for many years, corporal punishment had been resorted to, as a collateral counterpoise to the pleasanter parts of the " Reformatory " *curriculum*—such punishment, however, having been previously left entirely out of view in the published reports and laudations of Elmira.

In NEW YORK, also, in 1895, a leading journal devoted nearly a page of closely-printed type to a long list of recent " pardons," granted by the GOVERNOR of the State to atrocious criminals, after, in most cases, brief terms of imprisonment. In the three years, 1892-3-4, he pardoned 66 prisoners guilty of murder or homicide, 74 burglars, 115 robbers and thieves, 44 forgers, 20 violators of women, nine incendiaries and many others.

The New York *Observer* remarked, in 1895, that even as to the crime of murder, in the United States generally—

"Statistics show that, in this country, owing to the *general abuse of the pardoning power*, a nominal sentence to life-imprisonment, means, on the average, one of ten years."

Hence it is not suprising to find, in the last decade of the Nineteenth Century, in spite of increased "model" and "reformatory" prisons, a frightful increase of crime in the United States. Thus the New York *Sun* recorded twenty deaths by violence, in that city, within fourteen hours.

UNITED STATES MURDERS.

And in 1895, the *Chicago Tribune* (a journal which for many years has made a careful collection and study of American criminal statistics) stated that during the previous year, 1894, there were, in the United States, 9,800 murders; for which only 132 persons were legally executed, although 190 more were "lynched." Five years previously, in 1889, the number of murders was 3,567. Ten years previously, in 1885, there were 1,808 murders. So that the progress in the decade, up to *nearly ten thousand murders* in 1894, indicates an awful increase of homicidal crime.

Such are the very *cruel* effects, upon the community, of a general system of excessive laxity towards the most violent ruffians, together with gang-prisons, with the pleasantly corrupting companionship of their criminals and abundant indulgences, inaccessible to the average honest worker outside.

GENERAL EFFECTS OF CRUEL LAXITY.

As to other crime, in general, the experience of America has been similarly unfavourable. American crime has increased, during the last half of the Nineteenth Century, far beyond the proportion of increase of the population. And this is not at all to be wondered at. For suppose we take the case of an honest workman, say in New York, or San Francisco, toiling from morning till night, just able to get a living, but with few comforts and little amusement, for himself and his family. He may have, for a neighbour, on one side, a lazy, thievish loafer who never works, and on the other side, a violent bully, guilty of cruel assaults on man and beast, and of indecent outrages on women and children. Yet is it not a fact, that if either the loafer, or the bully, is sent to an American prison, the chances are, at present, that he will there find comforts of dietary, recreation, music, newspapers, novels, gymnastics, and professorial teaching even in the higher branches of education, which the honest worker can never hope to obtain? And not only so, but the bully and the thief, if obliged to work in prison, will probably be put to labour of a lighter character and shorter daily continuance than the other; and, perhaps, also, be trained to some fancy trade, or profitable art, which he, too, would most gladly learn.

Is such a system calculated to discourage the violent and the vicious, or rather to *attract* towards crime and pauperism the still honest toilers on the border-land of temptation?

On both sides of the Atlantic, this course has found plausible advocates. But their voices appear to have met with much more attention, hitherto, in America than in Europe.

The American people seem to be at last becoming conscious of the disastrous results of their penal system. For in 1895 there was a chorus of complaint from influential journals throughout the country, most of them demanding the introduction of Corporal Punishment, in place of the prison-failures and even of the "model" or "COLLEGIATE AND HOTEL PRISONS" of the United States. Thus the *New York Tribune* (1895) said:—

" A Bill was recently offered in the Legislature to punish, with whipping, men who inflicted brutal physical ill-usage

on others.   It was generally commended as the best means
of dealing with this class of people.   A little humiliation
and physical pain has been shown to be more effective in
dealing with the cowards who do not hesitate to inflict pain,
than any other method of punishment yet devised."

The *Detroit Free Press* (1895) remarked :—

" Under existing laws, a brute in human form, who has no
sentimentalism about the barbarities of the past, can maim a
woman or child and get off with a few months or years in
prison, where he will be well fed and cared for.   He can use
the lash or the bludgeon, but the State must not retaliate
upon him, even for the sake of deterring others from
imitating him.   It has long been thought by the practical,
that this is sentimentalism run mad."

The *Atlanta Constitution* (1895) observed :—

" The fetish of ' humanity ' must be bowed to, and the
greater inhumanity be perpetrated, of taking away five
years of a man's life, than giving him a good strapping and
letting him go, with the injunction that the application will
be redoubled on his next appearance."

The *Washington Post* (1895) wrote :—

" The creature who cruelly maltreats his wife or other
female dependent is, in nine cases out of ten, a worthless
vagabond, an habitual criminal and outlaw, for whom the
Prison or the Workhouse has no terrors whatsoever.   He
will serve his term under circumstances of greater physical
comfort than he is accustomed to at home, and then return
to freedom, to resume his hideous brutality without fear of,
if not with actual relish for, the consequences.   Meanwhile
the forlorn creatures who are subject to his evil moods have
absolutely no protection.   They lead lives that the dumb
brutes would shrink from."

Other contemporary journals expressed themselves similarly.   It may be hoped that while discriminative mercy
may be increasingly shown to the pitiable and unfortunate class of American offenders, a more effective humanity

may also be extended to the oppressed and violated victims of cruelty throughout the community, by giving to the ruffians who outrage them a penal treatment which shall have the truly beneficent effect of *reforming* them, by *intimidation* and real restraint.

BRITISH CRUEL LAXITY.

During the last years of the Nineteenth Century there has arisen in Great Britain, also, a specially cruel class of "humanitarians" so called, who seek to remove from penal treatment the *mercifully* deterrent elements which are so essential a condition of real reform and of crime repression. These unwise persons would render prisons as attractive as in some of the American States. Many of them, especially in the ranks of the local Magistracy, positively encourage and invite inhuman crimes, by their own criminally lax sentences upon ruffians of the worst nature. And yet, at the very same time, such persons, who are so indifferent to the sufferings inflicted upon others, are often needlessly harsh in their sentences and punishments for petty offences against *property*, or for poaching, or stealing a little food. Yet these people will lift up their hands and voices, in silly indignation at the idea of whipping a ruffian who has violated young children, or brutally maimed weak women, and will let off such wretches with two or three months' imprisonment, or a paltry fine!

One of the most humane and liberal of British philanthropists, Mr. HENRY LABOUCHERE, M.P., a gentleman hating oppression more than most men, although, quite consistently, advocating the whipping of ruffians, has for many years, in his journal, *Truth*, published a weekly "pillory" of unjust or inequitable sentences, showing the pernicious prevalence and disastrous action both of a cruel leniency to brutal criminals and of an extreme severity towards minor offenders against property.

He remarks:—"Apparently very little importance is

attached to a child's purity, or a woman's honour; and it is a regular practice to reduce the charge to one of common assault. Other offenders, for whom the quality of mercy is strangely strained, are those who, often through sheer lust for cruelty, starve, neglect, beat and torture helpless little children. There are dozens of instances in my record, in which perfectly fiendish conduct, on the part of parents and guardians, has not been thought deserving of more than a nominal pecuniary penalty. And it is the same with wanton cruelty to dumb animals."

Amongst Mr. Labouchere's *collectanea* (all during the last decade of the Nineteenth Century) are very many such as the following :—

One man, for breaking his wife's leg in two places, was fined ten shillings: another man (at the same date) for stealing a shilling, was sentenced to seven years' penal servitude.

One man, in Staffordshire, for kicking his wife out of the house, was fined a shilling. At the same court, and on the same day, another was imprisoned two months for stealing watercresses.

At a Warwickshire Court, one man was fined ten shillings for indecently assaulting a little girl of seven years of age. At the same date, another man, for stealing four shirts, was sent to penal servitude for three years, to be followed by five years' police supervision. At a Warwickshire Court also, another man was sentenced to one month for an indecent assault on a girl of twelve.

At a Shropshire Court, a man was fined forty shillings for an indecent assault on a little girl of six years.

In Lancashire, a man, for brutally kicking and wounding his little daughter, aged twelve years, was merely bound over to keep the peace for six months. On the same date, a boy of fourteen, for stealing two pigeons, was sent to jail for three weeks, and then to a reformatory for five years. On the same date also, a man was sent to jail for three weeks, for sleeping under a boat.

In Gloucestershire, a man, for repeated indecent assaults upon a married woman, in a field, was sent to jail for six weeks only. At the same court, on the same day, another man, for stealing nails, was ordered five years' penal servitude, to be followed by another five years of police supervision.

In Lancashire, two men, for indecently assaulting a girl of ten years, were discharged, conditionally on future good behaviour. At the same court, a man, who had previously been convicted twenty-seven times, was found guilty of a most revolting assault upon a poor blind girl, a cripple and paralysed, and was only sent to jail for eighteen months. But at the same court, on the same day, another man, for stealing tools, was sent to penal servitude for three years, to be followed by seven years police supervision.

In Scotland, most scandalous laxity is frequent towards persons guilty of rapes, or indecent assaults. Fathers guilty of gross assaults upon their own children, have been let off with a few months' imprisonment. And an influential Scotch journal, in 1894, under the heading of "A Severe Sentence," complained of an indecent assault on a young child being punished with as much as two months' imprisonment!

It is, of course, an almost necessary consequence of such criminal laxity, both in Europe or America, that assaults upon women greatly increase. At the Essex Assizes, in 1893, for example, the judge announced that there were thirteen cases, in which ruffians were accused of offences against women and children, some of which were of peculiar atrocity, the accused being the fathers of the victims of outrage.

JUVENILE RUFFIANS.

During the last quarter of the Nineteenth Century, partly as a result of excessive leniency, there has been

developed both in the UNITED STATES and more particularly
in AUSTRALIA, a pestiferous class of young ruffians who
have caused great suffering to the respectable, and especially
to the weaker, portions of the community, to whom they
have become a terror.

In AUSTRALIA they are popularly termed "larrikins,"
and in AMERICA, "hoodlums." An Australian writer, in
1893, thus described them—"At any street corner of a
colonial city, after 8 p.m., you may see crowds of them.
Tall and thin, with pale, animal face, constantly smoking
the strongest obtainable tobacco, dressed wholly in black,
with white linen, they take the pavement and pass obscene
remarks and comments upon the passers-by. On Sunday
nights, they gather in groups at church doors, expectorating
on the steps, and grossly insulting the worshippers, as they
go in and come out. Nothing can approach them for
language of the vilest, which they use habitually and
loudly. The 'larrikins' of one suburban district proudly
point to their record of at least three policemen and two
old women beaten to death by them, during the past year.
It is their joy to make savage assaults, in gangs, upon old
women, unprotected girls, Chinese, and especially solitary
constables in a lonely spot. They delight to thump their
victims, jump on them with brazen-heeled boots and beat
them brutally with sticks, until half or wholly dead."

Another writer, Mr. HENRY A. WHITE, an officer of more
than thirty years' experience in Australian prisons, writes
in 1894,—"Taking all things into account, the 'larrikin'
is, perhaps without exception, the most cowardly and
contemptible specimen of mankind. I have seen more than
one hundred of them attack a single policeman with all the
ferocity and brutality of savages."

But attempts to impose effectual chastisement upon them
have repeatedly been frustrated by Australian legislators and
authorities, amongst many of whom the "larrikins" have
relations and friends. Mr. WHITE continues:—"The usual

punishment awarded to ruffians of this class is from one to three months' imprisonment; but sentences such as these, unless accompanied by whipping, which alone strikes terror into the hearts of these criminals, are totally inadequate to the 'larrikin' class. The ordinary prison life presents no terrors to these young men. In fact, they appear perfectly indifferent to it. But they *certainly dislike the separate treatment* and they are terribly afraid of flogging."

Mr. White adds (in his work on "Criminals in Australia") that the too generally prevalent Colonial system of *merely secular* "education" has had a special share of influence in developing the "larrikin" class. Another powerful source of the evil is "GAMBLING, which is eating out the heart of our people."

Whether in Australia, or in Europe and America, the ruffian class cannot be repressed by ordinary or associated imprisonment. They *must* have *either* whipping, or the *separate system.* The latter, if strictly carried out, will sufficiently answer the purpose. Mr. White, after his long official observation, records this conclusion:—"The *only* system which, I believe, has the least chance of effecting reformation, must include *separate* treatment, not only for first offenders, but throughout the various grades. Let association, whether at labour or otherwise, *be the one thing carefully withheld*, except as a reward, after long periods of good conduct, and the jail will soon be regarded with terror, as it *ought* to be."

These are wise words, worthy of consideration everywhere.

But the modern and far too numerous school of *pseudo* "humanitarians" who, though with well-meant intentions, are so practically cruel to the community, are also, as a class, opposing prison separation, and urging the *retrograde* policy of associating criminals.

Indeed, generally, these shallow and unreflecting, as well

as too often ignorant, advocates of a lax treatment of ruffians, appear to assume, as a matter of course, that all prisoners and criminals are " poor prodigals." They practically ignore the distinction between petty and grave offenders, between the minor first offender and the professional criminal, or malignant villain.

They abuse experienced officials; they also abuse the Howard Association and those persons (possibly now a minority in some countries) who hold to the necessity of stringent measures to protect the community from that worst of all offences—cruelty. For not only are these *quasi* " humanitarians " practically indulgent towards the class of public ruffians, whether adult or juvenile, but they would also render prisons easy and attractive to the similarly dangerous class of private tormentors, who abuse the secrecy of home life to perpetrate abominable outrages there. In 1892 the Society (in London) for the Prevention of Cruelty to Children reported such instances of these domestic cruelties as the following :—" Punishing a child by putting pins into its nostrils; putting lighted matches up them; biting a child's wrist till a wound is made, and then burning the wound with lighted matches; burning the hands of a boy of six with matches ; throwing a little girl of two years, ill of bronchitis, out of its bed-room window, breaking its bones, and ending its life; breaking a two-year-old baby's limbs in three places, both arms and a thigh, leaving. them untended, when it moaned in its pain irritably taking it up from its cradle by the broken arms, shaking it by them, and throwing it down again; leaving a baby unlifted out of its cradle for weeks, till toadstools grew around the child out of the rottenness; leaving another to lie for days and nights on a mattress alive with maggots ; keeping the stumps of little amputated legs sore, to have the child with its little face puckered up in pain, to excite pity for begging purposes;" with hundreds of other similar instances.

The Law and Penal System should be an effectual "terror to evil-doers," of this description at least. And any system of utterly inadequate sentences, or pleasantly associated imprisonment, which deals in a lax and essentially ineffectual manner with the perpetrators of such outrages, is, in itself, a serious and cruel crime against the best elements of the community, however plausibly it may be advocated under the guise of a false "humanitarianism" or of specious "modern reform."

It is not in accord with the precepts of inspired wisdom, or with the example and operation of the Divine government.

CHAPTER V.

PRISON SEPARATION AND CLASSIFICATION.

THE FIRST ESSENTIAL.

THE separation of prisoners, *from each other only*, and for duly limited periods, is a first essential of good discipline, and an indispensable condition of success in penal treatment, whether intended as deterrent, or reformatory. It is also the best basis for Classification. It is the safest and ultimately, though not immediately, the cheapest arrangement, for adoption in criminal institutions.

It should involve, and this is always necessary to be borne in mind, the collateral condition, of the substitution of *good* personal influences for bad ones, together with constant useful occupation of body and mind. Mere cellular isolation should not be regarded as the sufficient condition for right separation. It has been one of the most pernicious and persistent hindrances to penal reform, in many nations, that *Solitude* has been so often considered as being identical with *Separation*. The terms " Solitary " System, " Silent " System, and " Separate " System, have been, in the popular mind, and even amongst many persons of general intelligence, confounded, as being three expressions for the same thing ; whereas they are *each different* from the other.

Silence may exist with the association of numbers; and effectual separation from evil association may be secured, in conjunction with the daily companionship of suitable persons.

The cell is most useful, and even indispensable, as a preliminary condition of separation. But it is only one element towards that end. When cellular imprisonment becomes absolute solitude, it is, if unduly prolonged, an unwarrantable cruelty. Solitude is one thing: wise separation is another. Continued isolation is unnatural, and ruinous to mind and body. Whereas, separation from evi association only, is most beneficial to its subjects.

THE VARIOUS PRISON SYSTEMS.

A few words of explanation, or repetition, seem here needful, respecting the several Prison Systems, because they are so often and persistently confused and misunderstood.

1. The CONGREGATE SYSTEM, in which prisoners have association with each other, by day or night, or both. This is still the unfortunately prevalent and general system in most European, Colonial, American, and other jails. It is emphatically and necessarily bad, especially with the common dormitories so frequent in the prisons of even civilised nations like France and Germany. An inmate of a Greek jail, on this plan, lately exclaimed, " The night is hell, when it is dark."

2. The SOLITARY SYSTEM, the opposite extreme, is also bad, under which prisoners are debarred even from good association, and are deprived, largely or wholly, of the helpful aids of labour, books, and adequate exercise. It is still occasionally used, for political prisoners chiefly, in Italy and Russia, as powerfully described and justly denounced by " OUIDA " for the former, and by various writers for the latter.

3. The SILENT SYSTEM. This is professedly adopted in

some British, American, and other prisons, with association. It is better than either of the former two; but it also is bad, because the silence is generally merely nominal, or confined to the absence of noisy conversation. If real silence is enforced, it leads to a large amount of punishment, which is unfair, and often cruel to the prisoners. In fact, the so-called "Silent System" is generally a pernicious delusion and pretence.

4. The SEPARATE SYSTEM, under which the prisoners are kept separate from other prisoners only, but have numerous visits in their cells from the officers, chaplain, schoolmaster, and from suitable persons from outside, together with industrial occupation, books, instruction, and daily exercise. With such ameliorating conditions as these, prisoners can enjoy good health of body and mind for periods extending from one to several years. Separation is at once more merciful and more severe than association. It is preferred by the better class of prisoners, and hated by the vilest. Hand industry in the cell is less competitive with free labour outside, than the large workshops, often with machinery, in American and Continental prisons, on the congregate plan. In the interesting autobiography of Mr. FREDERICK HILL, formerly H.M. Prison Inspector, and a veteran member of the Howard Association, he writes of the Separate System, "Though strongly opposed to an unlimited use of this system, I consider it greatly superior, even when carried to excess, to the indiscriminate association of prisoners, or to the Silent System."

5. The MIXED or COMBINED SYSTEM. Some prisons combine the separate, or cellular, with the associated plan. Many of the British jails are such. For long-term prisoners, such a modification is, in general, unavoidable, though it is disadvantageous, even in their case.

All sentences under *one* year, if not two, ought to be undergone on the Separate System.

Varying Meanings of the Term "Separate System."

The persistent injury which is often inflicted upon certain objects, by means of erroneous names, or objectionable ideas, which have somehow become associated with them, has long been illustrated in the history of what is usually termed "The Cellular System" of Prison Discipline. Owing to various misrepresentations, on the part of opponents, and in hardly less degree, to confusion and ambiguity on the side of its advocates, this name has too frequently conveyed the idea of a prolonged isolation of prisoners, without visitation, or companionship of any kind. In some countries, and to a comparatively very small extent, such a mode of treatment has been actually practised; and, as might be expected, with disastrous results. In several of the American States, formerly, and occasionally in some European countries, prisoners have been confined in separate cells, or underground dungeons, for years together, with little or no occupation, and with no association with their fellow-men, except the daily visit of a jailer. Thus pining between the dismal walls of their living tomb, their minds have, in many instances, given way, and they have become idiotic, or mad, or have gradually wasted to death. Similar results have ensued where, even under less rigid conditions, it has been attempted to substitute life-long separate confinement, instead of Capital Punishment. In such cases, many of the unfortunate objects of the experiment have not really been exempted from Capital Punishment, but have undergone that penalty, under the more cruel conditions of an execution prolonged over a period of years.

The fact is that the term " Cellular System " or " Separate System " has often been applied to *very different* modes of discipline. The name has represented a *variable* condition rather than a fixed one. The " Cellular System " of one country, or of one period, may not be at all identical with the so-called system of the same name, in another country, or at another period. Thus the original cellular treatment at Pentonville and Coldbath Fields Prisons, in London, was much more rigid than that of the Belgian prisons; whilst the corresponding system in New York State, during the term of its unfortunate experience there, was incomparably more severe than the Pentonville plan. The treatment in certain Dutch, Danish, Norwegian, and German cellular prisons has also undergone a series of modifications, in accordance with the experiences of successive years.

Hence the advocates and opponents of cellular separation have often, if not in general, assumed for it an identity and continuity of character which it has never really possessed.

Great impediments have been placed in the way of prison-reform, in this direction, by extreme opinions and hasty conclusions. Thus certain observers, having noticed the decided advantages of cellular separation for comparatively *short* periods, rushed to the unwarranted conclusion that the same discipline might be safely and beneficially extended over very *long* sentences, or even life imprisonment; an inference wholly unsupported by practical experience, and contrary to the laws of human nature. These extreme views, in support of the Cellular System, have produced equally exaggerated objections to its moderate and rightly conditioned adoption. And, on the whole, it is perhaps difficult to determine whether this great fundamental principle of all prison and penal reform, the separation of criminals from each other, has been most retarded by its friends, or by its foes.

HOWARD AND DUCPETIAUX URGED BY EXPERIENCE.

John Howard was awakened to the bad effects of prison association by his own personal experience of its disgusting evils, in a French jail, to which he had been consigned—

after his capture at sea by a privateer—during a time of war between England and France. Thenceforth he steadily advocated separation, industry and other conditions of improved prison discipline.

In like manner M. Ducpetiaux, the eminent administrator of penal reform in Belgium, was aroused to the necessities of the subject by his own sufferings, as a political prisoner, prior to the Belgian Revolution of 1830. Whilst in confinement, his feelings of decency and propriety were revolted by his enforced association with vile and filthy companions. He became profoundly convinced, from his own observation, that association renders imprisonment less punitory to the worst class of criminals, and more so to the less degraded. Just in proportion as a man is debased, he will enjoy the companionship of corrupt comrades. And it affords additional pleasure to the worst wretches in prison to corrupt others, who may at first be less familiar with evil than themselves.

After the Revolution of 1830, M. Ducpetiaux received from King Leopold I. favours and rewards, as some compensation for the imprisonment which his previous political partisanship had brought upon him. The office of Director of Prisons was ultimately conferred upon him. And thus, by a curious turn of events, he was placed in a position to give practical effect to the convictions which the mischief of associated imprisonment had so deeply impressed upon his own mind. But before committing himself to a decided and final plan of reorganisation, he instituted a further series of observations and inquiries as to the effects of the existing system. An overwhelming concurrence of testimony confirmed him in his conclusion that the associated plan was a welcome indulgence to the vile, a cruelty to the novice in imprisonment, and a corrupting evil to all.

From that time M. Ducpetiaux pursued a steady course of prison reform in Belgium, which placed that country in a leading position in this respect amongst the nations.   He received effectual co-operation from King Leopold I., the wise monarch whom he so faithfully served, and also from some able coadjutors, including, in particular, M. STEVENS, who for many years was the Governor of the cellular prison of Louvain, and afterwards of the great prison of St. Gilles, at Brussels.

BELGIAN EXPERIENCE.

The special progress of prison discipline, in Belgium and Holland, has been the result of long and carefully tested experience.   More than a century ago, their prisons elicited the repeated eulogies of the illustrious HOWARD, who visited them again and again, taking nine journeys to Holland, and nearly as many to Belgium.   In the former country he found the jails clean and orderly, with their inmates employed at useful labour (chiefly the manufacture of cloth), of the proceeds of which they received a share, to aid them on their discharge.   The Dutch motto, which became a favourite one with Howard, was " *Make men diligent, and you will make them honest.*"

At the same period, Belgium had established, in the great prisons of Ghent and Vilvorde, the system of entire separation by night, with congregate labour by day, which was a vast improvement upon the horrible and almost unrestrained contamination which then, and for a long time afterwards, formed a disgraceful feature in the jails of Great Britain and of most other nations.

It was in 1775 that Howard paid his first visit to Ghent prison, then newly erected, and was gratified with the large amount of useful industry, with piece-work and a share of the earnings for the prisoners, which characterised it.   On his sixth visit to the Low Countries, in 1783, he found the prisoners at Ghent in a miserable condition of demoralisation and ill-health.   For the Emperor Joseph, at the solicitation of a few private manufacturers, had ordered the useful productive labour of the establishment to be almost discontinued, on the plea of "unfair competition" with free labour. The results were such as might have been expected. The Governor spoke of them as "unhappy changes," and Howard, with his usual plainness of speech, termed the alteration a "vile policy." Two years afterwards, he had an interview with the Emperor, at Vienna, and, without any ceremony, complained sharply of the lack of wisdom in many departments of the prisons and other institutions in Austria. The Emperor asked, "Where have you seen any better institutions of the kind?" "There *was* one better," said Howard, "at Ghent, but (he added), not so now." The Emperor started and appeared displeased, but eventually parted from his honest-spoken visitor with cordiality and respect, and promised to carry out some, at least, of his recommendations.

The comparatively successful administration of the Belgian and Dutch prisons has continued throughout the Nineteenth Century; and the Governments of both countries have gradually, but decidedly, adopted the Cellular System.

M. Ducpetiaux, during his own imprisonment, had observed that any amount of association with other prisoners not only fostered evil communications whilst inside the prison, but, which was often more mischievous, ruined for life many of the inmates who had originally been committed for slight offences, by causing them to be *permanently recognisable*, after their discharge, by inveterate and evilly-disposed criminals. For example, Francis (to take any name), an apprentice, imprisoned at first for some theft, amounting to half-a-crown in value, might be, on his discharge, recognised by Alphonse, an old offender, who would thus have it in his power to brand the said Francis as a "prison bird," and blast for life his character and chances of getting an honest livelihood."

M. Ducpetiaux also ascertained that, in the boxes placed

in Belgian prisons to receive complaints from the prisoners, the majority of these complaints consisted of requests to be separated from the companionship of hateful and depraved associates.

His mind was further impressed with the amount of punishment *needlessly* afflicted on innocent wives and children by *very long* sentences of imprisonment passed upon their husbands and fathers—sentences which involved also unduly lengthened pecuniary burdens upon the honest taxpayer, whilst, in many cases, also greatly injuring the criminal by an unnatural and cruel separation from the ties of kindred and the softening influences of parental and conjugal relationships.

He reflected that if it should be found that the entire separation of prisoners from communication with others was a punishment to the worst class of offenders, and a safeguard to the better ones, the advantage would be double. The separation would be more punitory and more deterrent to the wilful, whilst more merciful and more curative to the penitent. Thus shorter terms, with cellular discipline, might safely, and with many advantages, moral and economical, be substituted for longer and less effectual periods of partially associated imprisonment.

It was also obvious that contagious and epidemic diseases would be greatly checked by cellular separation, whilst prison riots and rebellions would be rendered almost impossible. Nor would the sneers and laughter of reprobate companions any longer be able to efface from the hearts of the less hardened the impressions made by religious instructors or wise advisers; or to interrupt or prevent the exercise of *private prayer*, that most important and indispensable duty, as well as privilege, of every human being, both in and out of prison. Thus would there be a special inducement and prospect of success for frequent visitation by such persons, whether officially connected with the prison, or otherwise, as duty or desire might prompt to offer their aid to the prisoners. And finally, the inmates, anxious for occupation and variety, would become more diligent in their resort to useful handicraft labour (especially with the additional spur of a share in the profits), and would be more attentive to the instructive solace of well-selected books.

All these advantages, without any proportionate disadvantages, have been found to result from the adoption of the Cellular System in Belgium, Holland and elsewhere.

The Louvain and St. Gilles Prisons.

The prison at Louvain was opened in 1860, but has since been eclipsed in reputation and improved arrangements by the new prison of St. Gilles, in an elevated suburb of Brussels. The inmates of both establishments are chiefly occupied as tailors, weavers, shoemakers, bookbinders, and carpenters, the latter and the smiths having cells of double size to accommodate a bench or forge. There is a trades instructor for each branch of industry, as most of the inmates are found to be ignorant of any trade on entry. The warders are mostly conversant with some trade, and are chiefly selected, not (as has been too frequently the case in England) from the ranks of old soldiers, but on account of their experience and practical qualification for their special occupation.

In the Belgian prisons the inmates are treated with much respect and Christian consideration. In the female prisons the women are placed under the care of religious "Sisters," in the proportion of about ten "Sisters" per 100 women.

Many of the prisoners have, with perfect health of mind and body, spent from five to ten years in cellular confinement. In visiting Louvain prison, the writer observed a young man, aged twenty-seven, who had been in continuous separation in his cell for nine years. His crime was incendiarism, and he had been originally sentenced to death, which penalty was commuted to one of twenty years' imprisonment. But inasmuch as the Belgian Legislature has, since the introduction of the Cellular System, reduced the scale of all sentences, his term was rather less than ten years altogether. He had nearly completed it. Whilst in prison he had learnt shoemaking, writing, reading, and the French language (having probably only known Flemish before). He had earned nearly £16 for his use on discharge, in addition to as much more, with which he had purchased food of a better class than the rougher fare supplied gratis. Besides this, he had earned £40 or £50, or more, for the State, towards the expenses of his maintenance during his term. The Deputy-Governor remarked of him: " He is now a very good fellow ! "

Another prisoner there had earned for himself as much discharge money (£16) in the shorter period of five and a half years. His term would expire in six months. The officer remarked, " He is a very good man; he will not come again ! "

And certain it is that the comparatively large sums of money which the Belgian prisoners can earn (although the valuation of their labour is, as a punishment, much lower than its real worth) cause many of them to start well and easily in permanently honest careers, and in a more effective manner than the eleemosynary and smaller help of Discharged Prisoners' Aid Societies.

So far as may be gathered from a number of somewhat varying statistics, the average net cost of each Belgian prisoner is about £15 per annum. Hence the direct pecuniary results of the Cellular System are not nearly so considerable as those of American self-supporting prisons. But the indirect gain is much greater, by reason of the moral and preventive advantages, and the *shorter terms of imprisonment* which the system safely and effectually permits.

The money earned by Belgian prisoners, and retained

till their discharge, is never forfeited, even for mis-
conduct. Once earned, it is quite secure. They often
send a portion of their money to their relatives; thus a
parent in prison helps a child outside, or a child contributes to a parent's wants.

The articles which may be purchased with the immediately disposable portion of the prison earnings are
white bread, cheese, bacon, milk, paper, pens, tobacco,
etc. Smoking is only permitted as a privilege to the
better behaved, during their hours of exercise in their
separate yards, where they are obliged to keep in motion,
either by brisk walking, by gardening, or by paving
with heavy pounders.

As to the effect of the Belgian Cellular System upon
the health of the inmates, the official statistics show an
average mortality of about $1\frac{1}{2}$ per cent. per annum,
which is a lower rate than that of the partially congregate prison at Ghent.

In a recent decade of Louvain experience (with upwards
of 500 inmates on the average), there were only fourteen
suicides and fourteen cases of insanity, that is to say, less
than two per annum of each, in this large prison. This
state of things compares not unfavourably with some
English convict establishments, and similar congregate
prisons.

GHENT PRISON.

The great central prison of Ghent, with more than
1,200 inmates, is partly conducted on the Separate System
and partly on the Congregate. The life-sentenced prisoners
are in association by day. And considering the length
of their sentences, this is unavoidable.

The writer, on re-visiting this prison, in 1894, had
again the opportunity of conversing with some of the
inmates who were undergoing the longest terms of
detention.

One of these was a man who had been continuously in prison for thirty-three years, for attempted murder. He spoke intelligently and courteously, and appeared to be in good health, but was greatly disappointed that his punishment had not yet been deemed a sufficient one.

Another prisoner had been confined for thirty-one years, also for attempted murder.

A third had been brought to Ghent, after twenty-two years' cellular imprisonment at Louvain. This man might have come to Ghent twelve years previously, had he so wished, but he preferred the separation at Louvain to the association at Ghent. He said he had more personal liberty in his cell at the former prison, and could act and move about more freely, when at work alone, than when placed amongst other workers.

The writer was specially interested in the conversation of a Frenchman, then in Ghent prison. He said: "I have been in cellular separation here, by day and night, for six years. And I prefer it, because I am my own master in my cell; and I should not be so, if amongst other prisoners. I am strong, however, and can bear it, but I do not think that most men can be confined for such long periods, in a cell, without injury. For prolonged cellular imprisonment, even where it has not apparently injured the bodily health of its subject, tends to weaken the will and the brain power, and to destroy that vital energy upon which a man has to depend for success in life."

This prisoner said that when in France he had attended an "Anthropological Congress," where he had listened to the theories of such men as Lombroso and others. But he did not consider their views to be practical, or based upon real experience. He also spoke with disgust of the vile association of criminals in most French prisons. He had noticed that, as a class, French prisoners were more to be pitied than blamed. They had nearly all had bad parentage, or bad training. They were nearly all destitute of any idea of God, or Future Retribution. They despised religion and its services, and were without shame or moral sensibility. He considered the criminal class, at least in France, to be, on the whole, more intelligent than the non-criminal class of their own rank. Their wits had been sharpened by experience. They were very indolent and pervaded by a determination to get a living as easily as possible and without exertion. They saw no harm in theft.

On the subject of Capital Punishment, this prisoner said :—" I was previously confined in one of the largest prisons of Paris, where I came in contact with several thousand fellow-prisoners ; for two hundred of us were together at a time, and fresh prisoners were coming in daily. Being myself deeply interested in criminal matters, I used habitually to question my comrades there, as to their experiences and impressions. Amongst other things, we talked of Capital Punishment ; and I heard, from all of them, that its effect was just the *opposite* of that claimed for it. For these men were outcasts from respectable society. They had no further hope of its estimation or honour ; yet every one naturally desires the good opinion of his fellow-men, and if he cannot obtain the appreciation of the good, he will still value the admiration of the bad. Such is human vanity. But if there is anything the criminal class admire, it is pluck and daring defiance of authority and its penalties. Consequently even the guillotine is to them an object to be defied in actual life. And they do thus defy and disregard it, because it renders them heroes to their own class."

This intelligent prisoner, who had been a Parisian journalist, in answer to questions put to him by the writer, as to his own opinion of the most effective method of repressing crime, replied :—" My intercourse with other prisoners has convinced me of the desirability and value

of Corporal Punishment.   For the criminal class in general
need   something   powerful   enough   to   overcome   their
innate *inertia* and indisposition to honest industry.
Ordinary imprisonment has not this power.   It does not
give them a sufficient shake.   They need something which
can shake them out of their desperate indifference to
honesty and labour.   I think whipping will do this."

The same prisoner spoke highly of the Belgian Separate
System as contrasted with the debasing association in
most French prisons.

BELGIAN SEPARATION EXTREME.

On   the   whole,   and   notwithstanding   the   excessive
duration to which it is often extended, the Belgian Cellular
System is administered with wonderful skill and success.
It commends itself, by its nature and results, to the
Government, to the public, and to most of the prisoners
themselves.

The DIRECTOR-GENERAL OF BELGIAN PRISONS informed
the writer (in 1894) that about sixty-five per cent. of the
long-term prisoners prefer separation, and that many of
these, after having experienced the Association System at
Ghent, have asked to be again placed in separate cells, in
order to obtain the reduction of sentence which accompanies the Separate *Regime* in that country.

The cells in the Belgian prisons are comparatively large,
and are well lighted.   These are very important points.
The prisoners are frequently visited during each day, both
by their officers, priests, or other ministers, and also, at
least in the larger cities, by members of " Patronage " or
Prisoners' Aid Societies.   They have one hour's exercise
daily in a yard.   This allowance might with advantage
be increased.   It is admitted by visitors to the Belgian
prisons generally, that their inmates, including those serving for the longer terms, are generally healthy.

In order to secure the utmost vigilance over the mental

and physical health of the prisoners, the Belgian Government, in 1891, appointed three Medical Specialists, in addition to the local or resident physicians, who were to visit the prisons, and who were also to be summoned by telegraph in case of any sudden indication of dangerous disease or mental weakness amongst the inmates.

It is admitted that for periods of two or three years' cellular confinement, at least, the Belgian system works admirably. But, notwithstanding the official and other declarations that the longer periods are also borne advantageously, the writer ventures to doubt such statements. At any rate, he fears there is reason to conclude that, in more than a few instances, the longer terms of separation exercise an injurious influence upon the minds of the prisoners. He has been privately informed by various prison officers in Belgium, and by other persons also, that such is the case. One of the chief Inspectors of Belgium prisons has been understood to object to cellular detention beyond five years.

If the Belgian system were not so very carefully and wisely administered, a much shorter period of separation than five years would prove disastrous to its subjects. In some of the German prisons, with a Cellular System not possessing the ameliorations provided in Belgium, such unfavourable effects have been observed. In one of these establishments, a prisoner, undergoing the Cellular System by day and night, remarked to the writer, that he thought it was a good system up to two years, and that he had himself borne it well for a longer period, but that most prisoners confined there for three or four years were injuriously affected in their minds.

With ordinary care, as to visitation, employment, exercise, ventilation and light, the Cellular System may everywhere be carried out, with great advantage, for sentences not exceeding two years. But beyond that period it is certainly attended by serious risks and dangers. Though even so, it is incomparably better than the debasing and pernicious Gang-System.

SPECIAL ADVANTAGES OF THE CELLULAR SYSTEM.

For the general class of prisoners, under the Cellular System, sentences may safely and justly be rendered from 50 to 75 per cent. shorter than those for congregate confinement. The Belgian Legislature has enacted laws making *a general reduction* of sentences passed during the continuance of the Congregate System. For example, sentences of twenty years under that system are now reduced to less than ten years, those of ten years to six years, and those of five to three and a-half.

Briefly, the Cellular System, as distinguished from the rigours of the old American Solitary System, and as characterised by the substitution of good communication for evil, and by a much greater intercourse with officers, instructors, and visitors, than has hitherto been a feature even of English prisons, presents the following advantages :—

1. More deterrence than the Congregate or Semi-congregate System.

2. Infinitely more of reformatory effect and of freedom from corrupting influences.

3. More economy to the State, or the taxpayers, by reason of the much shorter terms of confinement necessary under it.

4. Less breaking up, or ruin, of the prisoner's family, by reason of shorter separation from them.

5. A better reception of religious and secular instruction in prison. More encouragement to reflection and especially to prayer.

6. General exemption from contagious and epidemic diseases.

7. Greater security from escapes.

8. Far fewer causes for prison punishment, than with either the Silent or the Congregate System.

9. Greater facilities for the observation and prompt detection of disease, or insanity.

10. Protection to the prisoner, on his discharge, from future recognition by other prisoners.

11. A greater eligibility for employment then, and a far more effectual qualification for a career of honest usefulness.

12. And last, but not least, under the Cellular System there is, in general, far less competition of prison labour with outside free industry. It is the busy workshops (sometimes with steam power and machinery) in the great prisons with association, where such quantities of goods are turned out as not unreasonably to excite complaints from Trades Unions, or other free workers. But the cell, with hard labour, presents a *minimum* of such competition.

NECESSARY QUALIFICATIONS OF THE CELLULAR SYSTEM.

Inasmuch as the best of methods may be liable to the worst abuse, if not rightly administered, so the Cellular System, to be accompanied by success, as in Belgium and Holland, must be everywhere as vigilantly and unceasingly guarded, as it is in those countries, against the neglect or mistakes which would convert it into the *rigid Solitary* System—which is *as evil* as the other is *good*.

Although a useful amount of separation has been introduced into the British prisons, yet up to the last decade of the Nineteenth Century there has not been permitted, in the United Kingdom generally, either that amount of suitable visitation, or that variety and encouragement of useful industry, or that daily exercise, each of which is essential for the success of any system with the *entire* separation of prisoners from each other.

When it is remembered that perhaps most of the reforms

in British criminal treatment have resulted from *unofficial* sources and *voluntary* visitors—such as John Howard, Mrs. Fry, Sir Fowell Buxton, Sarah Martin, and many others—it is evident that this great means of usefulness (suitable visitation) should be carefully encouraged, both for the sake of the prisoners and also for public interest.

AIR AND LIGHT.

Part of the opposition to the Cellular System, in some countries, has doubtless arisen from perversions and abuses of it, and especially from the very defective architecture of those prisons in which the cells have been constructed either cruelly small, or dark. There should be as much of sunlight as possible, and a due regard to ventilation. The Italians have a saying that " Where the sunlight does not enter, there the doctor must come." In some prisons these points are well attended to ; but in others a very unwarrantable neglect of them is manifest. M. RICHARD PETERSEN, the humane Governor, for many years, of a cellular prison at Christiania, in Norway, has invited particular attention to the importance of light and air in cells, as materially affecting the success of the system. Some years ago he visited several Danish prisons, where he was favourably impressed with the size and light of the cells. His observations and inquiries, during these visits, led him to advocate similar improvements in his own country, and with good effects. He has repeatedly protested against the cruelty of " caging " prisoners in cells too small and dark, a practice which, as carried out in some prisons, has tended to involve the whole system of separation in an indiscriminating condemnation by some writers.

M. Petersen, whilst urging a very decided adoption of cellular separation for first-term and ordinary offenders, has also expressed doubts as to its suitability for such a class as very ignorant, semi-savage Laplanders, for example. These are hardly fit subjects for rigid cellular discipline.

A merciful discrimination must always be held applicable to such cases. And the "falsehood of extremes," both in theory and practice, needs to be carefully guarded against.

Both for prisons on the Separate and on the Congregate Systems, a good supply of air and light is of great importance. Indeed in some of the crowded dormitories and workshops of associated jails, the ventilation is far worse than in the healthy airy cells of Belgian, Dutch and Danish prisons.

The general community, in most countries, is as yet very inadequately awakened to the necessity of a constant supply of fresh air, both by day and by night, in order to furnish to the lungs and blood that amount of oxygen which is absolutely necessary to maintain health and to obviate the various fatal forms of tubercular disease.

In his valuable work, entitled "*Consumption and the Air Re-breathed*" (London, Longmans), Dr. H. MacCormac remarks, "Scrofula and pulmonary consumption are much more frequent in Asylums for Foundlings and Orphans, in Reformatories and Prisons, and among artisans who work all day in close rooms, than in those who are much in the open air."

Dr. MacCormac points to the remarkable, the practically total, exemption from pulmonary consumption and other tubercular disease, enjoyed by the inhabitants of the Western Islands of Scotland, in spite of their very damp and misty climate. The reason is that, throughout the year, in summer and winter, the air from outside has constant access to their hovels, where a fire is always burning, a hole in the roof always open, and the door seldom closed. These islanders are incomparably more healthy than the generality of persons elsewhere, who shut out the air from their comfortable rooms, and hence re-breathe an atmosphere more or less poisonous, because largely deprived of oxygen. Warm and small rooms, with windows closed by day and night, slay annually, in most countries (says

Dr. MacCormac) more victims than war or the assassin. "The breath of man re-breathed is destruction to his fellows, pernicious to himself." There are thousands of houses and myriads of small bedrooms, in most places, which are literally murderous to those who dwell in them. And no medicines can possibly avail to prevent fatal tubercular diseases to their inmates. The "open-air cure" for consumption, by residence in tents, is suggestive of the vast importance of a free current of oxygenised air in every house, for the maintenance of health and the prevention of disease.

But if the dwellers in cities, in cottages, and even in palaces, are as yet so ignorant as they often are, of the necessity of this pure air, it is not to be wondered at that prison ventilation still needs much more attention than it has yet received in many quarters. The cellular prisons, in general, or at least in Europe, seem, however, to be better ventilated than the congregate ones.

Misrepresentation as to Insanity and the Separate System.

It has been said "There are three kinds of lies, namely, 'white' lies, 'black' lies, and *Statistics*." And, really, the originator of such a saying might derive considerable justification from the unfair manner in which "statistics," so-called, have been perverted and muddled, especially of late years, both by some British and Continental writers, with a view, as it would appear, of throwing undeserved aspersion and discredit upon the Separate System, by unfounded or greatly exaggerated statements respecting their alleged tendency to develop insanity amongst their inmates.

The old absolutely *solitary* imprisonment, as carried out in New York and other American States, about the year 1830, did, indeed, produce both insanity and death—owing to the absence of the most ordinary provisions for the health, employment, visitation and help of the prisoners. It was characterised by the grossest brutality and neglect.

Subsequently, both in America and Europe, the natural results of such wicked folly have continuously led to misapprehensions in the public mind, by confusing this system with the wise and beneficial *régime* of separation from evil companionship only.

Not long after the erection of the cellular prison of PENTONVILLE, in London, such misrepresentations were perseveringly promulgated in England. It was often urged, and by persons who ought to have known the facts better, that at that prison the system was a total failure. The incorrectness of these statements was authoritatively exposed by the Rev. Mr. BURT, the chaplain of that establishment, in his work on the Separate System. He showed that, during the period of *complete* separation of the prisoners, for terms of eighteen to twenty-four months, at Pentonville, from 1842 to 1848, their mental health was superior to that of a later and less stringent discipline. He observes, "The insanity under the altered (and relaxed) system has been *eight times greater* than during the four preceding years, when the original (cellular) system was in full operation." But the Pentonville System was always a defective one. Its assumption of the term "model" prison was unwarranted by facts. The rigours of separation were never, in this prison, accompanied by those necessary and merciful ameliorations, which other better conducted cellular establishments, in various countries, have adopted. But, incomplete as was the Pentonville plan, it was never so mischievous to the minds of the prisoners as has often been represented.

There are two important matters in connection with CRIMINAL LUNACY which are constantly apt to be over-looked. The first is that the habits and antecedents of criminals, as a class, always tend to produce amongst them a comparatively large amount of insanity *before* they come under the grasp of the law. And, secondly, both in Europe and America, it has been a frequent practice, on the part of magistrates or other authorities, to commit insane persons to jail, instead of sending them to Lunatic Asylums.

If these two leading facts are taken into consideration, they will effectually dispose of most of the allegations of insanity being specially caused by imprisonment. Whereas the real truth is that it is the criminal careers *before* imprisonment, or *outside* of the jail, which produce a special degree of insanity amongst this class. All well-conducted prisons tend to *diminish* such insanity, rather than otherwise.

Dr. MORSELLI, a writer on suicide, remarks: " The class of delinquents have more inclination towards suicide, as also towards madness, than the ordinary population." He adds that " Seventy per cent. of the suicides of prisoners are by those *without work*."

Passing from short terms of imprisonment to protracted ones, there is, however, a very real danger in the attempt to apply "Solitary," or even "Separate" confinement to Life Sentences, or *long* terms. Such a combination is inhuman. Yet it has continued, even of late years, to be exemplified in the treatment of a comparatively few prisoners, in certain Russian and other prisons. In Great Britain, France, Germany, Norway, Sweden, Austria, and even in Belgium, the longer sentenced and life-term prisoners are placed in association. This is an almost unavoidable evil even in such cases, but it is less mischievous, at least physically and mentally, than the total collapse which would ensue from prolonged isolation.

But speaking generally, as to ordinary sentences, more than three-fourths of which are under one year, in Great Britain, the statistics of cellular prisons, in respect to insanity, do not compare unfavourably with those of association establishments; and, in some cases, the amount of insanity is now greater in the latter than in the former.

SENDING THE INSANE TO JAIL.

Until and during the last decade of the Nineteenth Century, there has been a mischievous tendency on the part of many magistrates in England, Scotland, and Ireland, to send insane, or doubtfully sane offenders to Prisons, instead of to Lunatic Asylums. The PRISON COMMISSIONERS, for all three parts of the Kingdom, have had to complain of this.

It is doubly injurious and unjust. It is not fair to the persons thus imprisoned, and it is also unjust to the prison officials; for it has led the public to form unwarranted conclusions respecting the treatment of prisoners. Certain discussions, in the English newspapers, upon prison discipline, have shown that some persons had imbibed very mistaken ideas about a supposed connection between prisons and the insane. And the origin of these mis-representations is largely due to the number of insane persons who have been wrongfully sent to jails instead of to asylums.

The Howard Association has made many inquiries respecting this matter, and from these it is manifest that considerable popular misapprehension exists, which is quite opposed to the actual experience of prisoners and their officers.

In visiting a certain Scotch jail, its Secretary was informed that, during the preceding year, ten insane persons were sent to that prison. Their insanity was so evident that nine of them had to be sent away immediately to an asylum. The tenth was employed at work in the open air with some other prisoners, but he also had to be sent to an asylum in three weeks. It often takes weeks, or months, however, before the insanity can be proved, to the extent of warranting admission to an asylum.

In almost every prison visited by the Secretary of

the Howard Association, he has been informed that the ordinary system of British imprisonment, by separating the short-term prisoners from each other, tends rather to *improve* than to injure their mental health. Again and again has the statement been made, " Coming to jail prevents many offenders from going mad, for it is the drink that chiefly makes them insane. Here they get no alcohol, and hence many are saved from lunacy. Certainly they get better in jail, rather than worse, and there is no danger whatever of ordinary cellular separation, for short terms, injuring prisoners' minds."

The late Director-in-Chief of English Prisons, GENERAL SIR E. F. DU CANE, stated in 1894, that in those prisons where separation is enforced, " The cases of insanity, *not existing at reception* are very few ; and are much fewer than formerly, owing to the great pains we have taken." DR. R. M. GOVER, Medical Inspector of British Convict Prisons, has recorded " Separate confinement in a modern English prison, for two years, not only does not injuriously affect the mental and bodily health, but is frequently attended with benefit."

The principal Medical Officer of Wormwood Scrubbs Prison, London, DR. TENNYSON PATMORE, stated in 1894 : " So far from separate confinement in prison tending to produce insanity, my experience at this place for thirteen years tells me that, with the care and kindness shown and the preventive means used here, imprisonment tends to *restore* the mental balance, which a period of bad living *before* imprisonment has so often engendered."

At the present day there is comparatively little danger of insanity from the separation of ordinary offenders, in the cellular prisons, because the lessons of the past have widely awakened attention to the necessity for rational precautions in this direction ; such as constant industry ; daily exercise ; a supply of books ; instruction by chaplains and schoolmasters ; careful medical oversight ; and frequent visitation by the officers and other persons.

FRANCE AND PENAL SEPARATION.

Although in France most of the prisons, up to the end of the Nineteenth Century, have continued to be on the associated plan, yet beneficial progress is being made in that country, by the gradual introduction of the Cellular System for short sentences. Few countries need it more. For the evils of criminal association have long been specially noticeable in France. One striking example, out of a multitude of others, occurred recently, when two hardened criminals were arrested at Douai, after committing seven murders and various robberies. They had become acquainted with each other, whilst previously in a prison, and had there planned several of their subsequent atrocious crimes.

MIRABEAU, who became an early advocate of the Separate System, remarked on one occasion, after visiting the old Bicêtre—"I knew that the Bicêtre was both a hospital and a prison. But I was not previously aware that the hospital had been made to engender diseases, and the prison to propagate crimes."

In 1875 an important French Commission of Inquiry on Systems of Prison Discipline, of which BARON D'HAUSSONVILLE was a principal member, reported in favour of cellular separation for the great majority of short terms of imprisonment ; and the Government decided to adopt this system, for at least all sentences up to one year's duration. But the military demands and great National Debt of France have hitherto tended unduly to limit the outlay on cellular prisons, requisite to give full effect to this conclusion.

In so far as the principle of separation has been adopted in French prisons, as for example, in such admirable establishments as those of NANTERRE (Seine) and MENDE (Lozère), it has been very successful.

At a meeting of that very useful organisation, the

FRENCH PRISON SOCIETY, in Paris, 1894, a lady official of the women's prison at Nanterre, Madame D'ABBADIE D'ARRAST, said :—"I am happy to be able to testify to the good effects of the Cellular System, as it is carried out at Nanterre. When cellular separation is applied to women and girls, for periods of from a year to eighteen months, we do not observe that their health suffers from it, if the food is sufficient, and if they have work. They maintain their good humour and express a desire to lead a better life."

She added that the younger girls at Nanterre had remarked, in reference to their previous imprisonment in jails on the associated system, "If you had always kept us separate from other girls, we should not have learnt the bad things we have learnt, and we should not have become worse than we were, when we were first arrested."

This lady's laudation of the Separate System at Nanterre was limited to the maximum period, there, of eighteen months' detention. But so far, it had worked admirably.

AMERICAN NEGLECT OF SEPARATION.

It is a remarkable circumstance that whereas the people of the United States enjoy the reputation of being peculiarly shrewd in the pursuit of pecuniary profit, they they have manifested an almost universal disregard to the merits of the separation of prisoners from each other. They have, however, in one respect been wiser than Europeans, in that they have more generally compelled their criminals to maintain themselves by their labour during incarceration. They have practically said to them "You shall not rob your honest countrymen, whilst *in* jail, as you did when outside." But they have largely nullified this partial wisdom by encouraging pernicious association in their prisons. The result has been that crime has increased to a large extent, the cost of which has *very far exceeded* the *temporary* saving effected by the gains of congregate occupation in jails.

The Americans might with advantage act upon the emphatic words of their greatest Penologist, the Hon. EDWARD LIVINGSTON, who, it is to be remembered, was one of the few eminent authorities in the United States who have decidedly condemned the general prison system of that country. He thus shows the impossibility of adequate classification, except by cellular separation ("Criminal Code," page 309): "*Every* association of convicts that can be formed, will, in a greater or less degree, corrupt, but will never reform, those of which it is composed. And we are brought to the irresistible conclusion that classification once admitted to be useful, it is so in an inverse proportion to the numbers of which each class is composed ; and it is not perfect until we come to the point at which it loses its name and nature, in the *complete* separation of individuals. We come, then, to the conclusion that each convict is to be separated from his fellows." Mr. Livingston here showed his larger grasp of the question than perhaps any other American writer on criminal treatment. These are golden words, which might with advantage be inscribed on every prison, especially in America.

Both in America and in Europe, certain opponents of the Cellular System have objected to it, on the ground that it involves too much of reactionary influence upon its subjects, when their confinement comes to an end. But these gentlemen ignore the fact that the sudden discharge of a prisoner, from any kind of associated prison, to absolute liberty, involves, in most respects, as much reaction, or, to make a frequent comparison, as great a "rebound of the spring," as his release from a well-conducted cellular establishment. In each case, the measure of absolute liberty, immediately entered upon, is similarly trying and tempting. And for such sudden liberty, a previous prolonged association with corrupting wretches, is the very reverse of preparation ; it is the greatest disqualification.

Amongst the minority of Americans who have advocated the Separate System, may be mentioned the curious example of a Prisoner inside Elmira State Reformatory, who, in 1891, in the weekly journal there published, defended the Howard Association from some recent strictures by other Americans, and remarked : " If there is any one thing on which prison reformers agree, it is that prisoners should associate with each other as little as possible. What is said by the Howard Association, regarding criminals, is undoubtedly true."

In one of the last public utterances of that eminent American, RUTHERFORD B. HAYES, EX-PRESIDENT of the UNITED STATES, he spoke strongly (at Pittsburg) against the corrupting association of criminals in jails, and especially in reference to the disastrous influence of such evil companionship upon juvenile offenders. He said, " Surely almost any change, in dealing with the young, with the beginners in law breaking, would be an improvement on the prevailing system. Jails and prisons so constructed and managed as to keep their inmates separate, such as are found in several States of the Union and in Europe, would afford an adequate remedy for the evil."

CONCENTRATED CRIMINALITY IN PRISONS.

It is to be particularly remembered that the associated intercourse of prisoners is a *concentrated* form of evil. Even in the worst conditions of free society, there is some considerable admixture of persons who are more or less respectable and virtuous ; but the jail population is ex-elusively composed of offenders.

It has been proved again and again, that *no* system of supervision, however careful, can obviate the corrupting tendencies of the association of criminals. ·The British Convict Prison authorities have made strenuous endeavours, both by the number and discipline of their officers, and by attempts to classify their prisoners, to prevent the evil in question, but with little success. The ROYAL COMMISSIONERS on the PENAL SERVITUDE ACTS, with EARL KIMBERLEY as Chairman, remarked in their Report, in 1879 :—

"The evidence given by the great majority of witnesses, whom we have called before us, and the statements of convicts, of whom we have personally made inquiries, in our visits to the different prisons, have satisfied us that, *in spite of all the precautions* taken by the prison officers, communications can, to a considerable extent, be carried on between prisoners working in association."

FAILURE OF THE "CLASSIFICATION" OF PRISONERS.

No classification whatever, except absolute separation from other criminals, can obviate the intrinsic evils of association. That high authority on this question, the Rev. John Clay, observes : "I believe it to be *beyond human power* safely to classify prisoners. I dare not trust even six or eight prisoners in any class or association which leaves conversation free." (Life, p. 283.)

Perhaps this statement might be qualified, in view of some exceptional experiences in a different direction ; and it would not be difficult to adduce some illustrations of a comparatively harmless intercommunication of selected prisoners, of the better sort, whilst engaged in small parties, in agricultural or similar labours. But even with the aid of the most careful attempts thus to classify prisoners, their association will always be attended with dangers of combination, or mischief of some kind. A striking proof of this was afforded by the experience of CAPTAIN MACONOCHIE, at NORFOLK ISLAND. He regarded cellular separation as being unnatural; as indeed it is; and as *every* form of imprisonment must necessarily be. He also knew, by painful observation, the dangers and evils of associating large numbers of convicts in gang labour. He therefore devised a plan which he felt confident would succeed; inasmuch as it was designed to work with, instead of against, nature. This was to permit small groups of selected prisoners, of only half a dozen in each company, to live and work together, and be mutually responsible for each other's good behaviour. In this way, he hoped to bring into play those feelings of mutual forbearance, good fellowship, sympathy and resistance to temptation, which are to be found combined with healthful and favourable conditions of association in freedom. The desire was a noble one. And if any man could have made it succeed, Captain Maconochie was the one to do it. But even he failed at this point. One of his colleagues at Norfolk Island prison, Dr. (subsequently Archbishop) WILLIAM B. ULLATHORNE remarked, " These private associations (of five or six each) tempted to plots and conspiracies and gave all facilities for their execution. *They led, in fact,* to the outbreak in Norfolk Island; although the Catholic clergy warned Captain Maconochie of the very men, and of the game of hypocrisy which they were playing." (*Essay on the Management of Criminals;* by Dr. Ullathorne, p. 35.) Mrs. FRY also experienced very disappointing results, through her reliance upon the imaginary efficacy of similar so-called " classification " in prisons, by means of dividing their inmates into small groups.

If the dangers of combination and revolt are almost inevitable, even with such small groups of prisoners, how much greater are the risks incurred by the association of large gangs! The repeated outbreaks in convict prisons, and penal establishments, in all countries, illustrate this danger. But the Cellular System effectually prevents revolts and checks insubordination.

Pioneers of the Separate System.

In addition to the eminent Belgian advocates of the cellular treatment, its successful and rational application has been especially promoted by various other gentlemen, such as, in particular, by M. W. H. Suringar, of Holland, Rev. John Clay and Archbishop Ullathorne, of England, and M. Richard Petersen, of Norway. These practical men have worked out, in establishments more or less under their own official care, important problems connected with the question, in a moderate and common-sense mode, very different from the mere theories of inexperienced doctrinaires, or of extreme partisans of the system.

W. H. Suringar.

William Henry Suringar, a man superior in some respects even to John Howard, was, for about fifty years actively engaged, both as an officer of Government and as a philanthropist, in the visitation and administration of prisons and other institutions. He was Vice-President of the Directors of Prisons at Amsterdam, and was intimately acquainted with the other jails of the kingdom. In conjunction with his friends—M. Warnsinck, M. Nierstrasz, and M. John S. Mollett—he founded, in 1823, "the NETHERLANDS SOCIETY for the MORAL IMPROVEMENT of PRISONERS." He lived to see it enter on its fiftieth year of useful operation. In 1872 he recorded, as the result of half a century of special opportunities of observation at home and abroad : "I have become firmly convinced that whatever experiment may be made in the classification of prisoners, or in the use of all other means, the Separate System of our country, though decidedly not perfect, is *the best*, as compared with other systems ; and that it must be adopted."

He made a similar remark, in a conversation, shortly before his decease, with the SECRETARY of the HOWARD

ASSOCIATION. He then said, " I have spent nearly half a century in the discharge of official duties connected with the repression of crime. I have had constant and abundant opportunities of observation and information on this question. I have rooms in my house almost filled with the literature of the subject. And I have arrived at the most decided conclusion that the principle of the continued penal separation of offenders, from each other, is the only one effectual for its object. All other systems, however popular for a time, and however they may be supported by influential names, must, from their very nature and from their radical defects, prove ultimate failures."

Since that time the writer has conversed with many other practical authorities and observers, and has visited many prisons, in different countries, and read and thought much upon the matter, and he is increasingly convinced that M. SURINGAR was perfectly right in his conclusion. And probably no man in either Europe or America was, on the whole, more competent to form such an opinion than that gentleman, whose breadth of mind and absence of sentimentality were characteristic qualities which imparted additional weight to his extensive and prolonged official experience.

M. SURINGAR also remarked that the Commissioners of the large Dutch prison at Leeuwarden had made many attempts to classify prisoners, in smaller or larger groups, and by a union of cellular and congregate arrangements. They had instituted a careful study of foreign experiences by means of deputations sent to observe and investigate the prison discipline of other countries. " And what was the conclusion they arrived at ? With one accord they decided in favour of separate confinement. All the visitors and investigators came to the same conclusion; complete isolation of the prisoners from each other, but with regular work, the use of books, scholastic instruction, religious teaching, visits, and a daily enjoyment of the open air."

These latter adjuncts were always insisted upon, by M. Suringar and his colleagues, as of absolute importance. And he was careful to state, " It is not the cell *as such* that works the reclamation of its inmates. It is only the fittest —the indispensable receptacle for containing the healing potion. Religion must work the moral improvement of the criminals; religion the essence of humanity."

· M. Suringar and his Prison Society attached great importance to the visitation of prisoners by judicious members of their Association. The King of Holland granted these good men permission freely to enter the prisons and communicate with the inmates. This plan became a characteristic of the Dutch prisons, and rendered their system more complete than the Belgian mode. The visitors acted as unpaid schoolmasters, chaplains, librarians, and agents for obtaining employment for the prisoners on their discharge. Such functions, and especially the latter, are the special modes in which visitors may be of use in prisons. For one or two paid chaplains, or schoolmasters, however excellent and active, can never be adequate for the moral and intellectual requirements of hundreds of prisoners. Nor need there be any collision with the official staff, or any interference with their duties and prerogatives. On the contrary, it has been repeatedly acknowledged by the Governors and managers of prisons, that they have found their labours in the maintenance of the discipline materially aided and lightened by the influences of regular visitors. Nor was it the case in the Dutch prisons that the visitors were molested or injured. On the contrary, M. Suringar, speaking on the twenty-fifth anniversary of the Prison Society, said : In these twenty-five years, no visitor has had a hair of his head hurt."

M. Suringar and his associates obtained subscriptions from the public for the purchase of libraries of miscellaneous literature, including especially books likely to interest the ignorant classes of prisoners, and to attract them to a love of reading, and of the acquisition of knowledge. For devotional literature, a careful selection was made, to meet the respective tastes of the Protestant, Roman Catholic and Jewish inmates of the prisons. There being many Jews in Holland, in order to accommodate the religious scruples of this class, the authorities placed, as far as possible, all their prisoners of that persuasion in one jail. In every way the Dutch Society endeavoured to promote the success of religious instruction to criminals. They raised funds to send ministers to prisons where the State had not provided chaplains. They zealously encouraged these good men. M. Suringar says: " The preaching was not always in the desert. Prisoners have arrived in scores who had never prayed. They have been taught how to pray." But in order that such instruction should not be wasted, the Separate System was perseveringly urged. Again he declares that, where criminal association is permitted " One dispenser of the good news of the Gospel, who stays for an hour or so, is thwarted by scores of permanent teachers of evil." Such a prison becomes " an academy of sin," and especially for the younger inmates.

M. Suringar attached particular value to the oversight and aid of prisoners on their discharge. He and his colleagues instituted regular arrangements for bringing the discharged prisoners into communication with such of their relatives, friends, or local ministers, as might probably be of service to them; and for endeavouring to remove them from the influences of old acquaintances of the wrong sort. Clothes, tools, and travelling expenses were provided for those who needed them. Employers of labour were visited, on behalf of those anxious to find occupation. These and similar efforts were, in a large proportion of instances, encouragingly successful, though there were also cases of failure and ingratitude.

But even the failures were utilised. The Dutch Society of Prison Visitors found another important function in using its experiences with criminals, in and out of prison, as a means of impressing upon the public the necessity of preventive as well as restorative efforts. As M. Suringar remarked, "It is better to educate the young than to chastise the old. The new wine of instruction and virtue must be put into new bottles." Hence the Society laboured more earnestly to indoctrinate the public as to the value of extending general education and institutions for the reclamation of young offenders. Nor were they unsuccessful in these efforts.

The labours of these Prison Visitors were ultimately of great effect upon the outside world, as well as upon the inmates of the prisons. But it was owing to their experiences with, and knowledge of, the latter, that they became animated and qualified the more effectually to influence the former. This is a very important point to be borne in mind, in connection with public interest, elsewhere, in such matters.

Not until, in other countries generally, the Governments encourage, to a greater extent than hitherto, the visitation of prisoners by suitable volunteers from outside, will the general public become interested, to the extent necessary, in securing the best modes of the repression and prevention of crime. "Out of sight, out of mind" is a proverb applicable to prisoners. Until each community, by numerous voluntary representatives, thus becomes, in an energising manner, cognisant of its responsibilities in this direction, and zealous for their fulfilment, inadequate progress will be made towards the solution of the evils in question.

It was, then, the special contribution of M. Suringar and his friends, to the cause of prison discipline, that they advocated, after the practical experience of many years, the necessity of the Separate System; but under rational conditions, and in connection with organised and comprehensive arrangements for the regular visitation of prisoners by judicious members of the community. Since M. Suringar's decease, the progress of penal reform in Holland, has been ably promoted by his successors in the good work.

REV. JOHN CLAY.

In Great Britain there had been much discussion of the merits of the Cellular System previous to, or simultaneously with, its adoption in Holland and Belgium. But in the former, less decided results ensued than in the latter, owing mainly to extreme views and practices, on the part both of the supporters and opponents of the system.

The Magistrates of several counties, more particularly those of MIDDLESEX, SUSSEX, and BERKSHIRE, together with various individuals, such as the DUKES OF RICHMOND, SIR GEORGE PAUL, Bart., Rev. J. KINGSMILL, Rev. J. FIELD, Mr. CRAWFORD, Mr. WILLIAM MERRY, Mr. JOSEPH ADSHEAD, and others, had perseveringly endeavoured, for many years, to extend the practical adoption of separate imprisonment in this country.

As long ago as 1775, through the efforts of the Duke of Richmond, of that date, the local prison of HORSHAM, in Sussex, was rebuilt on the cellular plan, and was the first jail, on this system, in Great Britain. Marked success immediately attended the new arrangements. The Governor reported that whilst there had been constant re-convictions under the old congregate plan, only one prisoner had been re-convicted to that prison during the first twelve years of its cellular existence.

The REV. JOHN CLAY, for many years Chaplain of Preston Gaol, was one of the comparatively few Englishmen who took a broad and common-sense view of cellular separation, whilst at the same time he was one of its decided advocates. But certain other persons brought some ridicule upon this plan, by their excess of faith in the efficacy of merely shutting up prisoners in solitude, with their Bibles, and without due precaution against hypocrisy, idleness and ignorance. Mr. Clay, on the other hand, valued the cell only as a necessary condition to enable himself and others to influence the prisoner aright, without the certainty of all their work being at once undone by vicious association. His son and biographer remarks (in his *Life*, p. 197; London: Macmillan & Co.): "All that he asked from separation, was that it should guarantee the prisoners from mutual corruption and make them think. He definitely adopted the opinion that *individual separation* formed the *only possible basis* of efficient Prison Discipline; and year by year, with additional arguments and sharper urgency, he reiterated his plea for some system of non-intercourse." He observed that an expression most frequent in the mouth of prisoners separated from each other, was, " This is the best thing that ever happened to me."

Mr. Clay insisted on cellular separation, as far as possible, to prevent injury to that on which he most relied—the influence of the Gospel. He devoted his chief efforts to making his preaching impressive, loving, attractive, and effectual. He employed the service of song in the prison chapel, and adorned it with a fine picture of the Crucifixion, painted by himself. He was not a credulous or gullible man, but, on the contrary, was shrewd and wide-awake as to hypocritical pretensions to religion. He was a man of the world, as well as a clergyman. He attached the highest value to Christian influences, even upon the most depraved. He revolted from the ignorant, brutal scepticism of mere theorists, like that hasty and growling cynic, THOMAS CARLYLE, who ridiculed all efforts to reform a parcel of "rogues and vagabonds." On the contrary, Mr. Clay said, " I venture to affirm, as a minister of Him who came 'to call sinners to repentance' that what is objected, in bar of our sympathies, constitutes the strongest title to them. It is *because* prisoners are careless or wilful wanderers from the right way, that nothing should be left untried to reclaim them." But when he observed the very great amount of

utter ignorance of reading, writing, and figures, and even
of the simplest truths of the Gospel, which then characterised so large a proportion of the prisoners, he felt that it
was at least a just debt from society to these untaught
wretches, to utilise to the utmost the opportunity of their
imprisonment, for giving them intellectual instruction, and
awakening them to their responsibilities as Christians and
as parents and relatives. For his own Christianity had
taught him deeply the worth of single souls and the
sacredness of individual lives.

Even from a civil and economical point of view, he held
the reformation of offenders to be of immense importance.
He said, " A thief costs the community £150 a year while
at liberty. Reformation is cheap, at any price." Hence,
because the separate system was essential to reformation,
he regarded it as being eminently cheaper and more
economical than the association of prisoners. He repeats,
" Without separation and non-intercourse, a chaplain's
efforts would be comparatively fruitless. But, on the
other hand, separation and silence, unrelieved by the
benign influence of religion, are worse than fruitless,
positively injurious."

He added, " In every way, the work-room is an inferior
instrument, for reformation, to the cell. In whatever we
would desire for the prisoner, in regard to Instruction,
Reflection, Self-examination, and *above all, Prayer*, the cell
has greatly the advantage. Whatever good results have
been obtained in Preston House of Correction, I attribute
to the complete and effectual abolition of every kind of
prison intercourse."

Mr. Clay and the " Silent " System.

Mr. Clay strongly disapproved of and opposed the " Silent
System," which permits prisoners to be in association and
yet forbids them to converse. His biographer says of him,
" He always regarded the Silent as much the inferior

system ; and he was one of the first to point out its *incurable* faults." The biographer adds :—"The Silent System impedes reformation. It involves a constant duel between the prisoner's cunning and the officer's acuteness ; and thus the former is entrapped into systematic trickery and falsehood. The *incessant punishments*, too, harden and irritate the prisoners. Moreover the system requires such patience, sagacity, vigilance and honesty, in every member of the prison-staff, as is not to be purchased at any price." (**P.** 184.)

ARCHBISHOP ULLATHORNE.

The Roman Catholic Archbishop Ullathorne's long experience amongst convicts in Australasia, led him to study penal discipline very attentively He has remarked that the first sentence uttered by God to His intelligent creature was :—" It is not good for man to be alone." Solitude as to men, must involve communion with God ; or it becomes a source of evil. For, as the wise prelate adds : "Apart from God, and cast upon his individual resources, man is neither a light, nor a fountain of supply, to himself. The most rigid monastic discipline also, that of the Carthusians, with its protracted solitude and silence, is cheered by the little garden for each monk, and the long chantings of the brethren in the choir."

The Roman Catholic Church has held that, if the monk and the hermit need divine grace to rescue solitude from being disastrous, still more necessary are good influences for the isolated criminal. And on the partially cellular prison of San Michele, at Rome, erected in 1703, by Pope Clement XL, from the plans of his architect, Carlo Fontana, the necessity of combining the moral with the deterrent conditions of separation, was permanently recorded, in the motto, conspicuously inscribed over the prison, " *Parum est coercere improbos pœnâ, nisi probos efficias disciplinâ.*" (It is insufficient to restrain the wicked by punishment, unless you render them virtuous by corrective discipline.) This motto greatly impressed John Howard, when he visited Rome.

It is important to notice this broad view, taken by the Roman Church; for she was a pioneer of prison reform. Clement the Eleventh's prison became a model for a similar one at Milan. The long ranges of cells, and even the radiating arrangement of the wings and corridors, were planned by the Roman architect and the Pontiff. Long years later, they were imitated by Belgians at Ghent; then by Jeremy Bentham at Millbank, and also by some Americans in the United States. Oftentimes the latter have been credited with the origination of this system. Archbishop Ullathorne quotes M. Corbeer, who was sent as a Commissioner, from the French Government, to examine and report on Prisons, in 1839. He wrote:—"I feel it a duty to re-establish the truth. The correctional system is Christian. It is Catholic. It is no new system. It had its birth in the monasteries; and a Pope gave it its baptismal name when it came into the world. America did not discover it. America did not perfect it. She borrowed it from Ghent; and Ghent obtained it from Milan and Rome." It may, however, be here remarked that this positive statement by M. Corbeer, requires a certain degree of qualification.

Archbishop Ullathorne was profound in his analysis of what is meant by a system being in accordance with, or contrary to, human nature. He remarks that many modern advocates of political and social reform, are admirable in inventing expedients for regenerating human nature, if it were not that *the nature to be regenerated is missed* out of the calculation." ("Management of Criminals," p. 29.) That nature he held to be a very weak and corrupt one, and to be raised only through that which he describes as the "awful mystery of our Redemption, wrought through the innocent sufferings of the Son of God for the deliverance of man."

MRS. ELIZABETH FRY.

Whilst the Catholic Archbishop set forth a sound principle of penal treatment, as consisting especially in a judicious enforcement of separation from evil, the same fundamental feature of disciplinary reform also commended itself to the approval of that eminent Protestant lady, Mrs. Elizabeth Fry. Her two daughters remark, in their Biography of her, that " *Confinement which excluded from the vicious, but allowed of frequent intercourse with sober and well conducted persons, would have been, in her view, perfect.*" This admirably condensed and comprehensively descriptive sentence exactly embodies, it may be remarked in passing, the method of prison discipline perseveringly advocated by the HOWARD ASSOCIATION of Great Britain. Thus a recent Annual Report of that body records, " The Committee remain unshaken in their conviction that the fundamental principle of all prison efficiency consists in the utmost practicable amount of separation from evil companionship, with the provision of *as many good influences*, both by official and non-official visitation, as possible."

The horrible extremes of isolation exemplified in Mrs. Fry's day, in certain American and English jails, where prolonged solitary confinement, in semi or total darkness, without reformatory influences, was carried out with brutal inhumanity, justly shocked her compassionate heart, and led her to protest persistently against such a gross perversion of the principle of separation.

It is important to observe that the rudimentary condition of even British penal legislation, at that period, together with the structural defects of the prisons themselves, greatly impeded the progress in the reform of criminal treatment which Mrs. Fry, and the influential group of philanthropists who co-operated with her, so earnestly strove to promote. Her own praiseworthy labours to reclaim prisoners, by means of the Holy Scriptures and religious exhortation, were often counteracted by the absence of the special assistance which judicious separation would have afforded. Her first efforts in Newgate were based upon an approximation to this principle. She induced the authorities to divide the prisoners into small groups of ten or twelve, under the oversight of monitors selected from their own number. This secured certain advantages and a measure of progress; but, as was subsequently the case with Captain Maconochie's similar experiments with convict groups, so under these attempts at "classification," in Newgate, it was soon observed that, even the limited amount of evil association thus retained, was resulting in grave mischief, and contributing effectual checks both to the reformation and deterrence of the offenders. The sacred volume, which Mrs. Fry so highly honoured and valued, was afresh justified, even by the experience of these attempts at classification in groups, as to the permanent truth of its precept, " Evil communications corrupt good manners." For many of the women who had thus been grouped even in small "classified" parties, became the cause of grave public scandals, on their removal from Newgate. Much more satisfactory would have been the results under those wiser conditions which Mrs. Fry desired to see in operation, but which, owing to the imperfect development of prison discipline in her day, she did not witness on any adequate scale.

In some prisons, the function of Scriptural instruction, specially advocated by Mrs. Fry, was entrusted to very unsuitable officers. Thus at MILLBANK, at one period, the Bible was used by hypocritical and licentious warders, as a means of ostentatious imposition upon the authorities. A recent official writer on prisons appears to have regarded this as a proof of the failure of Scriptural instruction in jails! But this a most unwarranted inference.

MISCHIEVOUS REACTIONARY INFLUENCES.—CHARLES DICKENS.

In 1838 two of the most observant of English Prison Inspectors—Messrs. CRAWFORD and WHITWORTH RUSSELL —had issued a Report condemning the plan even of silent association in prisons, and decidedly recommending the cellular system. But subsequently the weight of public opinion was mischievously influenced, in a reactionary direction, by several writers, and especially by ignorant sneers at that system, on the part of that habitual cynic, THOMAS CARLYLE, and in still wider degree by the extensive publication of very fictitious statements by the more genial but easily impressible CHARLES DICKENS, based on ideas acquired during a very brief "call" at a single American prison.

The real circumstances of this most hasty and superficial visit were, at the time, carefully investigated by several competent authorities, whose observations were embodied in a work entitled "Prisons and Prisoners," by Mr. JOSEPH ADSHEAD (London, 1845), which, however, had a very limited circulation and excited little attention in America, and, therefore, some renewed reference to the subject may even now be appropriate.

Mr. DICKENS visited the "Eastern Penitentiary," or State Prison, at Philadelphia, in 1843, and spent two hours inside it. Subsequently, at a dinner which was given to him in that city, he expressed the gratification which he had felt in that visit. But when, shortly afterwards, he published his "AMERICAN NOTES," it was found that, in his account of the prison, he had freely given the reins to his imagination.

In the first place, he entirely overlooked facts, by his assertion that "The system here is rigid, strict, and hopeless solitary confinement." On the contrary, that prison has, from the outset, practically exemplified the important dis-

M

tinction between complete "*solitude*," and *separation* from evil
companionship only.   Its inmates have always been carefully guarded from "rigid solitude," and have been the
objects of humane visitation on the part of a large body of
members of the "PENNSYLVANIA PRISON SOCIETY" (founded
in 1787), one of the best organisations of the kind in the
world, and which still maintains its care over prisoners.   Its
Annual Report for 1894 stated that, during the past year,
upwards of *ten thousand visits* were made, by its committees,
to inmates of the State Prison.   Long previous to Mr.
Dickens' visit to America, there were, indeed, certain
prisons in that country, whose inmates were confined in
subterranean cells, in absolute solitude, without work,
books, exercise, or visits.   And, of course, insanity was
produced, in various instances, by such barbarous treatment.   The Philadelphia System was never thus solitary,
or cruel; nor is it so now.   But Mr. Dickens conveyed
the utterly misleading idea that it was such, and that it
was causing insanity amongst prisoners.   A recently issued
interesting description of the establishment by its Governor
says: "There is no ground for the charge that the Separate
System produces insanity; that idea was exploded long
ago."

In one of his novels, Mr. Dickens depicted prison chaplains
as a most gullible set of men; easily imposed upon by
cunning rogues.   But no chaplain was more imposed
upon than Dickens himself was, in the Philadelphia Prison,
by an artful German, named LANGENHEIMER, *alias* Morris,
who, in his native land, had excited a rebellion in a prison,
in which the association of the inmates was permitted.
(When prisoners are kept separate, they are easily
controlled, and cannot conspire for revolt.)   After Langenheimer's release in Germany, he emigrated to America ; and
on the voyage he robbed a fellow-passenger of a considerable sum of money, for which crime he was sent to the
Philadelphia State Prison for four years.   During that

period, Mr. Dickens' visit occurred, and the crafty rogue told the credulous novelist such an ingenious and piteous story that the visitor wrote in his " NOTES ": " My heart bled for him, when the tears ran down his cheeks." But the unsensational fact remains that this man lived forty-two years longer (surviving Dickens himself by fourteen years). Shortly before his death, in 1884, Langenheimer, still cherishing a sense of the real kindness of his custodians at the State Prison, presented himself one day at the gate, and *begged, as a special favour,* that, being a homeless, lonely man, he might be again received there and permitted an asylum for the brief remainder of his life. This strange request was granted, and he died a *willing* inmate of the very prison which, especially through his own misrepresentations to Mr. Dickens, the latter had so maligned, nearly half a century before.

Dickens described three young women in adjacent cells, who, " in the silence and solitude of their lives, had grown to be quite beautiful." These " beauties " were a negress and two mulatto girls, three prostitutes of the city, committed to prison for a robbery. One of these also wept when the novelist entered into sympathizing conversation with her. But this coloured girl who so impressed him, afterwards said to another visitor (PROFESSOR LIEBER, of Columbia College), " I feel very well here ; they treat me with much kindness. I have learned here to read and write and pray. Every Monday some ladies come to teach us. I should certainly prefer living here, than to go back and live where I was last. Here everything is clean, and all are kind ; there, was dirt, and drinking, and headache." It is stated that, after their imprisonment, these three women led respectable lives.

Another prisoner, described by Dickens was " Old Sam," a convict undergoing twelve years' confinement (of which he had served eleven), for the atrocious crime of rape. He, too, greatly excited the novelist's pity, who exclaimed in

indignation : "Eleven years of solitary confinement !"   But
in some other countries, this man would have been hanged
for the great crime of which he was guilty.   Old Sam was
soon afterwards discharged, in perfect health ; and, being a
sailor, he at once started on a voyage to the Pacific Ocean.

In the case of one prisoner, however, even Dickens
seemed to appreciate the value of separation.   This was an
English thief, " a villainous fellow with a white face, who
had as yet no relish for visitors, and who, but for the
additional penalty, would have gladly stabbed me with his
shoemaker's knife."   So that, as his fellow-countryman
made no attempt to excite pity, concocted no tearful story,
and had "no relish for [gulling] visitors," Mr. Dickens at
least tacitly recognised the necessity for separating him, as
a dangerous criminal, from others.

There was further an intelligent prisoner whom Dickens
noticed (under a three years' sentence for robbery), and
whom he passed by, with the remark that he was "a poet
who wrote verses about ships and the 'maddening wine-
cup.'"   That man became a reformed character, as a result
of his confinement, and, after his release, he wrote a
pamphlet in *defence* of the Separate System of imprisonment, in which he remarks : " Justice to a system of prison
discipline, which has received the severe and unjust
criticism of many intelligent persons, has induced the
writer to lay before the public the results of its operation
upon himself, as the best and most indisputable refutation
of the condemnation it has received.   He regards his confinement in the State Penitentiary as *the happiest event of
his life*.   It has dissolved improper connections, remodelled
his tastes, improved his mind, and, he trusts, made better his
heart.   He is neither morose, imbecile, dispirited, nor
deranged ; and whatever reformation his imprisonment
may have produced, he can attribute it to the *separate
seclusion from evil example and worse precept*, which must
necessarily follow the indiscriminate congregation of
offenders in a place of punishment."

This testimony is very important. For this reformed prisoner thus fully refutes the jail-fictions of the imaginative novelist. But their effect, both in Great Britain and the United States, on the popular mind, was very mischievous, as tending to diffuse most erroneous ideas of the nature and effects of cellular separation.

Such widely spread reactionary views also influenced, in too considerable degree, the executive authorities, and produced injurious relaxations of the wisely deterrent and reformatory discipline, which was previously becoming the basis of the prison system in Great Britain.

The " Irish Prison System."

The interesting experiments with the " MARK SYSTEM " and with associated groups of prisoners, which had already been advocated, and to a certain extent put in practice, by Captain MACONOCHIE and others, much impressed a Director-General of Irish Prisons, Sir WALTER CROFTON, a gentleman of great humanity, who for some years endeavoured to carry them out, in the convict establishments under his care. The prisoners, after spending the chief portion of their sentences in association, at Spike Island Prison, in Cork Harbour, were allowed, provided they had earned a sufficient number of good marks for industry and satisfactory behaviour, to be removed to two other establishments, termed " Intermediate Prisons." One of these was the Convict Farm of Lusk, near Dublin, where the inmates were employed in agriculture during the last portion of their restraint, and under conditions little resembling those of an ordinary jail. This " Irish system " did not, in its practical operation, materially differ from the English convict system, after making allowance for the exceptional facilities for emigrating the discharged convicts from Ireland, and for the especial influences of certain persons of superior ability temporarily employed in the administration of the system ; as, for example, the humane director; Sir

WALTER CROFTON, and the earnest Agent for procuring employment for the discharged convicts, Mr. JAMES ORGAN. Inasmuch, then, as it did not differ from other penal systems, in so far as it retained prolonged imprisonments and corrupting association, it failed to secure exemption from the universally accompanying evils of these arrangements. It was also conclusively shown that the great diminution of convicts which happened soon after the establishment of this " Irish " plan, was not at all peculiar to the prisons that were administered upon that system.

For a remarkable and rapid diminution also took place, simultaneously, in the numbers of the inmates of the *common* or *local jails* in the counties and boroughs of Ireland, where that special system was not at all practised, and where, indeed, *no change* had taken place in the previous routine of administration. The combined effect of the passing away of the Irish Famine and the subsequent vast emigration to America, at once tended to empty the numerous jails where the Maconochie and Crofton system had never been practised, and also the four or five establishments where it then existed. There was scarcely any virtual difference in the *comparative* results, either of the presence or absence, of that system, so far as the numbers of Irish prisoners were affected. Indeed, during the period in question, a similar diminution of the *free* population of Ireland took place. The famine had caused a rush of many of the starving people into all the prisons, both convict and local. When it passed away, their inmates again rapidly decreased. And further, it is to be noted that after Sir Walter Crofton ceased to direct the Irish convict prisons, they became worse than those of Great Britain, rather than superior. Sir W. Crofton wrote to the Prison Congress at Rome, in 1885 : " I wish it to be known at the Congress that I have had nothing to do with the Irish prisons for many years, and that I am entirely opposed to the system pursued by the present

Directors. The evil results of that system are shown in the Report of the inquiry recently made by the Royal Commission."

The " Irish " plan, at its best, then, was no exception to the *failure of all modes of congregate imprisonment.* Even the "intermediate" prison of the system, the open farm at Lusk, near Dublin, did not, in any very special way, prepare, for the ordinary conditions of free life, the very small number of convicts (from 30 to 50) there engaged in the cultivation of land and in quarrying. For although they were not surrounded by walls, and although they were occasionally sent into the village on errands, or to attend church, yet, for practical purposes, they were as completely shut in from the discipline and trials of ordinary life, as the inmates of other prisons. They were effectually watched and guarded by means of officers, police, and telegraphs, and all of them being near the expiration of their detention, any known misbehaviour would lead to the forfeiture of their money earnings, and would also involve an extension of their punishment under more penal conditions. Beyond all of which, the men were better fed and cared for, than thousands of the free peasantry outside. Grave charges were also made before the Royal Commission, in 1879, even against the morals of the selected convicts of Lusk. At the end of 1887 the Government abandoned this distinctive relic of the once unduly praised " Irish " convict system.

PARTIAL BRITISH HOMAGE TO THE MERIT OF CELLULAR SEPARATION.

The English Prison Acts of 1863 and 1878 did indeed maintain, as to the letter, a legal recognition of the superiority of separation in local jails. And in so far as this has been consistently carried out, or at least approximated, which has been the case in many of these establishments, great advantage has resulted to the community.

It is to be observed that some of the chief inconveniences
and evils, occasionally occurring in English Local Jails, arise
from relaxations of the legally enacted principle of the
entire separation of their inmates. For instance, at Armley
(Leeds) Prison, in 1888, one prisoner murdered another.
But how was this ? Because three prisoners were placed
in association in one cell.

As to the prisons of Scotland, that justly influential
journal, the *Scotsman* (Edinburgh), in an able editorial, has
pointed out the mischief of associating young persons with
adult offenders, either in the jails, or during the journeys
thither.

In 1886, the then chief administrator of English Prisons,
Sir E. F. DU CANE, in a letter to the SECRETARY of the
HOWARD ASSOCIATION, respecting the Local Jails, wrote as
follows:—" The Separate System never was more uniformly
and universally carried out than now, and never stood in
higher repute. All our [Local] prisons are on the Separate
System ; and if any are torn down, a fate to which between fifty and sixty have been consigned during the last
eight years, it is, so far as prison systems and management
affect the matter at all, a sign of the *efficiency of the Separate System.*" This was an important official testimony to
the merits of the principle thus eulogised. And the more
generally it is practically recognised, in regard to all classes
of prisons and prisoners, the better will it be for communities and for offenders.

BRITISH CONVICT PRISONS.

On the Convict " public works " the system of associated
labour has been general, and the results have often been
mischievous. It is, however, only fair to the chief authorities of these establishments, to state that they have made
many earnest and not wholly unsuccessful endeavours to
check or counterbalance the natural tendency of the gang
labour, by the aid of the " Progressive " or " Good Mark "

system of gradual amelioration of treatment, involving encouragements of hope and of immediate and prospective rewards, including especially the opportunity of earning the remission of a considerable portion of the original sentence by means of conditional release under certain arrangements for periodic police supervision.

The plan has also been adopted, with further success, of placing convicts undergoing their first conviction, in prisons distinct from those containing reconvicted ones.

In the British Convict Prisons also (where the longer sentences varying from three years to life-long detention are undergone), the inmates have had the opportunity afforded them of gradually obtaining for themselves, by means of good behaviour and industry, a remission of their original sentences, to the extent of about one-fourth of the time for men and one-third for women. Thus a man sentenced to twelve years' imprisonment can earn his liberation in nine years (but under police supervision for the remaining three), whilst a female convict may liberate herself in eight years, under the same original sentence.

In addition to this ultimate reward, the convicts may earn a succession of more immediate privileges and ameliorations of their condition, by working themselves out of the lower or more penal grades into the higher ones. The first year of penal servitude forms a " probation " period, of which about nine months are spent in cellular confinement. If, during this year, 720 good marks have been earned, the third class in associated labour is entered. The convict remains in this for at least one year. But when he has earned 2,920 marks he may pass up into the second class for a third year. Another 2,920 marks will bring him into the first or highest class, in which there is a further sub-class ranked as "special," which carries a slight extra remission of one week of the original sentence.

Eight good marks per day are the maximum attainable. In the third class, convicts may earn one shilling a month, with permission to receive one visit from their friends each half-year. In the second class one shilling and sixpence per month may be earned, with the substitution of tea for gruel, longer exercise on Sundays, and increased privileges of visits and correspondence. In the first class extended advantages of the latter kind, with a further improvement in dietary, more exercise on Sundays, and a half-a-crown a month, may be earned. There has also been instituted a special "Star Class," consisting exclusively of convicts not previously sent to penal servitude. These enjoy some particular privileges; and they carry a red star on their dress to distinguish them from other prisoners.

Convicts must, in general, have learned to read and write before they can be admitted to the highest class. Different dresses are worn in the respective classes. The adoption of this "Progressive System," it may be remarked, has led to a large diminution of punishments in these prisons. And this is a chief merit of the plan; namely, its aid to the officers and to the discipline. But it must always be re-membered that it affords *little test of either the character or the reformation* of criminals. In fact the greatest hypo-crites, and most cunning habitual rogues, may most easily avail themselves of its advantages. Nevertheless, and in spite of this, it is of great value. But the appendage of Supervision is also essential.

In the LOCAL JAILS of Great Britain (for short-term prisoners) four stages also may be passed through, in succes-sion, by the longer-sentenced prisoners, and a maximum of eight good marks per day may be earned. In the first stage the prisoner earns no money, has the hardest labour and the lowest dietary. When he has obtained 224 good marks he may pass into the second grade, where he may have school instruction and books. He may earn one shilling during the whole stage, and may have special exercise on Sundays.

In the third stage (reached after earning 224 marks in

the previous one), one shilling and sixpence may be earned ; and certain minor privileges. Another 224 marks will bring the prisoner to the highest or fourth stage, where, with some other privileges, two shillings may be earned. In certain cases of special good conduct, during the longer terms, a maximum of £2 may be reached. Increased privileges as to correspondence, reading, etc., are also now permitted. The *local* jails of Great Britain receive prisoners for periods ranging from one day to two years, the maximum. The *convict* prisons receive those sentenced to terms of from three years, the minimum, up to the remainder of life.

These regulations have hitherto applied, in general, to British and Irish prisons. The Irish convict prisons anticipated, by years, and in certain respects, this progressive system. But Captain Maconochie and the Bavarian prison authorities had, at a still earlier period, adopted a similar principle of grade-progression.

In 1895, a Committee appointed by the British Government, recommended the amalgamation of the Convict Prisons and Local Jails, a conclusion, however, of questionable wisdom.

Final Results the Real Test.

It is a wide spread and obstinately-seated popular delusion—prevalent amongst many influential and intelligent persons—that mere *length* of detention is the chief penal and preventive element. Whereas time tends to form habits of adaptation, and to diminish the really penal and therefore deterrent effect of that severity which can only be borne for comparatively short periods. It is rather the *continuously unpleasant memory*, of sharp but brief incarcerations, which tends to be effectual.

There have now been accumulated innumerable precedents for the adoption of a better system than that of either prolonged imprisonments, or frequently repeated but ineffectual short ones. In thousands of cases, especially in such of the English Local Jails as have rigorously enforced cellular separation—the effect of a first sentence to a few weeks or months of this punishment—has proved a life-long cure of crime. Whereas in scores of thousands of other cases, a few weeks of jail association with villains and prostitutes, has ruined for life young persons of both sexes, in Great Britain and other countries.

GLOUCESTER PIONEERING.

One county of England—Gloucestershire—under the prompting of that noble pioneer in various good works, the late Mr. THOMAS L. BARWICK BAKER, J.P., long proved the efficacy of short and sharp preliminary chastisements, as opposed to the costly and mischievous blunder of an indiscriminate application of prolonged imprisonment. The local magistrates, for a number of years, generally adopted the system of punishing ordinary felonies (with little distinction as to the amount stolen) with a rigid cellular imprisonment of a month or two, during which time the impressions of jail life were fresh and disagreeable. A second felony involved, according to circumstances, either two months in jail, followed by two years' police supervision, or six months of the former and four years of the latter. A third offence of similar nature entailed penal servitude for a term of years. Subsequent national legislation, however, rendered the treatment far too rapidly cumulative, and brought the intrinsically excellent and desirable system of cumulation (if only *gradual*) into undeserved disrepute amongst many persons.

The Gloucestershire authorities furnished facilities for the employment of their Discharged Prisoners. They constituted their local Superintendents of Police, the agents for distributing certain funds available for the assistance of such persons. But they expected all discharged prisoners themselves to *inform their employers* of their antecedents. If this was done, the police did not further interfere. But otherwise, the information was given by the police; *not by the subordinate members* of the force, but only by the *Chief* Constable. Mr. Baker reported, after years of experience : " The system works well. The Discharged Prisoners, in whatever part of the county they may be, have a Superintendent within reach, to whom they may apply, to assist them with money or work. All who are willing to work find nearly constant employment ; and the money given away is extremely small. The Chief Constable has not once in six years found it necessary to inform an employer of the antecedents of any one engaged by him ; and necessarily, where the truth is known from the first (from the employed person himself) no one is turned out of work in consequence of its being found out. The public appear to appreciate the being fairly dealt with, and many are willing to take a discharged prisoner—with a full knowledge of his character—who would have turned off one who was found to have obtained work without stating the truth."

In short, it was well and extensively proved by the Gloucestershire people, that their discharged prisoners were better off, under this system, than otherwise. They were not subject to the risk of losing their situations through the treachery of others. They needed not to fear either the further revelations of comrades, or of policemen. The police were felt to be their friends, and not their foes. Their masters knew the worst of them, from the beginning. And this knowledge, together with the police supervision, was a material help and mercy to the discharged prisoner, who was thus, in the great majority of instances, more effectually reformed and deterred, after his month or two of short and sharp cellular imprisonment, than he would otherwise be, by many years of costly, but pernicious, detention.

It is not to be wondered at, that the safety of life and limb, in Gloucestershire, has been at least as great as elsewhere, if not greater. That county was able, with advantage, to close six out of the seven prisons which it had contained, and which were at one time so crowded that it was feared more would have to be built.

Deterrent and Restorative Discipline: Distinct Stages.

The conclusion to which the prison and penal experiences of all countries appear to lead is that the special objects of deterrence and of reformation, whilst each of essential importance, cannot, with the greatest advantage, be simultaneously combined, except in very limited degree. An offender who leaves a prison, after a short term, really hating it and resolved never to re-enter its walls, is more effectually dealt with, *both* as to reformation and deterrence, than one who may have been confined there for years, but under such conditions that he returns thither again and again.

Even where the offence committed is a grave one, the principle of deterrence may be secured by dividing the sentence into several separate periods of *short and sharp* terms, each of which is to be inflicted, *if necessary*, in succession, but of which only the first need be undergone, *provided* its efficiency is proved by continued good conduct on the part of the offender, after his conditional release from that first term. Thus, for a robbery, the offender may be sentenced to one year's severe cellular imprisonment, of which three months may be rendered certain, and the remission of the other portions made conditional on his satisfactory behaviour, after his first discharge. He should be made to feel that his imprisonment, under any circumstances, will always be a real and most disagreeable infliction.

But to combine such deterrent cellular discipline with a special training for future self-supporting industry under the ordinary temptations of life, has not, in general experience, been found practicable. Either the deterrent elements tend to nullify the other training, or the latter weakens the former. Both are good, both are essential; but they should be administered, for the most part, in succession. Just as a physician, in prescribing for a patient, does not permit the simultaneous action of depleting and of tonic medicines, where both are needful, but in their due order.

Many officers of prisons have declared, from their own observation : " An habitual criminal effectually reformed, whilst *in* prison, is a very exceptional person. Such an one is occasionally to be met with, but very rarely." Others express their utter incredulity as to the prison reformation of such persons. In spite of sincere temporary impressions, tears, and much emphatic profession, they are sceptical as to ultimate practical results. Innumerable prisoners, too, have indignantly asserted the impossibility of their being won over to a love of self-supporting rectitude, whilst still being made to suffer the restraints of penal discipline. Prisoners are apt to feel like the negro slave, who said to a master who combined flogging with religious harangues, "Massa! if floggee, floggee ; and if preachee, preachee ; but not floggee and preachee too ! "

Further, the conditions of self-control and of resistance to the temptations of free life, which are essential to the reformatory principle in its entirety, and also some of the circumstances associated with the prolonged industrial training inseparable from such a discipline, are mostly incompatible with due prison conditions, and with their needful penal restraints. The two cannot be well combined.

Hence, the wise criminal discipline of the future may be

expected increasingly to separate what has hitherto been unsuccessfully sought in union. Penal deterrence, so essential to tame the ruffian, and to warn the dangerous elements in the community, must be rendered *more* penal than hitherto, instead of less, by means of an intenser, and therefore necessarily shorter, application, of strict and hated, but beneficial, cellular separation.

Then the process of restorative training for honest self-support may follow. And this should be sought, not mainly at the expense of the tax-payer, but by surrounding the discharged prisoner with all possible inducements to virtue and industry. *Continued Supervision*, either by the Police or by officially-authorised Societies or Committees—by either, or both, according to circumstances—must be especially looked to, to promote the end in view. The liability to a prompt recall to other brief terms of strict cellular discipline must hang over all habitual offenders—even, in some cases, during the whole term of their lives.

Again and again, they may have the option of trying an honest course. But a recall to comparatively severe treatment must be held in reserve. This may not be invariably efficacious, but it will surely succeed to a very large extent, and far beyond the extreme, or irregular, systems of the past.

CHAPTER VI.

A PROGRESSIVE SYSTEM OF SENTENCES.

.THE subject of a really Progressive System of Sentences is one of the most important which can claim the attention of Legislators, Jurists, and Penologists.

But the practical adoption of such a system has hitherto been a desideratum even in the most civilized countries. Yet it is essential for the increase of public security, both by the diminution of crime and the reformation of offenders.

It is indeed of far greater importance than even the general reform of prison discipline, as such.

It is always to be considered that the object of punishment is, admittedly, twofold, namely to deter and to reform.

. If a first sentence is not followed by any repetition of transgression, the desired object is secured, so far at least as that offender is concerned.

But if a first sentence is followed by a repetition of crime, it is obvious that a more effective impression needs to be made upon the offender, both for his own sake and for that of the community. And further, this second offence shows the beginning of a bad habit. Then the

N

reformatory object of imprisonment, or detention, demands time, in order to check this evil tendency and to afford opportunity for the development of good habits.

But it is unfair and unmerciful to one who has proceeded a very little way in the path of transgression to visit him with severe chastisement.   Only a moderate addition to his original sentence is warrantable.   If a first sentence, or any other, has manifestly failed to secure its object, it should not be repeated, unless after such long interval of good behaviour as indicated that the offender has made real efforts to avoid crime.

And certainly the repetition, many times in succession, of very short sentences on habitual offenders, has been abundantly proved to be worse than useless, a scandal to administrative authority, a positive encouragement to evil-doers and an utter failure both as to deterrence and prevention.

Nothing could prove this more than the fact that, in Great Britain and Ireland, a large number of drunkards and prostitutes have been committed to prison as many as twenty times each, in a single year.   Thus the machinery of legal administration has, in such instances, become a farce; and these poor wretches have been encouraged, if not compelled, to become habitual offenders, by the perversion of law itself.   In some instances the same offender has been imprisoned more than 250 or even 300 times, in succession.   What extreme folly !

In 1895, a wretched woman in London was brought before the magistrates for the 275th time for drunkenness, and disorder.   The *Evening News and Post*, in reporting this case, remarked : " She is a hopeless drunkard ; she rarely remains more than a couple of days out of prison ; and it ought to be evident by this time that all the imprisonment in the world will not save her from herself." She was sent to jail for a further short term, on which she exclaimed to the Magistrate, " You ought to be ashamed of yourself!" And certainly such utterly ineffectual sentences, in so very many instances, are a reason for national shame.

Another poor creature, who had been committed to the London jails nearly as many times as the preceding instance, became a hopeless, howling maniac in a lunatic asylum. The journal just quoted remarked of her case: " She went through the same successive periods of very brief imprisonments, until her brain gave way completely, and violent homicidal impulse seized her. Then, and not till then, did the authorities order her removal to an asylum. But *what a cruel and barbarous road* she travelled to get there !"

In certain Continental countries, such as Germany and Belgium, such frequent misdemeanants are detained, with advantage, for longer periods, varying from a few weeks to two years or more, in industrial establishments, partly of the nature of a Prison and partly of a Reformatory.

Popular opinion and action are both proverbially inconsistent ; and hence whilst there has been amongst many nations such a general neglect of the essential aid of a very gradual and progressive cumulation of sentences for the repression of ordinary petty offences, a most unreasonable extreme of cumulation has concurrently been resorted to, in certain other cases, especially in some of the United States of America and in England. Thus it has frequently happened that a criminal convicted of other offences than misdemeanours, has been sentenced, first to three or six months' imprisonment, secondly to two years, and on a third conviction to five or seven years penal servitude. Such leaps and bounds are utterly unnecessary, and therefore cruel. They are also very mischievous to the community, because they destroy that impression of regularity and justice which should always accompany the operation of the law.

Far too much weight has been attached, both by legislators and in the popular mind, to the supposed claims of vengeance, or retribution, whilst the main object of punishment, namely, the most efficacious method of *preventing a recurrence* of crime, has been comparatively overlooked.   Hence the superior efficacy of certainty, combined with very moderate increments of severity, has been generally neglected, both in criminal codes, and in magisterial and judicial action.

The writer, in 1884, suggested to a COMMITTEE, appointed by the English HOME SECRETARY (before whom he was examined), the following simple plan of a Progressive Cumulation of Sentences, both for habitual misdemeanants and for criminals, which could hardly fail, if adopted, to secure a large measure of practical success.

1.—GRADUAL CUMULATION FOR HABITUAL MISDEMEANANTS.

Habitual *petty* offenders, or Misdemeanants, are a class of whom, in Great Britain more than on the Continent, inveterate Drunkards and disorderly Prostitutes constitute a large proportion.   They are usually, and rightly, regarded as being, in large degree the victims of strong hereditary passions and frailities, or of early privation, seduction or neglect; so that it is generally felt that much more forbearance is due to them, than to offenders of greater Progressive personal responsibility.

But when such misdemeanants are permitted, by the absence of any effectual measures either for restraint or for reformation, to become a plague to themselves and to the community, such forbearance is, in itself, a gross evil.   And this weakness has most mischievously delayed (at least in some of the English-speaking nations) the adoption of a System of Sentences for this class.

In view of the extreme leniency hitherto extended to them, especially by English law and public opinion, it is perhaps inevitable that the measures essential for the reclamation of these offenders should be attempted, or attained, by means of concessions to the popular sentiment which may in themselves err on the side of undue laxity.

If, for example, progressive increments of only a *fortnight* upon each previous sentence were adopted, even this very gentle and gradual application of the cumulative principle would be much better than the too prevalent course of non-progressive sentences of a few days constantly re-inflicted for each offence.

The series of sentences might then run as follows : After a caution, only, for the first petty offence, the second should involve imprisonment, or detention, for a fortnight ; for the third offence, a month ; for the fourth, six weeks; and so on, until, by twenty-six of these very gentle increments, a year's confinement is reached—a term which would *then* be thoroughly deserved. The whole series up to that point, would have involved an aggregate of 702 weeks, or $13\frac{1}{2}$ years, detention, which, however, need not necessarily be within a prison, or merely penal establishment.

Meanwhile the misdemeanant would have had, at numerous intervals, abundant opportunities for " turning over a new leaf," on each successive liberation. The very gradually increasing periods of detention would also afford some facilities for training in useful industry and for the formation of good habits and the weakening, if not the extirpation, of bad ones. Whereas constant sentences of a few days only, or little more, render the reformatory processes impossible.

But, inasmuch as disorderly or incapable Drunkards constitute a large proportion of the misdemeanant class, longer increments than those of a fortnight are necessary for these. For experience has shown that when the power of intemperate habits has become established, a period of from one to two years of compulsory sobriety, in some suitable establishment, is the shortest time which will enable the subject of inebriety to be effectually reformed.

These unfortunate persons who, although pitiable in themselves, are great nuisances to public order, should justly be regarded as being the victims of disease rather than as intentional offenders; and hence their treatment should partake less of a penal than of a restorative and preventive character. But at the same time, it should be sufficiently prolonged to ensure its object.

Therefore it is needful that wherever public opinion becomes intelligent enough to sanction such a course, the offender, of this class, after having been previously discharged with a caution, should, on his second arrest, be detained in *some* suitable place for a week, and on the third arrest for a month, after which the detentions should be respectively three months, six months, a year, eighteen months, and two years.

Two years should be regarded as the *maximum* sentence of detention, even for the most obstinate cases of Drunken Misdemeanants. For a succession of several such periods of restraint, either in an Inebriate Asylum, or in some Industrial Establishment, with or without occupation in the open air, would pretty certainly effect a reclamation to habits of sobriety and order, in at least a large proportion of instances (as has been proved in the best Inebriate Asylums of Great Britain and America) a result not attained, hitherto, by any other plan.

In some cases, the detention or restraint, might safely consist in placing the offender under Probation, in the care of suitable persons, whether relatives or others, willing, with certain conditions of responsibility, to undertake his control.

The old idea that penal or reformatory detention should invariably, or throughout its extent, involve confinement in a prison, may advantageously be abandoned, in connection with petty offenders or Misdemeanants. *This is a point of special importance.*

The chief matter to be insisted on and secured, is the

certainty of *authoritative control*, either inside, or outside, of some place of detention, and increasing in duration with each repetition of the offence.

With the adoption of such a Progressive System, there would be felt, by the habitual misdemeanant, a consciousness that every fresh grasp of the Law would be certainly somewhat heavier than the previous one. And such a feeling could hardly fail, ere long, to exercise a salutary deterrence. Hitherto there has been a prevalent sense amongst this class of offenders that the Law can be trifled with, with comparative impunity. But with a certainty of cumulation, this impression will disappear. And the very gradual character of the cumulation will give it a feature of moderation and merciful consideration, to which, neither the offender nor the public, can reasonably object.

Any habitual misdemeanant remaining in one locality, would of course be recognisable, on being again brought before the court. And if he, or she, chose to flee to another part of the country, the use of the BERTILLON SYSTEM OF MEASUREMENT, with or without other similar means of identification, would, in general, soon enable the authorities to recognise the fugitive. But even where the latter might for a time elude detection, yet if he resumed his offences he would soon feel himself under the same steadily tightening grasp of law.

So that, in any case, there would be a prevalent power and efficacy in the adoption of such a system, especially as compared with the great evils inevitable, wherever and whenever, such system is absent.

Considering the minor nature of the offences of this class, the detention might be of a comparatively mild character. Educational influences might be specially introduced, and certain alleviations permitted, which might not be appropriate in the treatment of persons guilty of serious crimes.

II.—Gradual Cumulation for Habitual Criminals.

Secondly, in regard to Criminals, as distinguished from Petty Offenders, or Misdemeanants, the same principle of progressive or gradual cumulation is equally needful and similarly applicable, though under severer conditions.

This class may be generally divided into offenders guilty of crimes against *property* and those guilty of crimes against the *person*. The latter, in general, deserve much more severe treatment than the former, although too often they have been practically regarded as being less culpable. The brutal violator of women, the still more brutal violator of children, or the perpetrator of atrocious cruelty upon man or beast, such enemies of society are incomparably worse than the petty thief, or even than the persistent stealer of property, provided the latter never adds personal violence or intimidation to his crime.

To let off criminals guilty of personal violence, with light punishment, or brief detention, is in itself a serious crime against Society. It may especially be a cruel outrage upon the rights and the safety of every woman and child in the community, over whom, in particular, the law ought always to hold its ægis of effectual protection.

The Coroner of a large city once remarked, in substance: "When I think of the many corpses of the victims of violence, which I have had to look upon, such as weak women with battered faces, blackened or blinded eyes, arms and legs twisted or broken by kicks and blows; poor little children maimed and emaciated; to say nothing of their violation and ruin of purity; when I think on these terrible outrages, I feel indignation, whenever the law, or morbid public indifference, cruelly relaxes the rigour and certainty of just punishment against barbarous men who have wrought such awful misery upon lives and homes."

In regard to both classes of Criminals (whether against the Person or against Property), it is evidently just and necessary that even the first sentences should be of a severer nature than those passed upon Misdemeanants; and also that in case of serious injuries against public security being repeated, such a scale of cumulation should be adopted as will be adequate to secure the interests of the community, together with the reformation and deterrence of such offenders.

At the same time, it would be unwise and mischievous to allow any merely *arbitrary* classification of crime, hitherto laid down by the Law, to interfere with the adoption of the needful cumulation. For the object to be sought, namely, the repression of crime, will be hindered, if merely *conventional* estimates of the comparative enormity of particular crimes, such as Burglary, Forgery, Horse-stealing, and so forth, are permitted to interfere with the adoption of a scale of cumulation applicable to crime in general, and depending for its ultimate severity, or continuing operation, not so much on the nature of the particular crime committed, as on the evidence of intractability and depravity afforded by the criminal's relapse into evil courses. There must necessarily be some exception to the application of cumulation for crime, as in the case of persons guilty of Murder, or Rape, two offences of extreme gravity. But the ordinary run of crimes, to which the Law hitherto has attached varying penalties, may with great advantage be subjected to a uniform scale of cumulation, in proportion mainly to the repetition, rather than to the nature, of the offence.

When one of the highest legal dignitaries in Great Britain introduced into Parliament a proposal for the Codification of the Law, after setting forth some of the anomalies and artificial distinctions which abound in existing legislation, he said, "*I propose to make a clean sweep of all this rubbish.*" And in like manner, if a wise and effective system of Cumulation of Sentences is to be introduced it may be necessary to repeal certain laws, in regard to particular crimes, which, by their merely conventional character, may fairly be designated by that eminent Jurist's expression.

Such impediments being cleared out of the way, in Great Britain and, where necessary, in any other country, it would be practicable to deal, in a much better manner than hitherto with Crimes, as distinct from Misdemeanours.

But, at the same time, it is desirable to make only such changes in existing practice as may be necessary.

British law has long recognised two years as the *maximum* period for the infliction of separate imprisonment, as distinguished from detention in association, in the Convict Establishments, or "Public Works," where those under sentence are, for the most part, engaged in occupation in the open air. It may therefore be desirable to adhere to this limitation.

But, of course, many criminals especially those habitually or persistently such, require a longer discipline than two years. Hence the British convict system has retained this class under extended terms of from three to twenty years, or even for life. But it is becoming widely recognised that such very long sentences, especially with severity of treatment, are lacking both in mercy and in efficacy.

The two years' maximum of imprisonment, in the sense of separate confinement, should by all means be retained for those criminals whose sentences may extend to that period of detention. But all the longer periods, beyond the two years, might, with great advantage, continue to be spent in establishments for agricultural or handicraft industry, more of the nature of an adult "Reformatory" than of a Prison, in the strict sense of the word. And, not only so, but for certain classes of criminals, undergoing long terms of detention, Conditional Liberation under some effectual supervision, might be advantageously adopted (as, indeed, it is at present, to some extent, both in England and elsewhere), under prudent limitations, and as a reward for good conduct in the previous stages of detention. In proportion as a criminal repeats his crime, he should have longer sentences of restraint, with more severe conditions of treatment and in special establishments.

The element of CLASSIFICATION might be introduced with advantage for such offenders, by means of appropriating particular penal institutions exclusively to those re-convicted. So that a man thus re-convicted might find himself placed under a stricter *régime* than those who had only been convicted a first time.

In all cases of bad behaviour, either whilst under detention, or whilst conditionally liberated on probation or bail, the criminal should be again subjected, for awhile, to a further period of strictly cellular separation.

In England, and, perhaps, in certain other countries, some of the existing penal establishments might, with certain modifications of discipline and arrangement, continue to be available for the worst and most intractable criminals, whilst for those guilty of brutal cruelty, rape, or murder, special prisons might be set apart. These would not require to be very large or costly, for the class needing them would be comparatively few in number. But the discipline and treatment, for the long periods, should be of a milder character than that generally enforced hitherto. A main object of such prolonged detention should not be the punishment of the criminal, but rather his removal from the community, and the *protection of society* from a repetition of serious outrages upon it.

Crimes of such a character are too grave to allow the professed, or even the real, reformation of the offender to warrant any early opportunity of exposure to temptation which might result in a recurrence of former atrocity on his part. Hence the danger and unwisdom, for this class, of the crude systems of " INDETERMINATE " SENTENCES, (so-called) which, in certain American States, permit criminals guilty of the *worst* outrages an opportunity of returning to the community in periods as short as eighteen months or two years, in many instances. For even where any prolonged infliction of punishment, as such, may rightfully be deemed unnecessary, yet the safety and well-being of the community may still require a lengthy seclusion of the former criminal, solely for the sake of that community. Hence, while it may be just to remove from such criminals the specially punitory features of an earlier stage of treatment, it may be still essential, for the sake of others, that they should remain for a long time secluded from circumstances and temptations which would again render them dangerous. For most truly does the Bible declare that even " One sinner destroyeth much good." (Eccles. ix. 18).

It is important always to bear in mind that habitual offenders, whether criminals or misdemeanants, are, *when at liberty*, a chief source of contamination to persons not hitherto guilty of transgressions of the law. Hence it has been repeatedly found that the detention of small groups of such habitual offenders, in prisons or reformatories, has been followed by a remarkable diminution of vice and crime in the localities from which such pests have been removed for any considerable period. Hence, too, the mischief of very short detentions, under so-called " Indeterminate " Sentences, as at ELMIRA (N.Y.), for example.

Greater difficulty attends the apportionment of sentences to habitual Criminals, as compared with habitual Misdemeanants ; and it is obvious that. in regard to the former, a considerable liberty of discretion must be permitted to the Judge or Magistrate, before whom the facts connected with the criminal are laid.

But here also certain considerations may materially guide to a decision and to the adoption of some measure at least of progressive cumulation. In the first place, LARCENIES (or thefts more or less small in amount) constitute the greater portion, or more than half, of the cases coming before the British Courts. And of the remaining cases, another considerable portion consists of ASSAULTS, which, in general, arise more from sudden or drunken irritation than from deliberate malice.

As to THEFTS, the amount stolen is usually a matter of accident, and should not in general be made (as it too often has been made hitherto) a chief factor in determining the duration of the sentence. If a thief robs a man of his purse, the latter may contain only half-a-crown, or a cheque for a large sum of money. Again, another thief may break into a house, only expecting to find a small booty, and may, to his surprise, come upon much more valuable property than he had anticipated; and the temptation to steal the whole of this may be too great to be resisted. Hence the amount of theft is largely a matter of. accident, and should not be regarded as the measure of the criminality concerned.

An incomparably more important guide to the right measure of punishment, is the adaptability of sentences to produce the most salutary effect upon the criminal class as a whole. And these are most influenced by a knowledge that a certain progressive increase of punishment will follow repeated offences. Such a progression cannot be established whilst arbitrary and irregular sentences, sometimes very severe and sometimes very lax, continue to be given.

The efficacy, for most criminals, of a moderate first sentence, is proved by the fact that at least half of the criminals now brought before English Courts of Justice, and awarded from three to twelve months' imprisonment, are never brought up again, and do not enter the class of habitual criminals.

Hence the adoption of such moderate inflictions as three or six months, as normal first sentences for crime, is fully justified by experience, and may with advantage be generally accepted as a wise precedent, irrespective (with few exceptions) of the amount stolen.

But as criminals who are not checked by a first sentence, are also unlikely to be deterred by a second, of similar duration, therefore, in view of the seriousness of their crimes, whether of plunder or violence, reasonably prolonged increments of detention should be enforced.

It may be fairly assumed that a second theft or assault (within at least five years of a first offence of the kind) should be punished by one year's detention, and a second similar offence by two years.

Two years would exhaust (in Great Britain) the hitherto existing legal applicability of separate imprisonment.

The writer, after long and careful inquiry into the operation of separate imprisonment, in Great Britain, Belgium. Holland, and other countries, is of opinion that British legislation has taken a wise step in assuming two years as the maximum limit of separate imprisonment. He believes that the prolonged periods of ten, seven, five, or even four years, of cellular separation, adopted in certain Continental prisons, are not safe for the generality of prisoners. They may appear to be so, in many instances, while irreparable injury may nevertheless have been done to body and mind.

On the other hand, however, in 1875, a COMMISSION appointed by the FRENCH GOVERNMENT to consider the respective merits of separate and associated imprisonment, arrived, after the most careful examination of facts, at a decided conclusion to recommend that all prisoners detained for periods not exceeding one year, should be subjected to cellular separation. Even that limit, which may be assumed as an extremely mild one, in view of the general French dislike of separation, would include the great majority of prisoners in every country. But, on the whole, a *maximum* of two years' separation, may perhaps be assumed, as having the best claim to constitute a wise limit in this respect.

There is one form of industry which may be

especially recommended for its reformatory influence, whether in or out of prisons, and which, at the same time, has the advantage of only a minimum competition with the outside worker. This is the training in the general use of tools, chiefly for carpentry, to which the Norsk term of "SLOYD" is now generally given. It consists of a large number of graduated exercises in the use of saws, chisels, planes, and other tools, which would qualify unhandy and ignorant prisoners for future honest industry, and which at the same time would offer many incitements to thoughtfulness and self-education.

"Sloyd" is a suitable cellular occupation. And as its primary object is not to turn out a quantity of work immediately, but rather to acquire a capacity for skilful workmanship in the future, it is peculiarly adapted for prisoners, whom, as a class, it is not desirable to place in any unnecessary or excessive competition with free-workers.

Where the several progressive sentences of a few months, a year and two years, fail to prevent further reconvictions, the criminal should thenceforward have increments of two years' detention, with or without "probation," for each renewed crime.

If it be objected that such increments would be too small for obstinate criminals, a brief glance at their real extent will show that they would not afford opportunity to any of these to enjoy a career of impunity. For six progressive sentences, after the first, would run as follows:—One year, two years, four years, six years, eight years, ten years.

The sum of these six sentences would amount to thirty-one years' detention; which, generally speaking, would deal effectively with the lives of even the most inveterate criminals.

The detentions for periods after two years, might, or might not, consist of confinement in special establishments, of the nature of Adult Reformatories.

Some American authorities have proposed that on a third conviction, criminals should be sentenced to imprisonment for life. But this course would be unreasonable and cruel.

In view of the circumstance that the criminal is often the victim of social or parental neglect and of hereditary disqualification, his segregation, if necessary, ought, for the most part, to be merely *detention*, for prolonged *industrial* and *educational* occupation. In many cases, doubtless, a conditional liberation, or probation, might, with fairness and with safety to the community, be permitted, under *strict precautions* for Supervision and for Re-arrest, if necessary.

This plan is not a mere theory. It has (apart from its regularity of progressive cumulation) been already tried with much success in England, in the treatment of Juvenile Offenders, by means of Reformatories and Conditional Liberation, and a large diminution in juvenile crime has resulted; whereas the irregular and extreme cumulations of sentences on habitual adult criminals, with their long imprisonments, as in England, France, and America, have not answered their object. Many years ago, even the partial adoption of cumulative sentences for criminals, in Great Britain, and especially in the County of Gloucester, was attended by decided advantage. But that cumulation was too rapid and too severe; and hence it failed to secure either the needful increase of efficacy, or public approval. The *gradually* progressive cumulation here advocated, would be at once moderate, merciful, and efficaciously repressive.

It would also include the advantages often attributed to what are termed "Indeterminate" Sentences, a subject on which a great deal of unwisdom, not to say nonsense, has been spoken and written. For when we examine what is meant by "Indeterminate" sentences, it is evident that such inflictions must be either very arbitrary, or very delusive. It is contended that, in connection with certain American prisons, the plan of "Indeterminate" Sentences is already carried out. But what does this mean? It signifies that, after short periods, usually about a year and a half, or two years, criminals, many of whom have been guilty of most serious crimes, are liberated conditionally, on the basis and test, mainly, of their behaviour during such limited imprisonment. But such test is very unsatisfactory; because the worst criminals generally have cunning enough to pose as models of behaviour, whilst in jail. Then, when liberated, they can easily betake themselves to other States, or countries, out of the way of supervision, and may, by such very migration, be returned in "statistics," as amongst those who have ceased to be known as criminals. The expression "Indeterminate" is apt to be a mere euphemism for that which is vague and arbitrary.

Whereas, with such moderately progressive cumulations of sentence as are here suggested, the offender would have fair opportunities, after reasonable intervals, of entering the ranks of honest citizenship, under circumstances favourable both to his own reformation and to the protection of society. And neither his liberations, nor his re-convictions, would be based upon merely conjectural or deceptive inferences, but on reliable experiences and just conclusions.

Chapter VII.

ON SENTENCES IN GENERAL.

Cruel Extremes.

In a previous chapter, the mischief of extreme laxity to criminals, especially those of the class of ruffians, has been dwelt upon. But the opposite extreme of gross harshness towards minor offenders, is also an evil which has been too frequent. The following are a very few instances, by no means exceptional, selected from modern British sentences of this description, letters being substituted for the names of the culprits:—

"A," after two minor committals to a local jail, was convicted for stealing money, and sentenced to seven years' penal servitude, followed by seven years' police supervision. After all this he was re-convicted for stealing three shillings, and sentenced to another seven years' imprisonment, followed by a further seven years' supervision.

"B," for stealing a garden fork, was sentenced to ten years' imprisonment and five years' supervision. He had already, for stealing a rabbit-gin, had seven years' imprisonment and two years' supervision. The circumstance of his having undergone four minor committals to jail previously, does not justify the preposterous harshness of the subsequent seventeen years' detention, with seven years' further supervision for two such trifling thefts.

There is a monstrous disproportion and cruelty in such outbursts of vengeance on the part of legal " Justice " so-called.

" C," after some brief punishment in a jail, was sentenced, for stealing a cup, to five years' imprisonment and seven years' supervision ; another disproportionate and unjust infliction !

" D," furnishes a special illustration of the gross inequalities and anomalies which so often characterize English sentences. For stealing a piece of canvas, he was sentenced to twelve years' penal servitude, to be followed by seven years' supervision. He had already undergone six minor detentions in jail and three sentences of penal servitude, amounting to twenty-two years, and including one of ten years for stealing a shovel. So that this poor weak creature has been committed to thirty-four years' of imprisonment, with seven years' supervision, all for petty thefts; whilst few of the most atrocious ruffians, violators, or burglars, of England, have had half such an amount of punishment meted out to them !

" E," for stealing some water-cresses and shell-fish, was sentenced to eight years' imprisonment and seven years' supervision. He had already had, for stealing a hamper of potatoes, seven years' imprisonment and seven years' supervision. And before that, he had had sixteen minor convictions. But, here again, the very petty nature of most of the thefts committed by him indicate that a little common sense might have dealt with him far more promptly and effectually than by all this protracted and costly series of inflictions.

" F " was sent to penal servitude for his first offence (embezzlement). He then continued honest for sixteen years, when, for stealing some candles, he was sentenced to seven years' imprisonment and seven years' supervision ! Surely the sixteen years' interval constituted a claim for more mercy, and for a mild and moderate penalty.

" G," after five petty committals to jail, was sentenced, for stealing six shillings, to seven years' imprisonment. The same year in which he was liberated from the latter term, he stole a pair of boots, which offence brought down upon him ten years' imprisonment and seven years' supervision.

Is it any matter for surprise, that thieves have, of late, manifested an increasing disposition to carry pistols and shoot the police, or any one likely to cause their arrest? Are not murderous assaults the natural and almost necessary consequence of such shocking sentences as some of the above? For if the perpetrators of petty thefts find, by experience, that they incur punishments of from ten to twenty years' duration for stealing a few water-cresses, herrings, fowls, or boots, why should they not risk a violent self-defence against the police or others, inasmuch as their punishment, in case of arrest, can hardly be worse than that inflicted hitherto for comparatively harmless deliuquencies? The Law itself unwisely teaches them that atrocious crimes do not, in general, receive more vindictive retaliation, and very often not nearly so much, as little thefts committed to satisfy their hunger, or clothe their nakedness. Hence the extremely rapid and severe cumulation of long imprisonments, for petty offences, has been, and is, carried to such an extent, as to have become a positive temptation to dangerous crimes of brutality.

It is to be noted that the heaviest sentences for minor offences are not, in general, imposed by the superior or more intelligent class of Judges, but chiefly by the provincial or rural Magistrates and Chairmen of Quarter Sessions. For example, out of a list of 720 recent sentences to penal servitude, 240 were passed by the Judges, and only nine of these were accompanied by subsequent supervision. Whereas, out of the remaining 480 sentences passed at the lower courts (" the Sessions,") 209 involved supervision. Hence, the higher tribunals ordered this addition to less than four per cent. of their sentences; but the lower courts adopted it in 43 per cent. of cases. That is to say, the local Magistrates impose long periods of supervision, to an extent *eleven times greater* than that deemed needful by the Judges, the highest rank of legal administrators.

It has been pleaded, in justification of this special preference, by the lower Courts, for protracted supervision, that their members are personally better acquainted with the requirements of local offenders. It is alleged that the Judges know very little of the actual circumstances of the criminal classes, and that their previous training has only been a forensic and literary one. A magisterial correspondent of the writer remarks on this point: "Most of the Judges, when first called to the bar, held a few criminal briefs, drawn by a solicitor, not to show the culprit's previous habits or temptations, or causes of crime, or his thoughts or feelings, but simply to prove that he did the act. Has any one of them, in his life, had any talk with a prisoner, or with any labourer? Does any one of them know anything of the opinions or feelings of the criminal class, or how to affect them?" For such reasons as these, some of the local Magistrates argue that they are much better furnished than the Judges with that actual knowledge of the offending classes and of all their circumstances, which is requisite for guidance, in the imposition of sentences, within the wide limits of discretion, often permitted by the law.

And, unquestionably, this argument possesses some weight. But after due allowance for it, and for other adducible pleas, it is also undeniable that the numerous sentences of from a dozen to twenty years' aggregation of imprisonment and supervision, for a few repeated thefts— as of herrings, chickens, or boots—constitute a most disproportionate, unmerciful, and even crime-producing procedure.

A great change is therefore needful, at least in England,

in regard to habitual offenders of the less dangerous
class—those characterised rather by excessive laziness
and by propensities to pilfer, but not evincing violent or
ruffianly inclinations. These require a certain, but more
gradually cumulative, infliction than hitherto, of cellular
imprisonment. And for the proportion of them, probably
not a large one, for whom this will be insufficient, some
more protracted discipline, of a reformatory and industrial
character, will be further efficacious. But neither such
training, nor the police supervision—which may be either
its sequel or its substitute, according to circumstances—
should be characterised by excessive length of duration.
The whole process should be sufficient for its purpose, but
not extended so far as mercilessly to crush out hope, or put
the community to great expense, for a few peccadilloes; or
positively to furnish temptations to crimes of brutality.

CHANCE SENTENCES.

General Sir E. F. Du Cane has shown by official statistics,
that the graver sentences of long duration, upon English
convicts, have been, to a very great extent, a matter of
apparent chance, or, at least, that a sort of stereotyped
conventional fashion has largely prevailed with the Judges
in this matter. They have glided into a customary groove,
marked by certain favourite periods, especially five, seven,
ten, and fourteen years; whereas the circumstances of the
crimes to which these sentences have been so easily and
habitually attached, represent no such ratio. Just as, in
the eighteenth century, almost every crime was punished
by the gibbet, with the uniformly brutal addition " without
benefit of clergy," so, subsequently, with a painful disregard
of the real proportion of facts, the English Judges have
re-echoed their five, seven, and ten years' sentences in a
manner somewhat resembling the childish jingle of " Ding
dong bell; ding dong bell."

In proof of this, Sir E. F. Du Cane quoted official

returns showing that, in a recent period, the average number of prisoners under sentences of five years was 2,043 ; but of those for six years only 43. There was an average of 4,703 for seven years, and of only 366 for eight years ; 1,898 for ten years, and none at all for eleven years. It is evident that, in point of fact, there can have been no real necessity for this preponderance of the five, seven, and ten years over the six, eight, and eleven. Why, for example, should a sentence of seven years be at all more frequent than one of six or eight? Hence, great cruelty and injustice may often have been perpetrated upon unfortunate wretches, through this habit on the part of Judges, in yielding to the influence of an extensive idolatry of fanciful precedent, or even, unconsciously, to a mere numerical jingle.

In America a similarly unintelligent irregularity often characterises sentences. At the Toronto Prison Congress, in 1887, Mr. Z. R. Brockway, of Elmira, remarked that on one occasion, when he heard a judge sentence five felons to five very different terms of imprisonment, he inquired the cause of such a strange disparity of treatment under the circumstances. The judge was astonished at the question, felt very puzzled, and exclaimed, " Oh, ask me something easier; I don't know."

Several of the judges have publicly acknowledged the injustice which has too often characterised sentences, and their tendency towards opposite extremes, of cruel severity or of injurious leniency. But latterly some of them have manifested a laudable disposition to exercise more discrimination in this regard. Indeed, a much greater change for the better, in this respect, has taken place amongst the Judges than amongst the Magistrates.

ADVANTAGES OF CONFERENCE AND REFLECTION.

The existing inequalities of sentences might often be obviated by more systematic arrangements for a moderate

interval between the verdict of a jury and the decision of
the judge or magistrate. It occasionally happens, already,
that such an authority remarks in court, "I will take
time to consider what the sentence shall be, in this case."
The more regular adoption of this wise practice, thus
affording opportunities for reflection and conference with
other Judges or Magistrates, might, with much advantage,
be resorted to. There are also needed, in England at least,
various minor reforms in the conduct of trials, which
would facilitate just conclusions as to sentences. For
example, the forms of Indictment are often far too complex, verbose, and obscure. And further, the person
accused should be furnished with a copy of his indictment at least ten days or a fortnight before trial, as in
Scotland. It is very unfair to a prisoner to withhold a
copy of his indictment from him, as has often been done,
until immediately previous to the trial. Such matters
as these may materially affect both the defence and the
sentence.

Independent Action in Sentence and Punishment.

There has been, for the most part, too little connection, or
relation, between the functions of the authorities who pre-
scribe the sentences and of those who carry them into
execution. It may be remembered that it is always in the
power of the latter to modify, very materially, the original
intent of the former. An imprisonment of one year may
be rendered, by one set of custodians, as really penal as
double or treble the same period under the care of another
body of officers. It has sometimes happened that criminals,
sent to certain prisons with the express intention of being
there more leniently treated, have actually found themselves under a severer discipline than they would have
experienced in the establishments to which a more rigorous
purpose would have consigned them.

The almost necessarily hasty manner in which criminals

are often disposed of, at their trials in court—at least in England, as distinguished from Scotland*—largely precludes an adequate regard to their real character and requirements. Apparently conclusive evidence, as to the commission of the crime with which a prisoner is charged, may wholly fail to reveal some very material circumstances affecting the action itself, and the motives and antecedents of the offender. There is reason to fear that, even in England, actually innocent persons are more often convicted than is generally supposed. It occasionally comes to light that long periods of penal servitude have been undergone by such wrongly-accused individuals. And when once consigned to a convict prison, it is a matter of the extremest difficulty for these to procure any effectual attention to their cases. They are almost " buried alive," so far as help is concerned. This is a grave evil, which awaits a remedy in some way.

Again, the disproportion between the apparatus for arriving at a verdict, and the comparative disregard to the operation of the consequent sentence, has often been very great.

An able writer in the *Cornhill Magazine* has made some noteworthy remarks upon the sentences which often follow trials where immense pains have been taken, in regard to

* SCOTLAND has long enjoyed some great advantages, as compared with English procedure against criminals, especially in two respects. Firstly, in the opportunity, afforded to juries, of returning verdicts of " *Not proven,*" in cases where there is reason to hope for further evidence, and where it is desired to retain the power of re-arresting rogues, already put on trial, if occasion should arise. Secondly, the admirable arrangements both for officially initiating prosecutions, and for eliciting much important information, in a simple, sensible manner, by means of the functionaries styled " *Procurators Fiscal.*" The English law, by its excessive technicalities, affords thieves, burglars, and other offenders, numerous chances of eluding the grasp of justice. There are so many of these defects in legal definition and procedure, that a CODIFICATION OF THE CRIMINAL LAW has become a special desideratum for Great Britain.

the elaboration of evidence.   For the sentence is. to the trial, what the bullet is to the powder.   The writer alluded to, says: " A pack of hounds and a number of men, dogs, and horses, will spend hours in hunting a fox which, when caught, is abandoned to the dogs without an observation. So the criminal, when fairly run down, is sentenced by the Judge, and turned over to another set of authorities, utterly unconnected with and unrelated to him, who act upon different principles, and constantly pull different ways. It is just like a doctor, who, after spending all the morning in finding out that his patient was consumptive, should politely show him the door, saying, as he did so, ' Go and spend £25 in drugs, at such a chemist's.'   It is just as easy to say nine, as to say six, months ; to say seven years' penal servitude, as to say five ; and the question which of the two is to be said, has to be settled in a very short time, often without consultation, advice, or guidance of any description.   Yet the sentence is the gist of the proceeding. Unless it is what it ought to be, the counsel, the witnesses, the jury, and the summing-up, to say nothing of the Sheriff, with his coach, javelin-men, and trumpeters, are a mere *brutum fulmen.*   They might as well have stayed at home, but for the credit of the thing."

RESTRAINT NOT NECESSARILY DETENTION.

Sentences, in general, should determine a definite time, or a gradation of periods, during which their subjects should be retained under the power and within the reach of the authorities, for either penal or reformatory purposes.   But this should not necessarily, or even generally, involve the infliction of imprisonment throughout the entire term pre- scribed.   It should secure *liability* to imprisonment ; but the extent of the actual incarceration, and the nature and period of subsequent relaxed conditions of detention, or of strictly conditional liberation, should, within such period, be more largely left to the discretion of the officers charged with the custody of the offenders.

SENTENCES OF LIABILITY TO IMPRISONMENT.

Without any sweeping modification of the existing letter of the English law, and without materially interfering with the prerogatives of Judges on the one hand, or entrusting any dangerous punitory powers to the administrators of prisons, a much-needed reform may be generally secured, so far as the Statute Book is concerned, by changing, in each case, the expression " imprisonment " into "liability to imprisonment," or by enacting that " imprisonment " shall henceforth be deemed to signify such liability.

This would simply render the sentences pronounced, the *maximum* inflictions of penal *control*, without unduly limiting the mode of treatment during that restraint. It would be carrying out more fully the precedent and principle already adopted, with much advantage, in English jurisprudence, in the case of the " Conditional Liberation " of convicts. The executive authorities in charge of criminals would thus be afforded the needful means of discrimination, justly demanded by the different circumstances of each prisoner, and by his behaviour and progress during his preliminary training and subsequent conditional liberty under supervision. Several of the American States have modified their laws in this direction. The English " PROBATION OF FIRST OFFENDERS ACT," passed in 1887, constituted an important and decided recognition of this principle.

SPANISH AND OTHER EXPERIMENTS.

Long antecedently, either to the establishment of American " Indeterminate Sentence " Prisons, or of English " Conditional Liberation," the principle involved was partially adopted, and with success, at Valencia in Spain, and in Wurtemburg and Bavaria in Germany. Subsequently it found able advocates in Captain Maconochie, Sir

Walter Crofton, Baron F. Von Holtzendorff, Mr. Frederick Hill, Mr. Z. R. Brockway, M. Bonneville de Marsangy, and other penologists, in various countries.

In the year 1835, COLONEL MONTESINOS, being appointed Governor of Valencia prison, then containing 1,250 inmates, put in operation an old provision (previously dormant or neglected) of the Spanish Law, by which a prisoner could be enabled to shorten his period of incarceration, by good behaviour. The experiment was carried out during fifteen years, at the end of which the re-convictions had sunk from more than 50 per cent. to less than 10 per cent., whilst crime throughout that district had greatly diminished. The prison became a self-supporting establishment, through the variety and encouragement of industry there carried on, and the stimulus afforded to the workers, by giving them a considerable share of the profits.

A revised Criminal Code for all Spain was instituted by the Legislature, in which the exceptional clauses, which Montesinos had made such good use of, were omitted. No virtually indeterminate sentences were thenceforth allowed. This legal blunder at once struck the death-blow to a previously successful system. The elements of hope and reward were eliminated from it, and in consequence, of course, the plan collapsed. Despair, outrage, and increased criminality, again became characteristics of prison life in Valencia.

AGE AND SEX AS MODIFYING SENTENCES.

A French magistrate, M. EUGENE MOUTON, has justly remarked, in his interesting work entitled " Le Devoir de Punir " (Paris, 1887), that a systematic modification of sentences should be made, in regard to age and sex. He proposes that all legal penalties should be subject to a reduction of one-fourth of their amount for women, and one-half for persons under sixteen, or over sixty years of age ; also that these three classes should be exempted from

every form of corporal punishment. With some exception
as to the latter proposition, there is much to be said in
favour of these suggestions, in consideration of various
physical infirmities and temptations of the three divisions
in question.

The Final Object of Sentences.

It is to be desired that, in regard to Sentences, there may
be, in future, a more intelligent and practical consideration,
than in the past, of the *precise end sought* to be accomplished
by them. That experienced Gloucestershire Magistrate,
Mr. Barwick Baker, wrote to the author, on this point :
"Who can say whether a sentence is too long or too short ?
Before we can decide, we must settle what is the *object* in
sentencing ; I say, *the diminution of crime is the object ;* but
no Judges, and few Chairmen of Quarter Sessions, agree
with me in this. All hold that the true purpose is to give
an amount of punishment equal to the guilt of the
offender ; and as there is no measure for the punishment—
one man suffering three times as much as another, from
the same infliction—or for the guilt, each is sure his own
sentence is right, and we have ' *Quot judices, tot sententiæ.*'
No one can give, or does give, a test of what these
should be."

There are few things in which so much careful adaptation of means to end is requisite, as in this matter. The
time, or duration, of punishment is not the only element of
importance to be considered. But it has usually received a
too exclusive regard, irrespective of the varying demands
and conditions of criminal discipline.

CHAPTER VIII.

HABITUAL OFFENDERS AND SUPERVISION.

THE measures which have hitherto been adopted with Habitual Criminals (termed " *Recidivistes*," in France, and " Revolvers," in America), whether in Europe or in America, may be regarded rather as experimental than absolutely successful. For nowhere has there yet been carried out, in the treatment of this class, any system characterised by adequate regularity, certainty, and discrimination. Even in England, which has taken and maintained a leading position in this matter, the mode of cumulating sentences has been extremely defective and arbitrary; whilst, also, there has been a general practical disregard of the very important distinction existing between wilfully brutal ruffians, and the other class of habitual offenders who are weak and indolent, rather than violent or cruel. These require and deserve different modes of treatment.

A *sure* but very *gradual* cumulation of cellular imprisonment will *alone*, and without any provision for further industrial training, or police supervision, suffice for the effectual reclamation and deterrence of many offenders who, under existing irregularities of treatment, become habitual criminals. This is the conclusion decisively arrived at by practical observers. But what Government, or nation, has hitherto adopted it, on any complete or persevering scale ? *Not a single one.*

Criminals should not be regarded as belonging to the *habitual* class, until they have undergone several, at least, of the first stages of such a moderate but certain cumulation of penalty. In most cases the patience and majesty of the law might fairly afford them three or four opportunities of this kind. This course would greatly restrict the number of persons to be further and finally dealt with. But after these trials of the operation of imprisonments, such persistent offenders need, even when at liberty, a special vigilance and oversight on the part of the authorities.

Differing Opinions respecting Supervision.

But there exists on this point considerable difference of view amongst judges, magistrates, and prison-officers, who may, on either side, be regarded as competent to form some opinion. The writer once received, almost simultaneously, two letters, one from a most experienced magistrate, and the other from a veteran prison governor, conveying opposite views on this question of supervision, at least as now practised in Great Britain. And often many similar divergencies of opinion in regard to it have been noticed. Yet, on careful examination and comparison of these views, it will be found that they do not differ so much as at first sight would appear to be the case. They generally admit the value and even necessity of *some* kind of supervision, for some classes of discharged prisoners, but they differ as to its nature and extent.

Some of them decidedly object to its exercise by the Police, whilst approving it when entrusted to the operation of Discharged Prisoners' Aid Societies, or to private "patrons" of judicious character. Others, again, who still recognise the value of supervision, whilst exercised by the police, denounce as needlessly cruel and even mischievous, the protracted terms, such as five or seven years of surveillance to which many criminals are sentenced under existing law. In this matter, as in most other things, the best procedure will probably be found to consist in a medium course, or partial combination of the different views expressed by thoughtful and experienced observers.

Some of the possible disadvantages of Police Supervision* have already been obviated, in England at least, by confining its delicate and confidential functions, as much as possible, to the chief or superior authorities amongst the force, and by strictly prohibiting the subordinate or less intelligent members of that body from taking any part in the relations between discharged convicts and their employers. The co-operation of private benevolence— especially in connection with Discharged Prisoners' Aid Societies, and " Prison Gate Missions," has also been very advantageously united with the action of the police.

The question of the period of time over which the supervision of a discharged habitual criminal should extend, is also one on which differences of opinion exist, and which deserves more attention than it has hitherto received. It is probable that, at least so far as the police are concerned, a duration of one or two years' surveillance would, in most cases, be better than the more protracted terms of five or seven years ; though, of course, special prolongations would still be needful in various exceptional instances.

There should not be a too general or indiscriminate resort to police supervision. It should be strictly confined to *habitual* as separate from incidental offenders, two classes requiring very different treatment.

* POLICE SUPERVISION.—A sentence of "Supervision" in Great Britain requires its subject to report himself, in person, to the police once a month; and also to notify promptly to them every change of residence. Failure of compliance with these and some other conditions involves re-imprisonment.

There has been, on both sides of the Atlantic, a frequent expression of opinion, by prison officers and penologists, that Habitual Offenders, or Récidivistes, of the *violent* class, should, after two or three perpetrations of such crime, be imprisoned for life and never again be suffered to prey upon society. One of the ablest of American penologists, Professor FRANCIS WAYLAND, of Yale College, in an essay entitled " *The Incorrigible*," strongly urged this course. He referred to the numerous horrible atrocities committed by criminals who had previously undergone various periods, longer or shorter, of congregate imprisonment, and who, also, in many instances, had had such terms of detention shortened by remissions for presumed " reformation," or " good behaviour," on the mere ground of that obedience to prison regulations in which the most practised villains are apt to be the most exemplary, so long as it is their interest to obtain, thereby, any relaxation of their penalty or discipline. So many murders, rapes, arsons and burglaries have been perpetrated in America by these " reformed " criminals, that Professor Wayland suggests, in the interests of the community, that the only safe course is, on a third conviction, to shut them up for life in a penal institution.

Further, he deprecates, for this class, any reliance upon police supervision, as being insufficient. In the United States this surveillance is certainly very imperfectly organised, and perhaps, under their circumstances, almost unattainable there, to any sufficiently effective extent.

Professor Wayland says, " If it be argued that police supervision, after release, would avert the danger, I answer that it is far more easy, wise, and safe, to exercise it within prison walls. The authorities of a hospital might, with just as much show of reason, release a small-pox patient in the most contagious period of that dreaded disease, and then provide that while the dangerous symptoms continued he should remain under supervision. I believe that there

is but one cure for this great and growing evil, and tha
this is to be found in the imprisonment for life of the
criminal once pronounced incorrigible." He adds, " We
shall do no practical injustice to the criminal, if we provide
that a third conviction for such felony should establish
his status as incorrigible."

There is some weight in this objection to permitting
dangerous habitual criminals, of this particular class, to be
at liberty, even under supervision ; and on the whole, for
such ruffians and such morally inveterate desperadoes as
some of them are, it would be the better and safer plan
to have recourse to prolonged detention in institutions
specially adapted for the purpose, as on islands, for
example, or in places where escape would be very difficult,
but where, at the same time, considerable space would be
available for agriculture and other industry.

To a large extent this system of long detention for violent criminals has already been carried out, in England, in
the form of Penal Servitude. For such persons it is almost.
impossible to devise a course of treatment free from grave
difficulties and disadvantages. The British plan, although
requiring modifications, is one of the best yet adopted for
this particular class.

The writer ventures to differ from those authorities, such
as Professor Wayland and others, who advocate a sentence
of absolute life imprisonment for all desperate felons who
have been convicted a third time. For inflictions of detention, really for life, tend in practice to become a slow
form of the death penalty, and hence may be more cruel,
in the aggregate, than the immediate operation of the
gallows, or the guillotine. The writer believes that even
for violent criminals, it will be, on the whole, more
advantageous to all parties concerned, that gradually
progressive but definite sentences of confinement should
be passed, rather than of perpetual imprisonment. But
the gradation of sentences should be certain, instead of

uncertain and irregular, as hitherto. No sentence should ever be repeated a second time. Every successive infliction should mark a fixed advance upon the preceding one. Hence sentences on desperadoes should proceed on some such scale of increase as a moderate increment of two years in succession; having regard more to the number of repetitions of brutal crime, than to the character of each act.

A ruffian, knowing that the certainty of such a moderate scale of prolonged confinements awaited him, would be far more deterred than heretofore. A series of half a dozen of such moderately definite sentences would ultimately involve, to most, if not all of the worst characters, a lifetime of secure detention. After two or three terms of such protracted discipline they would, in general, have become incapacitated for further mischief; meanwhile they would have had always before them a ray of hope, useful alike for their own moral development and for facilitating the duties and permanent safety of the officers in charge. No country in the world appears as yet to have practically carried out a moderate, certain, regular gradation, such as is here advocated, for this particular class.

SPECIAL ADVANTAGES OF SUPERVISION.

In regard to a moderate, but not excessively prolonged, supervision of discharged habitual offenders, Mr. Barwick Baker remarked—" For myself I have no blind confidence in prison-effected reformation, and I should like to keep a watch for a long time on those who have gone wrong. I believe that such a watch is a more wholesome kind of punishment, as well as being far cheaper than an imprisonment. I am aware that some tender-hearted gentlemen will talk of the hardship of suspecting a man who has indeed stolen, but has since ' expiated his offence,' as it was once absurdly called, by an imprisonment. I have had much to do with criminals, and I know well that there is scarcely any time when a man requires a friendly watch so much as when he is just turned out of prison. Of all means of *punishment*, or *prevention*, I consider surveillance is the most valuable. As a punishment it is so slight, that it may be continued for a long period. If twelve months of surveillance be equally disliked with one month of imprisonment, the one will keep a man out of mischief for one month, the other for twelve. The jail more or less unfits a man for hard labour ; work under license especially accustoms him to it. No judge can tell how much each prisoner will suffer in the time allotted to him. One man will suffer acutely from that which another will hardly feel. But surveillance has this peculiar quality, that it adapts itself to the requirements of *all*."

It must, however, be always provided that the surveillance shall be friendly, as well as strict ; that it shall be vigilance for the *interests* of the former offender, and by no means exclusively for his relapses or failures. It must be a means to hold him *up*.

The more often a man has been in prison, the more likely he is to return thither. This is abundantly proved by experience. Statistics show that the first brief term of imprisonment, in cellular jails, is the most successful in general ; inasmuch as three-fourths of the persons who have undergone a first incarceration, separated from others, avoid prisons ever after ; but nearly one-half of the number who have been twice imprisoned, at least in association, have to be further re-committed. Nearly three-fourths of those who have been thrice in custody, return for a fourth time, or oftener. Hence the more habitual that any crime has become to any persons, the greater the necessity for maintaining some special supervision over them.

Licensing Out to Employers.

In many of the Reformatories for Juvenile Offenders, both in England and elsewhere, the practice has been adopted, with much advantage, of licensing out these young persons to private employers, under certain needful conditions as to supervision, payment and discipline. The State is thus relieved of a portion of their maintenance, whilst they are placed under a favourable but gradual preparation for a full restoration to the privileges of liberty. A similar principle might perhaps be beneficially adopted with certain classes of adult petty offenders, who, from the power of their evil habits, require a prolonged surveillance when outside the walls of prisons. In some American States, it is the practice to allow many of the criminals to exchange their imprisonment for the service of private employers, chiefly on the ground of immediate economy to the taxpayer. But, with a few exceptions, there does not appear to have been, as yet, a sufficient preparation or security for such a step, there.

Systematic Organization of Supervision.

In some countries, as for example in Great Britain, the adoption of a more regular and certain system of dealing with Habitual Criminals would necessarily involve a preliminary modification of the existing arrangements, or legislation, in regard to the special department of Police Supervision. But in any case, and in every land, the successful application of duly Graded Sentences and of Conditional Liberation, under Supervision, must largely depend upon the degree of organization of central and local action, for the adequate registration of convictions and for the recognition of habitual offenders, and also for a due cognizance of their location and movements.

A special staff of officers is needful for these objects. Considerable progress has been made, in London in particular, in this form of departmental organization, by the authorities charged with the supervision and registration of habitual criminals. There is always need for a more prompt and complete interchange of information between the

Metropolitan and Provincial officers, in regard to the constantly changing movements of the members of the class in question.

The greater co-operation of the local Magistrates and Patronage Societies may be very advantageously secured, by the police and prison authorities, for this object. It has been suggested that in each district, the magistrates should appoint a small committee to look over periodically, with the chief of police, the list of persons under supervision in their neighbourhood. In case of any of those under conditional liberty, removing to another district, this change of residence should be notified to the authorities in the Metropolis, and by the latter promptly sent down to the locality into which such new visitors have just arrived. By such a complete interchange of observations and registers, on the part of both local and central authorities, every change of residence by conditionally liberated offenders should be ascertained, recorded, and circulated, throughout the whole period of the vigilance imposed upon them. In so far as any system of supervision lacks this provision, it is defective in an important element.

The practice of placing some of the conditionally liberated criminals under the systematic supervision of private patrons, has been adopted with considerable success at NEUFCHATEL, in Switzerland. A former intelligent governor of the prison in that place, Dr. GUILLAUME, introduced this plan, together with other carefully designed efforts to reform offenders. When released provisionally, they are required to present themselves every week before a patron, who also receives regular reports of their behaviour from their employers, and transmits these to the authorities, as a guide in determining the period of each offender's absolute liberation.

CLASS PRISONS.

Not only should Sentences be graded, but also, where the

best of all classification, that of individualization in the cell, is not yet secured, some advantage may accompany the adoption of distinct prisons and discipline for each class of re-convictions. The convicts committed for the shorter terms should not be placed in the same establishment, or under the same *régime,* as those sentenced for the longer periods.

In particular, the class of ruffians, or criminals guilty of cruelty, might with advantage be generally placed in special prisons, with a more penal treatment than other offenders. For cruelty is the worst of crimes.

It was one of the former defects of the British Convict Prisons, that they intermingled all classes of criminals in the same establishments. Latterly some improvement has been introduced in this direction. Many of the re-committed convicts have been kept permanently apart from those undergoing a first sentence. With re-convicted desperadoes, under a certain and regularly cumulative system of sentences, a material part of the efficacy of their treatment, both as to deterrence and to security, would consist in their orderly distribution into prisons specially adapted for each stage of re-committal. This would, at least in some degree, facilitate the discriminative management of such peculiarly difficult subjects.

Throughout the terms of custody they should have opportunities, as at present in the convict prisons of various nations, of securing for themselves successive ameliorations of their treatment by " good marks." The cell or the whip might still furnish the ultimate resorts for special chastisement. As far as practicable, personal industry should be rendered (as outside, under the ordinary conditions of life) a basis of self support. For the skill acquired under long detentions would, in many cases, enable such prisoners to exercise very profitable industries of various kinds. They should, of course, as often hitherto, be permitted the stimulus of some present and prospective share of the results or value of their labour.

There is good reason to conclude that, on the adoption of the gradually cumulative system advocated by the writer, the first stages would generally suffice for their object, and that comparatively a small residuum of "intractables" or "incorrigibles" would remain to be dealt with, under the admittedly difficult problems of the final and most protracted terms. Indeed this result has been partially attained already in Great Britain, in so far as the plan here described has been approximated to.

But throughout, for every description of habitual offenders, whether of the less dangerous or the desperado class, the main element of repression must always consist in the certainty of a moderate gradation of restraint. Such certainty is the indispensable and primary condition of success.

Characteristics of the Chronic Thief Class.

And there is another matter to be borne in mind, both on grounds of justice and expediency. This consists in the general character and antecedents of Habitual Offenders, as a class peculiarly pervaded by hereditary moral weakness. They are, by nature as well as by habit, very irresolute, and easily tempted. To very many of them, society owes a special debt, of sustaining their attempts at amendment, and efficiently encouraging their good resolutions, by means of a kindly supervision and control. This just claim has been too often overlooked.

Mr. Percy Neame, a Chief Superintendent of discharged convicts in London, informed the writer that his experience of this class had especially shown him their inherent laziness and indifference to moral elevation. He estimated the number of the "residuum" of habitual offenders and vicious loafers, in London alone, at scores of thousands. They cluster chiefly in "nests" or certain low streets, and " rookeries " known to the police. They can easily supply all their wants by theft, at which they are adepts. One of them remarked to Mr. Neame, " I can rob ninety-nine pockets out of every hundred safely," that is without detection. If labour is offered them, they will not undertake it for any ordinary wages. They are content with their condition; they raise no " bitter cry," and only laugh at the philanthropists and legislators who desire to elevate or reclaim them. They prefer to remain as they are; they can exist on a few pence per day, and often do so. The product of one easy theft will maintain them for weeks, or months, in their fascinating idleness. A little fish, bread, or porridge is sufficient for many of them. They are not very drunken, as a class, but incorrigibly lazy. Work is the one thing they most abhor; they are often too indolent even to wash themselves; they prefer to be filthy; their very skin in many instances, almost ceases to perform its functions. Nearly all the discharge from some of their bodies is by the bowels; and if compulsorily washed, such people become sick. They neither know nor care for God. During their spells of imprisonment they are stupidly indifferent to the chaplains, and doze through their sermons; and they are often allowed to do so, for peace sake.

Many of them come out of their lairs at night, and prowl about like wild beasts. They watch for opportunities of theft; they crowd to conflagrations, or riots. Most of them are very ignorant; but the more dangerous of them are those who have been educated. Education tends, in general, to prevent crime; yet it renders a minority of this class more potent for mischief. If seven out of every ten young persons are prevented, by instruction, from becoming criminals, the other three may thereby be rendered more shrewdly mischievous. Mr. Neame stated that some of the worst thieves are those who have previously had a training in Board Schools, and that the most depraved girls and women are amongst the more educated ones.   He and other official observers would confine popular charitable and " Board School " education strictly to the " three R's," or Reading, Writing, and Arithmetic, with the Bible ; and nothing more.   But the Bible is just the essential element which is too often excluded from popular or State education.

" Adult Reformatories."

In 1868 Mr. Barwick Baker suggested a system of " Adult Reformatories," with special reference to their suitability for habitual offenders of the less violent description, and for inveterate drunkards.   He drew attention to the marked success which had already attended the system of partially indeterminate sentences and progressive liberation, in the case of the lads committed to ordinary juvenile Reformatories.   Their inmates were usually sentenced to five years' detention on a second conviction. They first underwent a short imprisonment of about a month or less, by way of a preliminary penal discipline. This was followed by two or three years of farm labour, under strict oversight ; after which they were placed out in situations, for the remainder of their terms of sentence, and permitted to earn their own living, but under certain conditions of supervision and liability to be returned to the reformatory.

It was at first regarded as a chimerical or Utopian idea to propose to retain disorderly lads at labour in open fields, and in buildings not surrounded by any high walls. Nevertheless the experiment was carried out with remarkable success.   The attempts to escape from such institutions were very few in number.   Mr. Baker therefore urged that the same principle should be tried with certain classes of older offenders, who should be sentenced, especially in the case of habitual thieves, to a term of years of " liability to imprisonment," to include a preliminary period in an " Adult Reformatory."

But their chief punishment and discipline would consist in prolonged vigilance and supervision *after* their liberation, and whilst maintaining themselves by their own labour, and not being supported at the cost of the honest taxpayers. They might also be required to pay, out of their earnings, a small sum of from sixpence to a shilling per week, or about the amount of their " beer money," during all their term of liability to imprisonment, as a salutary reminder and proof of their indebtedness to the community, and as some return to the State for the expense of their supervision.

The offender being thus steadily kept in check, but not inside a prison, would be an abiding visible witness for the disadvantage of evil courses. But when confined in jail, he is out of sight, and in a great degree out of mind, so far as his comrades are concerned. To make prisons self-supporting is desirable, but most difficult, and with few exceptions almost impossible. But to render the culprit self-supporting, whilst still under the restraint of an authoritative vigilance, is thoroughly practicable, and would tend to the best interests, both of himself and the public.

To a large extent, the increasingly popular system of *conditional* Liberation (both by the "Ticket of Leave" plan for convicts and by the holding of punishment in abeyance, through the application of the "First Offenders Act") supplies, without cost to the taxpayers, the place of Adult Reformatories.

But for certain offenders and especially for habitual drunkards, a prolonged detention in such institutions seems indispensable.

The Identification of Habitual Criminals.

Of late years, much aid to the identification of criminals has been derived from the adoption of M. Adolphe Bertillon's " anthropometric " system of measurement of certain bone dimensions of the human body, which, in the adult, remain comparatively unchangeable : such as the length and width of the head, at particular parts of it; the length of the left foot, the left fore-arm, and of the little and middle fingers of the left hand; the length of the trunk of the body, taken when seated; the full stretch of the arms, and the total height of the body. This is the best mode of identifying individuals of this cunning class which has ever been devised.

As a subsidiary assistance to the identification of discharged prisoners, the systematic adoption of photographic portraiture has been very useful in various countries. But it is only partially effectual, in consequence of the astonishing ingenuity of habitual criminals in disguising or changing their personal appearance and dress.

In the Criminal Museum of the London Police, there was a series of sixty photographs of one German girl, taken at many places and periods, but so varying from each other that it was difficult to believe that such exceedingly different aspects could ever be assumed by the same individual. But such was the fact.

Photographs of the thumb and finger marks of criminals have also been proved useful. But on the whole, photography is decidedly inferior, for re-detective purposes, to the Bertillon plan.

CHAPTER IX.

LAND CULTIVATION BY PRISONERS AND BY FREE MEN.

IT has long been a favourite idea with many philanthropists and penal reformers that the cultivation of land
by criminals and vagabonds may furnish one of the best
and most hopeful means for their reclamation. M. DEMETZ,
the founder of the Mettray reformatory, in France, used to
express this idea by his constantly repeated phrase,
" Reclaim the land by the man, and the man by the land."
And a benevolent citizen of London, Mr. CHARLES
PEARSON, sought and obtained the votes of a Metropolitan
constituency, chiefly in order to enable him to enter
Parliament as the advocate of this mode of employing
British criminals, though his subsequent efforts failed to
enlist the needful legislative and public approval.

Again and again, in various countries, attempts have
been made to carry out a similar idea. But most, if not
all of these persevering efforts have failed to attain the
desired object. Not only have the economic results been
of a very unsatisfactory nature, but that which is of
incomparably more importance, namely, the reformation
of the persons employed in this agricultural work, has also
not been secured, to any adequate extent.

The reason of this general failure is that the experiments have been made in defiance of that permanently funda- mental principle that the continuing association of criminals and vagabonds, whether on farms or in jails, is *essentially fatal*, either to their reformation or deterrence. This has been the constantly repeated result, even with the best managed arrangements for working companies of criminals and vagabonds together, in the cultivation of land or in occupation of a kindred nature.

The gang-labour of offenders is a source of loss or disadvantage, whether in farms or factories; as also it would be in any attempt to employ companies of criminals in shops, or other trading establishments. All such occupation is rather for the free man, under free and independent conditions.

The German " LABOUR COLONIES " (*Arbeiter Colonien*) appear, on the whole, to have been conducted in the best possible manner and with special advantages. They have, in particular, had the privilege of being managed by excellent men, of the type of M. VON BODELSCHWINGH, combining high religious character and motive with business ability and common sense. They have been administered with humanity, firmness and intelligence. They have secured the co-operation of State patronage and voluntary benevolence. And they have been tried on a large scale; for many thousand persons are annually received into them.

And yet the verdict passed upon them in an official report published by the British Government, entitled " *On Methods for Dealing with the Unemployed,*" 1893, is this—" The evidence seems to be wholly against the supposition that such institutions are reformatory. They form merely a receptacle for those, who, if they were free, would prey upon society and render means for relieving the deserving poor almost wholly futile." The report elsewhere says—" The repeated admission of the same persons into the German 'Colonies,' constitutes one of the features of the system." An instance was mentioned of a man who had been an inmate of one "Colony" nineteen times. The "Colonies" have become mainly resorts of discharged prisoners and ex-convicts, *but without reforming them.* And they are further stated to be shunned by respectable poor persons. Again, being almost necessarily unisexual, these establishments are at a moral disadvantage. For their inmates are either unmarried, or are separated from the moralizing influences of family-life and of the exertion necessary to maintain a home. And if, on the other hand, the attempt were made to introduce family-life, with wives and children, into such establishments, many and various difficulties would be added to those already existing.

However healthy, from a physical point of view, the cultivation of land by criminals and vagabonds may be, its reformatory influence is imaginary, unless other influences are secured. And the Report, just quoted, remarks, in spite of Mr. Demetz's favourite motto, "The reclamation of *land*, and the reclamation of *men* are two different processes."

The Belgian agricultural and industrial establishment, at MERXPLAS, has accommodation for nearly 4,000 of the vagabond class, and has been in existence for the greater part of a century. Yet it is officially stated respecting it, "The evil reputation of those who form the bulk of the 'colonists' sticks to everybody who goes there; and once within the gates of the Colony, everything conspires to keep a man there, or to force him back again."

Of the two large beggar-colonies in Holland, at VEENHUIZEN and OMMERSCHANS, containing more than six square miles of land, the latter, after many years' experience, had to be abandoned. Veenhuizen like Merxplas, does not appear to be either reformatory or deterrent in its general effect. Its inmates return thither again and again, after discharge. And the Dutch MINISTER

OF JUSTICE informed the Howard Association that he considered the discipline of a well-conducted prison, or factory, to be decidedly preferable to land-cultivation, for the class of persons usually sent to the "colonies."

The prison-farm at LUSK, near Dublin, had to be abandoned, although it was often held up to public admiration by some advocates of the long defunct "Irish Convict System," and although its inmates were exclusively of the better class of convicts, yet it was stated that the intercourse of the prisoners there, who were in association both by day and by night, was of a very demoralizing nature.

As to the agricultural labour at DARTMOOR, the dock-making at CHATHAM Prison (now closed) and other work "in the open" by English convicts, the mischievous association thus unavoidably fostered has been but too notorious.

And notwithstanding the utility of the farming, the roads, bridges, and other public works, on which the wretched gangs of convicts in AUSTRALIA and TASMANIA were employed in the old transportation days, a work which cost many times its actual value, the horrors inseparable from that system ultimately raised from the free colonists such a fierce cry, as against a modern Sodom and Gomorrah, that the British Government were compelled to yield before it, and put an end, for ever, to the deportation of offenders to those regions.

In ITALY, there has latterly been tried a curious experiment in criminal "colonization," under the name of "Compulsory Residence" (or "Domicilio Coatto"). Some thousands of vicious and idle men and women have been deported to several of the islands near the Peninsula, where they have been compulsorily detained, with a view to their partial self-support by labour. But the attempt has proved a costly failure.

Still, at intervals, some well-meaning but usually uninformed speakers and writers plead for the establishment of agricultural "colonies" as the chief and most needed *panacea* for the occupation of criminals and vagabonds. But experience condemns it. So long as it is necessary to deal with offenders by penal treatment or compulsory detention, they should at least be removed from conditions which tend to make them worse than they were before, or which prevent them from becoming reformed. And it seems impossible to avoid these evils, in greater or less degree, in the attempt to reclaim land by large companies of prisoners and vagabonds.

This occupation may, however, be advantageous for *small* parties, for classified and *selected* groups, of persons not of special criminality. Although even for such, it will be found necessary to hold in reserve the power to send the disorderly amongst them to the discipline of cellular imprisonment.

For, generally speaking, the satisfactory cultivation of land requires the conditions of freedom, or at least of liberty on probation, during which the best reformatory influences, namely, those of family life, self-control and ordinary competition with the labour market, can be brought to bear upon the worker. Punishment and reformation are objects which had best be attempted by distinct processes. They are not easy to combine.

In so far as the offender has deserved punishment, let that be inflicted by a preliminary stage of cellular confinement. But the reformatory process must almost of necessity be sought elsewhere than in a prison, or on a penal farm, or similar establishment, whether agricultural or otherwise.

BUT "BACK TO THE LAND" FOR "FREE" MEN.

Whilst land cultivation by gangs of criminals and vagabonds, under enforced detention, has been such a general failure, it is quite otherwise with the independent worker and the honest poor. For these, an extensively diffused occupation of small plots of land is one of the greatest of

Q

social needs. And it is one of the chief elements of national advancement.

The advantages of possessions of this kind are both economic and moral. A little piece of ground where a man can grow his own vegetables and fruit, or keep a pig and some poultry, will help many a poor family to stave off want and hunger. It need not be sufficient to enable the cultivator to raise crops or flowers *for sale,* even if the conditions of agricultural prices and railway charges for conveyance permit any profit on the disposal of the produce. But quite independently of this, vast benefits would ensue from the greatly increased multiplication of garden and land "allotments," by furnishing cottagers with the means of cheaply increasing their food supply, by their own exertions. Many a time of temporary cessation of wages might thus be tided over, without the necessity for applying for pauper-relief, and many a little comfort, both for health and disease, would be available.

The moral and sanitary advantages of land-allotments are also very great. The healthful exercise of digging the earth and cultivating its fruits and vegetables, would often take the place of worse than wasted hours in the pot-house, or tavern. The refining love of flowers would be promoted. Useful and profitable occupation for wife and child would be increased. And the better description of home-influences would in general be fostered.

The Agricultural Labourer Problem.

The immigration from the rural districts into the great cities has of late years constituted a serious evil. But the solution is perhaps more simple than many have supposed. What is specially needed is A BETTER SECURITY FOR THE HOME TENURE of the cottager. And this need not involve costly schemes for providing the labourer with small *freeholds,* at the ratepayers' expense. But it is essential that

he should be secured against *hurried or arbitrary eviction.*
For what inducement to efforts for home-neatness and
good tillage has the cottager, or the farmer, who is liable
to speedy and inconsiderate removal? This is a principal
reason why the British agricultural labourer is often so
miserably housed and so reasonably discontented with his
lot and location. If it were not for this, the annual produce
of meat, vegetables, poultry, eggs, fruit, &c., in Great
Britain, might probably be doubled, and replace much
foreign importation. The wrongs sometimes inflicted by
arbitrary evictions, hurried removals and uncompensated
toil, positively tempt the people to disloyalty and disorder.
The interests both of the community and of the landlord
and tenant would be materially promoted by wise measures
for diminishing these evils.

The *Contemporary Review* (1892) thus remarked on the
value, to the poor and to the nation, of secured home-
tenures—" In England the owners of estates above one acre
in size are about 300,000. In France they are seven
millions. In France there are *eight million acres of common-
land,* the *exact* amount which has, in England, been *taken
from the people* by successive 'Enclosure Acts' during the
last 170 years! In 1880 France *exported* 27 million
pounds' worth of food: England *imported* 80 million
pounds' worth."

In connection with the rural problem, it is too generally
forgotten that, in England, unjust legislation has permitted
an immense spoliation of the ancient rights of the poor,
over very valuable common-lands. The man who steals a
goose from the common is imprisoned; but the incomparably worse thieves, who have stolen the commons from
the poor man's geese and sheep, have been actually upheld
by the law in their crime!

With *security of tenure,* wonders may be accomplished;
but comparatively little without it. Mr. ARTHUR YOUNG
remarked, long ago, of the industrious French peasantry,

who are either freeholders, or small farmers on the sharing-of-profits system (*metairie*)—" An activity has been here that has swept away all difficulties before it and has clothed the very rocks with verdure. The enjoyment of property has done it. Give a man the *secure* possession of a bleak rock and he will turn it into a garden." And Miss Betham Edwards, in writing of "*France of to-day,*" speaks of :—" The almost entire self-sufficingness of very small holdings, making their little crops and stock almost completely supply their needs. Thus on a field, or two, enough flax is grown on which to spin linen for home use, enough wheat and Indian-corn for the year's bread-making, whilst pigs and poultry are reared for domestic consumption ; expenditure being reduced to the minimum." Again she says of the little farms—" Everything for comfort and grace is at their doors : wines, essences, jams, oil, vinegar, nuts, honey, linen (home-spun), dairy, poultry, sheep, horses, cows, fish, fruit, vegetables, strawberries, peas, figs, mulberries, grapes, asparagus, salads—all complete, all home produce." Nor is there any necessity for buying freeholds, to have such advantages. But some form of *security of tenure,* so long as a fair rent is paid, is indispensable.

Miss Edwards adds—" Nothing has done more to improve French industry within the last fifty years than farming on half-profits (shared with the land-owner). It is the stepping-stone from the status of hired labourer to that of capitalist ; and whilst the *metayer* is thus raised in the social scale, by his means vast tracts are brought under cultivation."

There is very little pauperism, comparatively, in the intelligent nation of Japan. And this exemption is chiefly attributable to the general possession of a piece of land, smaller or larger, by the inhabitants of that country.

Great is the increase of public safety, as well as of national wealth and individual happiness, health and morality, which everywhere must be promoted by the extensive multiplication of small holdings of land, amongst a people. This will ever contribute a mighty barrier against which the waves of anarchy and revolution will beat in vain. It is a material element for the diminution of crime and misery, as well as for the general prosperity of a country.

CHAPTER X.

PERPETUAL OR LIFE IMPRISONMENT.

FAILURE OF LIFE DETENTION.

EXPERIENCE proves that all long imprisonments tend, from various causes, to defeat their own object, whether for deterrence or reformation. The penal effect is necessarily counteracted by the unavoidable extension of such comparative indulgences as are needed to maintain life and health under such conditions of duration. These relaxations help to diminish the fear of punishment amongst the criminally-disposed portion of the outside community; and may render the lot of the prisoner more favourable than the gravity of his offence should permit. With the lapse of years, also, the power of habit operates with an effect injurious to the original purposes of detention.

But in the case of imprisonment for life, there are added to these objectionable features, further evils arising from the absence of hope and the pressure of despondency. The criminal who is sentenced for a very long, but definite, term of incarceration, even if for fifteen or twenty years, has at least a powerfully alleviating influence in the prospect afforded by the hope of ultimate restoration to the friendships and pleasures of free life. Whereas perpetual imprisonment is accompanied by the darkness of despair, at least as to this mortal existence. And as to matters of still higher importance, and the preparation for a happy eternity, it can hardly be seriously argued by any one really conversant with the unavoidable conditions of life-imprisonment, that the perpetual association of its subjects with other criminals, under a hopeless prolongation of the worst influences, renders spiritual conversion probable. Rather must it be a miracle, under such circumstances.

INCONSIDERATE SANCTION OF LIFE-IMPRISONMENT.

Almost the only possible justification for the horrors of life imprisonment is that it has been regarded as constituting a substitute for Capital Punishment, which many persons consider to be a still greater evil.

For more than a quarter of a century, the writer has devoted special attention to this question of Capital Punishment, and has been brought into much personal intercourse and correspondence with others interested in the subject, throughout the world. He has endeavoured to examine, impartially and broadly, all that can fairly be alleged for and against this infliction; not merely from the point of view of the reformation of murderers, but mainly in regard to the security of the community at large. And, on the whole, it appears that the great and inevitable difficulties peculiar to this penalty have rendered its infliction so universally irregular and unreliable, that a more certain but secondary punishment would, in general, be a safer one for the protection of society. (This may, perhaps, be considered apart from such very exceptional cases as those of wholesale murderers, like the Chicago anarchists of 1886, or other immeasurably atrocious enemies of the human race and of all law and government.) Meanwhile several impressions connected with this question have been forcing themselves upon the writer's mind, which he deems it his duty briefly to express.

In the first place, he has increasingly noticed, from observation and inquiry, that very few, comparatively, of

the persons who advocate the abolition of capital punishment, have been able, or have taken the trouble, to
make themselves acquainted with the extreme practical
difficulties attendant upon the provision of an effectual
substitute for that penalty. Very few of them have ever
devoted their personal attention to the actual features of
prolonged imprisonment, even under the most merciful
forms of its existing administration. Some of the advocates of that abolition have been remarkably ignorant of
matters connected with prisons or criminal treatment. It
is to be desired that those, as a class, who oppose capital
punishment, could have devoted much more serious and
practical consideration to the substitutes, proposed or
imagined, for that infliction, than has hitherto been given.
Especially should the real nature and evils of life-imprisonment be more studied and weighed.

The more this matter has been investigated by the
writer, the more has he become convinced that, in at least
a large proportion of instances, absolute life-imprisonment
is not so much a substitute for capital punishment, as a
slower and more disadvantageous method of inflicting it.
Cellular imprisonment for life is certainly a most cruel
mode of killing, by protracted torture. But this is seldom
resorted to, in modern times, even in the countries where
the great merits of short periods of separation for ordinary
offenders are partially recognized. Life-prisoners are,
almost everywhere, subjected to the milder system of
association, and with the ordinary conditions of labour and
general discipline undergone by other convicts. Unnecessary severity, towards this class, does not appear to be a
feature of the prison administration of most of the countries
of Christendom, apart from the duration of the sentence.
In the chief penal establishments of various nations there
may be observed a certain number of murderers, who, after
spending twenty, or even more years, continuously in prison,
still retain a good degree of health, both of body and mind.

The writer once noticed in the prison of Aggerhuus, near Christiania, in Norway, a murderer who had already spent thirty-seven years in prison, and who then appeared little the worse in consequence. In another prison, also in Christiania, he observed, at the same date, a murderess, who had undergone twenty-four years of her life-sentence. She was working with apparent contentment. Three years later, the writer referred to her, in a letter to the Governor of Christiania prison, who in his reply remarked, " The female prisoner, now 76 years of age, is in excellent health, because she is of a quiet nature. But, on the contrary, one of her two comrades and helpers in crime, died very soon in prison; whilst the other became lunatic, and was pardoned, after the lapse of many years." At Ghent, in Belgium, and at Leeuwarden, in Holland, murderers imprisoned for twenty and even thirty years, have come under the author's observation, and have proved to him the fact that it is by no means impracticable to carry out perpetual imprisonment, in some instances, without destroying the bodies and minds of its subjects.

PRACTICAL TESTIMONIES OF CRUELTY OF LIFE-DETENTION.

But with many others the results are most disastrous to mind and body; unintentionally cruel, in fact. It would perhaps be impossible to find any prisons conducted with more mildness and mercy than those of Sweden, under the Oscars. Yet, a former Chief Director of these establishments, M. ALMQUIST, in a general report in 1885, prepared for the Prison Congress at Rome, made the following observations respecting his intercourse with the class of convicts whose original sentences of death had been commuted to life-imprisonment, who had already suffered upwards of twenty years' incarceration, and whose applications for liberation had repeatedly been refused:—" I have found them in a condition of despair, and they asked me, ' Why did you spare us from the infliction of death, only to keep us here in association with the vilest criminals? You have buried us alive. The King's clemency to us is no real mercy. On the contrary, it is the severest aggravation of our punishment, to compel us to drag out our lives, without a ray of the hope of mercy.'"

A still more remarkable official statement, and one which deserves the most serious consideration by all advocates of life-imprisonment, was afforded by the report of the Directors of the State Prison of Wisconsin, contained in a British Parliamentary paper, on "Homicidal Crime" (C. 2849, 1881). The State of Wisconsin, it may be noted, had abolished capital punishment since 1853. And this is the description of the effects of the substitute there adopted, as given by the Directors: After protesting against what they term "*the indescribable horror and agony incident to imprisonment for life*," they add, "The condition of most of our life-prisoners is deplorable in the last degree. Not a few of them are hopelessly insane; but insanity, even, brings them no surcease of sorrow. However wild their delusions may be on other subjects, they never fail to appreciate the fact that they are prisoners. Others, not yet classed as insane, as year by year goes by, give only too conclusive evidence that reason is becoming unsettled. The terribleness of a life-sentence *must be seen, to be appreciated;* seen, too, not for a day, or a week, but for a term of years, Quite a number of young men have been committed to this prison in recent years, under sentence for life. Past experience leads us to expect that some of them will become insane in less than ten years; and *all* of them, who live, in less than twenty. Many of them will, doubtless, live much longer than twenty years, strong and vigorous in body, perhaps, but complete wrecks in mind. May it, therefore, not be worthy of legislative consideration, whether life-sentences should not be abolished, and *long but definite* terms substituted; and thus leave some faint glimmer of hope for even the greatest criminals?" (page 63.)

This statement must, however, be regarded as a some-what specially and exceptionally unfavourable picture of life-imprisonment. And further, there may, perhaps, have been some unusual features in the Wisconsin discipline, though it is stated to be " mild " in its character ; and the dietary appears to have been a liberal one.

British Testimonies.

In 1878, the then Chief Director of British Prisons—Sir E. F. Du Cane—said before the Royal Commission on the Penal Servitude Acts, " I myself do not think much of life sentences at all. I would rather have a long fixed term. I think all the effect on the public outside would be gained by a shorter period." Before the same Commission, a similar condemnation of life sentences was uttered by the then Chief Director of Irish Convict Prisons, Captain Barlow, who said, " My own individual feeling is this: I would be reluctant to keep men in prison for their lives ; but if they are to be kept all their life, the latter part of the sentence ought to be something like the treatment in a Luna-tic Asylum—comparative freedom and relaxation of rule."

It may here be remarked that even the condition of those murderers who have been consigned to some Lunatic Asylums, calls for the introduction of further improvements in those establishments. For example, one of the better-managed amongst Criminal Lunatic Asylums is that of Dundrum, near Dublin. But the Irish Government Commissioners have reported in a recent " Blue-book," on this institution, that, during the year, they had been " ap-prehensive of dangerous results from an accumulation of prisoners, fully three-fifths of whom had been charged with murder, some of them being *quite sane*, and many, though peculiar in their conduct and language, still intelligent, meditating schemes of escape ; whilst others, whose offences were less flagrant, coalesced with them—all yearning after freedom, and impressed with the belief that, do as they might, being inmates of a lunatic asylum, they would be irresponsible for their acts." This is a very suggestive official statement, from several points of view. It is at least indisputable that persons thus officially declared to be " quite sane" should no longer be detained in a Criminal Lunatic Asylum.

As to criminal lunatics, however, better oversight than that reported from Dundrum is secured in some other similar institutions; but at a heavy cost for the necessary super-abundance of precautionary arrangements. For example, the official returns of BROADMOOR, in Berkshire (for English Criminal Lunatics), show that one warder is employed for every six inmates, whilst at the Scotch Prison for Insane Criminals, at PERTH, the proportion is still greater, or nearly one to five! At Broadmoor the inmates cost about £70 each.

GRAVITY OF THE ALTERNATIVE.

The writer may here refer to the case of a young man who belonged to a respectable class of society, but who, under circumstances of special excitement and provocation, had committed a murder, for which he was sentenced to death. His father came to London, seeking to procure a commutation of the sentence. In the course of his efforts in this direction he called upon the writer to ask for information on certain points. Amongst other matters he was anxious to learn something of the ordinary conditions of convict life. When he was enabled to picture to himself something of the nature of the circumstances in which his unfortunate son would still be placed, if spared from the gallows — merely to spend the remainder of his life in association with the vilest and most atrocious criminals—the poor father bent down his head in prolonged silence, feeling perplexity as to the grave dilemma presented, and being dubious whether, after all, the infliction of death, before his son's mind had further undergone years of pollution and despair, might not be the less cruel alternative.

The nature of such an alternative has been too generally overlooked by many philanthropists interested in abolishing Capital Punishment, but comparatively indifferent or ignorant in regard to its substitutes. The writer once remarked to a Member of the English Parliament (since deceased), who took an active part in the public advocacy of this abolition, that in his opinion the reform of convict prison discipline was a needful preparation for the discontinuance of the death penalty. But that gentleman took a precisely opposite view, and said, "No, I regard the abolition of Capital Punishment as the basis of criminal discipline reform." This conclusion, which is opposed to that of the most experienced observers, has been, it may be feared, a too frequent one. And its tendency has been to delay the attainment and practicability of the very object desired—the ultimate safe disuse of the death penalty.

Sir WALTER CROFTON, after long experience with Irish convicts, stated, before the Capital Punishment Royal Commission of 1865, that, in his view, the due consideration of the question of abolishing Capital Punishment " entirely depends upon our having, in our secondary punishments, an effective substitute provided." He was prepared to approve the abolition of the death penalty, if special prisons and a special discipline could be appropriated to the murderers. And with such arrangements he believed life sentences could be properly carried into effect. Other authorities, however, were not so assured on this point.

ITALIAN LIFE IMPRISONMENT.

The country which has probably had the largest experience of life sentences, as to mere number, is Italy, where during recent years, many thousand prisoners, under this category, have been undergoing their detention, generally

in association with other convicts. The Naples correspondent of the London *Daily News* has described, in that
journal, a visit which he had made to the Ponzo Islands, near
that city, where, at St. Stephano,. many hundred life-
sentenced prisoners, chiefly murderers, were located. One
of the inmates had committed twenty-one murders, besides
robberies and other crimes! Other similar desperadoes
were also in the company. The visitor remarked as
follows :—" The chatter, the din of the chains, the confused
hum of 800 voices, the forbidding countenances, were indescribable. It was a very pandemonium. The director told
me that though he would have guards at the door, if I
wished to enter a cell, it was not quite safe to trust myself
amongst the convicts. Sentences of punishment for life
are carried out to the letter in Italy; therefore the criminal
has no hope of improvement, nor fear of rendering his
position more terrible; and murders have repeatedly
occurred within the prison."

The Italians have manifested an extreme regard for the
lives of atrocious assassins, but sometimes, also, as extreme
a disregard for those of respectable citizens. In their
hatred for capital punishment, they have substituted for
it a worse penalty, by such life-imprisonment as that
described above.

Injury to the Soul.

Too many of the opponents of death-punishment seem to
forget that it does not merely consist in the immediate
operation of the guillotine, the bullet, or the gallows.
This may be mercy itself, compared with the prolonged
injury inflicted upon the spiritual and mental powers,
extended over many years, by means of the hopeless misery
of the solitary cell, on the one hand, or by the corruptions
of filthy and blaspheming convict gangs, on the other. A
process thus continued, may ultimately be *as real* an execution of death, but by slow operation, as the more visible

and instantaneous deprivation of life. Nor, on the important plea of a better preparation for eternity, can much, if anything at all, be claimed in favour of permanent vile association with the refuse of mankind, as compared with a prompt ushering into the presence of God, who is the perfection of both mercy and justice, in His judgment of the past, present, and future actualities and possibilities of the lives of all. This has often been little regarded by some of the best-intentioned persons.

Of life-imprisonment, it may conclusively be pronounced, very bad is even the best form of it.

Years of inquiry and observation have increasingly pressed this conviction upon the writer; and he earnestly hopes that both the opponents and the advocates of Capital Punishment will devote a more comprehensive attention than has hitherto been given, towards ascertaining the most effectual means of diminishing the causes of the crime of murder, and of devising less objectionable methods of dealing with its perpetrators, than either the universally uncertain penalty of death at the hands of the executioner, or the horrible mode of punishment which has for the most part, and in most countries, been substituted, by the infliction of imprisonment for life.

Precedents for Twenty Years' Maximum.

The BRITISH GOVERNMENT has been compelled materially to relax, not only the certainty of execution in regard to capital sentences, but also the full enforcement of the life imprisonment nominally substituted. At least this has been the case in a considerable degree. It has been the practice of the authorities to bring under special official revision the case of each life-prisoner, on the expiration of a certain number of years of detention. Formerly this period was twelve years, but it has since been extended to twenty. After undergoing this amount of detention, many murderers have been set at liberty, under certain conditions, or precautions. And it does not appear that any serious inconvenience has resulted. Thus the utter hopelessness of life-imprisonment has been partially obviated.

In PORTUGAL, also, the term of twenty years has long been adopted as the legal maximum of imprisonment, as distinguished from banishment to Africa. That country has by disuse abolished capital punishment since 1843, and by statute since 1867; and it has been stated by various competent observers, that murders have not subsequently increased; although this has been questioned by others.

Certainly the period of twenty years, thus legally adopted for most of the worst criminals in Portugal, and practically favoured in Great Britain, has much to recommend it, as a suitable maximum of detention, even for criminals guilty of murder, rape, or treason. It may almost be said to be the only reasonable alternative to capital punishment, if it be admitted that life-imprisonment is merely a method of slow execution.

Its adoption by definite sentence, and with a provision, in general, against any commutation, would extend at least the hope of ultimate freedom to almost every subject of it, the exceptions being very few. It would furnish a basis for an easier administration of prison discipline and authority, than with absolute perpetuity of durance. Although it may be here remarked, in passing, that so far as the enforcement of obedience is concerned, life-prisoners are, as a class, found to be as amenable to it as others, if not more so. Nor has general experience confirmed the fears of those who object to the abolition of capital punishment on the ground of its endangering the lives of the officers administering life-imprisonment. This danger exists in the concentrated mass of murderous villainy in certain Italian prisons. But in the better managed penal establishments of Great Britain, Holland, Belgium, Sweden, Norway, Germany, and other countries, the murder of an officer by a life-sentenced prisoner is a circumstance of the very rarest occurrence. It is, in fact, remarkable by its habitual absence. Special inflictions, or deprivations, are always influential with any class of prisoners, and, indeed, more so, in some respects, with those detained for long terms than with others.

But a fixed limit of twenty years would greatly aid the discipline of its subjects. And what is of more importance, so far as the public are concerned, it would, in most cases, avail to practically incapacitate, or effectually deter the persons who pass through it, from any repetition of their crime. The mere natural operation of age, decay, and disease, would tend towards this result; and not only so, but it would, in a considerable proportion of cases, render the limit of twenty years a virtual sentence in perpetuity, by the intervention of death. But meanwhile the elements of hope and other desirable influences would be largely present, notwithstanding.

Under the wisest and best system of criminal legislation, even twenty years' detention would be only necessary for a small minority of offenders, such as murderers and a few others. If carried out under duly adapted and reasonable conditions, the character of the dietary and other allowances to the criminals of this class might usefully be made dependent, at least in some degree, upon their own industry and exertions. In many instances, if not in all, the convict might be required, or enabled, to contribute materially towards the cost of his detention, and occasionally, perhaps, be allowed to earn something for his family, or for his own future sustenance, in the event of his surviving the twenty years.

The establishments to be specially appropriated to this class, should, by means of an extensive area, admit of exercise, gardening, and agricultural or other labour, to a degree which " prisons," in the ordinary sense, have not generally rendered available hitherto. Of course, various modifications of the principle of a fixed maximum limit might be practicable. Some might suggest twenty-five years as the utmost period, allowing five of these to be " worked-off," or remitted, in reward for "good marks." But, on the whole, twenty is probably a better maximum than any other number of years, and one less open to objections, either as to undue prolongation, or too short limitation.

The re-infliction of brief terms of cellular solitude, during the twenty years, would be a constantly available and very powerful adjunct, as a reserve power, for the punishment of misbehaviour and the maintenance of discipline.

In the case of murderers, at least, their liberation, after this detention of twenty years, might be aecompanied by certain conditions as to future residence and supervision. It may here be remarked, however, that murderers, as a class, are not the most degraded or most hopeless of criminals. In many instances, their one terrible crime has been an entirely exceptional manifestation of passion or rage, called forth by some tremendous temptation.

Neither the above, nor any other plan whatever, would be free from some practical difficulties ; but, especially in view of the precedent of British experience with more than 40 per cent. of the convicted murderers, it is very desirable to adopt, more systematically and completely, some such arrangement, instead of the greater evils hitherto attendant both on life-imprisonment and on the inevitably irregular penalty of death.

Society would then be more effectually protected from murder and from similar crimes, because their punishment would be much more certain and general than heretofore. The claims of the criminal, to a just mercy, would also be met more largely and more humanely ; whilst the grasp of the law would be strengthened, instead of relaxed.

CHAPTER XI.

THE PUNISHMENT OF DEATH.

In addition to the remarks in the preceding chapter, on Capital Punishment, as specially connected with its ordinary substitute, life-imprisonment, a few general observations on this subject may be of interest to the reader.

A primary object to be kept in view, in considering the question of Capital Punishment, is the nature of its ultimate and general tendency, whether to increase or decrease homicidal crime. And in connection with this, constant regard must be had to that fundamental principle of Penology, that certainty is a more efficacious element in punishment than extreme severity.

As regards the presumptively deterrent character of the Death Penalty there is great diversity of opinion amongst practical persons. Indeed, absolutely opposite conclusions have repeatedly been arrived at by men of similar authority and experience. For example, the eminent jurist, Sir J. Fitzjames Stephen, declared before the Royal Commission of 1865:—" I think that Capital Punishment deters people from crime more than any other punishment, and that it deters them in two ways. I think that the effect of it is appreciable—and in some cases considerable—in a direct and ordinary manner; that is to say, when a man is going to commit a crime, he thinks, ' If I do this, I shall be hanged for it.' But besides that, there is a secondary effect of Capital Punishment. People are aware that murder is punishable by an ignominious expulsion from the world. They therefore get to consider murder as a very dreadful thing." Another experienced Judge, SIR GEORGE DENMAN, told the same Royal Commission, "My own feeling is that the law of Capital Punishment, as it exists, does not operate at all ; and that if you take the various classes of murderers, there is more, on the whole, done by Capital Punishment to induce murders, than there is to prevent them."

Now, unquestionably, there is some ground for each of these diverse opinions. But the writer ventures to think that they are reconcilable both with each other, and with a final conclusion as to the weakness of Capital Punishment, when the following consideration, urged in his own evidence before the same COMMISSION, is taken into account. He then said :—" I believe that the punishment of death is the most deterrent punishment possible to a certain class of minds, *provided* it be inflicted with absolute certainty; but I submit that that is merely an imaginary and theoretical condition, and that Capital Punishment never is, never has been, and, we may reasonably conclude, never will be, inflicted with absolute certainty.

" But (he added) on the other hand, I would also submit that there is another class of crime which altogether precludes the idea of any efficacious deterrence at all. I allude to the large proportion of homicidal crime which is committed under the influence of over-mastering passion, drunkenness, rage, or jealousy; there the argument of deterrence, which I admit in certain other cases, cannot apply at all."

SPECIAL OBSTACLES TO ITS INFLICTION.

If the punishment of death could be inflicted with as much certainty as prolonged imprisonment, then it might be more deterrent than the latter. But, as a matter of simple fact and experience, the world over, a number of circumstances, *special to this particular penalty*, conspire to render its infliction uncertain in a most extraordinary degree. Even in GREAT BRITAIN, where, perhaps, the law is carried out with less uncertainty than elsewhere, only about 25 per cent. of convictions result from committals for trial in capital cases ; and then, further, nearly half of these convictions are finally followed by commutations. In other countries, generally, a still smaller proportion of executions result. The official statistics of the various nations prove this clearly and strikingly.

Whence comes this peculiar obstacle contributed by this one penalty to its own enforcement ? From several sources. Partly because it is a *fatal* and *irreversible* punishment. Hence the highest degree of certainty in evidence is reasonably demanded by jurors and by public opinion, in murder cases, where, at the same time, there is usually *less* certainty of evidence procurable than with any other crime. For murders are generally committed in secret, and the only real witness, the victim, is destroyed in most instances. So that where the most direct testimony is needful, only indirect or circumstantial evidence is, in general, obtainable as to the simple matter of fact.

EXECUTION OF INNOCENT PERSONS.

In spite of the utmost care, it is known that even the strongest circumstantial evidence has sometimes led to the conviction and death of absolutely innocent persons. It may be admitted that in " the old hanging days," and when execution followed sentence, after a very short interval, there were greater dangers than in the present day, of executing the innocent. But, notwithstanding the anxiety on the part of modern judges and juries to avoid any mistake, yet, from time to time, fatal miscarriages of justice occur. The following are a few cases, from English experience only, during the last half of the Nineteenth Century, when judges and juries have been scrupulously careful, to avoid mistakes.

In 1865, one Polizzioni was sentenced to death in London. By dint of great exertions, on the part of his friends, he was proved to be innocent, and received a *free pardon.*—In 1865, another Italian, Giardinieri, was sentenced to death, at Swansea. By similar efforts, he was also just saved in time, and pardoned as innocent.—In 1867, J. Wiggins was hanged in London, solemnly exclaiming, when dying, " I am innocent, innocent, innocent." The woman he was said to have killed, had, the day before her death, intimated her intention of killing herself. And the coroner's jury, after examining twenty-six witnesses, had declined to inculpate Wiggins. The final evidence against him at his trial was most imperfect, and there is reason to believe that another person was the real murderer.—In 1873, two men (Hayes and Slane) were hanged at Durham, for a murder committed in a scuffle in a dark passage at Spennymore. Many persons in that county believed one of them, at least, to be innocent. Perhaps both were. A respectable lawyer, of Durham, wrote to the Howard Association : " Hayes is really innocent, and has been mistaken for another man who is now at large. Slane, unfortunately, was in the passage at the time the assault was committed. I have seen the place where the deceased was assaulted; and it is impossible for the boy (the chief witness) to have seen what he swore he did."

Speaking in Parliament, in 1869, the HOME SECRETARY said, that within half a year, out of eleven cases of capital sentences (each following very careful trials by jury) five sentences had to be set aside by him. Of two he stated,— " It is beyond all question that Sweet was an innocent man ; it is equally certain that Bisgrove was insane." In the three other cases it became evident that the persons concluded to have been murdered had died from accident or other causes. The Home Secretary was silent on one case : that of one of the remaining six who were executed — Priscilla Biggadyke, of Lincoln — who died protesting her innocence to the last, and some years later it was proved that she had been unjustly sacrificed. This poor woman was charged with poisoning her husband with arsenic, and the circumstantial evidence was strong against her. She protested her innocence in Court, but was not believed. On the morning of her execution, she exclaimed: "You are not going to hang me, are you? God knows I am innocent." But the hangman did his ghastly work and his victim's remains were interred in the murderers' burial ground, in the open space in the great round tower of Lincoln Castle. Some years afterwards, a man in the village where Mrs. Biggadyke had lived, became ill, and on being informed that recovery was hopeless, he manifested great anxiety, and said : " I cannot die until I make a full confession of my guilt. It was I who poisoned poor Biggadyke. His wife, who was hanged for it, knew nothing of it. I went into the house, while she was mixing a cake, and put arsenic into the bowl when she was not looking."

In the Home Secretary's speech just quoted, he added another important statement: "The judge is constantly obliged to pass a sentence of death when it is quite certain that the sentence *will not, cannot, and ought not to be executed.*" In other words, the English judges are constantly obliged to pass ·sentence upon the English law itself— law which should ever be honoured and upheld.

As showing the truth of this, it may be mentioned that at the Oxford Assizes in 1870, BARON MARTIN, in sentencing to death a woman for the murder of her child, three years old (not infanticide), said—" The killing of your child is, *undoubtedly*, murder ; and the sentence is death for such crimes." He added, " *But, as far as lies in my power that sentence will not be carried out !* "

HOMICIDE AND INSANITY.

Again, even where the fact of murder may be clear enough, the deadly issue of the penalty often raises special pleas as to just responsibility, in connection with homicidal insanity. For it is an unquestionable matter of scientific demonstration that insanity and homicidal tendencies are peculiarly and frequently associated. DR. WILLIAM GUY, F.R.S. (Vice-President of the Statistical Society), published a comprehensive series of observations extending over thirty years, and proving his conclusion that, "Insanity plays a conspicuous part in the terrible drama of homicide." He showed that whereas the proportion of insane persons was less than two to every thousand of the whole population of England and Wales, the ratio of insane to sane criminals in general was 57 per 1,000, but that amongst the particular class of criminals committed for murder, the proportion found insane was 145 per 1,000 (or $14\frac{1}{2}$ per cent.).

Juries who would willingly consign such unfortunate persons to prolonged confinement in a lunatic asylum, or even in a prison, naturally shrink from finding a verdict which would send them to a death on the scaffold, with its shame and horror. In such instances again, the capital penalty often seriously defeats its own object.

A STRIKING ILLUSTRATION.

And, in general, evidence is reasonably deemed sufficient to warrant a verdict resulting in imprisonment, when the same may not be felt to be adequate for a fatal and irreversible decision. In the event of subsequently discovered error, as to the former decision, some compensation can be made to the innocent, but not so in the latter case. Some years ago, five men were arraigned before an English jury for a very atrocious murder. To the public astonishment and indignation, they were acquitted. One of the jury, on being privately remonstrated with, replied in substance;

" We were almost certain of the guilt of the accused, but not quite. The law did not permit us to return a verdict of manslaughter, involving imprisonment. That we would have given. But we felt that nothing short of absolute certainty, which was unattainable under the circumstances of the case, would justify us in consigning five men to the irrevocable destiny of death. We therefore, had no alternative, but to acquit them." A similar result has occurred in many cases. Thus the capital penalty tends to promote the escape of the guilty, and so to encourage murder.

In other words, the superior deterrence which, it may be admitted, attaches in the abstract, to the death penalty, is practically counteracted, or nullified, by its unavoidable and special uncertainty of enforcement. That is to say, it has the (penologically) fatal defect of being *very weak in action ;* whereas the crime of murder should have the *most vigorously certain* repression.

The " Anthropologists " and " Mad Doctors."

Of late years, a certain school of thinkers, chiefly Italians, under the leadership of M. Lombroso, have started some theories respecting the responsibility or irresponsibility of many dangerous criminals and murderers, which have very properly been objected to by more practical observers—and in particular by an able Italian, Professor Lucchini. In England, a small group, popularly termed the " mad doctors," have propounded somewhat similar views.

Whilst, doubtless, these gentlemen have been warranted by the facts of the hereditary tendencies, the functions, and the environment of many criminals, in claiming for such circumstances a large amount of just consideration, yet they have, on the other hand, too often ignored the absolute and essential right of the community to be *effectually protected* from the criminal, *whether insane or not.* Even the inmates of lunatic asylums know well the dis-

tinction between right and wrong. And it is precisely upon
this knowledge that the government and discipline of such
establishments are based. Hence no theories of criminal
irresponsibility should be permitted to relax the security
and strictness of the detention of dangerous offenders,
whether sane, or partially insane, or wholly mad.

And it is important to observe that the treatment and
condition even of mad murderers should not be rendered
attractive to others outside.

A foreign medical "expert" (having large sympathy
with the Anthropological school of Lombroso), expressed to
the author his surprise at the luxuries enjoyed by the
English "criminal lunatics" at Broadmoor. He said: "I
cannot afford to have my rooms carpeted like theirs."

Of course, really insane persons, even murderers, should
be treated with a pitiful consideration; but the community
also is to be still more pitied, in view of its liability to
injury, if the treatment of murderers, whether mad or
sane, be not rendered effectually influential for the discouragement of homicide.

It is only fair to M. Lombroso, however, to say that he
deprecates undue laxity to actual criminals. He says of
the Italian prisons: "These prisons are, many of them,
little more than comfortable hotels, where the exaggerated
good treatment encourages the delinquent to return rather
than work like an honest man."

Defect of English Law.

English Law, by its unscientific and untrue definition of "wilful" murder and by its retention of capital
punishment, has imported great confusion into many
murder trials, and has often defeated its own object.

In 1864 the English "Association of Medical Officers of
Asylums for the Insane" adopted the following resolution:
"That so much of the legal test of the mental condition of
an alleged criminal lunatic, as renders him a responsible

agent, *because* he knows the difference between right and wrong, is inconsistent with the fact, well known to every member of this meeting, that the power of distinguishing between right and wrong exists frequently among those who are *undoubtedly* insane, and is often associated with dangerous and uncontrollable delusions."

If this law was modified and if capital punishment was abolished, murderers whether sane or insane, would be more readily convicted; and provided that they were safely separated from the community, it would be of comparatively minor importance, whether this was effected by a prison or an asylum.

MR. J. S. MILL ON UNCERTAIN EXECUTION.

In the House of Commons, in 1868, MR. JOHN STUART MILL made a speech in defence of capital punishment, which was an admirable specimen of merely logical argument, but it had the fatal defect of being very imperfectly based upon facts. Nor was this a matter for surprise; inasmuch as Mr. Mill had never been experienced in the procedure of courts of justice, nor a special student of criminal questions. In happy ignorance of the universally prevalent inefficacy of the capital penalty, he exclaimed : " When it is impossible to inflict a punishment, or when its infliction becomes a public scandal, the idle threat cannot too soon disappear from the Statute Book." But this supposed improbable state of things actually exists, on both sides of the Atlantic.

For a Parliamentary Paper, containing official statistics, collected by the British Government, on the motion of Sir J. W. PEASE, BART., M.P., (in 1881), stated that during the preceding decade less than half of the persons sentenced to death, in FRANCE, for murder had been executed—or only 93 out of 198 ; that in SPAIN, out of 291 murderers sentenced to death, 126 were executed, or less than half ; that in SWEDEN, out of 32 sentenced to death, only 3, or one-tenth,

were executed ; that in NORWAY, 4 out of every 5 condemned murderers escaped execution ; that in DENMARK,
out of 94 sentences for murder, during many years, *only one*
had been executed ; that in BAVARIA, 249 trials for murder
only resulted in 7 executions ; and that in GERMANY, generally, the proportion of executions had been similarly very
small.   These figures relate only to murder, and not to other
crimes, for which the infliction of the capital penalty is
still more unusual.   For example, the same " Return "
showed that in AUSTRIA, out of a total of 806 capital sentences in the decade, only 16 were executed.

The " Judicial Statistics " for ENGLAND AND WALES, for
twelve of the latest years of the nineteenth century (1881-
1892), show that during that period there were 2,105
verdicts of " Wilful Murder " returned by Coroners' Juries
which were followed by 775 trials, resulting in 322 convictions and 181 executions.   So that only a quarter of
those put on trial for wilful murder were hanged, and out
of those sentenced to death nearly half escaped that
penalty.   The chances of escape for female murderers
are still more extreme.   For out of the 44 women convicted of murder, in the above twelve years, only 7 were
hanged.   Thus 5 out of every 6 female murderers escaped
the gallows.

In the United States, in *one* year of the last decade of
the century, 1894, there were 9,800 murders, which were
followed by only 132 legal executions and 190 " illegal
lynchings." So that, even reckoning the latter as executions,
29 *out of every* 30 *murderers* in that country, escaped the
capital penalty; although it is enacted as the punishment
for murder in nearly every one of the States.

If this condition of things does not come under Mr.
Mill's supposition, "When it is impossible to inflict a punishment "—what worse eventuality is to be looked for in that
direction ?

This world-wide impossibility of carrying capital punishment into effect, with even a moderate degree of certainty, constitutes a principal reason for objecting to it. Such a general and intrinsic defect is fatal to its claim to efficiency. It may therefore be compared to a woman without virtue, or a soldier without courage.

Notoriety.

The special notoriety attendant on Executions and Capital Trials has a great attraction for many criminals, whose morbid vanity is excessive. But no such mischievous interest attaches to imprisonment. In the autumn of 1889, immense popular excitement was aroused by the death-sentences passed on a woman at Liverpool, and on a youth at Glasgow. Scores of thousands of persons signed petitions for commutations of those two sentences. When they were commuted, the excitement almost immediately disappeared. No other penalty, but that of death, produces such pernicious popular interest in murderers, or such interference with the enforcement of law. But this is *inevitable*, whilst that particular penalty is retained.

Experience of an Observer.

An habitual prison visitor remarks, as to the presumed superior deterrence of this punishment, in a book published by Messrs. Blackwood (Edinburgh, 1889), entitled "Scenes from a Silent World:"—"We desire to state, in the strongest words we can use, that this argument in favour of the death penalty is absolutely and radically false. We do not make this assertion without warrant; our practical experience has been very extensive. Crimes of violence are for the most part committed in the blind heat of passion, by persons who never give a thought to the penal consequences of the deeds to which they are driven by the frenzy of the moment. Apart, however, from this, there remains the fact, which we cannot assert too emphatically, that death is not the punishment which lawless men

dread the most.   Such men often fiercely desire death.
They seek it; they look forward to it as the cure for all
mortal ills—the sure and painless refuge from the agony of
life."

SUICIDES.

In confirmation of the latter statement, it is noteworthy
that the statistics of SUICIDE show that the number of persons
who kill themselves are many times more than those who
kill others.   It is stated that for every person who murders
another, there are seven who kill themselves.

AN UNWISE FRENCH " WIT."

A French " wit " has exclaimed " Abolish Capital Punishment !   By all means; but let Messieurs the assassins
commence ? " This is often quoted as a smart saying.   But
experience shows it to be bereft of practical wisdom.   *More*
atrocious murders are committed in those countries which
are still waiting for " Messieurs the assassins to commence,"
than elsewhere.   For example, the Tropmann *sixfold* murder
at Paris, in 1870, and the *sevenfold* murder, soon after, at
Uxbridge, in England ; also the multitudes of murders in
Corsica, Spain, and the Southern United States.   Devils do
not cast out devils, however long they may be waited for.
Only fools will wait for such a result.   Evils, whether
moral, social, or legal, can only be overcome by *good*
influences.

CONVICTIONS FACILITATED BY A SECONDARY PENALTY.

It is important to observe that in the countries which
have adopted prolonged imprisonment, under *reasonable*
conditions, as the punishment for murder, that crime has
not increased in frequency, whereas the convictions of its
perpetrators have materially increased.   In HOLLAND no
execution has taken place since 1860; in BELGIUM none
since 1863: in FINLAND none since 1824: in ITALY none

since 1876; in PORTUGAL none since 1843. Several AMERICAN STATES have also abolished the death penalty, and one or two of them have also restored it again. But the general prison system in America is not favourable to the repression of murder, whether with or without the death penalty. By far the chief proportion of American murders take place in States which have always retained the punishment of death.

ITALY, however, has not adopted other measures needful to diminish murder. And she has retained, in general, a most pernicious association of criminals in prison. Indeed many murders have been committed *inside* Italian jails. SWITZERLAND abolished Capital Punishment, and in 1879 accorded permission to the Cantons to reimpose it. But scarcely any executions, if indeed any at all, have taken place in that country since the nominal restoration of the penalty.

PROFESSOR FRANCIS WAYLAND, of Connecticut (where the death penalty continues), stated recently that "in twenty years of experience in MASSACHUSETTS, out of 173 trials for murder of the first degree, 118 were acquitted, 26 were pronounced guilty of murder of the second degree (non-capital), and only 29 were pronounced guilty of the capital offence. Thus the juries in more than two-thirds of the trials brought in no conviction; and nearly half of the verdicts rendered were for a less offence than that charged.

"In CONNECTICUT (with the death penalty), during the thirty years ending 1880, 97 persons were tried for murder in the first degree. Of these 13 were convicted of murder in the first degree, whilst 42 of these were convicted of murder in the second degree.

"In 1852 the State of RHODE ISLAND abolished the death penalty, substituting imprisonment for life. Turning to the records of the County of Providence, we find that during the thirty years next succeeding the date of the abolition of Capital Punishment, out of 27 trials for murder in the first degree, there were 17 convictions, or considerably more than 50 per cent."

GENERAL N. M. CURTIS, U.S.A., remarks hereupon: "The large number of acquittals in the trials for murder in the first degree, in States where the punishment is death, is unhappily no evidence that those arraigned were innocent and unjustly charged, but rather that their escape was almost wholly due to the aversion of juries to the infliction of the death penalty."

THE BIBLE AND CAPITAL PUNISHMENT.

THE BIBLE is often appealed to, in this question; and it may fairly be quoted on either side. The Old Testament unquestionably permitted Capital Punishment for murder and for other crimes. But there were no suitable prisons, as a substitute, in those days. The New Testament did not expressly condemn the death penalty; yet neither did it expressly condemn SLAVERY, or POLYGAMY. But its *spirit* is opposed to these. The general Scriptural argument on this subject may be narrowed to this simple point: Is it right to put men to death, unless experience proves that it is absolutely necessary to do so? Then the solution must depend upon the verdict of experience and history. God spared the life of the first murderer, though punishing him effectually. The Redeemer declared that He came "not to destroy men's lives, but to *save* them," both for time and eternity.

THE TESTIMONY OF EXPERIENCE.

The Right Hon. Joseph Henley, M.P., said in the House of Commons, in 1869 :—"I do not think that there is any man who, in the early part of his life, had stronger opinions upon this subject than I had. These feelings were created very much by the opinions of judges and others; but I have since watched the matter anxiously and carefully, and I cannot resist the logic of facts. When I look at the whole class of crimes from which the punishment of death has been removed, and am unable to find any increase in this class of crimes over murder, for which the punishment has been retained, I cannot bring myself to believe that capital punishment has that deterrent effect that some persons believe it has. The opinions of the judges and of the police are entitled to the greatest weight; *but they do not weigh with me against facts. You have now had before you the facts of more than thirty years;* and I do not think that any one who looks carefully into those facts can maintain that the crimes from which the penalty of death has been removed have thereby increased."

Earl Russell on Capital Punishment.

John Earl Russell, Prime Minister of Great Britain, recorded the following as his own conclusion on this question :—"For my own part, I do not doubt, for a moment, either the right of a community to inflict the punishment of death, or the expediency of exercising that right in certain states of society. But when I turn from that abstract right and that abstract expediency to our own state of society—when I consider how difficult it is for any judge to separate the case which requires inflexible justice, from that which admits the force of mitigating circumstances—how invidious the task of the Secretary of State in dispensing the mercy of the Crown—how critical the comments made by the public—how soon the object of general horror becomes the theme of pity—how narrow and how limited the examples given by this condign and awful punishment—how brutal the scene of execution—I come to the conclusion that nothing would be lost to justice, nothing lost in the preservation of innocent life, if the punishment of death were altogether abolished.

"In that case, a sentence of a long term of separate confinement, followed by another term of hard labour and hard fare, would cease to be considered as an extension of mercy. If the sentence of the judge were to that effect, there would scarcely ever be a petition for remission of punishment, in cases of murder, sent to the Home Office. The guilty, unpitied, would have time and opportunity to turn repentant to the Throne of Mercy."

The Weight of Evidence.

Whilst much may be fairly urged in support of, as well as against, the Capital Penalty, there appears to be a decided superiority of practical advantage in favour of its abolition. Yet it is a very serious matter either to retain or to abolish, Capital Punishment. In the event of its abolition, the most careful measures are indispensable to secure an effectual substitute, combining a due regard for public security, on the one hand, with avoidance of cruelty to the criminal, on the other.

Prevention More Efficacious than Punishment.

It needs to be remembered that punishment, of *whatever* kind, is merely one out of many elements, in the suppression of murder, as of other crimes. The countries where murders are comparatively few, are those where the two great influences of Prevention and Punishment are each rendered efficacious. Of these the former is very much the more powerful. Prevention is chiefly secured by the promotion of Religion, Education, Temperance, and the prohibition of the use of Weapons by private citizens. Even in England, an appreciable proportion of the murders and homicides perpetrated, were shown by a Parliamentary paper (issued in 1893) to have been the acts of persons carrying pistols.

The districts where there are most murders are those where private citizens habitually carry weapons; or where drunkenness specially prevails; where punishment, of whatever nature, is comparatively uncertain; or where ecclesiastical absolution is easily obtainable. Such countries are Corsica,* Spain, Italy, the Levant, and the Southern States of America. Capital Punishment is retained equally in Massachusetts and in Texas; but the difference in the amount of homicide in the two States is immense, owing to the free use, in the latter, of the pistol and bowie knife. There are several hundred "lynchings" annually in the United States; and nearly all of these occur in districts where the death penalty is retained. Preventive means are far more efficacious, everywhere, than those of a merely punitory character.

* CORSICA.—The experience of Corsica is very instructive. Owing to the hereditary practice of the *Vendetta* in that island, and the almost universal carrying and use of arms, there are more murders committed there than in any other part of Europe. In the five years ending 1850, there were 431 murders and assassinations in Corsica. Then a law was passed prohibiting the carrying of arms by private persons. What resulted? In the next five years there were only 146 murders and assassinations; truly a large total, but a great diminution from the previous state of affairs. This indicates that it is rather prevention, that avails, than an ineffectual, because generally impracticable, fatal penalty.

Chapter XII.

PRISON LABOUR.

Again Regard Mainly the Test of Final Results.

THE subject of penal labour should be mainly considered in reference to the chief end contemplated by criminal systems, and also in connection with the purposes of different prisons, and of successive stages of treatment. Through a neglect of this necessary discrimination, serious mistakes and grave injuries, both as to prisoners and communities, have frequently resulted. And the description of labour which may be eminently suited to minor offenders, or to the discipline of specially reformatory institutions, may be mischievous, if adopted for those violent and outrageous criminals for whom a deterrent or sternly repressive treatment is, at least for a time, needful.

It often occurs, that through the pursuit of delusive ideas of " economy," in regard to prison labour, great waste and loss are incurred. It has been repeatedly forgotten, in practice, that the most truly economical form of criminal treatment is that which eventually reduces the number of offenders to a minimum. It is *this final result*, this ultimate proportion of crime, which constitutes at once the test, and the real guide, as to the best selection of criminal labour, and, indeed, as to all other matters bearing upon penal discipline and prevention.

In some countries, notably France, Italy, and the United States, where this final test has been largely overlooked, and where the merely immediate profit of prison labour has been unduly regarded, there has been a far larger concurrent increase of general crime than in other nations, such as Great Britain, where the influence of the deterrent element has also been taken into view, as a material *part* of the real question of economy. An official " Report of the New York State Prisons," in 1886, declared : " The percentage of criminal population in the United States is excessive, in comparison with some other countries. It very much exceeds that of England and Wales. In the United States there are more than three times as many convicts, in proportion, as in the former country." Yet no community has been so apparently successful as New York and some other American States, in regard to the amount of immediate profit obtained from prison labour.

If a nation, by congregate labour in its prisons, gains, say £50,000 profit, but, at the same time, through the increased criminality occasioned by corrupting association in those jails, has to pay millions more of money in consequence, the alleged " profit " on the prison labour is utterly fictitious. Or, at best, it is an illustration of what is "*penny wise and pound foolish.*"

On the other hand, a nation which makes the ultimate *diminution* of crime the main object of its prison discipline, and therefore adopts the cellular system, with religious and educational instruction, and Sloyd training in handicraft skill, may, even with a greatly increased cost per prisoner, and with comparatively little or no profit on labour, nevertheless effect a large ultimate saving, by the decrease of crime thus promoted.

The principle of justice to the honest worker, and to the non-criminal pauper, should always have some consideration in the selection of occupation for offenders. The writer has visited a large town in North Europe, in one part of which he found the aged and unfortunate inmates of the workhouse toiling at very heavy mangling and other hard labour; whilst the criminals, in an adjoining jail, were occupied with exceedingly light and easy forms of industry, such as working with scissors, gum, and paste, in the fabri-cation of stationery, ornaments, and fancy goods. · In many. of the Continental prisons, similarly light occupation, more· suitable for poor, honest girls, is distributed, for months or years together, to atrocious criminals. This ought not to be. It is doubly unjust, both to the prisoners and to various classes outside. It is also injurious to the community, as a whole.

Distinctively Penal Labour.

The specially penal and deterrent stages of criminal treatment may require labour which would be injurious or useless in other stages, or for a prolonged period.

In certain cases, a few hours, days, or even weeks of cellular solitude, without any labour at all, may be a wise discipline; and one calculated to produce, in an idle offender, a salutary desire for work, as an alleviation of confinement. But a prolongation of such inaction would be unwise and cruel. Again, some forms of merely penal work, of little if any pecuniary value, may also be efficacious, but only for short periods. The writer on one occasion observed, on the treadwheel of an English prison, a gang of refractory vagrants who had riotously refused to pick oakum. They were accordingly sent to jail for a week or two, where they had some hours daily on the wheel, in addition to their previous oakum task, and with cellular solitude at night. This process was found to have a wholesome effect in that and similar cases. But to prolong either the treadwheel or the oakum picking for con-siderable periods, would be mischievous; though for brief initial stages of discipline, or for an occasional impressive reminder of reserve power, such modes of penal occupation, may be of service.

SKILLED LABOUR.

The teaching of a skilled trade to criminals, especially when young, is, for many of them, a very desirable thing. But an ordinary prison is not always the best place for imparting such a training. It is, however, to be noted that comparatively very few skilled artisans find their way into prisons, either in Europe or America. It is the wilfully or the unfortunately ignorant and unskilled who constitute the majority of their inmates.

And as, also, the larger number of offenders are only detained for short terms, it is often practically impossible to furnish a knowledge of a trade to them. Years of patient training are usually needed for such a process, and that, too, under circumstances, some of which are almost, if not quite, incompatible with the essential conditions, of imprisonment. Hence the industries practicable in most of the ordinary jails, are such as require little skill and few tools, as, for example, Mat and Basket-making, Net-work, rough Weaving or Spinning, Brush-making, Marble-polishing, the sorting and sifting of various mixed matters, Digging, Washing, Cleaning and the simpler forms of Masonry, Stone-cutting, Shoe-making, Tailoring and Carpentry.

Only in connection with long imprisonments, can skilled trades be effectually imparted. But long detentions are, at best, a mode of punishment which it is to be hoped may be of more and more limited application, as nations become wiser and more practical in their methods of preventing crime and of reforming offenders. But in so far as this extension of imprisonment continues, it is important to make the labour of those subjected to it as valuable to the State as can suitably be done. And this end may be accomplished better by various forms of skilled industry than otherwise. This problem has claimed considerable attention in most civilised countries of late years. In some of the European and American convict prisons many of the inmates have been brought from a state of previous ignorance to a skill and dexterity, which have subsequently enabled them to gain an honest and comfortable livelihood. Forty, fifty, or more different forms of occupation are carried on in these various establishments. Some of the products of their inmates are masterpieces of their kind. The specimens of work occasionally exhibited in London from the British convict prisons, and the handsome assortment of articles displayed in the Labour Exhibitions at Prison Congresses, have elicited surprise and admiration from many visitors. In a few places, special shops have been opened for the exclusive sale of articles of prison manufacture. A very interesting one was noticed by the writer at Christiania, where the clothing, carving, furniture, fishing apparatus, ornaments, and miscellaneous goods, showed remarkable care and skill on the part of the local prisoners and their officers.

VARIETIES OF PRISON INDUSTRY.

Amongst the great variety of work in which the prisoners of different nations are employed, may be mentioned the following :—

Masonry, Carpentry, Tailoring (with making of Uniforms, etc., with and without Sewing Machines), Boot and Shoe-making, Weaving and Spinning, Smithwork, Moulding, Metal Casting, Sawing, Printing, Bookbinding, Envelope Making, Painting, Tinwork, Ironwork, Cooperage, Making of Chairs, Carpets, Blankets, Cigars, Watches, Brushes, Baskets, Toys, Umbrellas, Sticks, Buttons, Coins, Harness, Hats, Caps, Portfolios, Sacks, Tiles, Slippers, Flags, Bedsteads, Boxes, Bags, Combs, Chains, Portmanteans, Saddlery, Gloves, Ships' Fenders, Mats, Ropes, Wheels, Upholstery, Porcelain, Girdles, Lamps, Tools,

Stoves, Utensils, Corsets, Fans, Accordions, Artificial Flowers, Tents, Carriages, Bottles, Pocket Books. The manufacture of Cloth, Linen, Muslin, Lace, Stuffs, Hardware, Plush; Work in Leather, Wire, Feathers, Cardboard, Hair, Straw, Mosaic, Gilding, Plating, Turning, Engraving, Enamelling, Lacquering, Embossing, Photography, Lithography, Polishing; Picking Coffee Berries, Grain, Oakum, etc.; Breaking Sugar, Stone-cutting, Stone-pounding, Marble-polishing, Oil-pressing, Wood-carving, Telegraphy, Clerkage, Washing, Knitting, Cleaning-up, Cooking, Wood-splitting, Cutting up Linen for Paper Mills, Gardening, Agriculture, Mining, the Construction of Dykes, Forts, Railways, etc.

PRISON LABOUR FOR THE STATE.

There are several modes of disposing of convict labour. They are as follows:

Firstly, Labour for the State. This plan, which has been adopted in the British convict prisons, has had a very limited acceptance in America. For whilst it possesses the important advantage of retaining the prisoners under the entire control of their own officers, it is seldom attended by pecuniary profit; and, in general, it results in heavy loss. Further, the nominal value of such labour is apt to be exceedingly delusive; as, for example, in the estimates placed in the Home Office Reports upon the work done by English convicts. There are also special facilities for official corruption and negligence, almost inseparable from this system. It has been the source of some of the most objectionable features of British convict discipline and disposal. It was tried, for a time, in New York State, but a Superintendent of Prisons there has referred to it as having proved a lamentable failure, in every sense. In Ohio, in 1884, the Legislature abolished the contract system, and adopted the plan of exclusively employing the convicts on State account, as in printing and the manufacture of hardware and woollen goods. But less than a‚ year's experience of this arrangement was so costly and unsatisfactory,‚ that it was relinquished in favour of " piece-work " labour, for sale to private or public bidders. In Great Britain, the convict labour for the State has been chiefly directed to the construction of fortifications, docks, harbours, and buildings ;‚ the cultivation of land, the manufacture of uniforms, clothing, boots, etc., for the‚ army, navy, police, and prison officers; together with printing and binding, for certain departments of the Government. Doubtless a portion of this work is of genuine value. But much of it has certainly been wasted. And some of the valuations of British convict labour, published in official " Blue Books," have been of an absurd character.

Leasing or Hiring Out Convicts.

Secondly, at the opposite extreme from the above system, is the mode of " leasing out " convicts to persons who entirely relieve the State of their cost and custody. This abominable system was long carried out in the Southern United States generally. But during the last years of the Nineteenth Century, it has been gradually abandoned in most of them. But several still retain it. Under this plan, the leaseholders take the whole charge of .the convicts, and in some States, re-sell their labour to railway companies, mining proprietors, and other large employers. The unfortunate wretches, thus leased out, are located from time to time in stockades or camps. The pistol, the lash, and the bloodhound are freely used to enforce discipline and to discourage escapes. Disease and death make terrible havoc in the convict ranks, which include many unfortunate children. The rate of mortality is enormous, and the permanent ruin to the health and faculties of the survivors most melancholy. The Superintendent of the convicts of one State reported that out of one hundred who had been pardoned by the Governor,. more than a quarter were children from ten to sixteen, years of age; and nearly another quarter "were hopelessly diseased, blind, crippled, or demented." Murder, rape, blasphemy, unnatural crime, and every form of vice, formerly prevailed amongst these gangs.·

THE CONTRACT SYSTEM.

Thirdly, there is the common "Contract System," by which, whilst the convicts are retained inside a prison, their labour is (for a certain sum of money paid to the State) placed at the disposal of a contractor, who is allowed to make his own rules as to time, occupation, and taskwork, with little, if any, restriction in these matters, on the part of the authorities. This system is also chiefly an American one, and has been largely adopted in the Northern States. It often tends to sacrifice the discipline of the prisons to the interests of the contractors; but it is not accompanied by the cruelties of the Southern "leasing out" system. Yet it is not wholly free from cruelty. For under it, there is a great inducement to over-work prisoners and to disregard the necessities of the weak or sickly ones. It also offers the contractors much temptation to bribe the prison officers, and to favour the stronger and more dexterous criminals, even when morally worse than the weaker or less skilful ones. It frequently throws the prisoners into too close communication with persons from outside, as messengers and others. But it has often resulted in large profits to the State; and it must be admitted that it has trained many thousands of men to habits of self-supporting industry.

LIMITED CONTRACT ARRANGEMENT.

Fourthly, there is another mode of contract labour which is subject to more rigid conditions, in the interests of the discipline and for the protection of both prisoners and officers. Under this system, the time and skill of the prisoners are let out, for a certain sum, to contractors, who are strictly limited as to the conditions of labour and as to the introduction of assistants and trade instructors from outside, or any special interference with that degree of discipline and regularity which the authorities may deem essential for the main objects of imprisonment. This plan of limited contracts is extensively adopted in the larger prisons of the European Continent, and occasionally in America. It differs rather in degree, than in essence, from the laxer system, previously described. And when the regulations are judiciously framed and firmly insisted upon, it is attended by marked advantages, both to the State and to the convicts. Also, it introduces, for the benefit of those prisoners who are willing to learn a trade, a class of practical instructors, much superior, as such, to the warders, who are usually devoid of special industrial knowledge and skill.

"The Piece Price Plan."

Fifthly, there is a further variety of the Contract System, which, in the United States, is usually termed the "Piece Price Plan." It enables the authorities to retain full control over the discipline and occupation of the prisoners, whilst disposing of the products of their labour to a contractor. But the latter agrees to buy from the prison authorities only those articles which they may choose to supply him with, and which must be finished to a certain standard of perfection; and he only takes such quantities of them as may accord with his own convenience and the state of the markets. This places the prison managers under great pecuniary disadvantage, as compared with the other and more common contract systems, under which the contractor pays a fixed price, per head, for all the labour of the prisoners, for a term of years, irrespective of changes in the outside markets.

On the whole, it appears that so long as large prison workshops, and extensive congregate industry in jails, are to be maintained, less evil and greater advantage will result from the moderately limited contract system, as long carried on in certain American States as, for example, in Illinois, and in many European prisons, than from either the "Piece Price," or the comparatively unconditional contract plans. The experience of the chief Continental nations confirms this conclusion.

COMPETITION OF PRISON WITH FREE LABOUR.

Both in America and Europe, but especially in the former, much difficulty has at times arisen, in connection with prison labour, owing to its real or imaginary influence upon the interests of the honest artisan outside. In the United States, opposition has been vigorously raised against remunerative prison industry of any kind. But it is to be observed that the only reasonable ground for such hostility has been furnished by some of the prisons, on the congregate system, in which large quantities of one or two particular classes of goods have been manufactured, especially by the aid of powerful machinery; thus causing a disproportionate concentration of criminal labour.

Considerable injury has at times been inflicted upon British free industry by the surreptitious importation of the products of the crowded prison workshops of the Continent, especially Germany and France.

Some years ago, when most of the work in the English jails was concentrated upon the single occupation of Mat-making, there arose a strong protest from the outside workers engaged in that handicraft. And there was a certain amount of justification for their plea. The Government then took measures for diminishing the proportion of this particular industry in their prisons, and in consequence the complaints of the free workers almost disappeared. But the Government went too far, and from a weak

yielding to party voters, totally abolished Mat-making in
many or most jails; thus causing an unjust treatment of short
term prisoners, for whom a moderate amount of Mat-making
is a peculiarly suitable occupation, and easily learnt in a very
brief time.   In France and Germany some difficulty has
occurred in connection with other trades; but the French
authorities have also endeavoured to conciliate the outside
workers by arrangements with the chief local representatives of trades, whereby the prices put upon the products
of prison-labour are, to some extent, regulated by mutual
agreement.   But this is not always an easy matter. to
secure in practice, inasmuch as the nominal prices of goods
may be materially modified by "discounts," or by some
private understanding between buyers and sellers.   And
the lowering of prices of prison products, even to a small
extent, may possibly affect the general markets over a
comparatively wide area.

It is important to bear in mind that the labour of criminals is, as a rule, less skilful than that of free men.   It
must necessarily be so, and in a large degree.   And, as
a matter of fact, the more thoroughly the competing influence of prisons, upon free labour, is examined into, the
more plainly does it become manifest that it is, and must
continue to be, of very inconsiderable proportion.

Any injury to free industry, arising from prison competition is, at the worst, a very limited inconvenience.   It
need never occur, to any noteworthy extent, with but a
moderate distribution of criminal labour over a variety of
industries.   This is obvious, when it is remembered that,
even in the countries where prisoners are most numerous,
they form a very small proportion, in comparison with the
free population.   In England there are less than one thousand prisoners, on a daily average, to every million of the
population.   Taking this as an approximate general rate,
it is obvious that the thousandth part of any community,
distributed over a number of occupations, cannot constitute

a serious industrial competition. This is still more evident when it is remembered that amongst the prisoners, the women form a considerable number, whilst many convicts, of both sexes, are very ignorant and unskilled; and a certain proportion are invalids, or unable to do any work.

So that the utmost amount of the rivalry of prison-labour with free industry is very limited, very exceptional and very local; and from general circumstances it can hardly ever be otherwise.

A curious illustration of the inconsistency of some persons is afforded by the fact that whereas, in Great Britain, almost the only trade affected by prison industry has been that of mat-making, it is this particular handicraft that American trades-unionists have approved for jail-occupation. A report on prison industry, issued by the "Bureau of Labour" of the State of Michigan, mentioned that a committee from the great Trades Union, named the " Knights of Labour," visited a Pennsylvanian prison to inquire into the crafts taught. When they found that mat-making was a principal industry there, "they went away perfectly satisfied," and said that the manager "had struck the right thing." How indignant the British Trade Union of Mat-makers must have felt, if they had been present to hear this verdict.

TRADE UNION INJUSTICE.

In several American States, sectional trade tyranny has occasionally succeeded in compelling the authorities to keep the prisoners in idleness. The results have been their demoralisation, with great additional cost to the taxpayers. The Governor of Trenton Prison, New Jersey, in 1883, most earnestly protested against the folly and cruelty of thus stopping the labour of the inmates, in the assumed and imaginary interests of a few politicians outside. He remarks "Only those acquainted with prison management, and who have repeatedly heard the piteous appeals of convicts, deprived of work, to be restored to the same, can form some idea of the terror of the punishment inflicted by the State upon its convicts, in keeping them in idleness, confined to their cells; and how the maintenance of discipline and the enforcement of the rules for health and cleanliness are made almost impossible, under such a state of affairs." Another prison governor reports, as a result of enforced idleness in his establishment, impaired health, disobedience, discontent, and general recklessness. Latterly many of the convicts at Sing Sing prison, New York, have been compelled to be idle, at the dictation of selfish but influential trades-unionists, who succeeded in obtaining unwise and timorous interference by the State Legislature with the prison administration. Great evils have consequently resulted.

Some of the anti-prison-labour agitators deprecate the absolute idleness of prisoners, and suggest their being employed in cultivating the ground, or on fortifications, etc. But these alternatives are not always practicable; and where they are resorted to, they almost invariably result in heavy loss to the community and are of little use to the criminal, as a training for an honest livelihood, instead of his easy and profitable thefts. For every penny which such substitutes may enable a few outside workers to gain, many shillings or pounds must, in consequence, be imposed upon the general taxpayers.

MACHINERY IN PRISONS.

It has been largely against the employment of machinery in prisons that the outcry, in regard to "competition," has been raised. And this is a principal point to be noticed. For there is some reasonable force in this objection; though not nearly so much as has sometimes been urged. It was recently observed, by the governor of one of the largest prison factories in America, that "the goods manufactured by us bear about the same proportion to the whole amount made, that one drop of water, in Lake Michigan, would to the whole amount of water in that lake."

Yet it is obvious that the employment of hundreds of prisoners, may, with the aid of machinery, produce, in certain localities, a marked influence on some occupations. And whilst each of these criminals has a positive natural right to compete with others, whether on behalf of himself, or his family, to say nothing of the tax-payer, yet, for the sake of conciliation, it may be desirable to abandon this special adjunct to jail labour, and to restrict the latter wholly to hand-work.

Sloyd for Prison Occupation.

Sloyd, or general training in the use of tools, is an excellent occupation for prisoners, especially in cells. It really teaches and trains them to get a future livelihood, or to become handy as emigrants and workers anywhere. Consisting, as it does, chiefly of a succession of graduated exercises in manual skill, where *ultimate dexterity* is the main object in view, rather than the immediate production of saleable goods, it renders prisoners less competitive with the outside market, or with free labour, than by ordinary jail-occupation hitherto.

The Danes, Finlanders, and Swedes, especially MM. Abrahamson and Cygnæus, have been the chief promoters of Sloyd, as an educational process of great value. M. Otto Salomon, a Swede, has written an excellent manual upon the system, entitled " *The Theory of Educational Sloyd* " (London, George Philip & Son). Mr. J. S. Thornton, of Leytonstone, has actively advocated the introduction of Sloyd into Great Britain.

The progressive Sloyd Exercises consist of such graduated practice as the following :—Use of Knife in long cuts, cross-cuts, oblique cuts; Chopping with axe; Boring; Use of Saw and Tenon, lengthways, perpendicularly and obliquely ; Chiselling and Paring, in the flat, perpendicular, and concave; Planing; Gouging; Bevelling; Punching; Nailing; Clamping; Dovetailing; Glueing; Screwing; Panelling; Slotting; Lock-fitting; Staving; Hooping, &c.

Amongst the simple objects which a beginner in Sloyd may try his skill upon, after a course of preliminary exercises in the use of tools, are such as making Pointers; Flower-sticks (round and rectangular); Pencil-holders; Key Labels; Rulers; Paper-knives; Pen-trays; Knife-boards; Thread-winders; Scoops; Clothes-racks; Stools; Boxes; Ladles; Bootjacks; Drawing-boards; Brackets; Picture-frames; Tea-trays; Buckets; Cabinets; Tables, &c. (See also the "*Handbook of Sloyd,*" published by George Philip & Son, London and Liverpool.)

Cellular Separation, with Hand Labour, the best Solution of this Question.

The Report of the Michigan "Bureau of Labour" records some instructive remarks by the Governor of the Philadelphia State Prison, Mr. Cassidy, who said that all the prisoners in that institution, about one thousand, were employed at hand-labour, in making shoes, hosiery, mats, chairs, and cigars; no steam-power being used. He considered such manual labour far superior, in its educational and training efficacy, to ordinary machine-work, "which furnishes neither brains nor muscles, the inventor of the machine providing all the necessary thought required." The inmates of that prison are taught to produce articles finished throughout by themselves. The exercise of some intelligence on their part is thus secured; and, in general, they are much better enabled to earn a livelihood afterwards than if they had been confined to some single process of machine-work, or to the making of one portion of an article, whilst having nothing to do with its other parts, or with its completion. Further, in that prison, the inmates are confined to their cells, both by day and night. The aggregate advantages of the plan there pursued are, that the prisoners are helped to reform, or at least are not depraved by evil association; their competition with outside craftsmen is reduced to a minimum, by hand-labour, without steam-aid; their intelligence is exercised by the avoidance of that subdivision of occupation which converts men themselves into mere machines, or parts of machines; and they obtain a better price for their work. Mr. Cassidy remarks: "All prison officers should be mechanics; and only employed regularly after a test of their capacity as such."

In the Philadelphia prison the industrious and well-behaved prisoner is required to perform a moderate minimum task daily, based upon the estimate of the work which may reasonably be accomplished in six hours, but which is found, in practice, to be equal to about three hours of free labour. On the completion of the six hours' task, no prisoner is obliged to do more for that day. But if he chooses to continue his exertions for several hours longer, he is credited with one-half of the profits of such extra performance, or "overtime." The money is not given to him until his discharge; but it may be, with his permission, sent to his family or relations. In addition to this, every prisoner there, may, by general good behaviour, earn a remission of one month off the first year of his sentence, and two months off each subsequent year. Beyond certain privileges of visitation and correspondence, no immediate rewards are obtained in this institution. The local authorities do not believe in the discharge of their prisoners on parole, or under supervision by the police. Mr. Cassidy observes, "Under that system, the worst professional criminals reap all the benefit." The Philadelphia prisoners are not allowed to be visited by mere idle sight-seers. This is a laudable departure from the custom existing in many American jails. A strictly limited contract system enables many of the products of the labour in that prison to be sold to a local firm of merchants.

On the whole, it is to be noted that nearly all the difficulties which have occasionally arisen in connection with the alleged, or partly real, competition of prison with free labour, have resulted from the *congregate*, as distinguished from the separate system, and from the use of *machinery*. The associated inmates of large penal establishments, especially when aided by steam and water power, can manufacture articles of various kinds, to an incomparably greater extent than the tenants of solitary cells.

The manual labour and separate discipline in the latter may be rendered more helpful to the prisoner, both technically and morally, whilst his competition with the outside worker is infinitesimal and perfectly legitimate. Whereas the crowded workshops of non-cellular prisons may interfere perceptibly with local free industry ; whilst at the same time their demoralising influences habitually tend to increase the total number of criminals requiring restraint, and so to involve the tax-payers in an ultimate expenditure far exceeding the apparent immediate profit resulting from the organisation of associated penal industry, and the aid of powerful machinery.

Thus the prison labour question, for its best solution, brings us back again to the advantages of the Separate System. *No associated prison industry, no corrupting gangs, no steam power.* With these simple conditions, the competition will always be an inconspicuous minimum ; even where the " Contract System " is retained, as it may be, with some advantage, under the reasonable conditions requisite to protect and maintain the discipline.

Chapter XIII.

PRISON OFFICERS, THEIR RESPONSIBILITY TO GOD.

DIFFICULTY OF OBTAINING WELL-QUALIFIED CUSTODIANS.

ONE of the numerous reasons for adopting, as far as possible, other means than imprisonment, for the repression of crime, consists in the great difficulty of selecting or training suitable custodians and instructors of criminals. A Government, or a State, cannot readily obtain, or constitute, a class of persons combining the qualifications needful for efficiency in this direction. Their most essential characteristics—those of a moral and religious nature—are precisely those respecting which a State Department is apt to be peculiarly unable, or even unwilling, to exercise discrimination. And yet the appointment of proper officers is one of the most important matters connected with any penal system.

Mr. FREDERICK HILL, who was for many years an efficient Inspector of British Prisons, remarks in his work on "Crime": "Of such supreme importance do I regard the appointment of good officers, that I should expect better results, in one of the worst built prisons, where no system of discipline was prescribed, but where there was an earnest and able governor, unfettered in his choice of subordinates, than in the best constructed building and under the most carefully devised plans of management, but where there was an incompetent head with ill-qualified assistants."

General Sir E. F. Du Cane observes that "The importance of selecting good officers for prison duties cannot be over-rated. The officer who has charge of prisoners has such power, for good or evil, over his fellow-men, that I do not think there are many positions more responsible than that which he occupies. Nor, on the whole, are there, I think, many in which the officer is exposed to more temptation to neglect his duty, or abuse his trust."

There is a special difficulty in procuring suitable men for the lower grades of prison service. It is by no means easy to train an efficient body of warders. Yet these are the class of officers who come chiefly into daily contact with the prisoners—sometimes almost exclusively so—and upon whom mainly depends the nature of the influence which can be brought to bear upon those under their care.

The Rev. J. Clay wrote to a nobleman, in reference to the discovery of the existence of unnatural crime, then extensively prevalent in a large British convict prison :— " The evidence now laid before your Lordship could only be given by convicts. The higher the rank of the official, the more ignorant he is kept of the true nature and extent of such evils as these papers describe. As the inquiry descends—beginning with the governor and ending with the ' guard '—it is met, in the first instance, by the conscientious disavowal of all knowledge of the abuses charged; and, in the last, by interested endeavours to conceal the real and appalling truth." These remarks confirm the often experienced fact that the Directors and Governors of prisons may easily and frequently be *the last* persons to be made acquainted with occurrences taking place within a few yards of them, and in the daily routine of the establishment with which they are presumed to be perfectly cognisant. They may be, in great degree, excluded from the sphere of influence in which their subordinates are concerned. Hence it is the more necessary that the latter class of officers shall be as carefully selected and as well trained as possible. Yet both the selection and the training are peculiarly difficult.

For, in the first place, it is not easy to meet with warders competent to discipline and handle large bodies of prisoners. It has been found, in the experience of most countries, that discharged soldiers possess this particular qualification in a degree superior to ordinary civilians. But then, on the other hand, the previous lives of soldiers, with their too frequently loose views of morality, and their by no means rare indulgence in swearing and intemperance, render them less suitable than selected civilians, to exert the necessary good influences required in a prison. When old soldiers are employed in prison administration, they should constitute a minority of the staff. Civilian common-sense should be largely called into requisition in the management of criminals.

The very discipline also which is needful to manage large bodies of associated prisoners is, in some respects, counteractive of reformatory influences. It was remarked by Captain MACONOCHIE: "In the management of our jails we at present attach too much importance to mere submission and obedience. We make the discipline in them military, overlooking a distinction, to which too much importance cannot be attached, between the objects of military and of improved penal discipline. The ultimate purpose of military discipline is to train men to act *together*, but that of penal discipline is to prepare them advantageously to *separate*. The objects being thus opposite, the processes should equally differ." But neither Captain Maconochie nor any one else could, with safety, dispense with an approximately military discipline, or with the necessity of attaching special importance to " mere submission and obedience," so long as prisoners are congregated in masses. Here, again, is indicated one of the many merits of the Cellular System, its superiority for disciplinary facilities over the associated plan.

Misused Official Influence.

Fearful have been the moral and physical injuries, in some instances, inflicted upon prisoners by their officers. For example, a few years ago it was discovered that the most shocking profligacy prevailed between the female prisoners and the male warders of the chief penal establishment of one of the leading Northern States in America. And unfortunately such occurrences have not been rare.

Even the Chaplains, the religious guides and lights of prisons, have sometimes been sources of evil instead of good. In going over a prison of North Europe, the writer was told by the schoolmaster, "Our Lutheran chaplain allows men to live and die here, with very little regard to them. *He does not care for their souls.*" How terrible must be the future responsibility of such a person, when summoned to meet the retributive judgment of God, and when, in the light of eternity, the awful retrospect of irrevocably lost opportunities for good, and of a worse than wasted life, may rest upon the unhappy spirit.

Crime and Sin.

Every prison officer, and indeed the general community, may profitably consider that whilst, for temporal interests, it is necessary to punish criminals, both for their own sake and for that of others, yet in relation to God and " the powers of the world to come " there is comparatively little, if any, difference between *Crime* and *Sin;* even as to those ordinary and constant states, or acts of sin, which it would be altogether inexpedient to visit with any human punishment. The most eminent personages, those specially honoured upon earth, are often quite as criminal in God's sight, as the lowest and vilest offenders against human law. For instance, a few years ago, one of the English Judges, whilst staying at a Midland county town for the Assizes, met with his death in a brothel. This offender against God thus passed into the presence of the Supreme with a weight of responsibility and culpability exceeding that of many poor ignorant creatures whom he had condemned to imprisonment. Yet it was only as by a mere physical accident that his moral depravity and unfitness for his post became known to the world. Probably many similar or worse offenders still exercise high authority in various lands. Hence prisoners and criminals, as such, are not to be considered as being at all more hopeless, or even more culpable, than multitudes of persons whom respectable and even religious society honours. Crime is a temporary and human distinction. *Sin*, whether it be punishable crime or moral disobedience, is the chief matter in regard to all wrong, whether private or public; for it is dishonour to God, and involves eternal consequences and interests.

That ornament of the Church of England, RICHARD HOOKER, usually surnamed "The Judicious," in a few weighty words, thus sets forth (in his "Ecclesiastical Polity") this truth, so essential for universal acceptation, and especially for those who have to punish and reform criminals. He says, "If we did not commit the sins which, daily and hourly, in deed, word, or thought, we do commit, yet in the 'good things' we do, how many defects are there intermingled? Let the holiest and best thing we do be considered. We are never better affected unto God than when we pray. Yet when we pray, how are our affections many times distracted? How little reverence do we show unto the grand majesty of God, unto whom we speak? How little remorse of our own offences, how little taste of the sweet influence of His tender mercies, do we feel? Are we not as unwilling, many times, to begin, and as glad to make an end, as if, in saying, 'Call upon Me' He had set us a very burdensome task ? The *best* things we do have somewhat in them to be pardoned. Our continual suit to God is, and must be, to bear with our infirmities and pardon our offences." That pardon can only be obtained as a result and most precious purchase of God's self-denying vindication of His own Moral Law in Christ. "For through this Man (or manifestation of the Highest) is preached unto you the forgiveness of sins." Through Him only is that costly and indispensable privilege attainable. The words of the great Anglican writer refer to that fear of God which is not only " the beginning of wisdom " to all men, but which is necessary to influence criminals, and equally so the persons placed over them. For very brief, and very little, comparatively, is the power of earthly sovereigns or authorities, either to punish or reward their officers and subordinates. But the Divine power, of reward and of punishment, endures for ever. The crystalline sanctity of God and His unapproachable majesty, except through Christ, the Mediator and Propitiation, demand a life-long, loving reverence. It is such considerations as these which must ever be the most powerful incitements to duty and to a good example, on the part of all who are engaged in the control of criminals and prisoners; as, indeed, amongst reflecting minds everywhere, and in all conditions of society. The prince, the pontiff, the prelate, the peer, the prisoner, and the pauper, stand upon the same humble level before God.

Good Influences over Warders.

If the chief officers of prisons, as the Governors, Chaplains, and Surgeons, are conscientious and intelligent men, they will generally be able to exert a powerful influence in guiding the Warders and other subordinates to efficiency in the discharge of their duties. For, practically, it is only in connection with actual prison service that the needful qualifications can be gained. Yet the best skill and ability in this direction require some more systematic modes of development than have usually been adopted. In a few of the chief prisons of various countries, Lectures and Classes have been instituted for the improvement of the lower officers; and in some instances they are assembled once a week, or oftener, for conference with their superiors. But, in general, an important desideratum, in the reform of prisons, consists in the necessity for a more practical regard for the intellectual, physical, and moral needs of those members of the staff who are most frequently and habitually brought into contact with the criminals.

In Italy, France, Switzerland, and elsewhere, special Training Schools for Warders have been instituted. These officers may be further helped by the adoption of a just gradation of rank and duty; by making pay and promotion strictly dependent upon proved efficiency; and, in short, by holding out more general *inducements*, than hitherto, to intelligent and hearty fidelity in the discharge of official service.

The duties of the Warders are so arduous, so trying to the temper, and their hours of service are usually so prolonged, that it is urgently requisite to provide them with more aid towards a conscientious, lively interest in their work.

They should not be discouraged and harassed (as has not unfrequently been the case) by too numerous and comparatively heavy Fines for very trifling acts of negligence. The best prison administrators are able to dispense with much resort to such impositions.

The services, in particular, of the Chaplain and Schoolmaster may be rendered very useful to the warders. These important functionaries can thus often exert a more practical influence for good upon the prisoners indirectly, by elevating the character and minds of the subordinate officers, than by their apparently more direct labours. At any rate it should be recognised, in every penal establishment, that failure in some of the main objects must necessarily result, unless the warders are regularly furnished with due educational and moral helps towards the discharge of their very difficult duties. They should be stimulated, by lectures and brief addresses, to take an intelligent interest in such subjects as Sanitation, Temperance, Thrift, Kindness to Animals, the principles and history of Prison Discipline and Penology, and generally in matters connected with the special occupations, or industry, of the inmates of their own prison.

LIBRARIES and READING ROOMS for the officers, as well as for the prisoners, should form a feature of every jail. And of course some reasonable opportunities for their use should be provided in the schedule of hours of duty and recreation. The assistance of persons of leisure and culture, in the neighbourhood, might often be successfully invited for the delivery of lectures and addresses to the officers. Probably in most districts there are well-qualified gentlemen who would gladly help, in this way, if asked to to do so. Facilities should also be encouraged for the enjoyment of Music, Athletic Sports, and Swimming, by the subordinates, where practicable.

The HOLIDAYS, PAY and opportunities of PROMOTION, should be granted on a scale of reasonable liberality ; and, in short, the general welfare and improvement, especially of the lower officials, should be a prominent part of the arrangements of every penal establishment.

PRISON SURGEONS.—DR. BROWNING.

In exercising a good influence both upon the officers and prisoners, the talents and benevolence of the jail Surgeons may be advantageously utilised. Even under the difficulties and horrors of the old Transportation System, a Surgeon-Superintendent of convict ships, Dr. COLIN BROWNING, exercised a marvellous influence for good. One of his sayings may be here quoted, as conveying a truth important for all prison officers everywhere to bear in mind, viz. :—" We hear much of various systems of prison discipline, as the Separate, the Silent, and the Congregate systems; but unless the CHRISTIAN system be brought to bear, with Divine power, on the understanding and consciences of criminals, every other system, professedly contemplating their reformation, must prove an utter failure. We willingly concede to various modes of prison discipline their just measure of importance; but to expect that human machinery, however perfect, can take the place of *God's own prescribed method* of reformation, involves not only ignorant presumption, but practical infidelity."

Between the years 1831 and 1848, Dr. Browning was engaged as Surgeon-Superintendent of Convict Ships, during the long voyages between England and Tasmania. Nine times he was entrusted with the direction of large parties of these wretched outcasts from their country. They always included a number of the most depraved and desperate characters. When these were congregated together, within a small space, on shipboard, for periods of four or five months, the difficulties of management were necessarily very great. Indeed, the voyages of convicts usually presented such scenes of horrible corruption and riotous insubordination, that the transport vessels were commonly spoken of as " floating hells." But Dr. Browning's parties formed a most remarkable contrast to the general rule. Yet he was not furnished with the slightest outward advantage, or facility, beyond other surgeon-superintendents. Whence, then, his exceptional success?

From his practical reliance upon, and application of, the power of the Gospel. From a daily and hourly maintenance of a combination of Scriptural exposition, fervent intercessory prayer, plain secular instruction and lectures, thorough cleanliness and order, and the strictest, but kindly, discipline.

When one of his parties, of 200 convicts, left Woolwich, for Hobart, 135 could neither read nor write. On their landing in the Colony, all could read. Seventy-six had learnt to write, 39 had signed the "Total Abstinence," and 150 the Temperance pledge. All were supplied with a Bible or Testament. And the Doctor mentions, "Out of their few remaining shillings, the prisoners, without my knowledge, subscribed among themselves the sum of £7. 8s. 10d., as an expression of their gratitude to the British and Foreign Bible Society. Had they possessed more money, the sum would have been greater. *Many of them gave all they had left in my hands.*"

When in charge of another party of 220 convicts, sent out from England in the *Theresa*, the Doctor established thirty-three schools, in active operation on board, and again landed all the men able to read. Not a lash, nor an iron, was laid on any convict throughout the voyage. During a voyage in another ship, Dr. Browning proved that his decidedly religious, whilst practical and strict mode of treatment, was also successful in the management of female convicts, who are generally even more difficult to govern than the worst of men.

But one of his greatest triumphs was his voyage from Norfolk Island (of horrible history) to Tasmania, in charge of 346 "old hands." A number of these had agreed to take a terrible revenge on some comrades who had been employed as constables over the others. But under the instruction and discipline of Dr. Browning, this purpose was entirely abandoned. (Murder was a common crime among the Norfolk Island convicts at that period.) The Doctor landed his large party at their destination without having had a single punishment. He remarks: "The men were given to me in double irons; I debarked them without an iron clanking among them. I am told this is the first and only instance of convicts removed from Norfolk Island having had their irons struck off during the voyage, and being landed totally unfettered. They are almost uniformly double-cross-ironed, and often chained down to the deck, everybody being afraid of them. I was among them at all hours, and the prison doors were never once shut during the day. To God be all the glory."

Three Governors of Tasmania—Sir JOHN FRANKLIN, Colonel GEORGE ARTHUR, and Sir WILLIAM DENISON (all practical and shrewd men) — expressed their high opinion of Dr. Browning and his system, and of its effects upon the *subsequent* behaviour of his convicts.

The sheet-anchor of Dr. Browning's reliance was on the inculcation, as a chief condition of any one's religious progress, of the *private, prayerful use of Holy Scripture*, as the record of God's infinite love to man, in the Incarnation of the LORD JESUS CHRIST, His dear Son. He writes—" The grand instrument which God has been pleased to ordain, for effecting man's conversion to Himself, is the truth concerning Jesus, as that truth is set forth in the Holy Scripture. But even this inspired Word of God derives its saving efficacy from the accompanying influence of the Holy Spirit." For " daily looking unto Jesus," the Bible is the helpful spiritual *Telescope*. But Dr. Browning knew that even preaching and Bible-reading must be accompanied by healthy practice, in every-day duties, decencies and industries, or the former will be fruitless; just as the best wheat, if sown on an undrained bog, will only rot.

In his advices to his officers, he records :—" You will remember that it is *men* with whom you have to deal ; God's creatures, like yourselves, whom He pities and loves, and whose interests He requires you, to the utmost of your power, to advance."

To his convicts, and officers and sailors, he said :—" The greatest snare to which you will be exposed, on shore, is the use of *intoxicating liquors ;* no vice is more calculated to lead you to the practice of other vices than drunkenness." He also advised serious reflection as to the temporal and eternal influences of a wise action in regard to Marriage ; and he urged " the vast importance of the uniform observation of the Seventh Commandment and all the other commandments of the Most High."

Like all good men, Dr. Browning had great faith in prayer—*public, private, and intercessory prayer.* He recommended and practised it constantly, and regarded it as a primary means of obtaining the indispensable aid of God's Holy Spirit, to influence the objects of his exertions.

Whilst strict in repressing offences, he always recognised and fostered the good qualities remaining in convicts, some of whom he knew to be not greater sinners than many free persons, respected in the community. And he strongly disapproved of the too-prevalent scepticism as to the reformation of criminals, especially seeing that it is only by Divine *grace* that *any* person can become a true Christian.*

MEDICAL SUPERINTENDENCE OF PRISONS.

The prisons of IRELAND have, of late years, shown, in special degree, the advantages which may be derived from medical officers being permitted to exercise a prominent share of influence in the arrangements of jail life. In Great Britain, during the same period, very valuable services have been rendered by the Prison Medical Staff to the sanitary condition of these establishments, and to the health of their inmates. These good results have been chiefly due to the efforts of individual medical officers, who have sometimes had to carry out their duty under difficulties which have been much greater in England than in Ireland. And in consequence, largely, of these efforts, English prisons have latterly enjoyed a wonderful freedom from zymotic diseases, and have had also a low rate of mortality. It is not unfair to other gentlemen to mention, in this connection, the peculiarly useful influence which

° *Vide* Dr. Browning's work, " *The Convict Ship and England's Exiles.*" London: Hamilton, Adams & Co.

has been exercised by Dr. R. M. GOVER, one of Her Majesty's Inspectors of Prisons.

But in Ireland, the labours of the medical officers of prisons have been even more successful than in England, especially in regard to the ventilation, dietary, invalid treatment, and other matters coming under their special direction, because, in this part of the kingdom, these gentlemen have not occupied such a comparatively subordinate situation as that accorded too generally in England to their class. An eminent medical man, DR. WOODHOUSE, has been appointed one of the chief Directors, or Commissioners, of Irish Prisons.

BELGIUM also has derived great benefit in her penal system, from the special influence rightly permitted to eminent medical men, such as, for example, Dr. MOREL, of Ghent.

In every country it is an essential condition of effectual prison discipline that it should involve the services of an intelligent medical staff enjoying the needful liberty of action and honourable recognition on the part of the Government.

THE PRISON CHAPLAINS.

The Chaplains, in particular, should be men feeling deeply the responsibilities of their position, in regard to all the custodians of the prisoners. They should especially seek to impress upon these a sense of the importance of Eternity, in reference to their own accountability to God, and as to the souls of those placed under them. The words and example of the officers either tend towards the salvation, or the moral injury of the prisoners. The former result will afford happy retrospects hereafter and the approbation of Christ. But the latter course will involve painful remorse and condemnation, when the present opportunities of faithful performance of duty, as in the all-seeing eye of God, shall have irrecoverably passed away. Both

the subordinate and the superior officers (as indeed the
managers of all institutions), may profitably ponder the
question once asked by a prison chaplain—" Will you be
content to replace such a treasure, as a human being, in its
former position, with nothing gained, during the whole time
you have had it in charge?"   From every officer (as from
every master, parent, or caretaker of others) Christ, the
omnipotent Final Disposer, may demand, "What did you do
with the souls committed to your control; the establishments, or households, over whom you ruled?   Did you
bring them to Me, or did you neglect them, or even lead
them away from Me?" .For, of course, some such requirement will be hereafter made by the Divine Judge, of every
prison official, as of all other men and women.   And it is
well to remember that God's authority is paramount over
all administrators, whether of prisons, communities, or
kingdoms.   No orders or regulations, whether of a Government or a State Department, can release any one from His
claims, as the Supreme Sovereign.   All earthly monarchs
and authorities are comparatively ephemeral influences,
whose powers cease when their bodies pass .to the dust.
But God, Christ, the Holy Spirit, lives and reigns for ever,
and will make absolute requirement of duty—a just and
thoroughly fair exaction, but a permanently sovereign one
—and with a gracious reward of His own eternal love, for
the humble and obedient.

BISHOP WILLSON, OF TASMANIA.

If, through the persuasions of chaplains, or by any other
means, earnest considerations, in regard to the inalienable
and certain responsibility of every person to God, can be
really brought home to prison officials of all grades, then
the most powerful and permanent of good influences will
be exercised upon them; and the happiest results may be
looked for, as to the prisoners.   One of the best examples
of effectual personal influence being brought to bear, from

outside, upon prison officers, both superior and subordinate, was afforded by that devoted and faithful minister of Christ, the late Dr. R. W. WILLSON, Roman Catholic BISHOP OF TASMANIA, who, in spite of excessive obstacles, accomplished more than any one else in mitigating the horrors of Australian Transportation, and in promoting the ultimate abolition of that system.

Bishop Willson was a man possessing wonderful influence over criminals and lunatics. He had previously been on the Boards of Management, both of the Nottingham County Hospital and County Lunatic Asylum. His personal appearance was genial and pleasant. His remarkably lofty forehead drew from a phrenologist the exclamation, " He has the largest development of benevolence that I ever saw on a human head." In Nottingham he was revered by all sects and parties.

His loving labours amongst prisoners in the Southern Hemisphere were fruitful in good results. The worst and most depraved of Norfolk Island convicts would exclaim: "God bless Bishop Willson!" His benevolence was more gentle and genial than that of John Howard. But, like Howard, he had also that hard headedness, without which benevolence so often fails. His biographer, Dr. Ullathorne (who was also a faithful worker amongst Australasian convicts), remarks:—" His eye was upon every abuse; his voice was raised against every custom that vitiated instead of reforming. His influence, in time, grew to be a great power."

The Australasian convicts, at that time, were treated worse than beasts. Wholesale floggings; men working in gangs, whilst burdened with chains of more than 40lbs. weight; punishment with the "tube-gag" (inserted into the mouth), and the "spread eagle," by which men's arms were painfully stretched out to ring-bolts; such were frequent occurrences. One day, at Norfolk Island, 39 men were flogged, and on the next day 14 more. Twelve convicts, there, were also executed in one day.

The Bishop had effected some reforms, but the very root of the system rendered cure hopeless; 1,900 convicts were there in association. He records this important and permanently reliable truth: "It may be taken for a certainty, that when criminals are constantly thrown together, the best among them, as a rule, will be corrupted *down* to the level of the *worst.*" Major Harrold, in command of the troops on Norfolk Island, exclaimed to the Bishop, with uplifted hands, "For God's sake, go home and let the British Government know the truth." Dr. Willson now saw how awful the state of things had become. Even death had lost its terrors for the convicts. Some of them actually sought execution, to get out of their living hell. When he was asked if the men had a dread of Capital Punishment, he replied, "I think not, they have very little fear of death."

The good Bishop took the long voyage home to England, in 1847, to urge personally upon the Government the total abandonment of Norfolk Island. This was at length secured. In Tasmania, also, his labours for penal reforms were arduous and not fruitless. But there, again, the system was hopeless. And it could only be effectually mended, by being ended. There, too, transportation ultimately ceased. But the Bishop had nearly worn out his life by his constant efforts. In 1865 he returned to England, paralysed and almost a wreck. The British Government, with that ingratitude and thoughtlessness which so often characterises the official attitude towards the most deserving of reformers, granted him no pension or reward to alleviate his condition, although he had worn himself out in the service. On June 30th, 1866, at Nottingham, this true servant of the Lord Jesus Christ peacefully passed to his rest.*

---

* *Vide* his biography, by Archbishop Ullathorne. London: Burns and Oates.

GERMAN COMBINATION OF OFFICIAL POWER WITH FREEDOM.

It is to be remarked, in connection with this subject, that Germany, although pre-eminent in its military organisation, has encouraged, amongst its prison officers of all grades, an intelligent freedom of mutual discussion and co-operation, hardly equalled in any other European country. For many years, annual or other periodical gatherings of prison officials have been held in the chief cities of Prussia, Saxony, Bavaria, Wurtemberg, Hanover, and Baden, for the discussion of matters affecting their particular profession and the various departments of penal treatment and prevention, and also for social recreation. By this means, these German officers have become characterised by a more intelligent interest in their duties, than the similar functionaries in most other countries. They appear to be, in so far, superior to the average of British prison officials. This result has been further promoted by the establishment of voluntary Associa· tions for the study of penal questions, in several of the chief cities, such as Hamburg, Dusseldorf, and Frankfort, and by the maintenance of several Journals and Magazines devoted to this department. Amongst these may be specially mentioned, the *Blätter für Gefangnisskunde,* for many years ably edited by the late M. G. EKERT, of Brucksal, and subsequently by his talented successor, Dr. OSCAR WIRTH, Director of Plötzensee Prison, Berlin. This Journal and the similarly excellent *Revue Pénitentiaire,* or monthly *Bulletin* of the French *Société Générale des Prisons,* together with the admirable *Japanese Prison Magazine,* conducted by M. SANO, of Tokio, are, hitherto, the chief journals of the world in this particular department of literature. In England some similar periodicals have hitherto failed to obtain the needful support from the public, or from the authorities.

But in Germany, and to some extent in Austria also, the officials and the supreme Government have actively encouraged both the literary and the verbal discussion of penal questions by their subordinates. The intelligent and lively interest thus manifested by the Germans, in matters relating to crime and prisons, has contrasted favourably with the comparatively mechanical routine which has too generally prevailed amongst the managers and subordinate officers of English penal establishments. Amongst these an excessive sternness has been too frequent. Whilst a certain degree of reserve has its disciplinary use, yet its excess tends to be ruinous to those moral and religious influences which every one in authority is called by God to exercise. Men and even beasts are repelled by undue reserve. At the Zoological Gardens, in London, it was noticed that one of the attendants was greatly disliked by the animals, some of which endeavoured to injure him. Yet it did not appear that he was cruel to them; he was simply and habitually silent; he scarcely ever spoke to them. Most creatures like to be talked to in pleasant tones, even though not understanding the words. And as regards human beings, excessive reserve is hateful, and renders a man disagreeable and of little use to his fellows, whether superior or subordinate. The Germans, with less of this defect than the English, have been, both as to their military and their prison discipline, at least the equals of the latter, if not indeed decidedly in advance of them, in their powers of authority. Familiarity is a mischievous extreme, but much reserve is an evil in an opposite direction. The best efficiency avoids both.

Superior Officers and their Opportunities.— Jerry McAuley.

The influence of the superior officers in the administration both of prisons and of the police, may sometimes be exerted with immense power for the temporal and eternal good, both of their subordinates and of offenders. Many of the latter do not furnish a very hopeful field for such endeavours. Indeed some of them appear to be almost irreclaimable. The good seed sown amongst them may be as that cast upon rocks, or among thorns. But, here and there, there will be some growth; and occasionally the fruit will be sixty, or even a hundredfold. For the resources of Divine Grace are infinite.

A most remarkable proof of this was afforded in the case of a well-known criminal, the late JERRY McAULEY. He was born in Ireland in 1839, but was taken to New York during his childhood. Having a bad example at home, he became an habitual thief and a ringleader amongst a number of criminals, men and women, of the lowest character. At length he was committed to the convict prison at Sing Sing, where he manifested some little appearance of religious impression, under the exhortations of a discharged prisoner named Gardiner, who, having become a reformed character, was occasionally permitted access to the jail, for reading the Scriptures and prayer with the inmates. No decided change in Jerry McAuley was yet visible. But at a later period, in 1862, the "Warden," or Governor of Sing Sing, adopted the plan of setting apart a few hours every week for private interviews with his prisoners, and especially with the object of giving them good advice under more favourable circumstances than during their association with the others. At one of these interviews a convict, named Jones, asked permission to teach a fellow prisoner to read. This was granted under certain conditions. Some time afterwards the same Jones petitioned that a few of the convicts might be allowed to meet for prayer, with the approval and in the presence of the chaplain. This also was sanctioned, and, commencing with an attendance of four, the gathering gradually increased to the number of about fifty prisoners. Amongst those who obtained leave to join in these meetings was Jerry McAuley, who had previously been specially urged to amendment by the Governor, in several private interviews.

He had hitherto been exceedingly morose and depressed almost to despair; but, through the personal sympathy of the Governor and one or two others, and being cheered by the hopes and comforts of the Gospel of Christ, he at length showed indications of sincere repentance and good resolve.

And these never passed away. For although, after leaving Sing Sing, he at first relapsed into evil courses, and this more than once, yet he did not relinquish the ordinary means of grace; and these ultimately gained a complete mastery over him. His soul was won for Christ. And now he felt called to prove his gratitude to the Lord, by endeavouring to rescue other poor creatures from evil and misery. His earnestness and evident sincerity gained him the friendship of a shrewd but benevolent banker of New York, Mr. A. S. Hatch, who showed his confidence in Jerry by making him the caretaker of a private yacht, in which position he manifested fidelity and trustworthiness. But the impulse to rescue others from degradation resting with abiding pressure on his soul, he obtained Mr. Hatch's help in this direction also, and was enabled to open a mission-hall in Water Street, in one of the lowest slums of New York. Here he was wonderfully successful in gathering for Christian worship many of the most depraved and hopeless men and women of the city. His notorious antecedents, together with the evident change in his character, and his humble, straightforward, sympathetic pleadings for souls, were the means of arousing the attention and permanently improving the lives of hundreds of outcasts. There were abundant proofs of the genuine nature of these results. Jerry himself had been too deeply experienced in the ways of imposture to be easily beguiled by mere hypocritical professions. But he loved the people, in view of their immortal capacities, and of Christ's love to them. It is recorded that "his perseverance was indomitable, and his faith in Christ boundless. His absolute confidence was infectious." His preaching was lively and natural. He believed in the efficacy of united prayer. Like Whitefield, Wesley, and Spurgeon, he relied especially on this influence. He encouraged another means of help, which, in every age, has been much blessed by God,—the practice of hearty and melodious Christian song. Hence his mission-hall became so attractive and crowded, that his friends furnished him with funds to open a larger one, named "Cremorne," in another similar slum. For sixteen years he laboured with extraordinary zeal and blessing until his death, in 1884, at the age of forty-five years. His funeral was one of the largest ever witnessed in New York, and was attended by many whom he had been the means of rescuing from temporal and future misery. He passed to his rest, having accomplished a grand life work, and having earned an abiding record, such as any monarch might envy. For of him it may be truly said, as of Barnabas of old, that by his fidelity and devotion, " Much people was added to the Lord." And what epitaph, or record, can be nobler than this?

A principal point to be here observed, is the distinct connection between Jerry McAuley's reclamation and the faithful labours of the Governor and Chaplain of Sing Sing prison, for the religious development of the criminals placed under their care. These efforts had also other important results; Jerry McAuley was by no means the only man then permanently reclaimed to honesty and a godly life, by the encouragement of religion in that establishment. Many of its inmates were practically changed into useful citizens, by the earnest conversations of the chief officers, and by the responses of Divine Grace to the petitions put up in the weekly prayer meetings held in the prison.

It was stated, by the New York *Observer*, that Dr. E. C. WINES, the eminent founder of the "National Prison Association" of the United States, was mainly induced to enter upon that important department of public service, in consequence of the deep interest in criminal reform awakened by a visit to the Governor of Sing Sing,.and to the prayer-meetings in his prison.   But the life and labours of Jerry McAuley, alone, constituted a thousandfold success, even if all efforts to reform other Sing Sing convicts had failed. And, from time to time, other individual successes will continue to compensate and to counterbalance, in every country, the numerous or general instances in which such good endeavours may have appeared fruitless.   To the prison officer who, by faithfulness to his opportunities of usefulness, seeks for eternal reward (and God judges rather by *motives* than results), the inspired words are peculiarly encouraging: " In the morning sow thy seed, and in the evening withhold not thy hand: for thou knowest not whether shall prosper, this or that; or whether they both shall be alike good."   (Eccles. xi.)

Good Lay Influence.

A layman, whether a prison official, a policeman, or in any other position, may exercise as much good influence as a clergyman, or priest, especially by familiar but judicious conversations with others for the promotion of Temperance, Kindness to Animals, Thrift, Sanitation, etc.   And, indeed, the non-professional and spontaneous character of lay efforts, for Christ, often imparts to them even a greater power than that possessed by the regular minister of the Gospel.   The example and words of a truly Christian prison officer, policeman, commercial traveller, tradesman, domestic servant, sailor, working man, or any other lay person, young or old, are often regarded, by those around them, with an interest much superior to that awakened by ordinary ministerial effort.

The Governor of an English prison informed the writer that before he came to that establishment he had desired larger opportunities of Christian usefulness than he had hitherto possessed. He found the prison afforded him the wished-for scope, for it became to him a virtual pastorate. He long exercised a kindly paternal care over the officers and the prisoners, and also over many of the latter, after their discharge. He was firm and humane; he exacted diligence and strict obedience; he habitually prayed for his prisoners and for himself. Many were the grateful acknowledgments of abiding benefits derived from his influence, which he received from the subjects of his former care. Nor was he by any means a solitary instance of such honourable fidelity to the Highest, on the part of prison governors. Many of these laymen, and at times their subordinate officers also, have found opportunities for the effectual exercise of genuinely pastoral labours, which have afforded to them profound satisfaction, and which also, it may confidently be believed, will redound hereafter to their rich reward.

. But, regarding men as they are, in the general, and in view also of the merely secular motives, often of a low character—which are so apt to characterise human governments and their whole system of patronage and appointments—it is hardly to be expected that the proportion of prison officers, distinguished by such exemplary goodness and efficiency, will be other than a minority. Too many State authorities seem to care but little for the religious and eternal interests of those whom they select for office, whether in prisons, or in other departments of the public service.

Hence, we are once more brought back to the conclusion to which so many investigations and observations lead us, that prison administration tends, for the most part, to be of such an essentially defective character, that the best economy of preventive and repressive effort must be that which reduces incarceration to the lowest extent compatible with public security, and which seeks its objects chiefly through influences to be applied *outside* the walls of jails, rather than within them.

Chapter XIV.

THE AID OF DISCHARGED PRISONERS.

DOUBLE OBJECT TO BE KEPT IN VIEW.

THE chief objects to be kept steadily in view, in any efforts
to assist discharged prisoners, should be such modes of
help as may combine the best interests both of themselves and of the community. This will involve two
things: firstly, that the direct aid to this class of persons
shall consist mainly in endeavours to obtain employment
for them, or to stimulate them to self-supporting industry;
and secondly, that those at least who have been imprisoned
more than once, shall not be allowed to enter situations,
especially those involving considerable responsibility, without their employers being made fully conscious, from the
first, of their antecedents. This course has been found to
be, on the whole, the most advantageous to all parties
concerned.

On the one hand, it is unjust to the community that
persons previously habituated to dishonesty, and not yet
proved to be reformed from past frailties, should, unconsciously to their employers, be placed in positions where
valuable property would be entrusted to their care; or that
individuals whose lives had, before imprisonment, been
characterised by vice and profligacy, should be permitted to

enter families or households, without the heads of such establishments being made aware of the necessity of some special care, in regard to these new comers. The neglect of such a precaution would be sure to lead, in many cases, to irresistible temptation and cruel injuries.

A case recently came under the writer's notice which illustrates this. One of his friends obtained a servant from a registry office, with good recommendations. For a week or two she worked admirably and her demeanour was most satisfactory. But on the family leaving her alone in the house for a few hours, she took the opportunity to plunder and run off with as many clothes as she could carry and a considerable sum of money. Her employer, on calling in a policeman, was informed, " This girl is a discharged convict, with ticket-of-leave; I knew who and what she was, but I was not at liberty to inform you." The girl obtained another situation as servant to a lady, whom again she soon cruelly robbed. She was then re-convicted to prison. In this instance, the excessive reticence and leniency of the police, in reference to a thoroughly depraved criminal, were the cause of serious injury to two households, and were of no benefit whatever to the ex-prisoner.

It is right that discharged prisoners, other than first offenders, shall be defended from such probabilities of further mischief to themselves and others. And, it is especially a kindness to these persons that they shall be, from the outset, relieved from all anxiety on the ground of betrayals by former fellow prisoners, or by the police. Their position, on obtaining situations where their antecedents are clearly understood by their employers, will be secure from the harassing apprehensions and fears which, in so many instances, have grievously perpetuated the sufferings of this class. The knowledge of a former offender's career will, of course, in many instances, render it difficult for him, or her, to obtain situations of trust; but then it may be justly considered that these persons should not be placed in such positions, until they have, by a steady course of perseverance, given proof of their fitness to occupy important posts and to be treated with full confidence.

Some of the less responsible descriptions of occupation are often found to be available for discharged prisoners, whose antecedents are, in a judicious manner, made known to their employers. It has, indeed, been repeatedly observed in practice, that some persons decidedly prefer to have servants of this class; because their circumstances furnish some special guarantees for good behaviour. They are anxious to regain a favourable character; they therefore strive to do their best. They are aware that their employers already know the worst about them, and therefore they are not under temptations to hypocrisy or deceit. Rather a lower than a higher standard of merit is tacitly assumed for their attainment. Hence their position is somewhat easier than it might otherwise be. The eyes of the chief police authorities (at any rate in England) are upon them, for a beneficent and not a malignant purpose. They are thus relieved from fear of the subordinate members of the force, whilst their masters feel that, in the privately-exercised supervision maintained in regard to these persons, either by the chiefs of the police, or by the agents of a Discharged Prisoners' Aid Society, or by some other delegated local authority, there is afforded a considerable protection against dangers arising from dishonesty.

Such a system is a combination of mercy and justice. This was proved, under the plan formerly adopted by Sir Walter Crofton and his agent, Mr. James Organ, in dealing with the better class of Irish convicts on their discharge. The circumstance that their antecedents were, from the first, made known to their masters, and that a kindly oversight was still exercised in regard to them by the authorities, facilitated the procuring of occupation for a large number of them.

UNION OF VOLUNTARY AND OFFICIAL ACTION.

A union of voluntary and official action is very desirable, if not indeed essential, in organising efforts for the assistance of discharged prisoners. If the arrangements are exclusively retained in the hands of the prison or police authorities, a certain amount of suspicion or reserve is liable to exist on both sides. Where, as in Great Britain especially, the co-operation of private individuals and philanthropists, or societies, has been encouraged by the Government, excellent results have been obtained. Much of· the recent diminution in certain classes of crime, in this country, is attributed, by competent observers, to this combination of effort. This is a material stimulus to unofficial charity.

There are in England more Discharged Prisoners' Aid Societies than prisons—and the Government distributes annually about £4,000 amongst these English Societies, on the condition than an amount equal to the sum granted, in each case, shall also be contributed by local private beneficence.

The Government practically doubles the amount allotted to a convict, on his discharge from prison, provided he consents to receive the whole sum in instalments, or in equivalent value, through the agency of a Discharged Prisoners' Aid Society. Thus if a convict has earned £3 whilst under detention, he is allowed £6 on discharge, if he consents that it shall be administered for his benefit by the local Discharged Prisoners' Aid Society.

It is of little use to prisoners leaving jail to let them have money to spend for themselves. In a large proportion of cases, they speedily squander it in drink and debauchery.

The BISHOP OF SHREWSBURY remarked (in 1893) that "There is no more important branch of the work of Discharged Prisoners' Aid Societies than undertaking the charge of convicts' gratuities after penal servitude. Of all persons they are the least fitted to be trusted with the money given to them on their discharge. When their gratuities are handed to a Society and laid out under the wise discretion of an experienced Agent, it contributes very largely to reclaim those men and to place them in a position which will prevent them from repeating their offence." The Bishop then mentioned a certain Discharged Prisoners' Aid Society in the Midlands which permits its discharged prisoners to have the spending of all their gratuities, and he added: "This Society, I may say without disrespect, is the worst Discharged Prisoners' Aid Society possible."

There is in England, generally, an exemplary union of the official and the non-official elements, in the management or distribution of the money available for the aid of discharged prisoners. In most cases, the governor and chaplain of the jail, with several of the neighbouring magistrates, clergy, and other benevolent individuals, constitute the working nucleus of any local society for this object. They usually, but not always, employ a special Agent to devote either a part or the whole of his time to visiting the discharged prisoners individually, and to endeavour to obtain lodgings and employment for them, and to disburse, on their account, in the purchase of tools, clothes, or in travelling expenses, the portion of money which has been allotted to them.

In an excellent Paper on Discharged Prisoners, contributed to the Prison Congress of Paris, in 1895, by Mr. E. J. RUGGLES-BRISE (Chairman of the English Prison Board) he suggests that all Visiting Justices might, with advantage, imitate the good example of those connected with WANDSWORTH Prison, near London, where the Visiting Committee, each week, after performing their duties as such, then form themselves into a Discharged Prisoners' Aid Committee for the coming week.

THE AGENTS.

The careful selection of Agents, where any such are employed, is a matter of great importance. Many of these officers are exemplary and earnest in the fulfilment of their duties. But, occasionally, complaints have been heard of collusion between them and the discharged prisoners, and of their mutually spending the money-grants in drink. Such abuses, however, appear to be exceptional. Nevertheless, some vigilance against these and similar practices is always necessary. Both paid and unpaid agency have, respectively, some particular advantages and disadvantages. Unpaid service is often the best and most genuinely effectual, but it also sometimes involves an undesirable irregularity and independence of action. On the other hand, a paid agent is more amenable to rules and order, and his responsibility can be more certainly and promptly enforced.

The Staffordshire Discharged Prisoners' Aid Society has employed two Agents, at a salary of £120 each, to give the whole of their time to the work. Other Societies pay their Agent a certain fee for each case successfully dealt with by him. In Dorsetshire, the county is divided into twelve districts, in each of which some benevolent person undertakes, gratuitously, to look after the interests of prisoners on discharge.

The Staffordshire Discharged Prisoners' Aid Society is a model one. The duties of its Agents are as follows :—

" To visit the local Prison weekly, or oftener, if ordered by the Hon. Secretary, to take his instructions as to dealing with cases selected for aid.

" To visit local employers of labour, taking every opportunity of seeing and becoming personally acquainted with foremen and other officials on works, explaining to them the objects of the Society, and endeavouring to secure their co-operation.

x

" To see the prisoners at the jail, and accompany them to the railway-station when needful, and to provide board and lodging for them, on discharge, for a limited period, until work is found.

" To visit constantly all persons under care of the Society so long as they are unemployed, and after employment is found.

" To enter daily, in a journal, all parties seen and places visited, such journal to be submitted to the Committee at the monthly meeting.

" To expend, under the direction of the Hon. Secretary, the gratuities of all ticket-of-leave men accepted by him, and to lose no opportunity of procuring them suitable employment.

" Cash payments must be entered up daily, and all vouchers submitted to the Committee at the monthly audit."

In every cell, of every prison, a printed notice is, or should be, placed, which informs the prisoner of the name and address of the nearest local Society for the Aid of Discharged Prisoners, and invites his having recourse to the good offices of such.

One of the chief desiderata of existing systems of aid to discharged prisoners consists in the need for more systematic communication between the agents, and for the exchange of information respecting applicants and cases removing from one district into another. Better arrangements in this direction will probably be introduced gradually.

Discharged prisoners are a peculiarly " feeble folk." The difficulties and temptations which beset them are powerful, whilst their own strength is very small. Hence, they specially require the kindly vigilance and wise help of the societies and individuals who devote themselves to this useful work. In some large towns in Great Britain there are philanthropic committees and agents who regularly visit the Police Courts, in order to become acquainted with offenders, and to render them assistance, whether convicted or not. In some instances these good persons have formed themselves into "Police Court and Prison-gate Missions," and by their systematic and kindly care of discharged prisoners, have constituted some of the most effectual of "Aid Societies."

TEMPORARY HOMES FOR DISCHARGED PRISONERS.

In a few places, as at Wakefield (formerly), Reading, Lewes, Northampton, Stafford and elsewhere, it has been found useful to establish temporary Homes for discharged prisoners, where they may obtain cheap lodgings, or a little work, whilst looking out for permanent occupation. But experiments in this direction require great care, and most of them appear to have resulted in failure. The one at Lewes consisted of two cottages, a work-room, and a large garden, and was supplied with a few beds, some books, cooking utensils, and a stock of tools for carpentry, shoe-making and gardening. The local prison Chaplain remarked of this little establishment: "Since the opening, many a man, destitute and ill-clad, on leaving prison, has earned for himself a decent suit of clothes and a few shillings to start with, and has expressed his rough gratitude for the assistance thus afforded him. Others about to emigrate, or proceeding to sea, have lodged there, awaiting, under friendly supervision, and removed from many temptations, the sailing of their ship, and being thereby tested as to their worthiness of this kind of provision."

Another Home, and one of the best of its kind, was instituted by the St. Giles Christian Mission in London, under the special care of that most devoted friend of prisoners, Mr. WILLIAM WHEATLEY. Its chief use has been to provide lodgings, and a few meals, together with oversight and advice, for discharged prisoners, during that peculiarly difficult and perilous period, the first fortnight or month after leaving jail. But to furnish their inmates with permanent labour is undesirable ; not only on account of the cost, but more especially because it is very objectionable to retain discharged prisoners together, even in small groups. They should, as soon as possible, be dispersed, and helped to scatter themselves over the industrial world. When supplied with work, even of a temporary kind, in the homes, they are too apt to relax their endeavours to obtain other and more satisfactory employment. But the chief danger arises from their association. Hence, some of such temporary homes have proved failures. The great fundamental principle, of the separation of offenders from each other, is again applicable here. And it also applies to the reclamation of Fallen Women. The employment of a motherly person to deal with these, one by one, and help them to find occupation, separately, has various advantages over the best attempts to classify these females in Refuges and Penitentiaries. A Birmingham philanthropist who adopted this individualising method with fallen women, was rewarded with an unusual measure of success in his Christian endeavours in his line.

Mrs. Susanna Meredith, of London, a lady of long and successful experience in the care of discharged female prisoners, said, at a meeting of that very useful Society, the "Reformatory and Refuge Union," (32, Charing Cross, London, S.W.) :—

" We have not at any time had a residential Institution. Women would be very much better not to be put in batches together in any kind of house, either Homes or Institutions of any description. They had better be treated in another manner. They naturally want some sort of a place that represents a home to them ; if they do not get it, they continue as bad as ever. They are naturally domesticated, and need a home to look after. We give them daily employment, but never keep them by night. When we know a woman to be anxious to keep the daily work, by coming regularly at proper hours, arriving at eight o'clock and keeping to the rules, we never, when she arrives in the morning, enquire where she spent the night. With the greatest earnestness, I say, I have left night work alone, because I thought I could not possibly do both; and we know by experience that it is best so; we do not reform them all at once; we must leave them alone till, by the grace of God, they become better. My experience is, that we have had at work every day, for more than twenty years, between seventy and eighty women. Indeed, the number varies, sometimes we have fifty, and sometimes over a hundred. We pay them every night, so that if they do not come the next day, there is no breach of contract between us. If they return at eight o'clock, prayer time, next morning, they get another day's work, and so on. The present condition of affairs is this : that we have some women who have been with us twelve years, six years, five years, and so on. All the Officers of the Institution have risen from the ranks."

The most effectual plan for the disposal of discharged prisoners has consisted in their being at once thus dealt with individually; and in their being facilitated in starting on their own separate courses of self-support, and, as much as practicable, at a distance from their former associates in evil, but under some friendly supervision. In fact, the principal help, and the chief need of a discharged prisoner consists not so much in pecuniary aid, as in finding a *friend* and a continuing sympathising adviser, or referee, for him, or her. Many Magistrates, Clergymen, and private persons, have rendered much kind assistance in this work, in many localities.

RESTORATIVE INFLUENCES OUTSIDE THE PRISON.

It is after his discharge from prison, that an offender can be best enabled to practise those social duties, and to exercise that self-control, which are essential for a healthy, moral life. These cannot, in general, be effectually developed in prisons, either in the solitude of the cell, or amid the concentrated villainry and temptations of the convict gang.

But after the discharge from jail, when the offender merges into the mixed good and evil association of free ife, where there is, at any rate, a considerable preponderance of decency, humanity, and honesty, then the needful conditions are available for the development of a wholesome reformation; especially if there be simultaneously afforded the guiding counsel and helping hand of wisely benevolent members of Patronage, or Aid Societies, or of sympathetic private individuals.

At this stage, the services of such bodies and of the Christian Church, are most timely and valuable. But they should combine firmness with kindness, and be so adjusted as to strengthen rather than enervate. They should encourage the repentant transgressor, but not with such unconditional or undue assistance, as reasonably to provoke the jealousy of the honest toiler, or to render the treatment of reclaimed criminals a source of envy and temptation to those around them.

It may be remembered that even the best Aid Societies do not deal with, or even reach, a considerable proportion of the persons discharged from prison. Some of the latter have friends who are well able to care for them. Others prefer to lean upon their own resources, or ability for self-help. And many, it is to be feared, are indifferent to any efforts to replace them in the paths of rectitude. These may be termed "the residuum"—those who will not work, and who prefer dishonesty and crime. The writer once asked the most successful of all helpers of English discharged prisoners, how he and his colleagues acted in reference to this latter class. The reply was: "We drop them, as we would a hot potato." This is certainly a very simple process, and one which relieves such helpers of any further trouble in the matter. Yet, it may be added, that just in proportion as an Aid Society, or other similar organisation, has to "drop" the subjects most in need of · reforming influences, in so far it fails in its own functions. An active worker in this field of charity, the Rev. C. Goldney, Chaplain of Stafford jail, has well remarked: "It is not the business of a Prisoners' Aid Society to shrink from an attempt to do good, because it is difficult. If you deliberately refuse to help a man on this ground, it is as good as to tell him to go again and steal; which seems a sad thing to do."

· Hitherto, to a considerable extent, Discharged Prisoners' Aid Societies have failed with this "residuum," the invete-rate·or habitual class of criminals. Such offenders must rather be dealt with by means of gradually, but certainly cumulative sentences, and by subsequent police super-vision. It is, however, to be noted that this failure with such subjects, points to the special importance of all efforts to secure the reclamation of those delinquents who have only undergone a single imprisonment. For, in the first stage of crime, many such persons may be effectually reformed, who, if they are left unaided, will ultimately swell the ranks of the more intractable residuum.

OBJECTIONS RAISED.

The various efforts so diligently put forth of late years, in Great Britain, for the aid of discharged prisoners, have materially contributed to reduce the number of criminals. But, like most other forms of beneficence, this good work is sometimes—and indeed often—made a subject of censure by ignorant persons, who raise the objection that when all the needs of honest poor men are provided for, then it will be the proper time to help the rogues, but not before.

Now, in the first place, it may be noticed that the people who raise these objections are generally such as never bestir themselves to help others, whether honest men or offenders ; and, secondly, discharged prisoners are a class who absolutely require aid, on grounds both of mercy to themselves and of the self-interest of the community. For if a criminal is not effectually rescued from his evil ways, and if he is not enabled to earn an honest livelihood, he will certainly return to his former courses. And few things are more costly to a nation than crime. Criminals, if unreformed, will soon involve the taxpayers in a disagreeable compulsory expenditure—often of hundreds of pounds—for each offender's detection, re-arrest, and punishment. Also the depredations and losses occasioned by a single thief, or burglar, are often enormous. And so many hundred thousand pounds are annually required for Prisons and Police, that the reformation of a prisoner, or the prevention of a crime, is one of the *cheapest* developments of social wisdom, and one of the most genuine operations of political *economy*.

And not the less is it a work of mercy. For a large proportion of criminals are more to be pitied than blamed, when all their antecedents of hereditary frailty, parental neglect, ignorance, poverty, and privation, are fairly weighed and examined. The Son of God declared that He "came not to call the righteous, but sinners, to repentance," and that "there is joy in heaven over one sinner that repenteth, more than over ninety and nine just persons that need no repentance." His parables, also, of the Lost Sheep, the Lost Piece of Silver, and the Prodigal Son, are fraught with permanent instruction to individuals and communities, in regard to this subject. A Continental penologist has even propounded the motto : "To know all, will lead to the pardon of all." (" *Tout connaître, c'est tout pardonner.*")

In proportion as, in the interests of the public, the plan is adopted of requiring that the antecedents of discharged habitual prisoners shall be made known to their employers, either by themselves or by some other persons, the difficulty of their procuring some kind of occupation may be thereby materially augmented. And hence the systematic carrying out of this practice involves, in common justice, an additional obligation, on the part of the authorities and of the benevolent, to make efforts to secure employment for such persons. Their lot is, at the best, a most arduous and discouraging one; and when their difficulties are further increased—though rightly so—by stripping off the protection of concealment from them, it is but fair to make them some compensation, by providing effectual assistance in other ways. Indeed it becomes the bounden duty of Governments and communities to do so.

CHAPTER XV.

PAUPERISM, SUGGESTIONS FOR ITS PREVENTION.

THE DIVINE METHOD.

IT is recorded in the Gospels that the LORD JESUS CHRIST chiefly aided the poor, in regard at least to their outward condition, by enabling them the better to help themselves, and by removing obstacles to healthy exertion. Thus He cured the paralytic, enabled the lame to walk, and rendered the withered hand capable of work. St. Peter, also strengthened the impotent man by curing him; whilst St. Paul urged that, "If any will not work neither shall he eat." Modern legislation and philanthropy cannot improve upon such principles of the highest sanction. And so far as they have been practically adopted, they have been successful.

A LABOUR OR THRIFT TEST ESSENTIAL FOR STATE RELIEF.

The wise framers of the English POOR LAW ACT of 1834 laid down the permanently efficacious rule, from which any departure must be hazardous, that the lot of the State-supported Pauper cannot be safely rendered superior to that of the ordinary self-supporting labourer; otherwise industry will be discouraged. They also practically recognised that "out-door relief" tends to injure the poor, as a class, by *lowering wages.* For, of course, if persons receive some small allowance from the parish, they can afford to work for a lower rate of pay than those who have to depend entirely on their own earnings. Hence an easy or general grant of out-door relief has always proved a cruelty to the poor themselves, as a class. But the Aged, the Sick, the Imbecile, and Children require special consideration. This has been effected, in the London district, by the provisions of the "Gathorne Hardy" Act of 1867; and these, in conjunction with the steady restriction of out-door relief, have already secured a very large diminution in the number of paupers. Loud popular outcries are, however, raised, from time to time, in favour of a return, in one form or another, to more general out-door relief.

It is too often assumed that persons who ask for work, will take it. But this is frequently a great mistake. Some years ago, in a season of distress, a multitude of men, at Birmingham, demanded work or relief. They were promptly and wisely taken at their word; and were informed that at the local "Test House," work would be provided for *all* applicants, by the local authorities. The result was that *not half-a-dozen*, out of the whole number accepted the offer.

Again, at a large town in the north of England, during special depression in the iron trade, many persons were out of employ, and much real poverty ensued. But exaggerated demands for gratuitous help were also raised. Large processions of claimants paraded the streets. The Guardians were almost besieged. They invoked Government advice. It was given, and consisted in this:—"*None must starve. But apply the Workhouse test.*" This was done, and with good result. The number of applicants for assistance shrunk almost to nothing. For very few of them chose to enter the Workhouse, although certain of receiving free board and lodging there.

Those who are willing to accept a real Labour Test will be always found to be a comparatively small number. For, as DR. CHALMERS remarked: "Pauperism is a bugbear which looks a gigantic hydra, when seen in the bulk, or from a distance; but vanishes into nothing when *dealt with at close quarters,* or piecemeal, and in small separate sections." So long as an efficient Labour Test is enforced, *Pauperism* (as distinct from Poverty) is never likely to assume giant proportions. But if that sound principle be abandoned, it will grow prodigiously and dangerously.

Nor must the Labour Test, of whatever kind, whether agricultural or manufacturing, be rendered more attractive, or easy, than the lot of the worker who is *not* aided by the State. This is the cause of the comparative failure of the BEGGAR FARMS of HOLLAND and BELGIUM. The inmates are made so comfortable that they return many times in succession to them, and actually *commit offences, in order* to be sent or remitted thither.

THE LANCASHIRE RELIEF PLAN.

For times of special distress and wide-spread temporary pauperism, the admirable administration of the Lancashire Distress Fund, by SIR ROBERT RAWLINSON, and others, in the Cotton Famine, during the American Civil War of 1861-5, remains a model for the relief of all similar privation on an extensive scale, inasmuch as it presented the spectacle of large private charity, acting through a central and judicious organisation, and dispensing *assistance without pauperisation.* The secret of this result consisted largely in the persistent requirement of some kind of labour, or effort, in return for every disbursement of aid. The same principle has been acted upon in some of the American cities, especially Chicago, with like satisfactory result. A portion of recent relief to the distressed in East London has taken the same judicious form; but in some parishes where it has been neglected, poverty has been increased and rents have risen, by the rush of mendicants from various quarters. Bounty, if unconditional, often becomes mischievous; and charity, to be real, must aid rather than lessen habits of self-assistance. Where pauperisation ensues, charity has failed; for it is too often true that "once a pauper, always a pauper." It has been observed that poverty and wretchedness peculiarly abound in places where large endowed charities, for promiscuous distribution, have been established. The Lancashire distress was judiciously turned to account by the promotion of habits of economy and sobriety, which had previously been glaringly neglected. Where a large proportion of wages is regularly spent in drink, poverty and demoralisation are certain to ensue.

Results of Experience.

The English counties which give *least* out-door relief, and impose the "house test" most strictly, have the least pauperism; whilst the counties giving *most* out-relief have the greatest pauperism. Mr. Francis Peek, Chairman of the Executive Committee of the Howard Association, has stated that "in one parish he found 1,339 persons on the poor-rates, costing the ratepayers 8s. 7d. in the pound, while in a neighbouring parish, with a population almost equal, there were only 150 paupers, and a poor-rate of 2s. 3d." The paupers in Yorkshire, Shropshire, Lancashire, Cheshire, Northumberland, Durham, and Middlesex, are much fewer than the number in such counties as Norfolk and Dorset, where out-relief is readily given. In Norfolk the proportion of pauperism is specially high, from this cause.

The Rev. Brooke Lambert, many years Vicar of Greenwich, and a Guardian of the Poor writes: "If it was better for the poor to have out-door relief, I would not allow the question of the rates to stand in the way. But I affirm, and I affirm it on the experience of some thirty years' work, that out-door relief does *not* benefit the poor as a class. It dries up the stream of family effort; it breaks down the self-reliance of the poor in the most insidious way; it *creates* pauperism."

Mr. T. L. MURRAY BROWNE (H.M. Inspector of Poor for N. Wales), wisely reported to the Local Government Board :—"Out-door relief may, or may not, be defensible ; but at any rate it is clear that the rate of pauperism over 60 years of age depends mainly, not on the *condition* of the poorer classes, but on the administration of relief ; in other words upon the comparative ease, or otherwise, with which out-door relief can be obtained. It would be perfectly easy to make the pauperism of Hawarden Union, within a year, as great as that of Holywell. [Holywell gave 50 per cent. more out-relief than Hawarden ; and, *consequently,* had more than double the proportion of paupers than the former.] Very few people will refuse a little pension, if it can be had for the asking."

A GOOD PRINCIPLE CARRIED TO AN EXTREME.

But a good principle may be carried to an extreme. The restriction of out-door relief is a wise measure, which has greatly tended to develop not only self-help among the poor, but also the exercise of filial duty and of natural affections. Many sons who would otherwise gladly place their aged parents upon the shoulders of the ratepayers, now support them. At the same time the refusal of out-relief in England is sometimes carried too far, and may even result in cruelty and in a positive discouragement to thrift. For it has been the weakest part of the English Poor Law that it has offered to the poor man scarcely any inducement to save. He has been virtually told that the only qualification for the receipt of assistance is *complete* destitution. Hence many have felt or said, "I can never save enough to secure an adequate provision for old age, so I may as well spend all I get. The parish will support me and my family, if I have nothing at all." Now, if wise means can be devised to reward a man for saving the little that may be possible to him, by *supplementing* it, this would be a very needful improvement. The Bible rule is, " To him that *hath*, shall be given." The Poor Law rule is *the reverse* of this, or " To him that hath *not* shall be given." Hence the poor have been virtually rewarded for *not* saving, instead of for saving. And, in consequence, the most reckless and drunken classes have been more willing to accept the "House Test" than the more respectable poor. The former are *too* kindly treated, even in English poor-houses.

But the poor must be properly looked after. And the more the "indoor test" is adopted, the more imperative is the necessity for also adopting a system of Unpaid Visiting Guardians (as in GERMANY (Elberfeld, etc.) and BELGIUM), to aid or take the place of the "Relieving Officers." These Visiting Guardians should be selected chiefly from amongst the men of competence, leisure, and education, in their respective localities. Their acceptance of office should be compulsory (with due exceptions), but, in return, the great value of their services should be acknowledged by some special honours and exemptions. They should be exempted from serving on Juries, and from certain Rates or Taxes; or they should have some other material privileges. Their duties should be the regular visitation and relief of a very few cases of destitution, say from three to six, according to the size of each local subdivision. In many cases these Guardians would voluntarily supplement public charity, with their own private aid, but judiciously and *intelligently*. They would also guard the public against the costly and myriad instances of lying vagrancy and imposture. They would obviate cases of starvation, now sometimes arising from overlooked and unknown suffering. And in various other ways their appointment would be a public advantage

Women Visitors of Poor.

In France the Bureau of Beneficence avails itself of the valuable services of religious women, "Sisters," for the visitation of the poor; and in London, some of the best results have been experienced through the similarly valuable services of the "Sisters" of the "Wesleyan West End Mission." All such lady visitors, however, work to most advantage when placed under the guidance or council of a Committee of men and women.

Edward Denison, M.P., on Pauperism and Vagrancy.

One of the wisest and most practical students of modern Pauperism was Mr. Edward Denison, M.P., who, desiring to understand the condition of the poor in cities, resided for about eight months, during winter, in the slums of East London. [See *Letters of Edward Denison, M.P.*, by Sir Baldwyn Leighton, Bart., London, Bentley.]

Mr. Denison cordially recognised the great value of the services rendered by the Guardians and other Poor Law Administrators, but he deeply regretted their too frequent rush through their business and their too general absence of deliberation and of local distribution of their Board Sittings. He records—"How many thousands of paupers have lived and died and been buried at the public expense, whom a little friendly advice, a little search for friends or relations, some pains taken to find proper work, when the first application to the Board was made, would have lifted out of the mire and set on the rock of honest industry."

Mr. Denison did *not* consider that the Poor Law Act of 1834 had broken down, but that its provisions and intentions were not adequately carried out. The "Gathorne Hardy Act" of 1867, for which he had laboured, was a great step forward in the promotion of discrimination. As to the large class of beggars and vagrants, Mr. Denison said, "There are homeless poor; there are criminal vagrants. The former must be assisted, the latter punished, and, if possible, reformed." He proposed that the Law should first take every pauper applicant, or beggar, *at his own word*, and detain him, with food and lodging, at the workhouse, long enough to investigate his story (a week or two, if needful), and then treat each case accordingly, with assistance for the deserving and certain punishment for the wilfully lazy. It would be important that the vagrant of the latter class should not have very short terms of imprisonment, but at least several months' hard labour. Thus the existing system needs to be made, as Mr. Denison urged, "at once more merciful and more severe."

In his East End lodgings, Mr. Denison saw much of the mischief of INDISCRIMINATE ALMSGIVING. He wrote: "The real truth is that sensation-writing and reckless alms are fast doing away with the great work of bringing up the people to providence and self-restraint. You will find all the men who really give themselves most trouble about the poor, are the most alive to the terrible evils of the so-called 'charity,' which pours money into the haunts of misery and vice every winter. If we could but get one honest newspaper to write down promiscuous 'charity,' something might be done. Things are so bad down here; and giving away money only makes them worse. By giving alms, you keep them permanently crooked. Build School-houses, pay Teachers, give Prizes, *help them to help themselves*, lend them your brains; but *give them no money*, except what you sink in such undertakings as the above."

Mr. Denison insisted on the necessity of *testing* all applicants for public relief. He wrote from the East End: "Once embarked on the system of giving outdoor relief, without the application either of a workhouse, or a labour test, there is naturally no end to it. Otherwise you take the lock off the door and have no means of

Y

discriminating applicants.   Organise a sufficiently elastic
LABOUR TEST, without which no outdoor relief to be
given."

Mr. Denison says very little about TEMPERANCE, which
is a main counteractive to Pauperism. It is perhaps the
most noteworthy omission in his recommendations.

He regarded the arrest and prevention of CHILD
PAUPERISM as a most important necessity, and considered
that no sentimental outcries about " parental rights " should
be permitted to injure the real rights of the poor children
of parents who deliberately neglected or ill-used them, or
who were habitually bringing them to the workhouse.   For
such young persons he advised training in separate schools,
or boarding them out, in carefully supervised homes.   So
long as the burden of maintaining the children is thrown
on the ratepayers, the latter should exercise their own
judgment as to the best way of dealing with such a task.

Mr. Denison advocated the German and Swiss plan of
" CONTINUATION SCHOOLS " for technical and other training.
He said, " We may build the most commodious school-houses,
we may train and pay the ablest and most zealous schoolmasters, and all will be in vain, unless the school period of
child-life is extended and regular attendance during that
period secured."   He pointed out that on the Continent
many parents get no profit out of their children until they
are twelve or more years old ; and he adds : " But isn't it
worth while ?   There are no Swiss paupers ; no poor rates ;
a Swiss can elbow his way all over the world and be sure
of always falling on his feet."   It may here be noted, that
during the last decade of the Nineteenth Century, the
Legislature has introduced "Continuation Schools" into
England.

Mr. Denison (unlike many framers of popular systems)
based all hope for social and individual advancement on
"the love of GOD MANIFEST IN THE FLESH " and on its
resulting love of His human and animal creation.   But

he deeply deplored the unscriptural separation between Religion and Morality, and the too prevalent substitution of abstract dogma, or mere ceremonial observances, for practical duty. He recorded his conviction that, in regard to theological beliefs, "the *only* valid test and proof of the soundness of those conceptions, the only test prescribed by Scripture, the only proof that will be admitted by the Judge at the Last Day, is the effect which those conceptions of God have produced by their dealings with *man.*"

SOCIALISM AND POVERTY.

Of late years, the questions of Pauperism and Poverty have been vigorously discussed by Socialists, "Fabians," and others. There is a reasonable, and there is also a foolish and tyrannical, Socialism. In so far as it is shown that the poor have been actually crushed and wronged by aristocracies or capitalists, the Socialist has a fair ground of complaint. But it is unjust to denounce wildly the rights of property acquired by honest industry and thrift, and to denounce such in the same terms as might be used against large tracts of land given, in former generations, to Court favourites, or to the illegitimate offspring of licentious monarchs.

To tax the propertied classes moderately for the education and health of the poor, and for Libraries, Parks, etc., is fair; but a tendency is being unduly developed, in the English-speaking lands, to carry such taxation to an extent cruel to the lower middle class and to industrious workers generally, by the practice of impecunious voters using legalised means to rob the pockets of the average taxpayer for indulgences and privileges which should be paid for by those who claim them. And even in connection with the intrinsically good work of civic Sanitation, costly and tyrannical interferences with the rights of individuals have been authorised by the

Legislature.   Such extremes are dishonest.   All honest
Socialism will recognise the rights both of Capital and
Labour, and their mutual necessary service to each other.
Not to do this, is to approximate the position of the criminal
Anarchist, or " Communist."

Holland and the Poor.

Few countries have surpassed, or indeed equalled, Holland
in wise methods of checking Pauperism.

A specially noteworthy feature of Dutch dealings with
pauperism consists in the prominent position taken by,
and indeed, legally imposed upon, THE CHURCHES in the
administration of help to the poor.   The Protestant, Roman
Catholic, and Jewish denominations, through their respective officers, discharge this duty with a discriminating
regard to the claims of personal character, and with an
amount of sympathy and privacy which can never be
expected from exclusively secular agents.   But the right
appropriation of the endowments and current contributions,
furnished to these Churches for this object, is promoted by
the action of the State in exacting, under penalty for non-
compliance, accurate reports of the amounts and distribution of all such disposable funds.   Thus waste and over-
lapping of aid are materially checked.

In regard to the large number of cases and localities
where the charity of the Churches is insufficient, or inapplicable, the civil authorities afford relief to the destitute
through the direct instrumentality of THE POLICE.   There
are not " Union Houses" for the poor, as in England, and
consequently no " House Test."   Neither is there now any
" Law of Settlement " for paupers in Holland.

The general principle kept in view in the extension of
assistance to the poor, both by the Churches and by the
police, is to furnish *a staff and not a crutch*, or, in other
words, to give as little as possible of continuous support,
and, while obviating absolute starvation, to allow the

needy to be still surrounded by strong but wholesome inducements to personal exertion. Most of the Dutch relief may be characterised by the Scriptural expression— "*Here· a little, and there a little.*" It is a series of gentle pushings and pullings, studiously designed to tide over temporary necessities only; though, of course, the absolutely helpless, such as the blind and the very aged, have to be maintained in hospitals, almshouses, or other refuges. The destitute are in general aided by a variety of gifts in kind, rather than in money, such as grants of food for so many weeks, supplies of clothing or fuel, provision of free medical attendance, or the rent of a small allotment for cultivation, or the payment of the burial expenses in the case of the decease of some member of an indigent family. In these and similar ways, applicants for relief are just kept going, but not much more, so far as material aid is concerned.

The Dutch also devote considerable practical regard to that very efficacious form of assistance which the eminent French philanthropist, M. FREDERICK OZANAM, designated "*l'aumône de la direction,*" or *the alms of wise counsel and personal influence.* By means of the Church committees, or of the police, much useful information and aid are afforded to many who apply for employment, and in other instances, by means of judicious advice and encouragement, the destitute are induced to turn over a new leaf in regard to some of those habits or actions which may have chiefly brought them into trouble. And where such efforts are insufficient without collateral assistance, there are provided, in various parts of the country, *bonâ fide* Workhouses, where money may be obtained by the performance of certain labour tasks, and in no other way. Of course, it is essential that the wages offered shall be lower than the average local rates of payment. Otherwise injustice would be done to independent workers, and further, the object in view would be defeated by an influx of more applicants than employment could be found for. But by careful sifting of the candidates, and by a judicious administration of discipline, many persons are thus provided, for longer or shorter periods, with occupation without pauperising them. For instance, the Author observed in a workhouse in Amsterdam scores of men and women, who did not reside on the premises, earning from 4s. to 12s. a week each, by weaving, or other labour.

The necessary element of non-attractiveness is secured in Dutch help to the poor, not only by associating the police with Church functionaries as relieving officers, but also by a general *penal policy towards Mendicants and Vagrants*, who are committed for periods of not less than one year to the "beggar colonies," in East Holland. But inasmuch as even there the treatment is found to be insufficiently deterrent, in many instances the committal of this class to cellular prisons is being increasingly resorted to, and with good effect.

In connection with certain aspects of the great principle that in regard to pauperism, as to other evils, *prevention is better* than cure, the Dutch encourage thrifty and provident habits, by their numerous INSURANCE OFFICES and SAVINGS BANKS, also by their increasing attention to POPULAR EDUCATION and to the TECHNICAL TRAINING of children, either while at school or afterwards. But they are behind the English people in a practical disregard of the preventive efficacy of definite RELIGIOUS INSTRUCTION, and in their comparative indifference to the discouragement of INTEMPERANCE—*that especial root and feeder both of pauperism and crime.* And herein they are holding back their country from progress and happiness that could be otherwise attained.

DUTCH GUILD LIFE.—THE "COMMON LOT."

It may be remarked that for the struggling, the poor, and the weak, of all lands, a great practical lesson was afforded

by a Dutch fraternity, the "Brethren of the Common Lot,"
or the "Common Life," who had their chief development
500 years ago, in East Holland; and of whom Thomas à
Kempis was an eminent leader.   These good men lived
secure from all fear of pauperism and of neglect in illness or old age.   For they constituted a noble co-operative society.   They were "Socialists" of a justifiable type
—being all voluntary workers to the best of their power,
and bound to support one another, only after the ability
for work was past. ,They differed from the Monks of the
same period, inasmuch as the latter were only partially
self-reliant; while the Friars were wholly supported by
the labour of others..   The "Brethren of the Common Lot"
earned a comfortable and absolutely independent livelihood
for themselves, and also maintained their superannuated
members by their industry, chiefly as copyists and schoolmasters.   They were the principal producers of Bibles and
good books, in the century previous to the invention of
Printing.   *Why should not similar guilds, entirely self-supporting and not necessarily celibate, be more often instituted in our
own day?*   The Belgian institution of Beguines is in some
respects an interesting surviving example of such associated
life.   English Trade Unions, by their useful charity and
co-operative spirit, also furnish some modern exemplifica-
tions of the same principle.   But that thorough co-operation
of the "Brethren of the Common Lot," with their combination of shrewd practical economy, with the powerful
aids of a genial and hopeful Christianity, was one of the
most valuable contributions yet furnished by the Dutch
to the social experiences of the world.

Pauper Farms—Sweden and Norway.

In Sweden and Norway some of the Paupers, both adult
and juvenile, are boarded out amongst farmers and cottagers, who are paid a certain sum for their maintenance;
others are placed in small groups on farms specially de-

voted to cultivation by this class. It is considered that, on the whole, these two methods are about as successful as the modes adopted in other European lands.

OLD AGE PENSIONS.

With the laudable purpose of encouraging the habit of saving, many schemes have recently been propounded for encouraging the thrifty poor, by means of State-aided pensions in old age. In some countries, as GERMANY and DENMARK, legislative action has already been taken in this direction; and such pensions are now in operation there, though not, as it would appear, with such decided advantage as was at first hoped for. All such schemes are beset with grave difficulties; but the problem need not be necessarily insoluble. Perhaps the best proposal, yet made, for Great Britain, is the suggestion that the poor should be encouraged to contribute voluntarily a sum, amounting to *about a penny a day*, towards a pension to commence at the age of 65, which pension the State might *supplement* to some reasonable amount. In case of the death of the pension-purchaser before attaining 65 years, all his own savings, for this object, to be returned to his family, or representatives. Further, in the event of his being obliged to suspend regular payment of the penny a day, or its equivalent yearly sum, he might be allowed a period of five years to replace such lapsed payments. The latter is a very important provision. For it is well known that at present the often unavoidable failure of poor persons to pay their insurance, or club-money, involves the loss of much meritorious saving in the past.

Any State-aided Pension scheme will, however, require great care to prevent it from becoming a source of pauperisation, or a means of undue rivalry or discouragement to some of the excellent FRIENDLY SOCIETIES and TRADES UNIONS, which already facilitate thrift and providence on a large and praiseworthy scale.

All ostentatiously advertised schemes of assistance tend to create the class they profess to diminish. There is hardly anything which requires so much discretion as the exercise of a charity that shall do more good than harm. Hence the Bible declares, " Blessed is he that *considereth* the poor." Some popular schemes promote reckless haste, like that of Professor Huxley's Belfast car-driver, who, on being asked, " Do you know where you have to go"? replied, " No, sir, but anyhow, I'm going fast."

There is something to be said against State-contributed Old Age Pensions, as well as in favour of them. In 1894 an influential Scotch committee, after a careful investigation of the matter, decided against any such system. Their report said : " With pauper-pensions by the State, there would· be no control, or supervision, as at present exists under the Poor Laws. The idle, the dissolute, drunken and depraved, if entitled to a pension, would drink or dispose of it, as soon as received, *and be as destitute as ever;* they could move about as they thought fit, and defy all authority; there would be almost a licensed system of begging to all who cared to go on the tramp. Without doubt, tramps would be more plentiful, and the public more annoyed than at present."

This document (Begg, Kennedy & Harper, Printers, Glasgow), by shrewd and practical Scotch specialists, merits a careful consideration. .

The Agricultural Labourer Problem.

Small allotments of land to the cottager, at moderate rentals, are of great value. Even if only enough to grow vegetables for home use, and to enable a pig and some poultry to be kept, they are an important boon to the poor. Such plots are often more serviceable than larger ones would be.

· As long ago as 1840, a remarkable illustration of this

was furnished by the Rev. THOMAS SPENCER, rector· of
HINTON · CHARTERHOUSE, near Bath. When he came to
the parish, there was no school, no library, much misery,
and drunkenness; with poor rates amounting to nearly
£1,000 a year. He introduced the Allotment System;
divided some fields amongst eighty labourers, at the ordinary farm rate of rent; signed the Total Abstinence
pledge himself, and then induced many of his parishioners
to do the same; instituted a Library and a Clothing Club;
and by these means succeeded, in a few years, in reducing
the poor rates more than 75 per cent., and in effecting a
beneficent revolution in his parish.

FRANCE has, happily for herself, set the nations an excellent example, in the distribution and division of the land
amongst the population generally.

A LABOUR BUREAU FOR EVERY DISTRICT.

Multitudes of poor persons seeking employment would
be much helped by the establishment everywhere of a
registry of vacant situations and of likely employers.
Some local and private experiments of this kind have
been made, as at Egham and Ipswich, with a certain
measure of success.

GOVERNMENT PAWN-OFFICES, WITH A LOW RATE OF INTEREST.

In various places on the Continent, the poor are greatly
assisted .by the establishment, by Government, of Pawn-
Offices (MONTS DE PIÉTÉ), where money is lent, on the
security of goods deposited, at a low rate of interest. This
is another desideratum for Great Britain.

ABOLISH MARKET MONOPOLIES.

In some places the poor suffer great disadvantages in
consequence of market monopolies. No such feudal-like

exclusive rights should be now permitted. They should promptly be abolished, and absolute Free Trade in local food substituted.

Enforced Public Audit of all Investment Companies and Societies.

Considering the misery and discouragement to thrift occasioned by the dishonesty of many Investment Companies and Societies which have invited and received the savings of the poor and of others, it has become imperative that every such body shall be obliged to submit every year to an independent Government audit, with a detailed annual publication of receipts, expenditure, and investments, and giving the names of all parties responsible for the same.

Some so-called " insurance " Companies have derived a large portion of their profits from the "*lapsed policies*" of poor people. This, also, ought to be checked in some way. And further, the Governments should facilitate the appointment of responsible State Trustees, and Executors, who should, for moderate fees, be rendered available for the service of private individuals and families.

Juvenile Pauperism.

This is best dealt with by Boarding-out, by small grouped Cottage Homes (in lieu of Union Houses) and by enforcing Parental Responsibility.

[*Vide* next Chapter, on " Child-Saving."]

Ministerial and Lay Relief.

Two very shrewd Scotch ministers, Dr. Chalmers and Dr. Guthrie, strongly enforced the principle that, in view of the almost inevitable temptations to hypocrisy and imposture, "the person who ministers in spiritual things should not be the one who deals out temporal charity to the poor." Lay agency, in this matter, they held to be far superior.

Even the Apostles delegated to Deacons the charities of the primitive Church.

Clergymen and Ministers are not usually persons of business habits, or capacities. They are peculiarly apt to take extreme views, to be either too "hard," or too "soft," and to entertain narrow prejudices.

Technical and Agricultural Education.—Denmark.

The industrial training of the children of the poor is a great means, in many cases, of preventing their becoming paupers. And in various ways it promotes their happiness and prosperity. Much has been done in many countries, of late years, in the extension of Technical Education, especially in Germany, France, Great Britain, Belgium, etc.

But the industrial education of the *agricultural* poor has not, in general, had sufficient attention directed to it; except, perhaps, in Denmark. Mr. J. S. Thornton, who has studied Danish institutions, states, that a work like that of the English University studies-extension, has for fifty years been carried on in Denmark with conspicuous success. For six months in winter, the ploughmen, the hedgers and ditchers, and labourers of all kinds, go to winter schools— as it were to a rustic University—and receive the best teaching. There are some scores of such schools in that small country, and many special Agricultural Schools. The aim of these Danish people is not to attain a different social position, but to do their ordinary duties with a higher motive and more thorough efficiency. There are, too, nearly thirty High-school Homes in Denmark, at which old fellow-pupils may meet each other, in after life, at holiday times. They are like hotels, and the tariffs are suited to the scantiest purses. A visitor's bill for five days was only 9s. 6d.

In France, the State makes grants in aid of establishments where the pupils are taught the cultivation of fruit and the best methods of preserving it.

OVERCROWDED DWELLINGS AND PAUPERISM.

There can be no doubt but that both Pauperism and Vice have been materially increased, in many large cities, by the overcrowded dwellings of the poor, a matter intimately connected with the laws affecting land and buildings. The subject is confessedly most difficult; but, considering its extreme importance, it should have more attention than it has had hitherto from Governments and Parliaments. It is one of the greatest of national interests. The evils involved demand that mere local and vested private "rights" shall be, wherever necessary, resolutely over-ruled. Ædiles are wanted, public officers armed with effectual powers to prevent the erection, or continuance, of all dwellings unfit for human habitation.

Such officers, as District "Surveyors," are now, to some extent, fulfilling the functions of ædiles in England. But it is also of importance to impose some checks, or oversight, upon these, so as to secure the public from possible abuses of their power, in order to extort bribes. Such abuses are not altogether unknown in connection with the office of district "surveyor."

The ancient Roman populace, on the occasion of the threatened violation of the purity of one young woman, rose *en masse*, and exclaimed with united voices, "Tribunes! we will have Tribunes." Incomparably greater is the need for ÆDILES in many modern cities. For the purity not of one, but of myriads, of women is being stained, or destroyed, by the extent of overcrowding. Lives also in thousands, both of young and old, are being sacrificed. And the bodies of those who continue innocent and virtuous are, in multitudes, ruined for life by the insufficient ventilation, the overcrowding, the defective drainage, the thin, damp walls, the leaky roofs, of the many "scamped" and "jerry"-built tenements (*not* homes) of the population of great cities. Innumerable young persons have been permanently ruined, in London alone, by rheumatic fevers, consumptions, etc., caused by horrible "run-up" buildings, and small and nasty ill-ventilated dwellings, with their mortar of half-baked clay, their raw, shrinking timber, gaping joiner's-work, foul chimneys, unsound roofs, damp basement-rooms, and inefficient drains.

The most bestial vices are being occasioned by this overcrowding, both in town and country. Thus the newspapers have reported such cases as the following:—A young woman having had three children by her own father and brother; another girl with several illegitimate children by her brother: a young woman having had four children by her own father. How can such horrible vice be unknown, under the conditions of life in many European and American cities?

Industrial Councils and Arbitrations.

Inasmuch as Strikes and Lock-outs have been, of late years, prominent causes of Pauperism, by throwing multitudes out of employ, both temporarily and permanently, and inasmuch also as both the workers and the masters have usually had some warrant for their respective action, it seems eminently desirable that there should be established, on a far more general scale than heretofore, standing Councils of Employers and Employed, for periodic consultation, and for Arbitration of disputes when practicable, so as to diminish these terribly disastrous strikes as much as possible. It is instructive to note that in Belgium, where Councils of this nature have been regularly established, strikes appear to have become less frequent.

Present Salvation.

Salvation has by many well-meaning religionists been made too exclusively a matter for the future. Whereas, in its reality, it begins now and is intimately connected with the physical conditions of this life. Christ devoted great attention to *bodily* helps. And the Psalmist instructively remarks, "That Thy way may be known *upon earth*, Thy *saving health* among all nations." (Psalm lxvii. 2.)

A London newspaper has remarked: "Our good people of the Churches are, too generally, all up aloft in the '*ations*.' They preach and talk about predestination, transubstantiation, justification, supererogation, and all the other '*ations*.' It would be a more *practical* work to preach sermons urging the duties of treating horses mercifully, and selling vegetables and fish honestly. With some noble exceptions, preachers comparatively seldom descend to the real sins and virtues of daily life and its citizenship." Yet it is truly a *work of God* to promote healthy dwellings, and to diminish vice-fraught overcrowding and pestilent diseases. Such physical civic improvement is a genuine ministry of sanctification and justification; that is, by tending to make men more holy and more righteous. More of the true GOSPEL is needed—the Gospel of the good tidings of *practical* every-day salvation from the evils of the *present* life, as a material preparation for the right reception of the faith and hope of a better life hereafter. The boundless grace and paternal goodness of God, in Christ, and the requirements of His crystalline holiness, alike call upon the CHURCHES, and on their individual members, for more practical exertions to serve Him by removing this great evil and stumbling-block from His people. For how can persons, crowded in fœtid dens and styes, be rightly prepared for the pure citizenship of Heaven?

However, progress is, happily, being made, in this matter also, on both sides of the Atlantic.

VAGRANCY.

In 1882, the Committee of the HOWARD ASSOCIATION instituted a careful inquiry into the extent and means of diminishing Vagrancy and Mendicancy. They collected the opinions and experiences of practical men in various parts of the kingdom, and then published them, with the addition of some general remarks and recommendations. In particular, they advised as follows :—" Every applicant for Poor Law relief, whether Vagrant or otherwise, should be absolutely certain of immediate compliance, and then of immediate investigation, by Parish Officers, or Magistrates, for legal decision and punishment if deserved. The needful powers and facilities for this investigation should be secured to the Local Authorities, by law and executive arrangements. Every recipient of relief should be afforded the opportunity of proving his honesty and industry. On producing such proof, or vouchers, he should be promptly speeded on his way in search of occupation elsewhere, or aided by any means available for affording employment in his present position. But if inquiry proves that he is a lazy and culpable vagrant, deliberately willing to prey upon society, he should be effectually checked in his purpose, either by a term of cellular imprisonment, or of detention in a workhouse.

"The public should be made to feel that every destitute person, without exception, is quite certain of obtaining, on application, prompt assistance adapted to his needs— benevolently adapted, if honest, and correctively and deterrently adapted, if the reverse. Then, and then only, will the public conscience be thoroughly at ease, in the steady refusal of alms to the unknown vagrant. Then, and then only, will the same public conscience permit a thorough and uniform enforcement of the penal provisions of the Laws of Mendicancy."

This Report of the Howard Committee attracted much attention at the time. Amongst other manifestations of public approval, it was, on two occasions, specially recommended to local notice, in Reports of the KENT JUSTICES, in 1883, signed by EARL STANHOPE, VISCOUNT HARDINGE, LORD SYDNEY, and several Members of Parliament.

THE DORSET VAGRANT CHECK.

In the English county of Dorset, vagrancy has been checked, at least in a greater degree than in most other districts, by the systematic adoption of gifts of bread to any vagrant applying for the same. Arrangements have been made, chiefly through the praiseworthy efforts of Captain AMYATT E. AMYATT, the district Chief of Police, that at sixty police-stations of the county, not more than five miles apart, a ticket for half a pound of bread shall be given to any beggar, or vagrant, asking for it. This is well known to the public, who are thus better satisfied than in other places, that no beggar need starve. Hence there is less alms-giving. And this must always be a chief preventive of Vagrancy. For in most counties and places, five out of every six vagrants, never come to the parish authorities, or casual wards, for relief, but rely entirely on the wheedling or intimidation of private persons. Hence nothing that does not induce the latter to withhold their mischievous alms, will effectually check vagrancy. But with the certainty of bread GRATIS (and lodging) at every few miles, all over Dorsetshire, the vagrants, whether in search of work (which most of them never wish to find) or otherwise, can always and promptly obtain a meal. The Dorset people willingly subscribe the necessary cost of the bread.

About 20,000 bread tickets per annum are distributed to vagrants in Dorset, at a cost of £130, which includes £90 for bread, £12 for printing, £16 gratuities to Police Superintendents for their extra trouble in the matter, and £5. 5s. for collector's commission. The local Mendicity Society have issued a large red poster which is pasted on walls, over the county, as follows :—" BEGGARS ! CAUTION ! The Dorset Mendicity Society being established throughout the county, NO WAYFARER CAN WANT FOR FOOD; whilst LODGINGS can be had on application at the Union.

"The Committee therefore earnestly request that the Charitable and Humane will NOT GIVE MONEY, or direct relief to Beggars, BUT GIVE ONE OF THE SOCIETY'S TICKETS, which ensure food being given. The Tickets can be exchanged for Bread at all Towns and most of the principal Villages throughout the county."

In addition to these posters, the Committee distribute small handbills of a similar character, and which also state that "Subscriptions in aid of the Society, not exceeding £1 nor less than 2s. 6d., will be received at the several Banks in the County. Tickets are distributed FREE to all Subscribers, and can be obtained by them, at the different Police Stations throughout the County, and also from Captain Amyatt, Honorary Secretary, Dorchester. By the adoption of this System, the annual saving to the Rates, both in the Jail and Unions, has been considerable; not to mention the amount saved to Public Charity, together with the Prevention of Fraud. As an illustration of the extent to which imposition is practised on the Charitable Public, a Clergyman lately resident in a suburb of Manchester faithfully searched into every case which applied to him for relief. He thus examined 200 cases; only two applicants gave him their right address, and one of these cheated him."

The Tickets are supplied in punctured sheets of twelve each. On one side of each ticket there is the following inscription: "DORCHESTER MENDICITY SOCIETY. Dorchester Union District. Half a Pound of Bread will be given for this Ticket at Dorchester, 43, South Street, or at Broadmayne, Maiden Newton, etc: [six places named] and at any of the places of Relief in the adjoining Union."

On the reverse of each ticket is printed: "The Shopkeeper is only to give Half a Pound of Bread for any number of Tickets presented by the same Vagrant. Persons living in the neighbourhood are not to be supplied with bread under any circumstances. The Shopkeeper to fill in the Ticket as below.

" Name of Vagrant ————, Date ————."

The Committee, in their Annual Report for 1895, stated that: " It is most desirable that there should be some uniform method of dealing with Vagrants :

" 1. A supply of food on the road, so as to take away all excuse for Indiscriminate Almsgiving.

" 2. A uniform task of work at all Unions.

" 3. Separate cells in all Casual Wards, as a deterrent to professional Vagrants, and a *protection* to *bonâ-fide Workmen* temporarily out of work. We must do what we can to prevent the latter from joining the ranks of the Tramps."

The Dorset System has been in operation for many years, and with fair success. It has also been adopted in certain other counties, such as Herefordshire.

The system of "Way Tickets" (other than bread tickets), adopted in some counties, is considered by the Dorset Society to be very objectionable, as tending to partake of a *License* for begging. But the bread tickets have not this tendency. On the *whole*, the Dorset plan appears to be the best Anti-Tramp System yet put in action in Great Britain, and it approximates Edward Denison's suggestion.

PUBLIC FOLLY AND VAGRANCY.

It is of special importance to bear constantly in mind that the great majority of vagrants do not come under the cognisance of the Poor Law authorities, or even of the Police. For every hundred tramps who apply at casual wards, probably nearly a thousand live wholly upon private alms. Hence measures of mere deterrence. do not touch the main body of vagrants, at least in Great Britain. For this great majority of tramps, who avoid all wards and poor-houses, and resort at night to private lodgings, will continue to form a vast social nuisance so long as the public, and especially the women of the poorer classes, persist in the cruelty of INDISCRIMINATE ALMSGIVING, and thus actually entice beggars and vagrants to remain in laziness and vice. The Chief Constable of Stafford says that from enquiries he has caused to be made, he finds that the average tramp gets two shillings and sixpence per day and plenty of broken victuals. Of course, if vagrants can thus obtain their fifteen shillings a week or more, with food in addition, and without any work, they are exposed to an irresistible temptation to remain idle and vicious. In view of this prevalence of positive temptation to evil afforded by multitudes of falsely "charitable" and self-deceived "good-hearted" people, who, under the guise of kindness, are leading their fellow-men into sin, it is evident that until public opinion, especially amongst the poor, is more enlightened in this direction, no effectual cure of the evil can be obtained.

Meanwhile vagrants are a perfect plague to the poor especially. They bully and threaten with violence women and girls, and sometimes carry out their threats into rape and murder. A recently published work states (from returns of the Scotch Constabulary) that there are in Scotland, alone, an increasing number of 50,000 tramps, who cost the public, at a low estimate, five shillings a week, or nearly two millions sterling per annum. It is added: "We have known them entering cottage kitchens with the simple order, 'Gie us some tea, half a pound o' sugar, and a joog o' milk,' and they get it." This intimidation of lonely cottagers, by tramps, is also a feature of various parts of England.

But the only effectual cure for it must come from the public. In cannot be suppressed by deterrent measures, but only by the community, and especially the poorer classes, abandoning their present too general folly of giving money to beggars, who, as a body, are rogues.

The CLERGY and MINISTERS of the GOSPEL, also the conductors of the NEWSPAPER PRESS, the CHARITY ORGANISA-

TION COMMITTEES and MUNICIPAL BODIES, may, with great advantage, and in every locality, further assist the education of the popular mind in reference to the mischiefs and cruelty of pernicious or unconditional almsgiving, a practice which instead of doing good, only increases evil habits and mercilessly hinders the recipients from being compelled to obey the Scriptural precept of honestly providing for themselves and their families.

Chapter XVI.

CHILD-SAVING.

Most emphatically in regard to both PAUPERISM and CRIME, "Prevention is better than Cure": and hence the utmost importance attaches to all methods of rescuing neglected youth, as early in their lives as possible, from circumstances which must neccessarily tend to their ruin and render them pests instead of blessings to the community.

These methods consist chiefly in the promotion of Parental Responsibility, Religious and Industrial Education, kindly but authoritative supervision on the part of the State, the Boarding Out System and the carefully limited use of Institution Life whether in small Cottage Homes, or Reformatories or Industrial Schools, together with aids to Migration or Emigration for some of the children.

Enforcement of Parental Responsibility.

It is recorded of a boy, named John Scott, that having been caught trespassing and stealing apples, his father was summoned before a magistrate and ordered to make compensation to the aggrieved person. This was done; but Mr. Scott also chastised his son, and looked more carefully after him for the future. That lad afterwards became Lord High Chancellor Eldon; but had he been punished by imprisonment, and his father allowed, with impunity, to neglect his responsibilities, the results might have been very different. This incident was rightly regarded by an able penologist, Mr. Alexander Thomson (of Banchory, N.B.) as being a suggestive one, in reference to the fundamental principle which should regulate the treatment of youthful offenders. So far as practicable, correction should be secured by enforcing parental responsibilities, and by bringing good influences to bear upon the homes. If these objects cannot be effectually secured, then only should other measures be adopted. Nature begins with the home and the parent. So should law and philanthropy. Well would it have been for innumerable parents and children, if the wholesome principle, adopted in reference to Lord Eldon's father, had been more generally regarded. [But, unhappily, the unwise and cruel practice of imprisoning young children, and of almost exclusively making them, instead of their parents, responsible to the law for their offences, became too frequent.]

ABUSE OF REFORMATORIES AND INDUSTRIAL SCHOOLS.

Gradually, a partial sense of the folly and injustice of this course led some good men to labour, with much ultimate success, for the establishment of Reformatories and Industrial Schools. [They had widely observed that not only are adult criminals very difficult of reformation, but that association with them tends to render the reclamation of young offenders almost as hopeless. Whereas, by wholly separating at least the one class from the other, they found that the probability of rescuing the young increased in a direct proportion to the early stage at which they commenced these wise efforts.]

The success of the class of institutions thus introduced for training criminal and neglected youth, and as substitutes for the prison, has been marked and decided. Large has been the consequent measure, both of prevention and cure. But, as time has gone on, there has also been manifested in this, as in so many other matters, a tendency to proceed to a mischievous extreme, and to develop what has been, not inaptly, termed an["INSTITUTION CRAZE."

It is right and necessary that orphans, or utterly friendless and destitute children, whether virtuous or delinquent, should be cared for, at the cost of the State, or of the charitable; but in certain countries, and especially in Great Britain and some of the United States, much more than this has been done. Wilfully idle, drunken and improvident parents, have been, in thousands, relieved of their natural responsibilities, and with mischievous effect.

Numerous establishments, some of great extent, have been erected and maintained, at a heavy cost to the honest and industrious portion of the community, in which pauper, criminal, and neglected youth have been received, with a facility and almost with an open welcome, which has practically put a premium upon parental vice and carelessness. These children of the deliberately improvident, or criminal members of the population, have often been loaded with comforts and advantages, far superior to those possessed by the offspring of the honest working man. Indeed, the latter has been taxed for the support of the former. This folly has been perpetrated on a large scale, and has constituted one of the most extensive perversions of originally well-meant philanthropy and legislation.

So far as Great Britain is concerned, a threefold mistake has been committed in this matter.]

[Firstly, the responsibility of the parent has been largely disregarded, or not enforced.] Official statistics show that, on the average, only about a shilling in the pound, or one-twentieth of the cost of the children, in English Reformatories and Industrial Schools, has been obtained from their parents or friends. Neither is their responsibility, in general, brought home to them in other ways, as by punishment.

Secondly, the multitudes of young persons thus taken over by the State, have often been crowded together, without due classification, and with a demoralising mixture of those of tender years with older and vicious youths. Hence the numerous outbreaks, riots, and incendiarisms, which have taken place in Reformatories and Training Ships. More than a few of these have, at one time or another, been set on fire by their inmates. Hence, also, the frequent complaints, by prison officers, that some of the worst convicts are those who have been trained in such institutions.

It has often been practically forgotten that the mischiefs arising from evil association may be as potently active in " Reformatories " as in Prisons. And a want of care, in this respect, has certainly been attended by serious results to the inmates of many such institutions, and has lessened the popular estimate of their efficacy, as places for advantageous training.

A Welsh High Sheriff has characterised some of the large " Training Ships " as " mischievous floating prisons, of one large cell." The chaplain of one of the largest and best managed of Reformatories, near London, wrote to the Secretary of the Howard Association : " The evils resulting from a promiscuous intercourse of the elder and younger boys in Reformatories can hardly be described in words. The corruption to which I allude is the root of almost every outbreak of insubordination, incendiarism, and so forth, of which we so frequently hear, in connection with Reformatories. You will be doing good service to the State, by continuing to draw the attention of the public to this most important subject."

Thirdly, it is to be noted, as a special blunder, that after spending large sums of public money upon the Reformatory and Industrial Schools of Great Britain, and after employing able and painstaking instructors to furnish a course of training, of several years' duration, a considerable proportion of the young people have been sent back to their parents, who have often proved to be their worst enemies.] These fathers and mothers have repeatedly undone all the good and costly work achieved in the schools, and have urged the boys to theft and the girls to prostitution. By a perversity of sentimental folly, the imaginary so-called "rights" of such parents have been allowed to sacrifice the *real rights of their children*, and to ruin the latter, for life, in body and soul. For example, at the large Industrial School for Middlesex, at Feltham, it was found that the relapses into beggary, or crime, amongst the former inmates who had been claimed by their parents, were three times more numerous than those amongst the orphans and other lads whom the managers had been able to place out in situations away from their relatives and old companions. The mother of a Feltham scholar, being remonstrated with for beguiling her lad away from some honest occupation, replied: "What is the use of children, if you do not get something out of them ?"

Recent British legislation has however tended, though not yet in sufficient degree, to lessen the control of vicious parents over their children, when the latter have been taken in charge by the State. In this matter, America is in advance of England.

The reports of the various Societies for the Prevention of Cruelty to Children, furnish abundant and most painful demonstration of the utter unsuitability of a certain class of parents to be ever again entrusted with any control whatever over their offspring, when the State has once had occasion to interpose for the custody of the latter. The writer recently saw a boy in a prison-cell who had been convicted of theft, perpetrated at the instigation of his mother, who used to turn him out on the streets, and give him a strapping if he returned empty-handed. Such parents are sadly too numerous.

Such blunders as these have materially limited the usefulness of Reformatories and Industrial Schools, though, happily, in spite of them all, these institutions have been a great improvement upon the old plan of committing delinquent children and youths to prison, amongst adult criminals of all classes.

[The French are, in regard to this particular, somewhat wiser than their British neighbours have hitherto been. For, in France, those parents whose wilful neglect, or bad conduct, causes their children to be taken charge of by the State, are thereby, very properly, deemed to have forfeited all rights and control over their offspring; and permanently so.]

It is important to bear in mind the distinction existing between the English "Reformatories" and "Industrial Schools." The former are for such youths—chiefly the elder ones—as have actually committed felony or other crime, and who have usually undergone a brief preliminary imprisonment. Whereas the Industrial Schools are for the reception of the class of young offenders who have not been imprisoned; and also for the rescue and protection of children who have not yet been guilty of any legal offence, but who, from their circumstances and surroundings, are in special danger of being ruined, unless promptly prevented by the interposition of the State and local philanthropy. On the whole, it may be briefly assumed that "Reformatories" are for *criminal youths*, whilst "Industrial Schools" are for *non-criminal children.*

[Where parental responsibility can be enforced, the training of children at home is incomparably better than the pauperising system of throwing the burden of them wholly or mainly on the State. Many a vicious or idle parent, who now complacently permits his offspring to be thus maintained at the expense of his hard-working neighbours, and even eagerly endeavours that such shall be the case, would promptly bestir himself, if obliged to perform a certain amount of labour for the State, or to undergo a term of cellular confinement for the neglect of his natural duties. The imposition of adequate fines, or of such chastisement as the above, in failure of payment for the institutional training, would often secure a lively and wholesome determination to take more efficient care of children, previously and voluntarily left in the way of temptation.]

TRAINING OF INSTITUTION OFFICERS.

In so far as it is absolutely necessary to have Institutions, whether for the care of youth or of adults, their officers should have some special training, or at least qualification, for their duties. Miss F. P. COBBE, writes: "On one occasion I visited an enormous Workhouse where there were nearly 500 sick and infirm patients. The Matron told me, with a toss of her cap-string, 'I never nursed anybody, I can assure you, except my husband, before I came here. It was misfortune that brought me to this!'" Miss Cobbe adds: "How many other Masters and Matrons receive appointments with as little fitness for them, or simply as favours from influential and easy-going Guardians, who may guess?"

TURBULENT YOUTH.

Both in England and in the Colonies, many youths are comparative veterans in crime and vice. Thus in AUSTRALIA much of the crime in cities is committed by lads, locally termed "LARRIKINS." Respecting these, it was stated by Mr. P. PINNOCK, a magistrate of Brisbane, Queensland: "In one year, there were 157 cases of young men, mostly under the age of twenty-one, few being above that age, who were brought before my Court, and who were stated by the police, to be living on the prostitution of women." Many Australian authorities attribute this "larrikinism" chiefly to parental neglect, or cruelty, or positively vicious training. As to young girls, Mr. Pinnock added: "There are facts which I dare not tell. We have to protect girls from their fathers; sisters from their brothers. It is something horrible."

The London *Spectator*, has suggested that for the class of turbulent lads who give so much trouble in England and abroad, more facilities and inducements should be provided for the application and exhaustion of their exuberant physical energies, by means of numerous PUBLIC GYMNASIUMS. Prizes for skill in athletic sports are useful inducements to such a class to devote their time to harmless muscular training. Even in many of the better disposed among these, the animal development so predominates over the mental and spiritual, that they resemble the American youth who shrunk from the idea of a Puritan "Heaven," saying: "Whatever could I do there? Unless they could employ me in some good hard work, such as hoisting up one of them Pearl Gates, or the like."

TRUANT SCHOOLS.

Both for many of the class of turbulent youth and for wilful and neglected children, other means than Reformatories may often be used with greater advantage. For example, in London, in particular, valuable results have already been secured by means of the "TRUANT SCHOOLS" of the Metropolitan School Board. An important paper by Mr. DREW, Chairman of the Industrial School Committee of that Board, remarks:

"After nearly thirty years of close acquaintance with the juvenile population of this great metropolis, I have no hesitation in saying that—*Truancy is to be credited with nearly the whole of our juvenile criminality.* The problem of the day, therefore, is to get all idle children out of the streets, and to save them from themselves and their evil surroundings by giving them a good sound secular and *religious* education."

Mr. Drew shows that in order to help this aim, there must always be the needfully deterrent discipline of Truant

Schools held in reserve for all wilful truants. He shows also the salutary influence of such compulsory detention on its subjects. A first detention of two months usually suffices to ensure future school attendance. For others, " a second dose of about three months seldom fails to cure altogether." But he adds that much good work in this direction would be done " if our hands were not tied behind our backs."

By this he means, partly, that the HOME Office has persistently disregarded the claim, so often urged, "for *special Magistrates* to deal with School Board cases, and in *other* places than Police Courts." Further and especially, he urges that the age of State control over both boys and girls should extend from sixteen to *eighteen years* of age.

Nor does Mr. Drew forget a much-needed word on behalf of a more stringent enforcement of *parental responsibility* than hitherto, wherever possible. [Even a fine of half-a-crown on a careless or reckless parent, for the child's first truancy, would often be of life-long benefit to both parties. For there are, unfortunately, thousands of parents who are too glad to saddle their children upon the honest taxpayers, for maintenance in Reformatories and Industrial Schools. And it is double folly to gratify such a vicious wish. Nor should it ever be forgotten that if parents are not their children's friends, they are apt to become their worst enemies.]

In Massachusetts, and in Australia, *special* Magistrates and special Courts are now set apart for dealing with Juvenile Delinquency. This is also urgently needed in European countries.

DAY FEEDING SCHOOLS.

Another means of child saving, especially in large towns, consists in the establishment of Day Feeding Schools. These may be, and in some places are, modified forms of

the ordinary schools, under the local "School Boards."
They were adopted, with much success, at ABERDEEN, as
long ago as 1841, through the exertions of the benevolent
Sheriff WILLIAM WATSON.

The children of the poorest and lowest class (and, it must
be noted, of this class only) were admitted, free of cost to
the parents, the expenses being furnished partly by voluntary subscriptions and partly by municipal or other local
grants. Four hours of lessons, five hours of manual industry, and three good meals, constituted each day's routine;
with the exception of Wednesdays and Saturdays, when
half-holidays were given. The attendance was wholly
voluntary, at any rate, during fourteen years; but subsc-
quently a few children, of a special class, were sent by
official order. But, generally, the free meals constituted
effectual inducements to punctuality and regularity of
attendance.

The instruction given was of a simple and practical
nature ("the three R's"), Reading, Writing, Arithmetic,
with some Geography and object lessons. Each day's proceedings began and ended with prayer, Bible reading,
and a little singing. A loving faith in God and Christ
was carefully inculcated, and constituted a most valuable
feature in the method, and one which honourably distinguished it from certain more ambitious schemes subsequently carried out on both sides of the Atlantic. The
simple manual industry was also a prominent element
which some later systems might with advantage have
adopted. The boys were taught Shoe-making, Tailoring,
Carpentry, Box-making, and other useful handicrafts, (as
in the common or "Slöjd" schools of Sweden and some
other countries). The girls were employed in Knitting,
Sewing, Box-making, etc. The cost of the food and
training, altogether averaged about £6. 10s. per annum.
Hence the net expense (after deducting the children's
earnings) was just five guineas a year, for each. This was

a much cheaper course than the subsequent development of costly institutions, " District Pauper Schools," " Board Schools," with elaborate systems, which have by no means surpassed, if, indeed, at all approximated, in efficiency, the simple plan, devised and so long successfully carried out, by those shrewd Aberdeen philanthropists, who had their reward in a most material diminution of local pauperism, mendicancy, and crime.   In another Scotch city—Glasgow —it was complained by the *N.B. Daily Mail*, that the erection of only six of the many Board Schools in that place had cost the rate-payers £174,000; that twenty-four of the teachers' salaries were not less than £400 each, and several were £500 ; and that the indebtedness of the local School Board in fourteen years had nearly reached the enormous sum of £800,000 !

" Day Feeding Schools" have subsequently been established in various other towns of Great Britain, but perhaps never with such complete and successful organisation as at Aberdeen, where the industrial, partially self-supporting, and decidedly religious training, was carefully combined with judicious elementary instruction, strictly limited to that which was necessary to render the children useful and contented in their ordinary sphere of life.

One or two other features in the Aberdeen schools deserve notice   They did not provide clothes for the children (with some exceptions) nor lodgings.   In so far, they insisted on the discharge of the responsibilities of the parents and friends of the scholars.   For some of the most destitute, however, a little special provision was made in these respects, but only as exceptional cases.

Day Feeding Schools are mainly advantageous in so far as they are only resorted to for the *poorest* class, and as substitutes for the *entire*, or almost entire, relaxation of parental responsibility, which accompanies long and costly detentions in Reformatories, Industrial Schools, and similar institutions.

It is to be particularly noted that, at Aberdeen and also in some similar schools at Edinburgh, the children *remained* under parental control, and no abrupt change took place, as between themselves and their homes. They were not, as in the English Reformatory and Industrial Schools, maintained as costly boarders, independent—or nearly so —of parental support, and then, on discharge, suddenly and completely returned to their homes, unconditionally, after a long and entire separation.

Boarding Out.

In Europe, America, and Australia, the practice of boarding out pauper children, especially orphans, in carefully selected cottage-homes, has long been practised. And as a mode of "Child-saving" it is in general far superior to any *institutional* training, besides being much cheaper. An indispensable condition of its success, however, is the necessity of the regular and efficient oversight, or visitation of the children who are placed out.

The English Poor Law system of 1834, excellent as it was in some respects, did not make sufficient distinction between the claims of the able-bodied paupers and of the children and the aged. Hence a certain measure of practical injustice to the latter, and especially to the young, ensued. And, of later years, the very efforts to amend this, have resulted in a grave departure from the fundamental principles of the system of 1834, by rendering the condition of thousands of pauper children, one actually to be *desired*, by hard-working, self-supporting parents, for their own offspring.

This is at once obvious from the circumstance that whereas labourers and mechanics, with wages varying from 15s. to 50s. a week, and with families of six or eight in number (though often more), manage to maintain them, at from one to three half-crowns a week (and thousands of them do this with marvellous skill and success), yet they see the pauper children, of the thief, the drunkard, the tramp, the idle scoundrel, and the wilfully improvident, maintained for years in costly palatial District Schools, or still more costly "Grouped Homes" and at an expense to the ratepayers of from three, or four, to six or even eight, half-crowns per head per week.   For some District Pauper Schools, "Grouped Homes," and Training Ships, run up to from £26 to £35, and occasionally even to £50 or more, per child, per annum!

Such outlay, for paupers, is not only outrageously unjust to the over-burdened rate and tax-payer, but also to the honest industrious class of the poor themselves.   It ought to be a fixed principle that every *pauper* child, as *such*, should not involve, to the State, an expense of more than *about two half-crowns a week.*

Now this is just exactly the average cost of the Boarding-out system.

In many districts of Great Britain and Ireland (as for example largely at Leeds, Glasgow, etc.), pauper children are boarded out, at a cost averaging rather less than two half-crowns.   And thanks to the care hitherto taken in selecting and supervising their homes, this class are *unsurpassed* by any other class of State-supported children, as regards their health, their morals, and their training for the common needs of industrial life.   *They* are not plagued by ophthalmia, as are so many of the inmates of costly "District Schools."   *They* are not exposed to the still more perilous contagion of immoral and dishonest companions in the masses of barrack-like institutions.   Ill-treatment is of rare occurrence amongst them—*rarer*, decidedly, than the occasional ill-treatment of children in Workhouses and District Schools.   And as to "Baby Farming," this is an evil which almost invariably is owing to *purposed* neglect, on the part of vicious *parents* of the *non*-pauper class. Boarding-out, as habitually regulated, is the *reverse* of "Farming Out"; though some persons have confused the two.

Boarding-out, then, is evidently in accord with the *wise* principles of the English Poor Law Reform of 1834. Hence it should be more extensively encouraged, both by the LOCAL GOVERNMENT BOARD and by the GUARDIANS OF THE POOR, but *always* with due regard to effectual supervision, to careful selection of the foster parents, and, last but not least, to the necessity of guarding the children (other than orphans) from the ultimate misery of again falling into the clutches of that class of unnatural parents (*worse* than the so-called "brutes") who regard their offspring merely as objects to be preyed upon and despoiled by themselves.

The AUSTRALASIAN COLONIES do not limit Boarding-out (as hitherto in England) to the class of orphan and deserted children. In SOUTH AUSTRALIA seven out of every eight pauper, or delinquent, children of the State, are Boarded-out. This saves the Colony many thousands of pounds per annum; with additional moral and other gain to the children also; and further, it is tending to decrease pauperism in general. Several hundred Ladies in that Colony (as also in New South Wales and Victoria), discharge *gratuit-ously* the duties of the selection and visitation of the homes of the boarded out children.

IRELAND and SCOTLAND practise the system more extensively than England, and with good effect. One of the CORK Guardians of the Poor writes to the Howard Association, that the Boarding-out-system has considerably reduced the number of pauper children in that Union, because: "Formerly, parents living in Cork made it a practice to send their children to the Workhouse, where they could see them every week. But, as soon as the Boarding-out system commenced, those children were sent out of town, and then, in one week, *no less than forty of them were claimed by their parents;* so that it actually operates as a deterrent plan."

The Cork Guardians report also that "when the children arrive at thirteen years of age they are invariably *adopted* by their foster parents, and then cease to be any further charge to the ratepayers."

Effectual supervision, however, is most essential; but even this should be arranged wisely and not be *over* done. An experienced lady, Miss JOANNA M. HILL, of Birmingham, writes, on this matter, to the Howard Association :— " The point needful, at present, seems to be to counteract a tendency to what is named ' thorough ' supervision ; that is, methods practised by supervisors, which force upon the child's mind, both that he is an alien in the family and that he is being used as a means of inspection of the persons whom he ought to regard as parents. Proper inspection should be carried on so that the child should not perceive this." These are timely words.

Nevertheless the necessity of thorough and searching supervision is everywhere indispensable.

In certain districts of CANADA, and especially in NOVA SCOTIA, terrible outrages have been committed upon boarded-out girls, in remote districts of wilderness and forest, far away from the needful oversight and control. In the western UNITED STATES, also, evils have occasionally attended the wholesale distribution of city children, in out-of-the-way ' homes '; and protests have been raised on behalf of better care and discrimination.

CHILDREN AND INSTITUTION LIFE.

The experienced Chairman of a New York Boarding-out Committee thus contrasts the defects of even the best institutional training of children with the advantages of family life under the Boarding-out system :—

" Children brought up in a well-systematized institution, must be made to conform to certain discipline and machinery of government essential to its good management. The same drill which makes a good soldier annihilates the individuality of the boy. His wants are all provided for, without care or responsibility on his part : he cannot realize that on his own frugality, his own industry, his own integrity, depends the future he may expect. How can girls prepare for cooking in a plain home, in a building where large ranges are used? How learn to wash and iron, in huge laundries, where the entire wash of a large establishment is done? Will not children used to the comfort of steam-heated halls and to being waited on, find it a hardship to break ice for water to drink or wash in, to bring water from a well, to chop wood, bring coals from a cellar, make fires at dawn,—all experiences likely to come to them in a hard-working after-life? In a word, does such treatment toughen a child, and give him strength to fight his way in the world? Does it not rather weaken him?

"But more serious than all this, is the want of fathering and mothering, 'the ride on father's knee, or the cuddle in mother's arms,' impossible even to the best-intentioned matron, except in the very smallest of institutions, say for eight or ten. How shall they attain the development of character gained in the rough-and-tumble of every-day life, with its petty annoyances, small discipline, little pleasures? No shut-in existence can fit a person for the battle of life; and these children are born to such a combat as surely 'as the sparks fly upward.' They need primarily the home life,—cuffs, and caresses, sympathy and reproof, self-restraint and self-reliance. These are not on the curriculum of any institution : even the little English Grouped Pauper Homes are but a substitute for a reality, and they come twice as dear. The matron at Magill said : 'I would never have a lot of young children together : they never develop. They only grow up into half-idiotic men and women. We have only five now, and they are as bright again as when we had twenty.' Children massed in large institutions are, as Miss Florence Hill, Mr. Brueyre and others have observed, singularly backward and stupid, showing a want of pluck, dependence on others, inability to shift for themselves,— characteristics which develop into the grown pauper. Again, there are many girls who are immoral from the barrack system; hardly any from foster-homes. They are ignorant of money, the rights and duties of property, the necessity for providence and economy. Sent out to service, they are called stupid because they have never seen the articles they are called on to use. Permanent children are subjected to the influence of casuals, and to association with corrupted children,—a class recognized in all institutions. Lastly, however good the institution, the children are still a class apart, looking naturally to the public for support.

"On the other hand, when we place a child in a home, by a small payment, with its share in the household work, it gives something for what it gets, and we place it in its natural surroundings. Children should be placed as nearly as possible in the same material conditions as those in which they were born. Rough conditions are as nothing, if the influence is good, morally and physically. Instance after instance, in many lands and in many tongues, is given of the attachment between foster-parent and child, to the extent of retaining the child without payment, and final adoption. One little fellow shouted out to the neighbours, 'I've got a father now.' Living the same life as his nurse, sharing the family joys and sorrows, brought up in the same cottage and without other treatment than that of his foster-brothers and sisters, the assisted child becomes an integral part of the family."—(*Report of Committee of U.S. Child-Saving*, 1893.)

How to Inspect.

Miss H. M. Mason, Government Inspector of English boarded-out children, says:—" Persons living on the spot, and seeing the children every day, may yet have no idea of their treatment, if they do not, by partly *undressing* them from time to time, ascertain their bodily condition. The *feet* are a better guide than anything else to the treatment of a child; for it is in the hollows of the ankles that strata of dirt accumulate most visibly. The removal of a stocking also often reveals broken chilblains, blisters and sores, nails uncut and broken below the quick, or growing into the foot. The neck, shoulders, and upper part of the arms also show dirt, bites and marks of vermin, skin complaints and blows. Beating is generally begun on the upper part of the arms. I sometimes find bruises there, evidently made by sticks; and where this is the case, I undress the child as much further as necessary. I have thus, now and then, found a child covered with bruises. . . . Continual or even daily visiting may reveal nothing of the true condition of things (*i.e.*, without actual examination by the visitors). *Questions* are so useless a form of investigation *alone*, that I wonder anyone can resort to it." Foster-parents often laugh afterwards at the credulity of the "good ladies," who believe all their replies to mere questions. *Women* are necessary for the inspection of children, whether boarded out or in institutions. Again, Miss FRANCES POWER COBBE has remarked :—"I have sat in an Infants' Ward when about two dozen gentlemen tramped through it for what they considered to be 'inspection,' and anything more helpless and absurd than those masculine 'authorities' appeared, as they glanced at the little cots (none daring to open one of them, while the awakened babies screamed at them in chorus), it has seldom been my lot to witness."

WHAT FOSTER-PARENTS TO CHOOSE.

Miss JOANNA M. HILL, who has been connected with the boarding-out of many hundreds of pauper children, remarks :—"That it is essential that no persons should be selected as foster-parents who have not an adequate means of livelihood, *independently* of the money they receive for the child placed with them, and secondly that the foster-parents should not derive a *profit* from the children. These conditions greatly tend to prevent unsuitable persons from offering themselves as foster-parents." Miss Hill also considers that boarded-out children should not be removed from one home to another, without urgent necessity.

CRUEL TREATMENT AND MURDER OF CHILDREN WHO ARE NOT PAUPERS.

The extensive FARMING OUT of lower and middle-class children, *not* of the pauper class, together with the abuse of BURIAL CLUBS, has long been a national scandal—though perhaps prevailing even more frequently abroad than in England. For instance, in France there are professional baby-starvers or suffocaters, styled " angel-makers." Some twelve murderers are hanged annually in England; but hundreds, if not thousands, of child-murderers wholly escape detection, or even suspicion. The old Canaanites used to pass their children through the fire to the gods. Too many people, both in Europe and America, quietly pass little children to the grave by " accidental " over-laying, or by " drugs," or more frequently by *slow* starvation, which no one can prove, and which is done so cunningly as to secure medical certificates of " death by consumption," or other " natural causes " ! Nor are these poor little children only those " farmed out " to be " nursed " cheaply. They are often thus slowly murdered by their *own* parents at home, either for burial fees, or to escape the cost of maintenance.

Mr. BENJAMIN WAUGH (well known for his good efforts for ill-treated children) and others have perseveringly exposed much of this terrible evil, but, it may be feared, that much of it escapes even suspicion. Dr. BARWISE writes to the editor of the *Birmingham Post* :—" You are, to my painful knowledge, absolutely within the truth when you state that *every* year, *hundreds* of parents are guilty of child-murder in *this* town. The fact is, there are *no* certain signs whereby starvation can be detected. Frequently, the first thing the mother says is, ' I suppose you will give me a certificate if *anything happens.*' Hardly a day passes without my hearing it, and I generally find that the parents would gain several pounds from some insurance office if the child died." Mr. JUSTICE WILLS has declared : —" Often it would be a much more correct definition of these so-called insurance societies to say that they are *death*-insurance societies." 300 deceased children's garments were recently found in one baby-farmer's house. Well may the *Globe* declare : "We are convinced that this cruel business flourishes in England to an extent of which the public is little aware." But little has yet been done to diminish these terribly numerous and unpunished child-murders.

PLACING-OUT *versus* INSTITUTIONS, IN AMERICA.— MICHIGAN.

In the United States a National Committee on Child-Saving report, in the last decade of the Nineteenth Century (1893), as follows :—" In *most* of the States dependent chil-dren are yet provided for in the *County Poorhouses,* which are admitted nurseries of crime and pauperism. In them the children often spend years associated with the insane, the idiotic, and with adult paupers, the mental, moral and physical wrecks of their own debased lives. In the larger number of the States there are no proper Reformatories or Industrial Schools for minor delinquents ; nor is there any classification of prisoners, the young child being placed in contaminating association with adult criminals in the same jail, workhouse, or prison."

However, in some of the Northern and Western States great progress is being made, either by the adoption of Boarding-out, or of the establishment of separate Institu-tions for the training and correction of neglected children.

It is important to note that whereas, in Great Britain,

boarding-out usually implies *payment* to the foster-parents, this is not the case, generally, in America, where the children placed out are mostly *adopted*, for their services, *without* other payment for them.

But it is to be especially noted that those States, such as Michigan, Minnesota, Wisconsin, Rhode Island and others, where the Placing-out system is chiefly relied upon, have far less pauperism than such States as New York and California, where the "Institution Craze" prevails.

MICHIGAN, through the efforts of Mr. C. D. RANDALL and others, has been an honourable pioneer in the great work of child-saving by placing-out. She does not board out her State-wards immediately on their becoming such, but first gives them a *preliminary training*, for a year or so, in a School, at Coldwater, consisting of a number of buildings for small groups of children. After they are educated there awhile, they are placed out amongst farmers and cottagers (who adopt them), under continuing State supervision, and the State reserves to itself the power of withdrawing any child, at any time, from the care of its foster-parents. The State, it is important to observe, does not allow parents who have ill-treated their children to resume control over its wards. Parental neglect forfeits all future right over the children, who are thenceforward under the exclusive care of the State until they attain the age of twenty-one years. (The European State of LUXEMBURG has a somewhat similar system.)

Whilst pauperism has enormously increased in New York, California and other States, it has diminished by fifty per cent in Michigan, whilst the population has meanwhile increased sixty per cent. since the establishment of the Boarding out system.

It is only fair to New York State however, to remember that, through the influence of Dr. WILLIAM P. LETCHWORTH and other citizens, her Legislature in 1875 enacted "THE CHILDREN'S LAW, which required that healthy children, over two years of age, should be removed from the poor houses and placed in families, orphanages, or large boarding - schools. This was a pioneering experiment which has subsequently been followed by other States of the Union, though not nearly, as yet, to the extent which is essential. New York has also limited the success of her experiment by relying too much upon institutions as compared with boarding-out.

A Cause of the "Institution Craze" in U.S.A.

It is stated that the reason why the "Institution Craze" prevails, so extensively and so mischievously, in New York California, and some other American States, is because it is specially encouraged by the Roman Catholic Church, as a means of enabling it to educate, at the taxpayer's cost, large numbers of children under its own exclusive care. This may be excellent policy from a mere sectarian point of view, but it is very bad economically. And further, it tends greatly to pauperize lazy and vicious parents.

Massachusetts Juvenile "Probation" Officers and Courts.

The evils inseparable from every system of imprisonment, either for younger or older offenders, have obtained such practical attention in Massachusetts, in particular, that its Legislature has, during recent years, enacted provisions for an extensive substitution of "Probation," or Conditional Liberty, instead of incarceration. This principle was first adopted there, with children and young persons, and being found successful with them, it was extended to adults, with satisfactory results.

From 1846 to 1866, Massachusetts had established a series of Reformatories or Industrial Schools, instead of prisons, for criminal and neglected children. These institutions proved to be useful, but also very costly, the expense of the inmates being often £50 each per annum. They also involved (as in Great Britain and elsewhere) some danger of collateral disadvantage, such as, for example, a risk of relieving vicious parents of their natural obligations, and of pauperising them and their children, at the expense of the honest tax-payer; and, further, of training young persons, in large masses, in ignorance of many of the lessons to be imparted only by family life.

Hence, in 1869 and 1870, the Legislature, with a view to more preventive effort, committed the general care of juvenile offenders to a special "STATE AGENCY," whose mode of operation is as follows. Every complaint against a boy or girl under the age of seventeen, must, before being brought into any Court, be laid in writing before a State Agent, or one of his assistants, for investigation. When the case comes into Court (and portions of the time in Courts are exclusively devoted to such juvenile cases) the Agent, or Sub-Agent, attends personally to act for the State, as watcher, counsel, advocate, or prosecutor, according as the circumstances require. If the complaint is a first charge against the accused, and for a light offence, nothing follows but a simple admonition, or the passing of a suspended sentence; a small fine for costs, being, however, enforced, if practicable, on the parents of the child, where the latter is not an orphan.

If there appears to be a prospect that the child will need some further restraint, or influence, than its existing care-takers seem likely to exercise, the Agent requests (and usually obtains from the Court) a sentence of "Probation" for a given time, he undertaking (for the State) to bring up the young offender again, if needful, and meanwhile to watch over him, or her, and devise measures for his or her benefit. Such sentence of Probation formally places the child under the oversight of the State Agent; but the child may still continue at home. The term is renewed when needful.

In cases where there is reason to apprehend an utter

absence of suitable home care or restraint, for the child complained of, the Agent is authorised by the Court to take it away for the State, and to put it entirely at the disposal of the Massachusetts " Board of Health, Lunacy and Charity." This body usually places its younger wards in private families, on the BOARDING-OUT SYSTEM, under due official conditions, and with regular supervision by a few paid, and numerous unpaid, but officially appointed, visitors. This plan is almost always tried, before having recourse to a Reformatory School. But the latter is used where boarding-out appears insufficient in disciplinary influence. Finally, where the subject of this care proves intractable, then, as a last means of control, a prison is resorted to. But comparatively few children are consigned to jail in Massachusetts.

Both the moral and economical results of this system are advantageous. The number of children in the Reformatory Schools has greatly diminished. The *chief* part of this economy, by prevention and reformation, results from keeping the children *out* of the "institutions" of all kinds, and securing their better oversight, either in their own homes or, in adopted ones. A State Report says: "Almost all juvenile offenders are to be found without homes, or healthful home influences. Rarely does one come from a good family."

THE PRINCIPLE APPLICABLE ELSEWHERE.

The principle of the Massachusetts mode of dealing with juvenile offenders, and with their parents, may be adopted in other countries, without involving the use of precisely the same means. Thus, instead of appointing a series of additional officers throughout any district, as State Juvenile Agents, the services of existing functionaries may be effectually utilised. One Magistrate in each locality might be requested, by the Government, to devote his sole attention to juvenile offenders. And in each place, this Magis-

trate should have one or more policemen, or, still better, one
or more volunteer helpers, placed under his orders, with the
object of watching over the cases of any criminal or neglected
children in the locality, specially requiring authoritative
influence. The chief purpose would be, in the first place,
to give the parents or relatives of the said children such
oversight or guidance, as might enable them to discharge
their responsibilities aright, and to avoid the necessity for
further compulsion. But, persuasion failing, fines or other
forcible influences would have to be used. If these proved
insufficient, the magistrate should be empowered to have
recourse, at his discretion, and according to the circumstances of each child, to Boarding-out, or Emigration, or a
Reformatory, or, as a last resort only, to Imprisonment.
But, as in Massachusetts, it should be the *first* aim to promote the *voluntary* efficiency of the parents ; the second, to
prefer selected and supervised Family training (by Boarding out, or Emigration), to the costly and congregate life of
large Institutions ; and the third, to use such Institutions
in preference to the Prison, so far as possible.

European Union Tyranny over American Youth.

The large number 'of American children who are boarded
out are generally able to obtain an honest livelihood afterwards by farming, gardening, and land cultivation. But
American youths who seek for handicraft occupation,
find cruel and generally insurmountable obstacles placed
in their way by the injustice and tyranny of Trades Unions,
chiefly officered by European immigrants.

A leading American journal *The Century*, thus complains
(in 1893) of this very serious infringement of the national
rights and liberties :—" Under the present conditions of
trade instruction and employment in this country, the
American boy has no rights which organised labour is
bound to respect. He is denied instruction as an apprentice,
and if he be taught his trade in a trade school, he is refused

admission to nearly all the trade unions, and is boycotted if he attempts to work as a non-union man. The questions of his character and skill enter into the matter only to discriminate against him. All the trade unions of the country are controlled by foreigners, who comprise the great majority of their members. While they refuse admission to the trained American boy, they admit all foreign applicants with little or no regard to their training or skill. In fact, the doors of organised labour in America, which are closed and barred against American boys, swing open, wide and free, to all foreign comers. Labour in free America is free to all save the sons of Americans.

"In the earlier days of the Republic, the American mechanic was everywhere known as one of the sturdiest representatives of American character. He was an honest man, a good workman, a loyal, faithful citizen. To-day he is an almost extinct species. As a nation, we lead the world in mechanical skill, yet we are the only nation in the world that has almost ceased to produce its own mechanics. We not only take the great mass of ours from other countries, but we accept their poorest specimens, and, having accepted them, we allow them to control the field against our own sons."

Such a serious state of affairs is a cause of much of the great mass of Vagrancy and Pauperism which already afflicts this comparatively young Republic.

THE LONDON "CITY CUSTOM OF APPRENTICES."

The New England "Probation System" was not altogether a novelty. It had, in part, been exemplified in the Capital of the Mother Country, for centuries previously, in a form established by the wisdom of our forefathers, and known as the "City Custom of Apprentices." By this "Custom," which has had the force and sanction of Law, the semi-private Court of the Chamberlain of London, at the Guildhall, has exercised a controlling power over all

apprentices in " the City " properly so-called.   This tribunal
has long afforded a prompt, cheap, and excellent mode of
dealing with their delinquencies, except such as may be of
a graver nature ; and it has been much valued by the
citizens.   A master, having a ground of complaint against
an apprentice, obtains for the nominal fee of one shilling,
a summons for him to appear before the Chamberlain, who
quietly and impartially investigates the case, and gives
such advice or warning to the parties concerned, whether
apprentice or master, as often suffices to prevent further
trouble.   But where the misbehaviour, or obstinacy, of the
youth, appears to call for something more stringent, he is
sent, for about a fortnight, to a private "Bridewell,"
belonging to the Municipality, specially appropriated to the
detention of these young persons.

Several days of quiet reflection usually suffice to accom-
plish the desired end, and, on the apprentice expressing
regret, or apology, for the past, and promising amendment
for the future, he is, in most cases, liberated by the
Chamberlain without further infliction.   This mode of
treatment involves no public trial, is not reported in the
newspapers, is not attended by demoralising contact with
criminals, and is, in short, a valuable form of " probation "
and a substitute for ordinary imprisonment.

It is further to be observed that the experience both of
the " City Custom of Apprentices," and of Massachusetts
"Probation," alike furnish good ground for believing that
the *long and costly* detention of juvenile offenders, in Reformatories and Industrial Schools, might, in many instances, be
safely dispensed with, through the adoption of some form
of probation or supervision, useful alike to the young
people themselves and to their parents or friends, and in no
wise so expensive as the Institutional plan of disposal.

Recent proposals for the unification of London Government render it doubtful whether the Chamberlain's jurisdiction over the City youth will be permitted to continue.

But during the term of its continuance, it has been, on its limited scale, a great benefit. Some of the youths " saved " by it, have subsequently become honoured civic magistrates, instead of being ruined by committal to jail.

THE SHEFFIELD SYSTEM.

In some towns in England, the pauper children have been placed in " grouped homes," or clusters of cottages, each containing a score or so of children and under a house father or mother. But these groups are very costly, and they continne the undesirable feature of separating their inmates from the surrounding population as a distinct pauper class. An improvement upon this plan has lately been instituted at Sheffield, through the efforts of Mr. J. WYCLIFFE WILSON, J.P., and others. It consists in distributing the children in cottage homes in different parts of the town, in the midst of the working population, under foster-parents, acting under the constant supervision and direction of the central Board of Guardians. The children go to the public schools with the children of the working population around them, and are as much depauperised as possible. This excellent system is in fact, a sort of " Boarding out," under specially advantageous conditions of control and inspection. And it is worthy of extensive imitation in other localities.

JUVENILE EMIGRATION AND " BOARDING OUT."

In connection with this subject there may be added a few words on the Emigration of young persons, whether of those who have been in Reformatories, or those of a pauper or neglected class. In Great Britain, considerable attention has recently been directed to this method of permanently facilitating the interests of these wards of the State or of philanthropy. Thousands of them have been sent to Canada and the United States, through the efforts of various benevolent persons and societies. It has been found that although there is an increasing jealousy, in the

United States and Canada, against any form of pauper emigration from Europe, there is much readiness, on the part
of farmers and householders there, to receive partially-
trained children and employ them in industrial occupation.
This arises from the comparatively high value of labour
in those younger and less crowded countries. But in any
arrangement for the systematic emigration of the young, it
is important to secure two things. Firstly, they should
have a preliminary training, for about a year, before being
sent abroad, and secondly, some effectual means should
be taken, for their due supervision and visitation, in their
new homes. Otherwise, serious abuses may arise; as has
indeed sometimes happened, both in regard to children
sent from Great Britain, and also as to some of those
migrated from the crowded American cities of the Atlantic
sea-board to the Western States. The need for the training does not so much apply to those who have been
inmates of Industrial, or similar Schools, but rather to
the young paupers from Workhouses, or waifs and strays
from the street. The necessity for very careful selection
and visitation of the homes, applies to every class of
young persons thus sent abroad, or to distant localities.
It is a matter of essential justice to the inhabitants of the
countries where such young emigrants may settle, that
they should be placed out under such arrangements, or
after such training, as to secure them from becoming
nuisances to those around them. Some of the American
people are becoming very jealous as to this danger. And
not without reason.

It is too generally forgotten that the disadvantages
arising from a want of oversight, or supervision, are far
greater in the case of children brought up in the slums of
cities, or even in the wards of workhouses, than in regard
to those from rural homes, selected with reasonable care,
either in Great Britain or the Colonies. The pestiferous
life in the slums, with the too general promiscuous crowd-

ing of both sexes in one room and one bed; the by no means infrequent cruelties and demoralisation in Workhouses and Pauper Schools; and the occasional revolts and incendiarisms in the best Reformatories and Industrial Schools; all these things demonstrate the far greater dangers of the congregate than of the individual training of delinquent or destitute youth.

MILD CORPORAL PUNISHMENT.

The English law, in certain cases of juvenile offences, permits the infliction of a few strokes with a birch rod, instead of other punishment; and he must be a bold man who will dare to deny that it may be more merciful, in various instances, to impose such a short and mild infliction, rather than to have recourse to incarceration in a jail, or even to a long and costly detention in a "Reformatory" or "Industrial School."

The Town Clerk of an English borough, of more than 12,000 inhabitants, wrote to a public journal: "It has been our rule, for five and thirty years, that no boy and no girl under fifteen years, shall go from our Town Hall to prison." The substitute, at least for boys, was a birching. In case of repetition or obstinacy, another birching has been given; in one instance three whippings were inflicted, with a couple of days' interval between each. It is added: "The result is that we have not a known juvenile thief in the place. Thieving is unpopular and contemptible, in the eyes of the boys who do not want to be birched, but who probably might not object to become heroes of 'penny dreadful' depredatory adventures."

All corporal punishment, whether for children or adults, should be free from cruelty, and not administered under sudden impulse, but after deliberation. An additional means of impressiveness, and also a provision against undue severity, in inflictions of this nature, may be afforded by regulations insisting upon the presence of some independent witness, or a local authority. The chastisement of children by blows on the head, or "boxes" on the ear, is altogether objectionable. Serious injury has resulted from these, in many instances. Whenever corporal punishment is to be inflicted, whether in Schools, or by a Magistrate's order, some rules or arrangements are requisite, to prevent its becoming a mere result of passion, or other incapacity on the part of those who impose it.

Brief Solitary Confinement.

Those who still object to the infliction of any corporal punishment whatever, may perhaps approve the substitute, both for that chastisement and for imprisonment, which has been advocated by a Middlesex Magistrate—Mr. W. Knox Wigram—who, in his "Justice's Notebook," protests against affixing the jail stigma upon either boys or girls, and also objects to an excessive resort to Industrial Schools. He says: "It would be an immense boon if there were some legitimate way of ordering a boy or girl to be locked up, in solitude, for twenty-four hours," either at a police-station, or at some other place, perhaps still more suitable. He adds, "There would be no romance about it; nothing heroic, no prison experiences to boast of. The 'obstreperous' boy or Board-school truant, locked up alone for twenty-four hours or so, with nothing in the world to do, bread and water in extreme moderation, and a plank for the night, would have tasted punishment in its purest form. He would understand that he had been treated as a child. He would not have liked the treatment, nor the being delivered at his father's door next morning—like a parcel—with one shilling to pay." This is a suggestion, worthy of consideration. It might obviate, with advantage, much prolonged and costly detention in prisons and reformatories.

A somewhat similar plan was tried, with success, for many years, with refractory French lads, by M. Demetz, in a special house in his establishment of Mettray, near Tours.

It should constantly be borne in mind that the faults of the parents are the *chief* causes of juvenile delinquencies of all descriptions. Hence, the former should have the larger share of punishment and of executive pressure. A short imprisonment, would more often do good to a vicious father, and through him benefit his family, than sending the latter, at the public expense, to training institutions for a long period.

Help of Youth after Leaving Institutions.

In reference to the extension of some further care over the young persons who have ceased to be inmates of Reformatories, Industrial Schools, Pauper Schools, or similar institutions, it may be appropriate to mention the benefits which have atended a practice long adopted at M. Wichern's establishment at the "Rauhe Haus," near Hamburg. When any of the children who are being trained, approach the time when their stay there must come to an end, their instructors endeavour to secure, for each one, a patron, or *special friend*, in the neighbourhood, who may be willing to make some endeavour to obtain employment for his young ward, or at least, to render him, or her, some little help and kindly oversight, after finally leaving the schools. Much willingness to undertake such good offices has been shown by the respectable inhabitants of Hamburg and its vicinity, and many young lives have thus been effectually aided and guided to happy and useful careers. Nor has the benefit been one-sided. The exercise of this benevolent friendship has been very helpful to the patrons themselves. The cultivation of a similar principle might, with great advantage, be adopted for the assistance of many young persons, on their leaving institutions where they have received an education and oversight which it is very desirable should not wholly or abruptly cease with their departure from such places. Not merely juvenile offenders, not only friendless and pauper

children, but all classes of young persons beginning the
battle of life, may be greatly benefited by some such
arrangement, wherever practicable. The ancient, but unfortunately too generally merely nominal, office of "God-
father" and "Godmother," was wisely intended to meet
this need.

In London and elsewhere, of late years, some excellent
efforts in this direction have been put forth, on behalf both
of youths and girls requiring sympathy and friendship
amid their loneliness and temptations; as for example by
"the M.A.B.Y.S.," or " METROPOLITAN ASSOCIATION FOR BE-
FRIENDING YOUNG SERVANTS," and " THE GIRLS' FRIENDLY
SOCIETY "; also by the " CHURCH OF ENGLAND SOCIETY FOR
PROVIDING HOMES FOR WAIFS AND STRAYS," which has
boarded-out, emigrated, or otherwise trained and started in
life, some thousands of poor boys and girls. The Anglican
Church has taken an honourable leadership in this class
of effort.

LIMITATION OF HOURS OF LABOUR.

Undoubtedly multitudes of young persons, of both sexes,
are, in our own day, driven into vice and pauperism, and
into disease and death, by the excessive strain and exhaustion resulting from prolonged hours of labour, from early
morning till late at night, in crowded shops, offices or factories. Thus many of them become incapacitated for
taking any profitable interest in intellectual improvement
or religious truths. They become also, in consequence, the
easy prey of the tempter. Hence one of the most useful
forms of service to God and to man, on the part of philanthropists, and especially of the employers of juvenile
labour, consists in efforts to restrict, within reasonable
limits, the hours of occupation, and to promote those conditions of sanitation, harmless amusement and moral protection, which are essential for the physical and spiritual
salvation of the young.

CHAPTER XVII.

INTEMPERANCE—ITS DIMINUTION.

AVOID CAUSES OF REACTION.

A PECULIARLY "vexed" question is—"HOW TO DIMINISH THE CRIME AND MISERY CAUSED BY INTEMPERANCE?" To this end, numbers of good men have long been labouring, and undoubtedly with some success. Earnest Total Abstinence advocates have been urging their countrymen to "go to the root of the matter," and become *total* abstainers from intoxicants, inasmuch as, in their view, there is no other safe or justifiable course, however moderate. Yet prisons and poor-houses, asylums and hospitals, are still filled, in great degree, by the victims of intemperance.

It is therefore useful to consider whether the repression of this great evil will not be more rapidly, as well as more effectually, attained, by a practical recognition of the truth conveyed in the wise saying of an ancient writer, "*The half is better than the whole.*" For, paradoxical as this saying appears, it is often eminently true of political progress. Public opinion is produced and set in operation very slowly. To urge it too rapidly to adopt sweeping changes, involves disappointment and reaction; just as the attempt to fill narrow-mouthed jars, by deluging them with buckets of water, results merely in the waste of most of the liquid and the hindrance of the desired object; whereas gradual advances, in accordance with the readiness of public opinion to support them, are at once more easy of attainment, more secure when reached, and more widely beneficent, by their general voluntary acceptance.

There are several means, involving comparatively little innovation upon existing arrangements, which, it is likely, would be followed by a considerable improvement on the present state of things, and might comparatively soon be attained, if the friends of Temperance would concentrate their efforts upon the attempt in such a manner as to encourage the co-operation of thoughtful public opinion.

And it needs much more consideration than has hitherto been generally given, by would-be reformers, to the important fact that all measures of mere legal compulsion are easily evaded. A prevalent public opinion against forcible liquor-license restriction readily devises means to secure its wish.

The diminution of Licenses for the sale of Drink, and also laws to enforce the Sunday closing of public-houses are intrinsically good objects. But their compulsory operation is already largely nullified by the sanction of unlicensed drinking clubs, and by individuals supplying themselves with barrels of liquor at home for use when the taverns are closed. At Cardiff, for example, the " Welsh Sunday Closing Act " has caused the establishment, not only of scores of illegal " shebeens " for the clandestine sale of alcohol, but also of many drinking clubs, which are permitted by law, and are not subject to ordinary regulation, or supervision. On one Sunday, 5000 persons were observed entering twenty-one of these clubs at Cardiff.

Again in London, the increase of the well-meant, and indeed laudable, efforts of the County Council to limit the licensing of certain music-halls, frequented by prostitutes, has developed, at the West End in particular, an abominable class of "dancing clubs," usually opening after midnight. A visitor thus described them in a London newspaper, in 1894: "Here you can, unfettered by the County Council, become a member of the club, by payment of a fee at the door. Here you can dance with the best and the finest of the *demi-monde*, with music, and with vitriolised drink supplied to you at fabulous prices, while the master of the ceremonies will come up to you with suggestions not to be repeated. It was at one of these places, kept by an ex-convict, that I saw a poor fast woman felled to the ground by the fist of a pugilist. It was at another of these places that I saw another poor creature, well soaked in drink, persuaded to divest herself of every vestige of her clothing, and dance to an applauding crowd of shameless card-sharpers, and well-dressed rogues and vagabonds. It is at these dens that the licensing laws are openly defied and the lowest form of human scum is allowed to gather, under the legalising ægis of a 'club.'" Such is the state of affairs in London, and probably in other British cities, in the last decade of the Nineteenth Century.

For practical and social purposes, the chief question to be considered, in relation to this subject, is what measures for promoting Temperance can the *general public* be induced to adopt, with such concurrence of opinion as is essential to render them effectual and abiding?

Now it is about as certain as anything can be, that, all teetotal arguments notwithstanding, the Anglo-Saxon race, on both sides of the Atlantic, will *not*, as a people, abandon their mild beers, nor the Continental nations their light wines. The ordinary French wine ("Bordeaux") is practically non-intoxicating and healthful. And the French are generally a more temperate people than the English.

A writer in the *St. James' Gazette* remarks: "The very large majority of customers frequenting public-houses, in working-class districts, do not get drunk, even on a Saturday; yet they spend a *monstrous* proportion of their earnings on liquor; injure their health and keep themselves and their families in a constant state of impoverishment. The essential point to them is, that the public-house represents amusement and distraction in the handiest shape. They want amusement, and take it in the way that gives them the least trouble, whether they can afford it or not. It happens to be drink."

In view of such considerations and facts, it is desirable to make efforts for such aids as the following means would afford.

LIMITATION OF LIQUOR LICENSES.

A limitation of Liquor Licenses would, at least in some degree, lessen temptation; because, as it has often been remarked, a man may be able to pass several taverns without entry, but not a score or more, in quick succession. The limitation could be secured partly by the licensing authorities ceasing to grant any *new* licenses beyond those already existing. The latter also, where, as is usually the case, they are numerically excessive in proportion to the local population, might be gradually taxed more and more until their number was materially reduced—the money thus gained to be appropriated in compensation to those taverns which had been obliged to succumb. In view of the enormous increments of property which the grant of licenses confers upon the persons receiving them, and in view also of the detriment to the community largely occasioned by drink, especially as tending to fill the jails, asylums and hospitals, for which it (and not the publican or brewer) has chiefly to pay, it is unreasonable to suppose that the public should also be taxed for any further gifts to the liquor trade.

But at the same time those persons who have made the largest profits by that trade ought to compensate their less fortunate brethren who may be "weeded out" by the gradual increment of taxation. And that increment ought accordingly to be thus applied.

No Appeals.—No Clerks' Fees.

Licensing Committees, whether appointed by County Councils, Municipalities, or otherwise, should not have their decisions open to appeal to any other body. And their CLERKS or SECRETARIES should have no fees dependent upon licenses, but should be wholly paid by fixed salaries.

Regulation of Drinking Clubs.

All clubs where drink is sold should be registered, and the names of their members should be open for inspection. Their hours of usage should be the same as in licensed houses. And they should pay a license duty in proportion to the rateable value of the premises. A special police officer should be at liberty to enter them at any time.

No Double Licenses.

Music and dancing halls should not be also, or doubly, licensed for the sale of drink. Their temptations are thus unduly increased. Private inconvenience should give way to public interest, in this matter. A music-hall manager, on being asked for the free admission of certain applicants, replied, " Let them in ; they'll drink like devils." Prostitutes cannot in general be kept out of music and dancing halls. But prostitutes *plus* drink are more than a community ought to allow any capitalist exploiter of public amusement to avail himself of, for his profit, but for the ruin of men and women.

Discouragement of Strongly Alcoholised Liquors.

Seeing that nearly all the evils of intemperance arise from the *strongly alcoholised* beers and ales, and from *spirituous* liquors, such as brandy, whisky, gin and rum, it is of importance that all such beverages should be discouraged by being made the objects of *special taxation* and *restriction.*

LIMITED TEMPERANCE PLEDGES.

A Dutch gentleman once remarked to the writer: " We, in Holland, are not like those poor Westphalians across the Rhine, who drink on empty stomachs and so get easily upset with the liquor. We line our stomachs well with good food when we drink." There is some sense in this course. And hence a certain English Temperance Society encourages three forms of Temperance pledges, namely, firstly a promise never to drink alcoholic beverages except at meals, or with some solid food. Secondly, not to drink them in the presence of children, and to dissuade the latter from liquor. Thirdly, total abstinence.

Some persons who will not take the latter are willing to adopt one or both of the former pledges. And in either case something is gained.

The old-fashioned " Temperance Pledge," against " spirituous " liquors, or " strong " drink only, was also a good and helpful one.

LONGER DETENTION OF INEBRIATE OFFENDERS.

The treatment of habitual drunken offenders requires alteration, so that they may not be sentenced to a useless succession of five-shilling fines, or of a few days' imprisonments, almost *ad infinitum*, but they should be detained either in Inebriate Homes or on Industrial Farms, long enough to form sober habits, or otherwise be only left at liberty, on satisfactory bail, for good conduct, being offered.

INEBRIATE HOMES—REAL AND SHAM.

In case of the committal of inveterate drunken *offenders,* to Inebriate Homes, it is of essential importance that these shall only be consigned to institutions of this kind, conducted by authorities who have full powers of strict detention, and of immediate re-arrest (without magistrate's warrant) in case of escape, and who, in particular, will most rigidly exclude all intoxicating liquor from the premises.

This is the more important, in view of the fact that, already some of the so-called " Inebriate Homes " are mere shams and impostures, where the inmates, either through bribing the servants, or by other means, obtain alcohol readily. In some of these establishments, also, the inmates merely lounge away their time in idleness and card-playing, with little or no encouragement to self-improvement and industrial occupation.

Habitual drunken offenders had far better be retained in ordinary prisons (with special adaptations to their class) than consigned to sham Inebriate Homes.

A genuine example of an Inebriate Home (but not for offenders) is the Dalrymple Home, at Rickmansworth, Herts. (Vide " *Inebriety or Narcomania,*" by Dr. NORMAN KERR. London: H. K. Lewis, 1894.)

VIGOROUSLY ENFORCE EXISTING LEGISLATION.— INDIVIDUAL EFFORT.

The example of the success of the Magistrates in some places, in greatly diminishing local crime, by means of resolutely carrying out the provisions of the " Prevention of Crime Act," as applicable to low public-houses harbouring disorderly characters, shows how much might be similarly effected in other districts, if combined popular opinion were brought to bear upon the Magistrates and the Police.

It is local action, and especially on the part of a few active and well-concerned individuals, which is most effectual in this direction. Members of Parliament are, too often, apt to be of little reliability for combating popular vices. They are so " weak-kneed.". So too, sometimes, are Home Secretaries and other Ministers of State. Years ago, when a Law for suppressing Burial Clubs was under discussion, in the British Parliament, a Committee of its members examined, amongst other witnesses, the Rev. John Clay, Chaplain of Preston Jail. As he walked away from the House of Commons, he said to his son:—"They'll do nothing. The pot-houses back the burial clubs; and I have long ceased to hope for anything from M.P.'s when the pothouse interest has to be meddled with. They daren't offend the publicans and so risk the loss of their seats. They'll slur the matter over, you'll see, in their Report." His son adds:—"Which, accordingly, they did."

INDEPENDENT INSPECTORS.

The appointment of INDEPENDENT INSPECTORS, by the Government, to act as general supervisors (similar to Inspectors of Factories), and to report to the Central Government on local Magisterial or Police laxity, would be a further check on existing evils, without involving any startling change of current arrangements. But at present it is a curious circumstance that the effect of diminishing Licenses has, in a number of localities, been followed by additional drunkenness, inasmuch as the increased value of the public-house property, previously licensed, has rendered the Magistrates less willing to sanction the heavier penalties on the publicans involved by a rigid carrying out of legal supervision. INDEPENDENT INSPECTORS, *in no way responsible to the local authorities*, but only to the *Central* Government, would be able to stimulate a more strict oversight. And such Inspectors should be required to visit, not only Taverns and Public-houses, but all Drinking Clubs and Music and Dancing Halls. The ordinary Licensed Houses or Inns, are now, in general, the best conducted, or least disorderly, of all these classes of establishments, precisely because they are more subject to control.

MODERATE FINES, OR PENALTIES.

In England, hitherto, the penalties to which liquor sellers are liable, for proved abuses on their premises, have tended to defeat their own object by being too severe. Milder penalties would be more frequently enforced, and would, therefore, be more certain and effectual in their operation.

THE GOTHENBURG LICENSING SYSTEM.

At Gothenburg and some other places in North Europe, the Municipality has taken the retail sale of spirituous liquors into its own hands (but without compensating the previously licensed sellers), and has employed vendors at fixed salaries. Some reduction in local drunkenness is reported, but it is does not appear that the system has the decided advantages which some persons at a distance have claimed for it. It does not interfere with the sale of malt liquors. The profits arising from the sale of spirits in Gothenburg and the other towns are devoted to town improvements and the reduction of taxation, etc.

LIMITATION OF SUNDAY SALE.

Whilst the stoppage of the Sunday Sale of Liquor, if attempted on a general or sudden scale, in advance of local opinion, tends to develop worse evils, yet a limitation of the Liquor Traffic on that day, if well supported by the public, is most desirable. A wise and an active philanthropist writes to the Howard Association on this point: "Observation of many years has made me believe that no single step is likely to effect so much good." But in case the public are not prepared for so decided a course, the sale might reasonably be confined to a smaller number of houses than during the week. This might be effected by issuing SPECIAL SUNDAY LICENSES, at a considerable EXTRA CHARGE. And even if publicans are willing to pay such extra charge, only a certain proportion should be thus permitted to open on that day.

Non-Alcoholic Restaurants.

Great benefit has already resulted in London and other cities from the establishment of cheap and good restaurants, where no intoxicants are sold. These have been found to be very profitable undertakings, also, to their projectors. Thus the £1 shares of the Aerated Bread Company (one of the best of these restaurant companies) have been sold at £6 premium, and have returned handsome dividends.

Squalid Dwellings and Intemperance.

Over-crowded and unhealthy dwellings have often contributed something to the causation of Intemperance, just as nagging wives have tended in a similar direction. But the influence of poor dwellings has been greatly exaggerated. For drunken, intemperate people make their dwellings dirty, disreputable and unhealthy, by their own habits. In some cities where, by local changes of residence, the good houses of prosperous merchants have been converted into tenements and let out to intemperate tenants, they have become as squalid and dilapidated as ordinary slums. A drunken family will spoil any dwelling. Whereas orderly and decent temperate persons will not, in general, abide in wretched dwellings. Their habits enable them to afford houses more in accordance with their tastes. Just as pigs would soon convert a parlour into a sty, so drunkards ruin even sanitary abodes. But abstainers, as a class, will not stay in squalid dwellings. They either rectify or quit them.

At the same time there is, in every city, decided need for increasingly vigorous efforts to improve the undrained, ill-ventilated, sunless dwellings which unquestionably contribute a certain share of inducement to habits of intemperance amongst those who reside in them.

RELIGIOUS MOTIVES AND TRAINING.

Religious motives and training will always be the chief power of God against Intemperance, as against other evils. An experienced prison chaplain remarks that "Drunkenness, Sabbath-breaking and profligate companions are but *secondary* causes of crime. The source of these and of their consequences is the neglect of religious training. Criminals are not brought up in 'the way in which they should go.'" In proof of this he mentions that out of 1,224 prisoners whom he had examined, 674, more than half, could read fairly ; but *only six* possessed a good knowledge of the Holy Scriptures. The training thus needed implies, in particular, the early formation by parents, of the *habit of prayer* and of the fear of God, in their offspring.

As God is honoured by a *main* reliance upon Him and His Gospel, for the means of checking this evil, He will bless such efforts. Numbers will recognise the claims of Christ's love upon them as an obligation to Temperance, in the sense of abstinence from *drunkenness*, when those claims are perseveringly urged and not extended to merely conventional, or strained, interpretations of the word "Temperance." The CHRISTIAN CHURCH, by its manifold organisations of Ministers and Evangelists, City Missionaries, Bible Women, and District Visitors, is, and ever must be, the *greatest* of all agencies for promoting Temperance and many other social reforms—even when not directly aiming thereat. And notwithstanding much shortcoming in these respects, so considerable a measure of success has attended the past and existing labours of the Churches, as to point with encouragement to the value and necessity of a far greater extension of organised social aggressiveness on their part—in humble and prayerful reliance upon the all-seeing and all-present God, who will bless endeavours to gather souls to Him, and to snatch from destructive influences those for whom the Redeemer has died.

Chapter XVIII.

PROSTITUTION

Importance of Checking its Sources.

THE vast evil of female Prostitution is not only a vice, but also the direct and indirect cause of many crimes. For example, the thefts perpetrated by abandoned women are innumerable. The jewellery, watches, and money stolen by them, both inside and outside of brothels, amount to many thousands of pounds annually, in every large town. Many murders have been caused by quarrels with, or concerning, prostitutes. And these women are often accomplices in burglaries and violent assaults.

Mr. RUSKIN, in a lecture on the rivers of Lombardy, sharply criticises the Venetians and others, who in their endeavours to restrain the wide-spreading shoals and pestilential marshes produced by those streams, have confined their operations to the *mouths* of the rivers, where their current is unmanageable and irresistible, instead of giving attention to their *sources* amongst the mountains, where remedial measures are more available. So, to a very great extent, has the overflowing evil of Prostitution been treated. Its sources have (with comparatively little exception) been made very secondary objects of notice and effort.

The causes of Prostitution are various, and deeply rooted in the social system. Absolutely extirpated they can never be, whilst human society remains as it is at present constituted. But the prominent sources may be greatly restricted, wherever strong ·Christian interest is excited to efforts in this direction, and whenever strong vested interests are vigorously grappled with.

It is the more important that preventive means should be resorted to,. in connection with this particular evil, because of the peculiarly difficult task of reclaiming women when they have entered upon a life of shame. Both they and the men who share in their vice are more rarely reclaimed to virtue than almost any other class of evil-doers. The writer of the Book of Proverbs wrote a too prevalent truth when he said of "the strange woman, who forgetteth the covenant of her God," that "her house inclineth unto death and her paths unto the dead. None that go unto her return again; neither take they hold of the paths of life." And again : "Her house is the way to hell, going down to the chambers of death." "The dead are there."

The poet BURNS, too, had observed of this or its kindred evils :—

> "But oh! it hardens all within
> And petrifies the feeling."

In a very literal sense, even physical death soon follows a life of Prostitution. The poor women perish like rotten sheep. Every year sweeps away a multitude of them. It has been stated, by medical men, that the average duration of a prostitute's career, as such, is less than four years. And the ravages of the horrible disease of syphilis, both among the guilty and the innocent, are terrible, enduring, and far-reaching. Many an innocent wife, with her offspring, is rendered a life-long sufferer, in consequence of sexual immorality on the part of her husband, even if many years before his marriage.

IRRELIGIOUS EDUCATION—THE DIVINE CLAIMS ON MARRIAGE AND HOME LIFE.

Among the chief sources of Prostitution, must be placed foremost, NON-RELIGIOUS EDUCATION, of boys and girls. Ordinary secular education is powerless, if indeed it does not rather tend to facilitate early sensuality.

In the Puritan communities of England and New England, and amongst the Mennonite districts of Holland, Pennsylvania, and Western Germany, as also amongst Quakers, as a body, where a careful religious training in a sense of the Divine Sovereignty has prevailed, very little of the evil of Prostitution has existed.

It was, we may well believe, with a special design to set forth the sanctity of the Home and the truly Sacramental character of Marriage, that our Saviour wrought His first miracle at a wedding. He thereby placed His authoritative seal and sanction on the great truth that the most religious influences of human life are intended to be promoted and developed by family love, and responsibility; and that the most blessed Priesthood is that of Parentage. The Prophet Malachi, also, referring to the institution of marriage, as being in its best form, the union of one man and one woman, says: " And wherefore one ? That He might seek a *godly* seed."

This is, then, the Divine purpose, that every home should be pre-eminently an abode and training school for godliness. This is the greatest source, at once of human happiness and qualification for duty.

What does more to soften men's hardness of heart and to develop their sympathies, than married life, with its mingled joys, sorrows, and claims of affection ? And what a great crime it is for any man to ruin and desecrate a woman's body, which is meant to be the shrine of godliness and of the purest and life-long happiness.

The grand fact of the Divine Sovereignty teaches us that

God will finally hold every man and woman responsible for their obedience, or disobedience, in regard to the consecration of their sexual relations and functions—relations which so far from being in any way incongruous with the highest interests, are designed to be subservient to, and promotive of, the happiest and holiest developments of man and woman.

But through a terribly prevalent neglect of godly education, and the resulting wide-spread ignorance of every person's inalienable and individual responsibility to God, these claims of His Divine Sovereignty over marriage and sex are too often disastrously ignored. And this is one of the chief sources of Prostitution, and can only be dealt with, by more fidelity on the part of the Churches and their members, in the promotion of training the young in the fear and love of God.

If there was a more general sense of this Divine Sovereignty in the matter of sex, there would not be heard from young men the foolish and wicked plea: "I am only obeying the instincts of Nature, in indulging my passions." For the instincts of Nature are given by God for subordination to His own wise and gracious purposes. A gluttonous fool may just as reasonably plead his liberty to gorge himself to disease and death, in obedience to an appetite implanted by Nature. For God's sovereignty extends over the appetites.

And this Divine Supremacy over all human duty, function and enjoyment, is, and will be, a great *final reality.* " All His commandments are sure. They *stand fast for ever and ever* " (Psalm cxi.). The pleasures and capacities for enjoyment of this world are given by God for man's blessing, but not in reference, only or chiefly, to Time and to this brief mortal life, but rather for Eternity. A certain nonsensical and quasi-religious sentimentality often condemns earthly enjoyments as " worldly," and therefore wrong. But what is worldly is only wrong in so far as it is separated from its relation to the *Eternal* world. And it is in this sense that the Holy Spirit has to convince us of the certainty of Divine Judgment: "Because the Prince of *this* world [merely as such] is judged."

All that is of "*this* world" only, passes away. Its end is corruption. Empires, Kingdoms, Aristocracies, Democracies, Parliaments, "fade as a leaf," by certain ultimate decay. But there are other "things which *cannot* be shaken." And the Divine Sovereignty, with its irresistible requirements of future and final responsibility, is one of the sure and "last things." It may be forgotten, or ignored now, but all who thus neglect it, will, infallibly, have to submit to it hereafter. And to ignore this, for temporary indulgence, is supreme folly.

If the Churches, in general, had, like the old Puritans, more faithfully promoted the education of youth, in some real sense of this glorious but awful fact of the Divine Sovereignty, what immeasurable amounts of Prostitution and other Vice would have been prevented and arrested at the source.

And to a vigorous and uncompromising resort to this great principle, must every community betake itself, in proportion as Prostitution, with other evils, is to diminish.

Give no Quarter to Exploiters of Vice.

Secondly, the large measure of legal and social protection to the capitalist dealers in vice, must be withdrawn. It is in vain to harry and worry poor prostitutes, whilst the far worse men and women who exploit them and enslave them in their brothels are allowed to prosper, and are positively encouraged in their diabolical trade. The law, in every country, should deprive brothel-keepers, and owners of houses of assignation, of all rights of property, in so far as the users and inmates of such houses are concerned. They should forfeit all legal power of enforcing payment for *any lodgings, food, clothes*, or other accommodation, supplied in such houses. For they have no *moral* rights in these things. And when convicted of any offence, brothel-keepers should never have the option of a fine. They should always have strict cellular imprisonment, or corporal punishment. In England, in 1894, a man was fined £20 for keeping a brothel. He had already been fined £220, within the year, for the same offence. He paid the last fine with a smile. And well might the fellow smile at the legal and magisterial folly which thus encouraged his wickedness.

But so long as British, American and Continental law permits, as hitherto, the nastiest and vilest of human kind to derive a profitable trade from the ruin of female virtue and the causation of cruellest misery to myriads of pitiable creatures, so long will prostitution flourish.

Legislators and administrators themselves have too often been criminally lenient to vice-capitalists, because of their own sinful participation with them.

POLICE AND PROSTITUTION.

Hitherto all police supervision of prostitution has more or less failed. In many cases the police have favoured or abetted it. The women have successfully defied the " Contagious Diseases Acts " and medical examinations. These may, indeed, have frightened some and checked others. But the mass, both of vicious men and women, have triumphantly evaded them.

If a tithe of the legal and police vigour against prostitutes had been directed against brothel-keepers and owners, and against their agents and procurers, such efforts would have met with no inconsiderable success.

The police, or some other authorities, however, ought everywhere to have a power of entry into brothels for the purpose of taking down the names of their managers, their owners and all their frequenters, which names should be regularly published by authority. This, also, would be some check on the evil.

In Liverpool, Manchester, and some other towns, the police, by an increase of vigilance and with magisterial and public support, have been able to shut up many houses of ill-fame.

INTEMPERANCE AS A CAUSE.

Another source of prostitution consists in the excessive facilities for intemperance. Licensed houses for the sale of drink have become so disproportionately numerous, that, to use the words of a Chief Justice, " Amongst a large class of our population, intemperance in early life is the direct and immediate cause of every kind of immorality, profligacy and vice—and until the beershops and all taverns and public-houses are placed under some sufficient restraint and regulation, there can be little hope of effecting any material reform in the habits of the people."

Special temptations to prostitution are offered by many establishments *doubly* licensed as music halls and drinking-houses, whose visitors are importunately pressed to drink, and are at the same time plied with the worst seductions to vice. A license for music and for the sale of drink· should never be given to the same premises. Doubtless this would occasion inconvenience and annoyance to some of their frequenters. But this is not for a moment to be weighed against the disadvantages and increased tempta-tion attendant on double licensing.

LARGE STANDING ARMIES.

There are in Europe millions of men in the vigour of life, kept under arms, for the most part homeless, and in enforced celibacy. Even in the British army, only a very small percentage of marriages are sanctioned. No regula-tions can possibly prevent prostitution from largely resulting, whilst *this* source continues. But, it is replied that these large standing armies are indispensable for national security. Are they indeed? History proclaims quite the contrary. A nation of virtuous, free people, having homes of their own, will always overcome, even when suddenly called under arms, a much larger number of homeless, wifeless hirelings, demoralised by camp and barrack life, just as the American volunteers routed the trained troops of George the Third; as, also, undisciplined Swiss and Caucasians have repeatedly worsted large armies of French and Russian regulars. And in the United States Civil War of 1861-5 the Federal farmers and tradesmen of the North similarly conquered the Southern "Chivalry," trained to arms, but debauched by slavery.

LACK OF SYMPATHY AND FAIRNESS.

Prostitution is increased by unsympathetic and unfair treatment of Women. Professingly Christian society too generally reserves for the fallen woman relentless severity, whilst smiling on the "gentleman" who seduces. The latter, however rich, is perhaps fined some half-a-crown a week for a short time, whilst the weaker offender is too often abandoned altogether and driven to hopeless ruin, and often to child-murder. The crime of *deserting* seduced women should be specially punished.

An eminent Physician has exclaimed, not without some reason: "I wish to say a word in reference to Ladies' Purity Associations. Is it not Ladies who, in many instances, drive young women to the streets? Let a young person make a false step, and that moment her mistress becomes a very dragon of virtue."

PUBLIC SENTIMENT AND SEDUCERS.

In some communities the seducer of female innocence is regarded, too generally, as being still a "gentleman." And the vile fellow who has seduced a number of poor girls, boasts of his wickedness and is admired by others like-minded. But in certain countries also, a healthier state of public opinion obtains, and its effect is greatly to diminish seduction and to protect young females. For example, in the United States this is generally the case. Practically, in the South, the seducer may be, with impunity, " shot at sight " by the relatives of her whom he has injured ; and in the North also this is largely the case. The punishment is sharp, but it acts as a great shield to women and children.

Domestic Service.

From want of a little consideration by their mistresses, virtuous girls in household situations are often suddenly dismissed without sufficient cause, and this has repeatedly led to their ruin. It is also stated that a high average of insanity prevails amongst the class of female ser-vants, and that it is mainly produced by severe anxieties respecting the uncertainty of employment and the sudden loss of situations, when without other means of support.

To lessen such anxieties and dangers, it is important to urge upon domestics the early formation of habits of foresight. The Post-Office Savings Banks afford a facility for aiding such habits, which would be made use of by many who only need a little persuasion, or information, to avail themselves of the advantage. When once formed, the habit of saving easily becomes a source of permanent self-assistance. The provision made by some of the most respectable business-firms for the moral and intellectual improvement of those in their employ, of either sex, united with the practice of early closing, and with arrangements for comfort and order on the Sabbath, is a further exemplary means of lessening temptation. But in some establishments, the assistants (boarders) are not permitted to remain in the house, on Sundays, from breakfast time till late at night, but are expected to find entertainment with friends, or at taverns, " tea " gardens, etc.

It is a grievous fact, and well established, that the majority of prostitutes do not come from the ranks of street-hawkers, or factory girls, but mainly from private families, where, as servants, their subordinate position has been taken advantage of in a wicked and cowardly manner by the husband, or some other man, or youth, in the household. This root of the evil can only be reached gradually by godly education. Though, perhaps, systematic public exposure (exempted from charges of libel) might have some deterrent efficacy.

ABUSE OF REGISTRY OFFICES.

Of late years, a considerable amount of Prostitution has been caused through the misuse of Servants' Registry Offices, by the agents of brothel-keepers and seducers, who thus become acquainted with girls, and by means of tempting offers and high wages, lure them to their ruin. It is very difficult to suggest a means of checking this abuse. But something might be done by publicity, visitation and warning.

GIRLS' AID SOCIETIES AND PATRONAGE.

Much also may be accomplished, for the prevention of Prostitution and female ruin, by organised and individual efforts to look after and help young girls. An admirable and successful attempt in this direction is the "M.A.B.Y.S." —or "Metropolitan Association for Befriending Young Servants." It has done much good. So, too, has the somewhat similar "Girls' Friendly Society."

Mr. WYNDHAM S. PORTAL, a Hampshire Magistrate and Guardian, well remarks:—"Until we can find that *each* child has at all events one friend, we must not rest satisfied. Whether Lady Visitors, 'Sisters,' Deaconesses, Bible-women, District Visitors, or by whatever other name they may be called, let us ask them to come and help us. It was but the other day that a penitent young woman, when on her bed of sickness, was asked if she could give a reason for having fallen when little more than a child, and replied that had she then possessed even one friend in the world in whom she could have confided, and to whom she could have gone for help and advice, her life would probably have been a far different one. May I not, then, put this question to you? Will you befriend *one* poor friendless child?"

Great would be the "Home Mission" work, if amongst the *un*fallen, the poor but still *un*pauperised children of England, as well as amongst the pauper and boarded-out children, *each* individual boy and girl, could be offered the friendly care of some one kind lady visitor.

THE RECLAMATION OF FALLEN WOMEN.

The means of rescue which appear to have been the most efficient, are the exercise of *strictly private* efforts, to assist with employment and kindly visitation those who have fallen or are in danger of so doing. One of the most successful labourers in this direction is a philanthropic person who, in a large town, has employed a Christian woman to devote her whole time to the visitation and industrial assistance of this class, but with the utmost privacy, so as to uphold the character and self-respect of the persons thus aided. This single agent has reclaimed 335 girls in six years; only one relapse having been known. Privacy, complete *individualisation* and subsequent *silence* as to the past, are special elements of success in this work. Yet "Homes" and "Refuges" have their use also, especially if rendered more or less self-supporting.

"PREVENTION BETTER THAN CURE."

But such remedial agencies as "Midnight Meetings," and "Homes" for reclaiming the fallen, however excellent, can only diminish prostitution in the ratio of "a drop from a bucket," whilst the main *sources* of the evil are practically permitted free and overwhelming operation. On these sources, therefore, attention and effort should

be chiefly and perseveringly concentrated. The motto
" prevention is better than cure," applies with thousandfold
emphasis to prostitution. *All attempts at suppression will
certainly fail, except and only so far as the roots and sources are
diminished.*

For instance, in great military and naval stations like
PORTSMOUTH, PLYMOUTH, ALDERSHOT and WOOLWICH,
where multitudes of unmarried men promote vice by wholesale, a few " Rescue Homes " for the poor fallen women
must have their benefits immensely overwhelmed by
counteractive influences.

CHAPTER XIX.

SUBSTITUTES FOR IMPRISONMENT.

FINES AND RESTITUTION.

EVEN the best prisons are, in a certain sense, evils. And one of the chief aims of a wise Penology is to devise means for advantageously and safely dispensing with them.

As one form of substitute for imprisonment, in certain cases, the infliction of Fines possesses several advantages. It obliges the offending person to make compensation to the State, or injured party, entirely at his own expense, and not at that of the honest tax-payer. Nor does its operation preclude its subject from continuing his ordinary exertions for the maintenance of himself and family. The chief objection to this mode of punishment, as now inflicted, consists in its arbitrary nature, by reason of the penalty being a definite sum of money, to be imposed irrespectively of the pecuniary position of the offender. Hence the rich and poor are often inequitably dealt with in this matter, precisely because of the nominal equality of the imposition. A more just and efficient principle might be found in taking as a standard, for at any rate certain classes of fines, the amount of a man's income, as indicated by his salary, wages, or ordinary assessment for taxation and local rates. Thus, if instead of fining rich and poor alike, so many pounds or dollars, the punishment consisted of so many days' income, or so much percentage on the regular taxation, a principal objection which has hitherto applied to this form of penalty would, in great degree, be removed. There would be some difficulty, at first, in ascertaining, for finable purposes, a man's income or taxation. But certain legal facilities and arrangements for registering at least the taxable status or assessment of the persons in each district, might perhaps be made fairly available.

It is desirable, under modern conditions of society, that a more general resort should be had to this mode of punishment, than to imprisonment. The English Legislature has already considerably extended its operation, by the "Summary Jurisdiction Act," of 1879.

The enforcement of RESTITUTION, made under ordinary conditions of life, as sanctioned by Mosaic and ancient British Laws, and by Apostolic precept, is, to some extent, contained in the principle of Fines.

THE INTERESTS OF THE INJURED PARTY.

Even modern England, with all its progress, has not surpassed, if indeed equalled, the primitive JEWS and WELSH BRITONS in the very important matter of making the interests and compensation of *the person injured* by a crime a more prominent object of attention than the punishment or reformation of the offender. Those wise ancient peoples made it the first point to right the wronged party, at the expense, as far as possible, of the evil-doer, or those associated with him. RESTITUTION was one of the many noble features of the MOSAIC CODE. Even now, in England, of all countries, an injured person has to incur much expense and trouble, in order to prosecute those who have robbed or wronged him, and even when he has secured their imprisonment or fine, there is no thought of compensating him. At the very least, the law ought to undertake the trouble and all the cost of prosecutions, by some such arrangement as the appointment, in every district, of officers like the Scotch PROCURATORS-FISCAL.

At the International Prison Congress at Stockholm, in 1878, Sir GEORGE ARNEY, Chief Justice of New Zealand, and Mr. TALLACK, the Secretary of the HOWARD ASSO- CIATION, both advocated a more extensive adoption of this just principle of Restitution to the injured. It was also, and more fully, advocated at the subsequent Congresses of Rome and Paris, by M. GAROFALO, and others.

NEW ZEALAND AND RESTITUTION.

In NEW ZEALAND, the British Government systematically, and with much advantage, adopted this course, in the treat- ment of offenders amongst the Maori aborigines. It was specially inexpedient to imprison those warlike and freedom- loving people. In cases of theft, they were therefore required to pay, either to the injured party or to the local authorities, four times the value of the articles stolen; the same standard of restitution adopted by the publican Zacchæus, in the Gospel. In various instances, the chiefs of the tribes to which these thieves belonged, promptly paid all or part of the fines. And this had the useful effect of securing an increased exercise of tribal influence in favour of honesty.

FINES ARE SOME OF THE BEST " LABOUR SENTENCES."

Under a systematic scale of application, and for certain offenders, fines constitute the most practicable mode of carrying into effect the ideas underlying the schemes of " Labour Sentences" recommended by Dr. Paley, Arch- bishop Whately, Captain Maconochie, Mr. C. Pearson, and others; whilst the serious difficulties, inevitable with any attempt to enforce such sentences *during* imprisonment, are thus obviated. The application of just measurement to labour tasks and piece-work, whilst in detention, is a matter of perplexity and sometimes of impossibility. Even in reference to the simpler forms of exertion, such as agricultural occupation, it is difficult to impose a uniform and fair standard of measurement. For instance, if a number of men are required to dig so many square yards of land per day, it will continually happen that some of them will have to deal with more tenacious, more stony, or otherwise more intractable ground than others. Also, as to such operations as cleaning, watching, serving, repairing, and so forth, the application of the principle of piece-work is impossible, except under conditions of mere arbitrary valuation. The same objections already apply, in some degree, to the apportionment of "good marks" for prison labour and conduct. This plan works tolerably well in some British and other prisons; yet it is, at the same time, a very imperfect one, and is attended by certain dangers and objectionable modes of operation.

The exaction of a portion of the money-earnings, under the competition and valuation of actual life, is a more generally available basis than imprisonment, for estimating both the punishable capacity of a man, and also his powers of restitution to an injured community, or to aggrieved individuals. Whether the offender be a ploughman, a mason, a shopkeeper, a servant, or a physician, the scale of his ordinary earnings, or assessment, may furnish a fair foundation for estimating an amount of punishment which shall be really penal, but free from the demoralisation of the concentrated felonry of prison life. There can be little if any doubt, that to this mode of penalty, in conjunction with a vigilant police supervision, a resort might much more generally be made than hitherto, with advantages moral and economical, deterrent and reformatory, not possessed, in nearly the same degree, by imprisonment.

FINES ARE IN HARMONY WITH NATURAL CONDITIONS.

Punishment by fining has the important recommendation of being in harmony with nature. For the subject of it is

D D

retained under the conditions of family and social life, and under those salutary influences which are, for the most part, exerted by wives, mothers, and daughters, but which are precluded by incarceration.

The adoption of Fines, on any extensive scale, should always include arrangements for their payment, at any rate by the poor, in weekly or monthly *instalments*, extending over a considerable period, so as to allow the offender to work out his imposition at such a rate as may be reasonably practicable.

The Efficacy of Fines Enhanced by the Alternative of the Cell.—Fraudulent Debtors.

As a stimulus to continued exertion for the payment of fines, it is necessary to hold in reserve the alternative of a prompt infliction of cellular imprisonment. Much indeed of their efficacy depends upon their being regarded as a desirable *substitute* for confinement. And unless the latter be known to be a really disagreeable infliction, it will be chosen in preference, in many instances. Cases have often occurred in England, where Fraudulent Debtors and persons arrested for the non-payment of fines, have deliberately allowed themselves to be sent to jail, even when able to pay immediately. The reason was that they confidently reckoned upon the pleasant and jovial companionship with other debtors, to be enjoyed in the common wards usually allotted to this class of prisoners. A veteran Governor of a jail informed the writer that he had adopted an effectual scheme to disappoint such expectations. He imposed, as far as possible, unpleasant conditions of restraint and strict separation. Consequently, in a day or two after entrance, the debtors were almost certain to exclaim, "I have had enough of this; I'll pay. Let me out." In instance after instance, the money was promptly paid in that prison, after a little profitable isolation and meditation.

But in other prisons, where less wise measures are

adopted with Fraudulent Debtors, they willingly allow the authorities to substitute, instead of cash payment, an easy detention in the association wards, at the cost of the taxpayers. In one such case, a man who was brought to jail for the non-payment of a small sum, was found to have in his pockets five times the amount of the debt. But he loved his money more than he feared the lax restraints of association in confinement, without work. All such persons should simply have the alternative of paying their fines whilst in a state of liberty, or, as an equivalent, serving a duly limited term of cellular imprisonment. It is indispensable that the latter must be salutarily penal.

CONDITIONAL LIBERTY, OR PROBATION.

Of recent times, the most civilised nations have very advantageously adopted, as a substitute for imprisonment, .the system of Conditional Liberty, or Liberty on Probation, for certain classes of offenders. It may be here observed that there is a distinction between Conditional *Liberty* and Conditional *Liberation.* The former applies to persons who are permitted to escape imprisonment altogether, on the condition of their continuing good behaviour for a certain period. The latter refers to offenders who have undergone a portion of their sentences of imprisonment, and who have then been discharged " on ticket of leave," or otherwise on some conditions implying a liability to prompt re-arrest and re-imprisonment in case of their relapse into evil courses.

It is to be remembered that the *principle* of Conditional Liberty (as distinguished from Conditional Liberation) had long been practically recognised in England under the forms of BAIL, or personal RECOGNISANCES; and in the " BINDING OVER " of certain quarrelsome or offensive persons to " keep the peace " towards their fellow-subjects, for a given period, as an alternative to imprisonment.

In GERMANY this plan is carried out by means of

sentences of *Deferred* Imprisonment. That is to say, the
offender receives a certain sentence, but at the same time
he is permitted to be at liberty *until* some further misbehaviour on his part, when he becomes at once punishable
both for the original transgression and the subsequent
offence.

In BELGIUM, FRANCE, AUSTRIA, the UNITED STATES, and
other countries, various modes of Conditional Liberation
are also now being increasingly adopted, with advantage
both to the State and to the individuals concerned.

MASSACHUSETTS ADULT " PROBATION."

After the State of Massachusetts had (as already
mentioned) successfully adopted the Probation System for
Juveniles, it extended it to Adults, by a Law, passed in
1880, which instituted as a special class, "PROBATION
OFFICERS" for ADULTS, to be appointed in every district,
by the respective Municipalities. It was then enacted, in
regard to each of such functionaries, as follows: "He
shall, in the execution of his official duties, have the powers
of Police officers, and may be a member of the Police Force
of his city or town. Such Probation Officer shall carefully
inquire into the character and offence of every person arrested for crime, for the purpose of ascertaining whether
the accused may reasonably be expected to reform without
punishment; and shall keep a full record of the result of
his investigation. The Officer, if then satisfied that the
best interests of the public and of the accused would be
subserved by placing him upon Probation, shall recommend
the same to the Court trying the case; and the Court may
permit the accused to be placed upon Probation, upon such
terms as it may deem best, having regard to his reformation."

"When the Probation Officer considers it advisable for
any person placed on probation to be sent out of the State,
the local authorities may make the necessary appropriation

for the purpose, to be expended by him, under the direction of the superintendent of police."

"The Probation Officer shall, as far as practicable, visit the offenders placed on probation by the Court at his suggestion, and render such assistance and encouragement as will tend to prevent their again offending. Any person placed upon probation, upon his recommendation, may be re-arrested by him, upon approval of the superintendent of police, without further warrant, and again brought before the Court; and the Court may thereupon proceed to sentence, or may make any other lawful disposition of the case. It shall be the special duty of every Probation Officer to inform the Court, as far as possible, whether a person on trial has previously been convicted of any crime."

The above are the principal clauses of the Massachusetts Law of 1880, permitting the experiment of Adult Probation, and which at once went into operation. It may be observed that it is *permissive* in its nature, and entrusts large powers of discrimination and decision, both to the Courts and to the Probation and Police Officers. Such must necessarily be the case, from the very nature of probation.

The Secretary of the Massachusetts Commissioners of Prisons informs the writer that "The success of the (adult) probation work is unquestionable." He adds: "It is the 'ticket-of-leave system' simplified to suit the circumstances. Most of those here released, on such probation, are drunkards, or night-walkers (prostitutes); and the results have been gratifying."

In the smaller towns of Massachusetts, Probation usually continues for a year; in the large towns, often only about two months. The latter period is quite inadequate for many cases.

One of the Boston Probation Officers reports that one of the best results of their system is the stimulus which it affords to the relatives of the offending parties, to seek

employment for them, and to exercise some effectual influence and vigilance on their behalf. He remarks: "The
best success has been secured by making it a condition with
their friends that employment be provided for the persons
probated, before they are bailed and set at liberty."   The
fees paid on liberation are stated to be nearly sufficient to
cover the expenses incurred in carrying out the system."

In one of the Reports, an Agent relates an incident which
is not without instruction. He, one day, received a sharp
lecture from a wealthy and influential Bostonian, who was
indignant with what he regarded as the undue laxity of
the State towards offenders on probation. He said: "I
would have every one of them punished, to the extremity
of the law." But some time afterwards this gentleman
came to the officer, in great grief, to implore aid on behalf
of his son, a youth of eighteen, who had got into trouble
by embezzling money from his employers. On investigation, it was found that the lad's previous character had
been good, and that he had fallen under great temptation.
The Agent reported favourably to the Court respecting
him, and he was placed on one year's probation, to obviate
the disgrace of imprisonment. He afterwards returned to
his former employers, who eventually took him into part-
nership. His father, meeting the Agent subsequently in
the street, grasped his hand, and exclaimed with emotion,
"My son is safe; I was wrong." The same Agent remarks:
"I have learned to believe that none are so good that they
may not err; and none so bad that they cannot reform."

PROSTITUTES AND PROBATION.

The class of "unfortunate girls," or prostitutes, often
derive effectual benefit from the "probation" system, by
reason of the opportunities which it affords for inducing
them to return to their friends, or to enter some suitable
shelter. The Massachusetts Laws are nominally severe
against certain forms of unchastity, in both sexes alike;

but there, as all over the world, the women generally have to bear the brunt, both of the shame and the punishment. The men usually secure impunity. A Probation report mentions a girl, with whom six different men, in one evening, had been observed to go off, for an immoral purpose. But it adds, " Six to one. Who ever saw one of such men in the prisoners' dock, as an accomplice ? Who ever saw one of this class of men on the witness-stand, in his own defence ? "

For female prisoners, the Massachusetts Laws permit a special form of probation, or conditional liberation. The State Board of Commissioners are authorised to bind out in domestic or other service, for the concluding unexpired portion of their terms of imprisonment, such women as they consider suitable to be thus liberated, on condition of good behaviour. Failing this condition, the licences are revoked, and all the original sentence is carried into effect. Such remissions usually amount to about one-third of the full terms of sentence. The great majority of these women are reported to behave well, and to furnish no occasion for re-imposition of penalty. But it is noticed that longer powers of sentence, and of subsequent control, are still needed for the female criminals, as a class.

The Old English " Ticket-of-Leave " Imposture.

It is important to observe that, although one of the Massachusetts Agents compares probation to a "ticket-of-leave" plan, yet neither that nor the present English system of Conditional Liberation, under supervision, is identical with the original mischievous "ticket-of-leave" practice, as adopted for British convicts, under Sir Joshua Jebb. That officer discharged his prisoners by wholesale, with the *form* of "Tickets," but *without* the all-important elements of adequate supervision and inquiry. The men were simply released with wild recklessness. The results were just what might be expected, and occasioned an outburst of robbery, burglary, violence, and other crimes, until the very name of "Ticket-of-Leave" became deservedly offensive to the public. Unfortunately, too, the memory of that blunder has ever since constituted a chief obstacle to the progress of any system of "conditional liberation" or "probation" on each side of the Atlantic. But both Massachusetts and Great Britain have since been able to remove some of this popular misapprehension, by more cautious experiments.

THE HOWARD ASSOCIATION AND "PROBATION."

The Committee of the HOWARD ASSOCIATION in London, in 1881, issued a paper, drawing British attention to the advantages of the Massachusetts Probation system, especially for Juvenile Offenders. As the plan was then almost unknown in Great Britain, the HOME SECRETARY had that document reprinted in a Parliamentary Paper. Subsequently, Colonel HOWARD VINCENT, M.P., expounded the system in an interesting manner at a meeting of the Social Science Congress. Later still, he introduced a Bill into the House of Commons with the object of securing the legislative sanction of an English "probation" system for misdemeanants, somewhat similar to the Massachusetts mode. This measure passed in 1887, and is entitled "The Probation of First Offenders Act."

PROBATION BY BRITISH LEGISLATION.

Of recent years, the public mind in England has been awakening, in some degree at least, to the advantages of inflicting other modes of punishment than imprisonment. This impression had, even previously to the passing of the Probation of First Offenders Act led to the enactment of the "Summary Jurisdiction Act" of 1879. That excellent measure not only increased the power of magistrates, already existing under the Juvenile Offenders Act of 1847, to dismiss young persons, on admonition, and without imprisonment, in certain cases, but also permitted the substitution of Fines instead of dètention, for various offences under the Acts relating to Poaching, Vagrancy, Public Health, and even some Felony. The previous scale of sentences for several crimes, was also reduced by this Act. And it obviated many imprisonments of poor persons, by authorising the fines to be paid gradually, by Instalments. In these and certain other respects, the Summary Jurisdiction Act was a very valuable measure of penal reform.

The "Probation of First Offenders Act," 1887, effected further progress in a similar direction. Its provisions are as follows :—

"In any case in which a person is convicted of larceny, or false pretences, or any other offence punishable with not more than two years' imprisonment, before any court, and no previous conviction is proved against him, if it appears to the Court before whom he is so convicted, that, regard being had to the youth, character and antecedents of the offender, to the trivial nature of the offence, and to any extenuating circumstances under which the offence was committed, it is expedient that the offender be released on probation of good conduct, the Court may, instead of sentencing him at once to any punishment, direct that he be released on his entering into a recognisance, with or without sureties, and during such period as the Court may direct, to appear and receive judgment when called upon, and in the meantime to keep the peace and be of good behaviour.

"The Court may, if it thinks fit, direct that the offender shall pay the costs of the prosecution, or some portion of the same, within such period and by such instalments as may be directed by the Court."

These two Acts, together with the collateral measures for the committal of delinquent and neglected youth to

Reformatories and Industrial Schools, have materially contributed toward that diminution both of prisoners and of jails, in Great Britain, which is a gratifying feature of the age. Especially satisfactory is the approximate abandonment of the imprisonment of children, in this country, of late years. ˙

In proportion as the jail has been less used than at a former period, it has proved that other ways of disposing of offenders, at once less costly and less degrading, have been found practically advantageous. May this lesson be profitably pondered. And may it lead to further advances in the adoption of more economic, more reformatory, and more effectually preventive modes of dealing with transgressors against the laws, than by an excessive resort, as in the past, to either the solitary cell, or the corrupting convict gang.

CHAPTER XX.

CORPORAL PUNISHMENT.

DIVERSITY OF OPINION.

ANOTHER advantageous substitute for imprisonment, in
certain cases, may be found in Corporal Punishment.
The authority of Solomon, and of other ancient writers,
has been invoked in favour of this means of correction,
whilst many instances of failure and of increased perversity
have been adduced in counter objection. And certainly the
opponents of flogging appear to be so far justified in their
position, when they object to a brutal or general infliction
of this punishment; when, for example (as often occurred
in military floggings), the flesh of the sufferer was so
lacerated that the surface of the body became a mass of
bleeding wounds. Such a spectacle is brutalising to all
parties concerned. It is savage and wicked, and is calculated to quench any remaining spark of self-respect, or
hope, in the person so punished. Further, it tends to
produce cruel and criminal dispositions, in those who have
to take part in its administration. Such an infliction is,
in short, barbaric torture, rather than just chastisement.

The frequent and habitual resort to flogging, as a punish-

ment, has been a failure, and has always proved incompe-
teney on the part of the authorities. Its subjects have
then become reckless and irreclaimable.

Two Missionaries of the Society of Friends, JAMES
BACKHOUSE and GEORGE W. WALKER, who visited the
Australian penal colonies in 1834, when flogging was in
constant and abundant use by the authorities, recorded—
" Most prisoners have a dread of flagellation, till they have
once suffered the punishment; after this, the generality of
them exhibit a decided deterioration of character." This
statement agrees with the remark of the Author of " Six
Years in the Convict Prisons of England," who says, " You
will never find a man doing much good, *after* being flogged.
It may make him quiet under authority, but it ensures
the very opposite when he is free." Mr. SHEPPARD, who
was for thirty years Governor of Wakefield Prison, one of
the largest in England, stated that during all that period it
was not found necessary to flog any prisoner there. He
added " It is never necessary, when other right means are
tried." Even in Tasmania, where flogging had long been
in frequent, or rather constant use, as a means of convict
discipline, there came a period of excellent government,
under Sir WILLIAM DENISON, of whom it is recorded by
his wise counsellor and friend, Bishop Willson, that " for
some years previous to his departure from the island, not
one convict had been subjected to the odious lash."

This question of flogging is one respecting which there
is a peculiar diversity of opinion amongst practical men, of
similar experience and humanity. And especially in regard
to it, the old proverb may be quoted—" Who shall decide,
when doctors disagree ? " Still, this difference of view
will be found, on examination, to be not quite so perplexing
as at first sight may appear to be the case; for there
is corporal punishment *and* corporal punishment. And
some persons who most decidedly object to the brutal
form of its administration, where the flesh is mangled or

the body disfigured, do not entertain an invincible repugnance to the comparatively mild and only occasional, or exceptional, infliction of such whipping, or "spanking" with a leather strap, as merely produces transient but stinging, pain on cruel offenders who are insensible to reasonable persuasion.

As to the utility of this description of punishment, in certain cases, there is an extensive concurrence of view amongst men whose acquaintance with the criminal classes is based upon long and close observation. Many prison officers are able to adduce instances where ferocious and otherwise intractable men have been subdued by a whipping, or strapping; or even by the knowledge of its being available, as a reserve power, to be certainly inflicted if called for. It is reasonably argued by such experienced authorities, that they have found this castigation, when inflicted as a rare and exceptional resort, a peculiarly merciful penalty, as obviating a much greater, though less impressive, aggregate of punishment, by prolonged imprisonment, or special privations.

The Mercy of Moderate Corporal Punishment.

And indeed the chief defence of corporal punishment, of a moderate description, consists in its *mercifulness*, both direct and indirect, especially when inflicted upon the particular class of cruel and brutal men who are apt to despise other influences, and from whom it is necessary that their ordinary victims, weak women and tender children, shall be more effectually protected. For example, a wretch was recently brought before an English court, for having so habitually beaten his wife upon the face, that she had been disfigured with " black eyes," in consequence, twenty-seven times! Another flung his little child violently against the ceiling. Another, because his young brother, twelve years of age, refused to go out and beg for him, stripped the boy naked, lashed him to a chair for fifteen hours, and struck him with a strap and buckle thirty-four times. Another horrible ruffian committed outrages, on various occasions, upon twenty-two little girls, whom he had enticed into lonely places by offers of sweetmeats. Other men have kicked their wives and children with their hobnailed boots until they have broken their bones, or have disfigured them for life; others have assaulted inoffensive persons with crow-bars and knives, or gouged out their eyes; others have scattered death and misery amongst peaceable citizens, by means of dynamite or similar explosives.

These are the sort of outrages, and their number is legion, constantly committed by a class of wretches who are at once the most cruel and the most cowardly of the community; creatures compared with whom the ordinary thief is a paragon of virtue.

Such despicable miscreants are more effectually cowed, and more promptly held in check, by smart corporal punishment than by other modes of restraint. It is absurd to talk about "degrading" them by this infliction. *They have already degraded themselves to the uttermost.* Any process of treatment which either checks their crimes, or brings them to some sense of wholesome fear or shame, is at once an *elevation* and a *mercy.* Even floggings of the old sort, are inflictions which *they,* at least, would have no right to deem unjust. But, for other considerations, that description of punishment is not to be advocated. To these inhuman foes of their own kind, the adminstration of a moderate but stinging castigation with rods, or a whip, or leather strap, on the bare back, for a reasonable number of times, at intervals, according to the enormity of the offence, is a much more dreaded, and therefore a more effectual, punishment, than months and years of mere imprisonment, with the encouraging association of other wretches, and under comparatively comfortable conditions of food, lodging, and indulgence, and all at the cost of honest tax-payers.

It must be remembered, too, that many of this particular class have already done despite to a vast amount of kindness and patient forbearance, on the part of too-loving relatives, as mothers and wives. They have become deaf to remonstrance, and hardened to ordinary persuasives. Professor HENRY ROGERS remarked many years ago, in the *Edinburgh Review*, in reference to such persons: " Too many of them have deliberately advanced along their career of crime, in one perpetual outrage on all the best and holiest impulses of humanity ; in contempt of that passionate domestic love which outlives the worth of its object, and the dictates of reason itself; in spite of infinite sacrifices and never-wearied forgiveness ; in spite of the spectacle of comprehensive and all unutterable misery, caused by their perseverance in evil. To suppose that such natures as these are to be subdued by leniency, is to hope that rocks will melt in the sun."

It is for such a class of criminals, those characterised by the most hateful of all crimes, *cruelty*, that corporal punishment is here advocated.

EITHER CORPORAL PUNISHMENT, OR THE CELL.

For this class of ruffians, either Corporal Punishment, *or* the Cell, is indispensable. The latter, with moderately certain cumulation for repeated offences, would in many instances be effectual, and perhaps be even preferable to the former. But whilst the almost universal alleviations of modern prison life, necessitated by unduly prolonged detention, and by associated labour, are retained, there will be a constant danger that such conditions of existence will become a positive attraction to lazy and reckless offenders, or will at least fail to hold out a repellent or deterrent aspect to the criminal and the ruffian, unless some decidedly disagreeable elements are added, or, at any rate, held in reserve, for ultimate adoption.

ANCIENT WISDOM.

Our forefathers were not so bereft of wisdom, in regard to their treatment of certain offenders, as it has become, of late years, the fashion to represent. They often proved, by experience, the efficacy of the very brief, very sharp, and very cheap infliction of a whipping, in such cases as have been mentioned. They believed the old Book was not in the wrong when it prescribed "a rod for the fool's back," at any rate for the *cruel* class of fools.

For some trivial transgressors, our ancestors used the "STOCKS." And here, again, it is fairly open to question whether the cause of mercy has been served, by substituting the prison for that short and simple mode of warning. Is it not a harsher thing to inflict the life-long stigma of "gaol-bird" for certain petty offences, together with the involved withdrawal from family support, for weeks or months, rather than to place such persons upon the "stool of repentance," with legs in the "stocks" for an hour or two, amid the not always, or altogether, unsympathising, if somewhat rough, criticisms of their neighbours; and then to have wholly done with the affair, so far as the interference of authority is concerned ?

Public opinion is apt to vibrate from one extreme to the opposite, and from one folly to another. Hence, as soon as men began to perceive the brutality of such inflictions as the rack, the knout, the thumb-screw, or the pillory, they rushed to an opposite mode of dealing with offenders' and, under the delusion that all corporal punishment was wrong, proceeded to substitute prolonged, costly, demoralising, and hardening imprisonments, which ultimately were, in many cases, *more* cruel, to spirit, mind, body, and estate, than, at any rate, the more moderate modes of short and sharp castigation, which had previously been in vogue.

Many imprisonments have permanently ruined men, and thereby cruelly punished their innocent families also; when, by the simpler and common-sense methods of our forefathers, much of this mischief might have been immediately nipped in the bud, at the cost of a few shillings in money and a few hours in time.

CHAPTER XXI.

CRIMINAL STATISTICS.

STATISTICS OF CRIME AND PRISONS.

As respects the Statistics of Crime and Prisons, it may be observed that the measure of imperfection, which is more or less inherent to all matters pertaining to humanity, is apt to be somewhat specially characteristic of this class of figures.

Many years ago, a friend of the writer, Mr. JOSEPH JOHN FOX, F.S.S., of Stoke Newington, read before a meeting of the British Association, a paper on the *necessity of uniformity of basis for statistical calculations.* This principle is one of great importance; but it is very apt to be disregarded. This neglect involves much practical difficulty in various directions.

Thus, in reference to Crime, it is to be noticed that the legal definitions, and therefore the statistical tabulations of "Murder," "Burglary," "Forgery," etc., not only vary considerably in different countries at any one period, but have also undergone consecutive changes in each particular nation. Hence, for example, if a statistician makes a collection of the English official returns, in regard to the number of burglaries, or forgeries, committed during successive decades, in this country only, it will be found, on careful examination, that owing to the progress of legislation during the later periods, certain new forms of these crimes have become included under the categories in ques.tion; or, otherwise, certain old forms have been excluded from them.

In the first issue of the English Judicial Statistics in their reorganised mode of presentation, in 1894, it was remarked by Mr. JOHN MACDONELL, that from year to year, the statistical student, or writer, should note, as is done in the Italian *Statistica Giudiziaria Penale*, changes in criminal procedure law, or in other parts of criminal law likely to affect the returns: *e.g.*, extension of summary jurisdiction; alterations in the definition of crimes; decisions of great consequence; and the formation of new Courts. But it is often very difficult, if not impossible, to adapt statistically such changes to previous or existing figures.

Thus, if it is attempted to compare the statistics even of Murder, in different countries, it will be found difficult, if not impossible, to ascertain how far the respective figures include, or exclude, cases of manslaughter and general homicide, as distinguished from deliberately "wilful" or premeditated "murder." The legislation of the principal States of Europe and America differs so considerably, in regard to such points, that, at the best, only approximate accuracy can be secured in any calculations or inferences. based even upon the official penal statistics of these coun-tries, as compared with one another, or as generally sum-marised.

Further, the departmental organisations for the collec-tion and determination of statistics, in the respective nations, vary so much, in reference to their efficiency, as to import additional elements of imperfection and perplexity into the matter. Nor is there much reason to conclude that under the existing circumstances of States, a satisfactory avoidance of these difficulties is likely to be arrived at, at any early period. Hence the whole question of Inter-national Statistics, especially in regard to penal matters, must be regarded as essentially defective, and of merely elementary development, from the point of view of mathematical accuracy.

And yet, essential as is this numerical accuracy, it only forms one portion of the materials requisite for arriving at a uniform basis of statistics. An elaborate machinery for the collection of figures and enumerations may be performing its duty, with a fair degree of completeness, within its own province, and all the while, it may be conveying a very erroneous final impression as to the real condition of affairs, for want of collateral and qualifying information on other connected matters.

For example, the statistical returns of various districts of the British Metropolis indicated, to a certain student, a special mortality in several parishes. So far as the figures were concerned, this indication was perfectly correct. Nevertheless the impression, at first naturally received, was altogether and most properly modified by the subsequent discovery that these apparently very unhealthy districts contained large hospitals, or infirmaries, where patients, in dangerous stages of illness and injury, were collected from the surrounding parts, and the deaths of many of whom gave an exceptional character to the local mortality in question. Again, there was a very healthy place in Cornwall, in which, during a certain year, only four deaths were recorded. One of these was by public execution. It would, therefore, be perfectly correct, so far as mere mathematical accuracy is concerned, to remark that twenty-five per cent. of the deaths, there, in one year, took place at the hands of the hangman. But, at the same time, such a statement would tend to convey an impression unjust to the people of that virtuous and orderly locality, in which the execution of a criminal was probably an occurrence so exceptional, that it is doubtful if any other individual, from there, had been hanged for half a century or more.

The above are extreme illustrations of the possible dangers of reliance, upon mathematically accurate statistics. But some such danger often, if not indeed always, exists in this department; and it is intensified by the prevalent deficiency, even of the single element of numerical accuracy of registration.

In consequence of these almost unavoidable features of statistical defect, throughout the world, more or less, it is needful that Penologists, everywhere, should not attach too much importance to mere numerical returns. For it may be fairly concluded that, in view of the actual circumstances of the collection and condition of International Criminal Returns, their general value is much overestimated in many quarters. Some Penologists, it is true, are hoping great things from a further development of this class of Statistics. But there seems to be very little real ground for an expectation of early or considerable advantage arising in this direction.

It would have been well for some nations, if portions of the large sums of money and of the great amount of time, long devoted to the collection of minute numerical details, in reference to prisons, police, and arrests, had been appropriated rather to the study and exposition of a few simple principles, to be practically regarded in the treatment and prevention of crime.

Government Departments are apt to manifest undue favour to such excessive statistical registration, for two reasons; firstly, because it gives easy routine work to many officials; and, secondly, because it affords a great show of attention to duty, and at the same time often furnishes a convenient excuse for indefinitely postponing more laborious, but more essential, performances for the public welfare.

A very serious defect in the criminal and other official statistics, even of some of the chief nations, is that they are not seldom characterised by culpable omissions. Where there is not the positive *suggestio falsi*, there is sometimes to be found, and not always in a small measure, the *suppressio veri*.   In some ostentatious volumes of Departmental Returns, the careful Penologist may look in vain for important information which he ought to find there, but which is studiously withheld ; whilst at the same time, a tedious minuteness, in comparatively trivial matters, is thrust upon the reader, to the extent of many pages of figures.   The class of numerical statements, sometimes known as "cooked accounts," is not such a rarity as it ought to be, even in Returns issued officially to Parliaments and the public.   And where, when, or how, may we hope for a generally effectual remedy for this ?

CHAPTER XXII.

THE POLICE:

Especially in Relation to Pawnbrokers, Publicans, Prostitutes and the Prevention of Crime.

The Police More Influential than Prison Authorities.

Not only has there been manifested, in most nations, a too prevalent tendency to over-estimate the general efficacy of Imprisonment, but also and especially, a disposition to form an exaggerated idea of its influence, in comparison with that of the Police. The latter have been too exclusively regarded as mere instruments of arrest and of detection ; or as a body of men whose chief function consists in being the outside servants of the prison authorities.

In reality, the position and powers of a wisely organised Police Force are much more efficacious and comprehensive in their operation than those of the other class. The officers of Prisons have, for their special duty, the infliction of punishment, and to a certain minor extent, the application of reformatory efforts, in regard to those persons placed under their charge. But such constitute only a very small proportion of the community. Whereas the Police are more or less brought into contact with the great body of the population; and if rightly directed and trained, they have unlimited opportunities, both for the exercise of

preventive influences in regard to crime, and for the promotion of various modes of social improvement.

Yet, in most countries, hitherto, the splendid possibilities
and powers of a beneficently organised Police, have been
largely ignored, or very inadequately regarded.   For
example, throughout the greater portion of the European
Continent, the governing authorities appear to have had
little idea of making their police anything but a mere
agency for the purposes of political or criminal espionage
and arrest.   The detection, rather than the prevention, of
offences, has too exclusively constituted the function of
these officers.   But this is a grave mistake.

For in proportion as such a one-sided course is adopted,
it becomes the interest of the police to abstain from
influences and exertions which might, by destroying or
obviating criminality, at the same time deprive themselves
of the opportunities of earning reward and promotion.
The motive and principle resemble those of the cunning
rat-catcher, when paid in proportion to the number
of animals which he secures in his snares, and who therefore, takes, also, effectual measures that the supply of such
creatures shall never fail, or be reduced in such a degree as
to put an end to his own occupation.   But when his
services are utilised in a more intelligent manner, by his
employers, and when he is remunerated in proportion to
the success of his endeavours in keeping places altogether
and permanently clear of the vermin, it is observable that
he manifests resources of skilful efficiency, which appeared
to be beyond his power, so long as he was paid only for
the capture, rather than for the continuous absence of the
rats, as tested by the discontinuance of their depredations.

ABSENCE OF CRIME, A CHIEF TEST OF POLICE EFFICIENCY.

Similarly, a decisive test of the success of the Police
system of any country, is the general comparative amount

of its crime. This is not to be chiefly measured by the number of criminals arrested, but by the known and felt absence of violence, theft, and vice. Certain countries, or districts, could be named, where there is a notorious prevalence of serious crimes, whose perpetrators remain, in many instances, undiscovered and unpunished. This indicates a double inefficiency of the local authorities. They are, in such places, comparatively impotent, both for prevention and for detection. Whereas the characteristic of able police administration, is skill in *both* directions. But the prevention requires much *more* ability than the detection. And hence it is found, as a matter of fact, that the Police who are best trained in *preventive* efficiency are also the most skilful in *detective* ingenuity.

Distinctively Military Police are the Less Intelligent.

The comparative efficiency and popularity of the British police are in a great degree to be attributed to the progress already made, in efforts on the part of their chief officers, to develop amongst their men the faculty of individual thoughtfulness and general practical aptitude. They are encouraged to use their own wits, and to think for themselves. This they are the better qualified for, inasmuch as they have not, for the most part been subjected to previous military training. It must, however, be acknowledged that much more of this intelligence is still to be desired, even on the part of the Metropolitan police.

One of the chief and most successful of British Police Authorities has remarked to the writer,—" *Soldiers, in general, make the worst police*, precisely because they have usually been trained *not to think for themselves*, but simply to obey commands implicitly. If you order an old soldier to perambulate a certain street, he will just ' cover the ground,' and do nothing more. He simply goes where he is told to go, and sees what he is told to look at, but is apt to

direct his attention to nothing beside, and to allow all else
to elude his observation ; because he has always been taught
to do nothing but *to obey orders in a mere mechanical spirit.*"
The same officer added, "If one of my men asks me to give
him precise directions for the detection of a certain crime, I
know that he is not adequately skilful. I expect him *to
think out and to devise, for himself*, the best means of detection, in accordance with the special circumstances of each
particular case. But unless he has been trained, or accustomed, to think for himself, he is incompetent for such
mental exertion." And *hence* it is that mere military police
fail in the highest functions of a first-class organisation.
Their antecedents, as a body, have not only not qualified
them for the lively, independent exercise of their own
intellects, in the double work of detection and prevention,
but have positively unfitted them for such important
services. In other words, the very foundation of military
efficiency is one of the chief sources of incompetency,
as respects the highest police functions. This important
truth is, however, greatly disregarded by many authorities,
both in reference to the police and prison officials.

Efficiency of the British Police.

It is no undue boast, on the part of Englishmen, to assert
that, notwithstanding some decided defects, the police of
their own ·country are amongst the most efficient in the
world, and are indeed probably unequalled. One reason for
this high position is that the central and municipal authorities in Great Britain have, at any rate of late years,
chosen for their chief Directors or Commissioners of Police,
gentlemen of high qualifications, and have not permitted
the elements of political partizanship to usurp a prominent
influence in this selection, in comparison, at least, with the
extent to which such inducements have operated in regard
to some other appointments. It is true that these able
chiefs have, in general, had a military training ; but then

this has been of a very different nature from that of the comparatively uneducated private soldiers. The former have been men of much intellectual development, through collegiate or university advantages, and have thus been accustomed to think and act for themselves. Some of the foremost among them have been, and are, men of piety and morality. They have been in sympathy with the people, and have insisted upon their subordinates cultivating this spirit. The British police, as a body, are therefore popular. And herein consists much of their power. An experienced Director of the police said to the writer :— " We are ' in touch ' with the people. Otherwise we could not get on at all; or, at any rate, we could not maintain order with anything like our present numbers."

Moral Functions of the British Police.

The attainment of success, in the eminently important service of preventing or diminishing crime, imperatively demands the cultivation of moral qualities and human sympathies, in addition to detective intelligence. And in this department, also, many of the British police are exemplary. They have approximated the honourable standard described by an observant magistrate, in the following words :—" The Police should not be a separate body, antagonistic to the people, but more citizens than police ; respected and valued by their fellow-subjects, and specially fitted to keep a friendly watch on liberated prisoners."

Many of the English Police, both in the superior and subordinate ranks, are to be numbered amongst the practical philanthropists of the nation. They are kind to the children and dumb animals, and courteously helpful to the citizens in the streets. And they may fairly be credited with some share in securing that marked diminution of serious crime, which has taken place in Great Britain of late years.

The Police and Receivers of Stolen Goods.

There is a form of evil, in Great Britain especially, to which legislation and public attention have not been adequately directed, and in regard to which the interests of the community demand that more power should be given to the police, or at least to the Superintendents, and more intelligent officers amongst them. This is a most fertile root of crime, and consists in the insufficient control over the Receivers of Stolen Goods and similar " Crime Capitalists." It has been repeatedly observed that, if there were no receivers or dealers in stolen property, there would be very few thieves. There are, amongst the Pawnbrokers, many respectable persons who afford considerable assistance to the police in the detection of crime, but there is also amongst them a minority of a very different character. And the business of even the best class of Pawnbrokers, for want of more stringent regulations, may render them unconscious instruments of facilitating crime. There has also arisen, of late years, a body of men who advertise for large or small consignments of goods from distant places, for which prompt payment is promised and no questions are to be asked. This mode of doing business places great temptations in the way of dishonest servants, workmen, and others.

It also aids the operations of " The Long Firm," a name given to individuals, or groups, who, whilst pretending to be legitimate merchants, are in reality base thieves, often on a wholesale scale, inasmuch as they obtain, by regular order, goods for which they have no intention whatever of paying, but which, through the help of other dishonest traders and receivers, they promptly turn into cash, at a very cheap rate, and at a good profit (having incurred no expense for the same), and then disappear, or become bankrupt, or in various ways manage to elude the grasp of the law. Very extensive injury is thus inflicted upon the public, and cruel wrong done to many respectable dealers. But hitherto, when any attempt has been made, in England at least, to impose an effectual check upon such dishonesty, some of the offenders, or their agents, have been able to mystify the public, and frustrate the needful legislative changes. They have pointed to the danger of increased police power, and have pleaded that only a minor portion of their business is connected with fraud. And, like the young woman who excused her having an illegitimate baby, because it was "so small," so by raising a somewhat similar plea, some of this class have succeeded in averting that vigorous repression of their operations which is essential. There can be no doubt but that a vast amount of property is annually stolen with impunity, in every country; and somehow, it finds purchasers. Individual thieves are often apprehended, but it is a *rare* event to see one of the wholesale receivers convicted. Yet these are *incomparably more dangerous*, more intelligent, and more culpable, than the open thieves and robbers. In regard to this, as to other public evils, the sources and roots of the mischief should be mainly dealt with. But, with some exceptions, this has not yet been the case.

It ought not to be an insuperable difficulty, in England, to secure measures for destroying the confidence between thieves and the cunning receivers of their plunder, the men who have their secret melting furnaces in readiness to promptly convert stolen gold, silver, and jewellery into a condition beyond the power of identification by its legitimate claimants. It has been suggested that special inducements, through a reduction of sentence, or of punishment, should be held out to thieves to furnish such information (often only known to themselves) as might tend to bring to justice the chief agents and abettors of crime, these more wicked dealers in plunder. The Police have long been obliged, through defect of the law in this direction, to refrain from arresting persons whom they have good reason to consider the most dangerous and effective sources both of local and distant crime. It was stated by Mr. M. D. HILL, that for one such person punished, five thousand have escaped.

It is also to be desired in England that the Police, or, still better, some Magisterial authority, such as the Scotch Procurators Fiscal, should be furnished with greater powers for the INITIATION of Prosecutions, both of the receivers of stolen goods and of other criminals in general. This too generally devolves upon private persons, to the great injury of the public interests.

POLICE INSTITUTES.

Most valuable aids to the moral elevation and general efficiency of the Police, as a body, have of recent years been afforded by the establishment of Police Institutes, in Great Britain, the Colonies, and the United States.

The extension of these Institutes, or Clubs, has been greatly promoted by a philanthropic lady, MISS C. GURNEY, whose labours in this direction have been most praiseworthy. From the Central Institute at Adelphi Terrace, London, branches have been established far and wide. The principal Institutes combine Libraries and Recreation Rooms, with arrangements for the encouragement of Temperance, Thrift, Excursions, Meetings, and Entertainments. Police Orphanages and Convalescent Homes have also been instituted.

By means of correspondents and travelling agents, an active organisation of a model character has been formed, which has already conferred great benefit upon the Police and the community in many lands. The chief authorities have helpfully encouraged these Institutes, the further extension of which is desirable in every country.

In America, a similar movement has been greatly helped by the New York "CITY VIGILANCE LEAGUE," and kindred bodies.

THE POLICE AND KINDNESS TO ANIMALS.

In Great Britain, the Police render excellent service in the promotion of kindness, and the discouragement of cruelty, to animals, especially horses and dogs. The shocking treatment of such poor beasts in France, Spain, and Italy, ought to be checked by the Governments of those countries, where, also, the Police should be requested to devote special attention to the repression of an evil which is so dishonourable to any nation.

THE POLICE AND THE POOR.

The Police can, and often do, render valuable assistance to the poor, in the manifestation of various modes of practical sympathy. In EDINBURGH, for example, in conjunction with a local benevolent association and certain philanthropists, such as Mr. KEITH MURRAY, Mrs. MAC-DONNELL-LEMMI, and others, and with the active encouragement of CAPTAIN WILLIAM HENDERSON, the local Chief Constable, the Police have greatly improved the condition of poor children in that large city, by their services in connection with admirable arrangements for lending clothes to the most destitute families, under wise conditions.

POLICE MATRONS.

Both in the United States and Great Britain, of late years, a long-needed reform has been introduced, by the employment of middle-aged women, as Matrons, at Police Stations and Police Courts, for the care of prisoners of their own sex, and of children under arrest. Many philan-thropic ladies, such as Miss FLORENCE BALGARNIE and others, have already laboured for this reform; as also has the Howard Association. The more general, not to say universal, employment of Police Matrons is, however, very needful.

THE POLICE AND TEMPERANCE.

A number of " Temperance Unions " have been formed amongst the London and Provincial Police. They have been greatly helped by Mr. JOHN KEMPSTER and other energetic workers, and have been joined by some of the principal officers. A fine example of the latter was the late Mr. JOHN ROBINSON, Detective-Superintendent of the Birmingham Police, an able and universally respected man, and a practical Christian. In one period of five years, he induced one hundred and thirty-seven policemen to sign the Total Abstinence pledge. Many members of the Force, with their wives and families, were largely indebted to his influence for the happiness of their lives and homes.

Some excellent remarks on the importance of Temperance amongst the Police were made at a meeting at the Mansion House, London, by Mr. JAMES MONRO, then one of the principal Commissioners of the Metropolitan Police. He said—" I must not lose sight of a special temptation which is caused, not by the work that the Policemen have to do, but by the action of others. I think most of you will bear me out in saying that there are not many places in London where a Policeman cannot get his beer, pretty well all the year round, for nothing. This is very much more insidious and dangerous than the temptation which is afforded by the performance of hard work, because yielding to it means the omission to perform duty, shutting a man's eyes and holding his tongue. If, by Total Abstinence, you overcome this evil, then I am perfectly certain you will be better policemen and better men."

In America also, the temptations put in the way of Police by drink-sellers are very great. Dr. HOWARD CROSBY states that the Chief of Police, in one city in the United States, earned some thousand pounds sterling annually " by his carefulness in leaving the license-law breakers alone." It is further stated by Rev. JOSIAH STRONG, Secretary U.S.

Evangelical Alliance, that in New York, until recently, the liquor vendors collectively possessed such power, through bribery of some of the Police officials, that, in certain cases, punishment was secured, not for the violator of license laws, but for the conscientious subordinate of the Police who might venture to arrest such a one.

In order to extend Temperance, whether amongst policemen or the general community, a principal condition of success is the contrivance and adoption of such details of arrangement, as render the desired object *readily practicable*, and prevent its becoming too difficult of attainment. Thus the movement in favour of popular sobriety amongst the general community has of late years made very considerable progress, chiefly through the opening of numerous self-supporting establishments for the sale of cheap and good substitutes for intoxicating liquor; or otherwise, for the provision of light, warmth, books, music and recreation, as attractive rivals to the tavern, or gin-palace. Comparatively little advance was made in the Temperance cause, until these facilities for its more general observance were secured.

And, in like manner, if the Police authorities are to encourage sobriety amongst their men, and to protect them from the very severe temptations to which they are subjected, it is necessary for them also to institute such detailed arrangements in connection with the stations, lodgings, and duties of their men, as shall bring the desired object within their reach, easily and generally. Hot tea, coffee, or cocoa, should be provided at all Police-stations, for the men during the night and early morning; and they should be allowed to fortify themselves with such non-intoxicating beverages during prolonged hours of duty. Soldiers and sailors have, in many instances, been greatly assisted and cheered by having such refreshments served out to them in the early mornings, and also just before going on guard at night.

Need of Public Co-operation.

In every country and town, the efficiency of the Police greatly depends upon the interest taken in them by the general community, and upon the wise vigilance exercised in regard to them, by the People and the Press.   In several cases, where there has been a temporary exertion of special Police efforts in the direction of Temperance, Sanitation. or Kindness to Animals, it has been observed that these endeavours were intimately connected with the stimulus furnished by certain local Philanthropists, Editors, or Associations; and that when these relaxed their diligence, the Police also relapsed into comparative inertness.

The Police, the Public, and the Press, are three collateral and mutual influences, neither of which can become inactive, without loss to all parties concerned.   In Great Britain there is an increasing development of this beneficial and truly patriotic union.

Public Women, Public Houses and the Police.

It is with regard to public women and public houses that Police failures, or corruption, chiefly and most often arise; because here the men themselves are most open to temptation and bribery, through the strong inducements of appetite.   Even in the cities where the Police are most efficient, as in London and Berlin, they are *never reliable—never safe*, as the sole or chief protectors of society from the evils of prostitution, whether as to its degrading vice, or its constantly connected robbery and violence. The Police are always under special—sometimes almost irresistible—temptations, to levy blackmail on the frail sisterhood, either in money, or in compliance with evil.

Vigilance over the Police, as well as by Them, Indispensable.

In the interests both of the Police and of the Public, the latter should be well protected, by the law, against any abuse of authority, or needless violence, on the part of the former. This is largely the case in Great Britain, where the Police are legally punishable for such transgressions of duty as the unnecessary use of their truncheons, or for making wrongful arrests, or for perjury, drunkenness and other offences. But, in some other countries, they are practically permitted to become instruments of oppres-sion and even of brutality. This is a very unwise policy on the part of the chief authorities, for it tends to destroy the popular sympathy with the Law and with its agents, and deprives the Police of that support and respect, on the part of the public, which are of such material service for the facilitation of their duties.

UTILITY OF "WATCH COMMITTEES" OVER THE POLICE.

Neither Prostitution nor Drunkenness can be effectually put down by the Police, or by mere legal Prohibition. The experiences of Paris, Berlin, Brussels, and other cities where the "Police des Mœurs" have been glaring failures, and sources of rank demoralisation, prove this, as to the former vice. And the wide-spread evasion of "Total Prohibition," in some of the United States, conclu-sively demonstrates it as to the other. Nevertheless, in each case, certain checks, or powers of control by the Police, are very needful. But, in view of the ordinary human frailty and special temptations of these officials, it is essential to public morality that some *independent* or collateral authority should be instituted, both for the assistance and for the control of the Police themselves, in reference to these special tempters, before whom they so often fall prostrate—the public woman and the public-house keeper.

In London the authority of the Chiefs of Police is comparatively autocratic. It is partially influenced by the Home Secretary in the "Metropolitan District," and

by a small Committee of Aldermen in " the City " proper ;
but generally these collateral elements of control are of
very limited activity.   The Civic supervision, however,
appears to have been more satisfactory and effectual than
that supposed to be specially exerted by the Home Office,
in the wider " Metropolitan District."   But in many of the
provincial towns there are vigilant and efficient bodies,
appointed by the local Municipalities and named " Watch
Committees."   Their function is to guide and watch the
guardians of public security.   Most valuable, in many
places, is this independent check and support.   And it has
often prevented the police from getting themselves, and
others, into difficulties.

The highest Police efficiency, in every department, but
especially in reference to Morals, is essentially dependent
upon the measure of collateral control possessed, and of
vigilance exercised, by the local Municipalities, or County
Councils, or similar Boards, and by the Press.   And it
is to be particularly remembered, in this connection, that
the importance of the Police, as a body, will continue
to increase, in proportion as, in various countries, Conditional Liberty, instead of Imprisonment, and Conditional
Liberation, after a certain measure of detention, become
more and more resorted to, as means of effectually dealing
with offenders, rather than by an undue resort to the
Prison, with its numerous disadvantages.

CHAPTER XXIII.

JOHN HOWARD'S PRACTICAL PRINCIPLES.

THE present volume seeks to render homage to simple but great and fundamental principles, both for the Prevention of Social Evils, and the maintenance of Social Good. And it may be useful to some readers to remind them how practically the illustrious Howard based his actions upon these or similar principles.

JOHN HOWARD, F.R.S., was born in 1726, at Hackney, educated in London, engaged in business pursuits in the City (Watling Street and Old Broad Street), resided, before and during his first years of married life, at a house (still standing, in 1895), in Church Row, Church Street, Stoke Newington, but subsequently dwelt chiefly at Cardington, near Bedford. He became High Sheriff of Bedfordshire in 1773, and died at Cherson, in Russia, in 1790, aged 64. He travelled about fifty thousand miles, and expended £30,000 of his property, in efforts of mercy. During his life he received the thanks of the British and Irish Parliaments, and the homage of Europe, from the prince to the peasant. His death was officially announced in the *London Gazette*, and occasioned lamentation throughout the civilised world. He chose for the single motto of his epitaph, the words, "CHRIST IS MY HOPE," and requested

that the text for his funeral sermon should be Psalm xvii.
15 : " As for me, I will behold Thy face in righteousness.
I shall be satisfied, when I awake, with Thy likeness."

It has, perhaps, been too common to regard him merely
as a man of one object, as an indefatigably persevering
visitor of prisons, at home and abroad, and a keen-eyed
investigator and exposer of their abuses. But he was
much more than this.

A leading feature in his character was his comprehensiveness of aim, together with an unimpassioned, practical
circumspection of the *pros* and *cons*, and the associated
bearings, of all the subjects which interested him. In this
he was an eminent example to philanthropists, that
excellent class of men whose besetting weakness is, not
unfrequently, to pursue their objects so rapidly and
impulsively as to lose sight of the guiding posts of
surrounding fact, and to plunge into difficulties which might
otherwise be obviated, or diminished, by a due regard to
the real state of things around. This width of outlook was
the more creditable to him, inasmuch as he never had the
advantages of a University education, and was born amid
some of the narrowest sectarian influences. But his combination of Scriptural study and meditation, with London
business training, much travel, and long intercourse with
Churchmen, Roman Catholics, Quakers, Unitarians, and
others, more than compensated for this disadvantage.
A decided Congregationalist himself, he regularly accompanied his two successive wives to the services of the
Church of England, once each Sunday. A staunch Protestant, he dwelt with delight upon the manifold charities of
self-denying Roman Catholics, witnessed by him on the
Continent, and on their efforts for the reform of prison
discipline, which anticipated his own, by the establishment
of several prisons and reformatories in Rome, in 1655 and
1704, possessing improvements far in advance of any
Protestant institutions of the time. And he expressed dis-

approbation at the harsh treatment of aged monks by the Emperor Joseph II. He habitually cherished intimacy with many members of "his favourite religious sect, the Society of Friends," as his biographer, J. Baldwin Brown, terms the Quakers. To some of these, and, in particular, to Dr. JOHN FOTHERGILL, the founder of the large Quaker School at Ackworth, in Yorkshire, he was indebted for many suggestions and much useful assistance in his prison labours. His admiration of civil and religious liberty, simplicity, and useful industry (the latter specially enforced in the Dutch jails and schools) attracted his interest more to Holland (which he visited nine times) than to any other foreign land. But, plain and simple as he was, he was also so eminently polite, so gallant to ladies, and so neat in his attire, as to be most welcome in company, and he was once mistaken for a French dancing master. He pursued his inquiries abundantly amongst ministers of state, magistrates and other authorities; but he also visited and questioned the prisoner, the criminal, and the outcast. He moved an honoured guest amongst nobles and even monarchs; but he records, "Let this maxim be a leading feature in my life,—*constantly to favour and relieve those that are lowest.*" Kings honoured him, Senates thanked him, the Pope blessed him; yet he was literally " a hero to his valet." His faithful attendant, John Prole, charged his children to imitate his " good master," " that worthy, benevolent and good man, Mr. Howard, with whom I enjoyed all the happiness that a rational mind could wish."

His comprehensiveness of effort was by no means confined to Prisons. He was a pioneer of SANITARY REFORM. His last great journey was undertaken, not to visit prisons, but to investigate into, and acquire the most accurate information possible in relation to, the Plague, its nature, origin, treatment, cure and prevention. HOSPITALS and LAZARETTOS claimed a vast amount of observing study from him. He not only urged the importance of a great increase of attention to cleanliness, diet, and regular nursing in these institutions, but far outstripped his contemporaries in the perception and inculcation of the value of *ventilation*, and exposed prevalent errors as to the inert and poisonous tendency of confined or vitiated air. He urged also the necessity of a *good water supply* and *thorough drainage*, for all buildings. Nor did he overlook the sanitary advantages of light and sunshine, but denounced the window tax. All his study was practical; not mere library erudition, or book-shelf knowledge. Everywhere his plan was to visit personally—see for himself—measure, weigh, note, record in every detail. He was, as Dr. William Guy remarks, a most eminent STATISTICIAN—indeed, a model statist.

A model LANDLORD also was he. Not in mischievous, poverty-perpetuating alms-giving to his tenants; but by liberal, intelligent beneficence and well-calculated charity. He mainly aided the poor by inducing them to *help them-selves.* He made his bounty generative, as George Peabody did, a century later. He greatly encouraged POPULAR EDUCA-TION in his vicinity, but did not believe, as some modern School Boards seem to do, that education of the head is much real help to the children of the poor, apart from education of the *heart* and *hands*, and training to industry. One of Howard's principles, in the education of children, the reformation of offenders, and the prevention of crime, was remunerative industry—his again and again repeated motto was the Dutch saying: "*Make men diligent and you will make them honest.*" He encouraged the village girls to knit stockings, the boys to plough and dig, to chisel and hammer. They should read and write, but not learn to dislike labour. He did not believe that even sermons and tracts would make men and women good, or moral, whilst herded in styes. Hence he built (and got the neighbouring gentry to do it too) clean, *healthy cottages* for the poor, pulling down the unhealthy and dilapidated ones. Sound sanitarian that he was, he made good drainage, and freedom from damp, the main object in his cottage building. He greatly encouraged that important counteractive to popular discontent—the ALLOTMENT SYSTEM. If he did not sup- ply his poor neighbours with Lord Beaconsfield's useful triad—" an oven, a tank, and a porch,"—he endeavoured to secure, for each, a potato patch, a flower plot, and a clean dry floor. But none of these boons to the poor were to be enjoyed gratis, or without useful *conditions.* The rents were low; but they must be paid. Further, he stipulated that these advantages should be partly conditional on regular church and chapel going, and on abstinence from pot-houses. He liked to give the poor children halfpence ; but even these must carry the condition—"Wash your hands and faces, and be good boys."

Again, long before the modern TEMPERANCE movement, Howard actively promoted its principles. He was too shrewd to be befooled by cries of " Rob a poor man of his beer," for he saw that, oftentimes, intemperance was robbing the poor man of home and food, of virtue and liberty. Abstinence from ale-houses was a frequent con- dition of his bounty, during life. And at his death, he left legacies of £5 each, to a number of poor cottagers " if they had not been in an ale-house for a twelvemonth." He drafted a Bill to exclude all intoxicating liquors from jails. He records, " I have often wished that in all Bills for small debts there was a clause to prohibit arrests for debts contracted in public-houses." He adds : " For I have observed that the great number of ale-houses is one chief and obvious reason why our prisons are so crowded." Yet did he not intemperately condemn moderate drinkers, or ignore the just claims of publicans. Although most abste- mious himself, yet, whenever he arrived at an inn, he ordered meat, wine, etc., " for the good of the house," but gave the same to his servant, or attendants, whilst he con- tented himself with tea, milk, bread, fruit, and vegetables. Here, again, one sees his liberal mind.

As a PRISON REFORMER, he showed the same breadth and comprehensiveness; avoiding extremes, weighing all *pros* and *cons*. He was one of the earliest advocates of the SEPARATE SYSTEM, which St. Paul indirectly defends when he declares that "evil communications corrupt good manners." Howard characterised jail gangs and congregate prisons as "filled with every corruption which poverty and wickedness can generate between them." But he also wisely deprecated *prolonged, idle* solitude as "more than human nature could bear." He vigorously exposed and protested against every species of TORTURE, in jails or elsewhere, and repeatedly took pains to collect and publish statistics showing the tendency of frequent CAPITAL PUNISHMENT to increase rather than diminish crime. Whilst he was never weary of urging, on moral, sanitary, financial, and penal grounds, that criminals should be compelled to work hard in jail, and so be trained to virtuous industry on their release, and that honest ratepayers should not be compelled to carry about on their shoulders (as it were) lazy and vicious offenders, who have already injured and plundered them, he objected to making pecuniary profit, or mere safe custody, the sole aim, irrespective of moral reform. Hence he foresaw the evils of the Australian Transportation System, then just beginning under specious pleas. The convict "hells" and gangs of Norfolk Island, Port Arthur, etc., had not yet commenced. But he had already denounced "the expensive, dangerous, and destructive system of Transportation to Botany Bay."

What, then, was the motive power, the great driving-wheel, whose steadily sustained force kept in action the machinery of his widely energetic life? For Howard was not the man lightly to forsake English comforts, home and wealthy ease, for the innumerable privations and annoyances of his arduous toils and journeys. He was too sensible to care much for human praise. He had no ambition for transient fame. Nor did his philanthropy arise from very sensitive sympathies, or impulsive excitement, at sights or tales of woe; for he was cool and slow in temperament. Indeed, impulsive sympathies by no means necessarily accompany real beneficence. That surgeon, who shudders during an operation, is not so practically humane as he who, with unquivering eye and muscle, plies the needful knife. So it was with Howard. He was not, and could not have been, impelled to his tremendous exertions and dogged perseverance, by mere excitement, or by emotions which were not natural to his calm, cool temperament. Nor did he appear to trouble himself about those requirements of a mere *intellectual* theology which have no more practical effect upon men's daily lives, than a knowledge of the exact heights of the mountains in the moon, would have for them.

But he was ever sensitive to one grand motive—THE LOVE OF CHRIST, with the hope of immortal joy in His presence. That was the secret power, the sustained and mighty impulse of his life. Again and again he acknowledged it. When at Naples, he wrote of "the honour and glory of God, my highest ambition." At Lyons he recorded, "My soul, may it be thy chief desire that the honour of God, the spread of the Redeemer's name and Gospel, may be promoted. Oh! consider the everlasting worth of spiritual and divine enjoyments! Then wilt thou see the vanity and nothingness of worldly pleasures. Remember, oh, my soul! St. Paul, who was determined to know nothing in comparison of Jesus Christ and Him crucified. Oh, the glorious hope of an interest in the blood and righteousness of my Redeemer and my God!" Similar expressions occur throughout his life. He endured, therefore, "as seeing Him who is invisible," and as daily dwelling upon the infinite love of God in Christ, and the consciousness of the infinite importance of ETERNITY, as compared with the brief span of man's mortal life. Daily religious meditation and prayer, persistently maintained everywhere, supported his arduous toils. Thus Howard's self-denying life, fruitful in good works, proved that he was not deluded by that which is perhaps a chief snare of modern Protestantism, namely, a willingness to rest satisfied with religious knowledge and *intellectual* "orthodoxy." He knew that "the devils believe and tremble," though they do not show love to Christ by good *works*. Our Saviour met with very "orthodox" devils, who, amid an unbelieving generation, could call Him, "Jesus, Thou Son of God most High," and "the Holy One of God." St. Paul, again, had to cast out, as an evil spirit, one which, through the girl at Philippi, could yet exclaim, "These men are the servants of the most High God, who show unto us the way of salvation." But that spirit did not walk in the way thus shown, by the faith which *worketh* by love. Howard's was not such mere barren head-knowledge, but a loving service of Christ, working actively and laboriously for the good of His human family. He felt the inseparable connection between "Lovest thou Me," and "Feed My sheep." Howard loved and aided the repulsive and the ungrateful, not so much for their own sakes as FOR THE SAKE OF THEIR LORD, who loves all and despises none of His creatures, and "who will have all men to be saved." And, through the operation of that Lord's Spirit upon the souls even of the most degraded, Howard recognised in them, as in others, *glorious capacities of immortal growth*, even as, when walking in his groves at Cardington, he saw in each acorn the germ of a noble oak. Similar motives and similar principles will ever be essential to prolonged and effective efforts for the social elevation of mankind.

CHAPTER XXIV.

CHRISTIANITY THE CHIEF BASIS FOR MORAL REFORMS AND RESTRAINTS.

HOWARD, then, adopted a thoroughly scientific basis, both for his Penology and his Philanthropy, when he placed his chief expectation on the only abiding foundation, the Lord Jesus Christ, as the great hope for individual and collective humanity. This great "CORNER-STONE" has far too frequently been disregarded by Politicians, Statesmen, and Social Reformers; and, in consequence, their schemes and arrangements have often failed.

The best operations of civil Government and the most effectual means of preventing offences, restoring the erring, and promoting the happiest developments of social organization, must be, it is generally admitted, inseparably and specially connected with a reverence for Law and Order, and with a wise combination of the influences of Fear and Hope, of Reward and Penalty.

But it is precisely and pre-eminently in the Gospel of Christ, that we find these powerful principles most authoritatively embodied and exemplified. For it reveals, with a clearness elsewhere unequalled, the absolute sovereignty of the perfect Moral Law of God; inasmuch as the vindication of the majestic inviolability of this, constituted the necessity for the atoning sufferings of the Redeemer, as the Incarnate Justice and Love of the Highest, "magnifying that Law and making it honourable."

Even the laws of human monarchs and States require
to be maintained with unrelaxed power and sanction. If
they can be set at nought, or transgressed with impunity,
the authority of the ruler and the security of the people
alike suffer. Much more, then, may we conclude that the
Supreme Creator does not permit any of His Moral Laws
to be broken, or disregarded, without some effectual manifestation of majestic vindication. We see already, that
in the case of His physical ordinances in outward Nature,
any infractions of them are certainly and universally followed by penalty, or by proofs of their absolute dominion,
in some form or other.

Neither in Nature, nor in Grace, does God pardon, unconditionally, the transgression of His laws, or permit their
authority to be, in the slightest degree, impaired.

The Holy Scriptures declare that "God, sending His
own Son, in the likeness of sinful flesh, and for sin, *condemned* sin, in the flesh." This self-sacrifice of the Highest,
in the Person* of Christ, rendered it compatible with the
sovereignty of His own law of perfect sanctity, to pardon
all humbly repentant sinners, even to the very uttermost;
and so to afford them *honourable* access to Himself, in peace,
and to the blessed influences of His own Spirit of immaculate purity. As Dr. Allon has well remarked: "The
Atonement does not leave Law a dishonoured thing." But
the Sacrifice which thus combined the sublimest inflexi-
bility of regnant majesty with an immeasureable tender-
ness of righteously paternal compassion, constitutes also a

---

* "PERSON."—Professor Max Müller and other writers have well
shown that the original theological meaning of "Person" (from *persona*,
a mask) did not imply separate individuality, but only a special or
collateral *manifestation of the One*, undivided and unchanging identity,
of the Eternal God. We must not regard Christ as a Being *other* than
the Supreme Father, selected as an innocent *creature*, to bear penalty.
No! The Highest vindicated in His *own* incarnate Person, the majesty
of His own Law. And, eternally, "Jesus Christ is Lord, to the glory
of God the *Father*."

forecast of irresistible chastisement, impending over those who wilfully reject the humbling but gracious terms of acceptance and shelter, thus offered to them in the Gospel.

Substitutionary remission (as distinct from the mere, or mainly, *penal* atonement of the ultra-Calvinists and *pseudo-* "orthodox") is not unknown in the ordinary government of States. Thus the eminent merits of the patriotic JOAN OF ARC, caused the exemption of her birthplace, Domremy, from taxes, for centuries. Year by year, the local tax-collector inscribed in his books, opposite the State's claims on that place, the words " Remitted, for the Maid's sake."

Similarly, the services rendered, during the American Civil War, by JOHN BRIGHT, to the cause of the North, were so appreciated by President Lincoln, that when, on one occasion, he received, from the English orator, a request for the pardon of a man condemned to death, it was at once gladly granted, by a document commencing with the words, " Whereas, John Bright, of England, has asked for the life of ———," etc.

Christ, being the Son of the Highest, and filled, without measure, with the Eternal Spirit, and also having suffered His human life to be taken from Him, when (*un*like all the martyrs) He could have struck His enemies dead in an instant—the merits of His Incarnation, with His whole Life, Death, and Resurrection—are boundless, and, therefore, in God's great pity, they avail for the pardon of all sin, but with simultaneous honour to God's Majesty.

This *substitutionary* merit of Christ is a great gift of grace to man, who is in himself so weak. This free *gift*, from an inexhaustible treasury of Divine goodness, is just what is needed by poor *weak* humanity, as such, whilst at the same time glorifying to the Highest. Christ, as the Good Shepherd, leads His frail sheep, and carries His tender lambs. And just as the setting sun throws, far and wide, a warm glow of crimson and golden light on the shining windows of whole terraces of houses on a hill-side, or on the high, reddened trunks of the mountain pines, so the merits and pardon of Christ, given to man, diffuse honour and blessing on a redeemed race. Well may the ascription be reverently, and eternally, raised, "Thanks be unto God for His unspeakable *gift.*"

Not only does Christianity reveal a reason for wholesome fear, amongst individuals and communities; it also furnishes the brightest and surest source of hope and virtuous encouragement to our race. For it conveys the proof of the infinite love to man, shown by the God of immaculate holiness. The Incarnation was (as the poet HAWKER, of Morwenstow, has concisely expressed it) that exceeding gift of Divine Grace :—

> " Where woke to breath and beauty, God's own birth,
> *For men to see Him by.*"

The previous revelations of the Highest, whether in outward nature, or by comparatively vague spiritual impressions, had not adequately manifested the depths of sacred sympathy existing in the Supreme Father. As Lord MACAULAY has remarked, "God, the uncreated, the incomprehensible, the invisible, attracted few worshippers. A philosopher might admire so noble a conception ; but the crowd turned away in disgust, from words which presented *no image* to their minds. It was before Deity embodied in a human form, walking among men, partaking of their infirmities, leaning on their bosoms, weeping over their graves, slumbering in the manger, bleeding on the Cross, that the prejudices of the Synagogue, and the doubts of the Academy, and the pride of the Portico, and the swords of thirty Legions, were humbled in the dust."

And this "express *Image*" of the Divine Personality, once revealed, is never to be withdrawn from manifest existence. As the all-victorious Redeemer, He lives on for ever, in His risen "spiritual Body," whence He irradiates, by the vitalising energies and individualising visitations of His Holy Spirit, the hearts of His believing children, one by one, thus granting to their souls the inestimably precious gift of separate, loving recognition. Even the old Pagans craved and earnestly sought such private and distinguishing links between themselves, their homes, and "the Immortal Gods." Hence their "Lares and Penates," their "Household Deities." Such aspiration was a measure of the natural desire, which springs up, in every earnest heart, for an abiding communion, special to itself, with the Divine and Everlasting Father of Humanity. And He, having honoured in His own incarnate Person, the claims of His awful majesty of Supreme Sovereignty, then opened, freely and without limit, the measureless resources of His love to men, not only collectively, but separately. Hence, from the holy risen Christ, flow forth, for ever, the blessed emanations of the Eternal Spirit, shining into each heart and bringing there also the growing impress of His Image, with His light and sunshine of celestial fire. This priceless gift of the individualizing manifestation of Christ, spiritually, brings into each soul, singly, a treasure, as of home sweetness, which shall never experience the bereavement of the beloved object. It kindles a glow as of a paternal and private fireside, which shall never be quenched. And it tends, by similar links with the beloved souls of kindred and of others, to reunite, in indissoluble brotherhood, the members of the one "whole family in Heaven and in Earth."

But to individuals and to the race, these unspeakable blessings are communicated, as is God's way generally, by gradual development. This is to be prepared for, and patiently wrought out, in the first place, by the calling and training of the Christian Church and its elect members, even that body of chosen and disciplined souls, to whom, in every age, the Holy Spirit has granted special visitations and peculiar privileges, not for any private merit or selfish interest, but for present or ultimate service to their fellow creatures. For Divine Election is a great

and blessed historic fact; although Calvinistic "Reproba-
tion" is a pernicious delusion.

The Incarnation of Christ manifests God's justice and
fairness, in taking into full consideration, not only the
demands of His own Law of spotless sanctity, but also
the natural claims, upon His compassion, of every human
being, as inheriting, from the First Adam, inevitable tendencies either to actual sinfulness, or to moral disinclination
and weakness, in consequence of which men are universally
born, as on to an inclined plane, and not placed in a position where it is, from the first, possible for them to make
an unbiassed choice of virtue, or to tread the path of right
with equal facility with that of evil. The Apostle Paul
again and again declares, and even five times in one
chapter, that Christ the Second Adam, shall "much more"
than make ultimate "restitution of all things," not only to
the few, the Church of the First-born, to whom distinctive favours have been given for the subsequent benefit of
others, but also finally to "the many." For, as he again
records, Christ is "the Saviour of all men; *specially* of those
that believe." And we may trustfully expect everlasting
developments of "the manifold wisdom of God, according
to *the eternal purpose*, which he purposed in Christ Jesus
our Lord." (Eph. iii. 11.)

There is a verse in St. Paul's Epistle to Philemon, which,
while apparently unsuggestive of any high significance,
may really be interpreted in a very instructive sense.
It is "Prepare me also a lodging." If these words are
imagined to be addressed by Christ Himself to every
Christian and Social Reformer, in reference to each individual's opportunities of facilitating the entrance and
growth of the Holy Spirit in the hearts of other men, then
they may be regarded as an important and stimulating
practical precept. It is indeed a grand work, and one for
which eternal results and rewards may be confidently
expected, to prepare and secure, by wisely beneficent efforts

and measures, the dwelling of Christ's Spirit in human hearts and communities. For such visitation, amid present terrestrial conditions, will lead on to eternal mansions of celestial blessedness hereafter.

John Howard was but one of myriads to whom the hope centred in Christ has been the great sustaining power of life, and the chiefly animating impulse of philanthropic action. A similar hope has generally characterised the good men and women who have been the chief instruments in efforts for the diminution of Crime, Sin, Poverty, Slavery, and Wretchedness; such as the Suringars, Buxtons, and Wicherns; the Clarksons, Wilberforces, and Shaftesburys; the Borromeos, Fenelons, and Vincents de Paul; the Andrew Reeds, George Peabodys, Dr. Charles H. Parkhursts, and Samuel Morleys, of the world. These, and innumerable others, of noble efforts and aims, have, for the most part, based their lives upon definitely Christian principles and hopes.

Hope in Christ is the soul of Philanthropy and of individual, national, administrative and penal amelioration. It is the great stimulus to beneficent effort, whether in Social Reforms at home, or Missionary Evangelisation abroad; because it involves the promise of the highest rewards— those of Christ's everlasting love and peculiar favours—to the persons who, in whatever sphere of life or action, become His willing instruments, in His own great work of the permanent education and moral development of the human race. This, we may infer from past and present experiences and analogies, will be always carried on, chiefly by His servants; of each of whom, however humble, it may still, for gracious purposes, be declared, "The Lord hath need of him." And as God has, in general, wrought out His dispensations amongst humanity, by prayerfully dependent *instruments* and reverently *volitional* agents, so may it probably continue, through the unending Future. To this principle, so stimulative of useful and happy activity, seem applicable the familiar words, "As it was in the beginning, is now, and ever shall be."

Hope in Christ is as sunshine, to the race and to the individual. But to what similar hope, light, or power, can the unscientific Agnostic, or the vaguely credulous Positivist, point mankind? These turn us but to blanks, or failures, in the present, and to dense clouds in the future; to no effectively victorious influence over evil, and to no animating relief from despair and gloom. But the Christian is furnished with the grandly *scientific* basis of innumerable historic verifications and personal experiences of the fruitful power of the love of the Lord Jesus, in moulding the best lives and in overcoming, throughout the world, obstacles otherwise insuperable. Even in modern missionary successes alone, as for example, in China, Burmah, India, Africa and elsewhere, the initial triumphs of Christianity, through the labours of very few and very feeble instruments, prayerfully leaning on God's Spirit, have effected results in the reclamation of criminal, vicious, and miserable lives, and in developments of social progress and civilization, as marvellous as any miracles recorded of old time, and as demonstrable, in point of fact, as any matters of physical or mathematical science.

This great spiritual force ever advances to victory. It was never more widely diffused, or more hopefully active, than it is to-day. The present, more than any preceding century, is "the Age of Saints," notwithstanding various and vigorous collateral operations of evil—operations, it is to be noted, which are in large degree being overruled, even already, for benevolent ends, through the moral discipline, for which a certain antagonism and contrast appear to be essential concomitants. Hardly one, if any, of the departments of the Christian Church, has any reasonable ground for regarding its human Fathers and Founders as having been better, or more privileged, than its existing members. To all Churches and to every Christian, the Lord still proclaims, as hopefully as to the Jewish remnant in the days of Haggai, and indeed, incomparably more so now, " My Spirit *remaineth* among you." The voice of the Pessimist, or of the Agnostic, is the cry of the blind. But Christianity, with all its beneficent energies, upon communities and individuals, is manifestly destined to magnificently progressive developments, throughout the boundless ages.

APPENDIX I.

THE INTERNATIONAL PRISON CONGRESS OF PARIS, 1895.

THE proceedings of the fifth (quinquennial) INTERNATIONAL PRISON CONGRESS, held in PARIS, in July, 1895, indicated, in a very cheering manner, that the principles advocated in the preceding pages of this volume, have, of late years, been receiving greatly increased practical attention amongst the chief nations of the world. This Congress, like its predecessors, by no means confined its labours to matters connected with Prisons, but also embraced more important subjects, such as the Prevention of CRIME and PAUPERISM.

So far as PRISON DISCIPLINE is concerned, the Paris Congress gave the weight of its sanction to the separation of prisoners from evil (but not from good), association. And it was informed that France, Germany, and some other leading nations are building all their *new* prisons on the cellular plan.

But it is much better than any system of Imprisonment, however good, to be able, with safety to the community, to substitute CONDITIONAL LIBERTY, or PROBATION, under friendly but efficient supervision, for incarceration. And the Paris Congress afforded gratifying evidence that, both in Europe and America, the adoption of this substitute for the Prison has already made very extensive progress

The eloquent addresses of the fine body of delegates from the UNITED STATES, to the Congress, and in particular of General BRINKERHOFF (Ohio), Major MCCLAUGHRY (Ill.), Mr. C. D. RANDALL (Mich.), Mr. CHARLTON T. LEWIS (N.Y.), Mr. M. HEYMANN (La.), and Rev. SAMUEL BARROWS (Mass.), bore testimony to the considerable degree of success which, in their great country, has attended the experiment of thus exercising a reformatory influence over offenders of the less criminal grade, whilst obliging them to support themselves by honest industry, under the natural conditions of free and family life, instead of being continuous burdens upon the taxpayer, and amid the unavoidable disadvantages of the jail.

It was, however, pointed out, in a specially interesting manner, by Professor PESSINA, of Italy, that the system of Conditional Liberty, or Probation, ought to involve more generally than hitherto, in Europe, the collateral appointment of *Probation Officers*, as in Massachusetts.

The American Delegates were able to report some gratifying results from the partial adoption, in the United States, of INDETERMINATE SENTENCES; and they mentioned that the discipline in such establishments as PONTIAC and ELMIRA, under this plan, is rendered more deterrent, as well as more reformatory, than it has generally been reputed in Europe. They said that the obligation imposed upon the prisoners, in such institutions, to raise themselves, by mental as well as industrial labour, into higher grades, as a necessary condition for liberation, is felt, by many of them, to involve so much exertion, that they would rather be consigned to some ordinary prison, where self-improvement is not specially enforced.

A large and influential RUSSIAN DELEGATION, headed by the courtly M. GALKINE-WRASKOY (Chief of the Imperial Prison Administration), attended the Congress, and afforded encouraging proofs of recent active efforts to reform the Russian and Siberian penal establishments. M. Wraskoy had just returned from a journey across Asia, and had taken measures for a reorganisation of the Exile System, and for a sweeping reduction in the number of persons to be sent thither in future. The Russians did not deny some of the charges made against their prisons, by Mr. KENNAN and others; but they felt that, in justice to them and to their country, more credit should have been given them for their improvements and sincere efforts at amelioration. M. Wraskoy has recently issued an interesting and comprehensive Report of Russian progress, in this department.

The UNITED KINGDOM was officially represented, at the Congress, by Mr. E. J. RUGGLES-BRISE, Chairman of the Prisons Board of England and Wales, Mr. E. R. SPEARMAN, J.P., Mr. JAMES L. GIBBONS, Chairman of the Irish Prison Board, and Mr. A. BEATSON BELL, Chairman of the Scotch Prison Board.

The influence of good WOMEN, in the work of PRISON VISITATION, and in connection with REFORMATORY and PREVENTIVE EFFORT generally, was abundantly recognised by the Congress. In particular, Mr. E. J. RUGGLES-BRISE, in one of the two valuable papers contributed by him to the Congress, remarked: " I should like to see an Aid Society, consisting of Ladies, in connection with every prison exclusively occupied by women. We have already, in many of our prisons, such Lady Visitors, whose zeal and kindness cannot be too highly praised."

M. PUIBARAUD, and others, bore testimony to the special success which has, both in France, Luxembourg, and elsewhere, attended the placing of Reformatories and Houses of Correction, for boys, entirely under the care of religious ladies, Catholic and Protestant. Thus at Frasnes-le-Chateau (Haute Saône), a band of Alsatian " Sisters " have the complete management of 400 youths, of from twelve to twenty years of age, with wonderful success. And, without assistance from male officers, they secure obedience and good discipline.

The Congress revealed a large extension, during recent years, of CHILD-SAVING efforts, in various countries: especially in connection with REFORMATORIES and INDUSTRIAL SCHOOLS of various kinds, as substitutes for the pernicious system of juvenile imprisonment. Renewed evidence was also given of the preventive value of DIS-CHARGED PRISONERS' AID (or "PATRONAGE") SOCIETIES, and of the need which still exists, for a much larger increase in their number, in most countries. ENGLAND, however, occupies a peculiarly honourable position, in this matter.

The Congress, being held in Paris, afforded the best opportunity, to its members, for studying the practical application of the BERTILLON SYSTEM OF ANTHROPOMETRIC MEASUREMENT, which is an honour to its inventor and to France. Its advantages have been specially brought before the English people by Mr. EDMUND R. SPEARMAN, and in America by Major MCCLAUGHRY, formerly the efficient Chief of Police at Chicago.

The Delegates were also permitted to visit the various Prisons, in and around Paris. At *La Santé*, in particular, they were interested in the WARDERS' SCHOOL. Every year, forty-eight of the principal warders of the French provincial prisons come to La Santé, in two parties of twenty-four each, who stay for six months, during which time they receive a course of lectures and lessons in subjects useful to them in their prison duties. They are also practically instructed in the application of the Bertillon system of criminal identification.

Some animated discussion, in the Congress, on the subject of PROSTITUTION, revealed the existence of an extensive practice of inveigling respectable young women (under false pretences of employing them as governesses, type-writers, travelling companions, or otherwise) into immoral lives, and it was shown that an extensive traffic in "white slavery" is being carried on by the transmission of girls,

especially from Belgium, Holland, and Austria, to Egypt,
Turkey, and other countries, even to America and Australia,
for prostitution.   M. YVES GUYOT reported on the valuable
efforts to check these practices, which are now being made
by local Committees of benevolent ladies, who meet friendless girls at railway stations, provide them with temporary
lodgings, and insert advertisements in newspapers, warning
young women against the snares so industriously set for
their ruin.   M. LECOUR, a former Chief of the Paris Police,
stated that the Law and the Police cannot do much in
these matters, the means of evasion being so numerous and
subtle.   Mr. HEYMANN (U.S.) eloquently pleaded for efforts
to raise the general moral tone of the community and to
excite public disapprobation of seduction, as being a chief
means of diminishing such evils.

Much consideration was devoted to INTEMPERANCE, and
it was urged by Dr. MAGNAN, of Paris, and others, that the
excessive alcoholisation of spirituous or "strong" liquor
was a principal cause of it, and that a more general use,
and cheapening, of ordinary light wine, tea and coffee, as
substitutes, would be beneficial.   It was contended by him
that the "natural" light wine of France is, practically,
a temperance drink, there being scarcely any intoxication
amongst those who use it as their ordinary beverage.
Professor DYMCHA, of Russia, advocated a general extension of INEBRIATE ASYLUMS, for habitual drunkards, the
time of detention to be sufficiently long.   The institution
at Ellikon-sur-Thur, near Zurich, was mentioned as being
a model institution of this nature; also the Dalrymple
Home, at Rickmansworth, as described by Dr. NORMAN
KERR, in particular.

The very important question of SENTENCES on HABITUAL
OFFENDERS, or "RECIDIVISTES," claimed attention at the
commencement of the Congress.   A paper by Mr. TALLACK,
advocating a very *gradually* progressive, but *certain,*
cumulation of sentences, both for habitual misdemeanants

and criminals, was, in fact, placed first in the group of papers arranged for discussion in the First Section. Professor VAN HAMEL (Holland) advocated Indeterminate Sentences for these classes of offenders, but Professor KIRCHENHEIM, of Heidelburg, preferred the moderately progressive gradation of sentences. Valuable papers on this subject were also contributed by Professor FOINITSKY (St. Petersburg), Dr. GARCON (Lille), M. ARMENGOL Y. CORNET (Spain), M. GAROFALO (Naples), and other specialists. Ultimately the Congress recommended the adoption of Gradual Cumulation, as of special efficacy.

Another very important question was, after considerable discussion, postponed for further consideration by the next quinquennial Congress, to be held at Brussels in 1900. This related to the COMPENSATION OF INJURED PARTIES by their offenders, and also to the general subject of RESTITUTION to plundered or assaulted victims of crime. Valuable essays on this topic were furnished by M. ZUCKER, of Prague, Dr. POET, an accomplished Italian lady, of Pignerol, M. GAROFALO, and M. FLANDIN.

It was shown, in an admirable paper, by M. PRINS, of Brussels, that under the Greeks and Romans, as also later by the Anglo-Saxons and Germans, the chief and usual punishment for crime consisted in the enforcement of COMPENSATION to the injured. But the Feudal Barons and the Ecclesiastical Authorities of the Middle Ages substituted, for this, imprisonment and torture. A return to the practical wisdom of the earlier ages, in this respect, is now one of the chief needs of modern Penology. And the Twentieth Century can hardly work out the solution of a more useful problem in this department.

Altogether, thirty questions were discussed by the Congress and with much interest, utility, and harmony. They were introduced by 240 papers, extending collectively over 2,500 pages (distributed weeks previously, amongst the members of the Congress). Most gratifying proofs were adduced, showing a general progress of late years, in the modes of dealing with and preventing crime, not only in Europe and America, but in the more distant regions of Australasia and India; and not least in far Japan. The Congress was admirably organised by the standing INTERNATIONAL PENITENTIARY COMMISSION (of which Dr. GUILLAUME has long been the very able Secretary), aided most efficiently by the FRENCH GOVERNMENT, whose hospitality and general good offices were most praiseworthy. In particular, the excellent arrangements made by M. LEYGUES. Minister of the Interior, and M. J. DUPLOS, Chief Administrator of Prisons, to promote the efficiency of the Congress, will be gratefully remembered by those who had the privilege and pleasure of taking part in it. And it afforded many opportunities for the revival of old friendships and the formation of new ones, which were highly appreciated by its attenders.

APPENDIX II.

A GLANCE AT NINETEENTH CENTURY PROGRESS.

A VERY brief (*fin de siècle*) glance at the progress made, during the Nineteenth Century, in matters affecting the Treatment and Prevention of Crime, is sufficient to indicate that, in spite of remaining evils and defects, there is much substantial reason for encouragement, on the part of the numerous body of good men and women, who have been labouring in this and other departments of Philanthropy and Humanity.

THE UNITED KINGDOM.

At the commencement of the century, the Gallows was in constant requisition for the punishment of many crimes. Highway robberies were frequent. The detection of offences was very difficult. Travel was most insecure, as well as slow and difficult. Prisons were dens of disease and cruelty. Justice was slow and uncertain. Wars were almost incessant. Pauperism was rampant. Food was dear; so were Bibles and other Literature, in general. Schools were comparatively few. Religious doctrine was strongly and narrowly sectarian.

Whereas, at the end of the century, through the great

social revolution effected by a CHEAP PRESS, by the introduction of STEAM POWER for Railways and Navigation, by the ELECTRIC TELEGRAPH, by FREE TRADE, with its results of an abundant supply of FOOD from abroad (especially aided by REFRIGERATING PROCESSES), by the extension of the FRANCHISE and POPULAR LIBERTY, by UNIVERSAL EDUCATION, by a wonderful development of CHURCH and MISSION ORGANISATION, by beneficent FEMALE influence and activity, and by BIBLE and TRACT SOCIETIES and similar means, a milder, more intelligent, and more Christian civilisation than formerly, has permeated every rank of society.

EXECUTIONS have become very few. PRISON DISCIPLINE has been so ameliorated, that there has even arisen a danger lest its repressive object should be lost sight of. The INSPECTION, VISITATION, and INSTRUCTION of Prisoners have been organised systematically. An efficient body of POLICE, throughout the kingdom, have taken the place of the old " watchmen " and untrained constables. DETECTIVE means have been vastly increased. PROGRESSIVE STAGES of treatment, aided by rewards and appeals to hope, together with CONDITIONAL LIBERATION, after undergoing a portion of the original sentences, have been adopted in many Prisons. The CORRUPTING ASSOCIATION in jails, although not put an end to, as is most desirable, has been much restricted. PENAL LEGISLATION, as a whole, has had a large share of attention. But the great work of a CODIFICATION of the Law still awaits accomplishment. And no regular GRADATION OF SENTENCES, on Habitual Offenders, has yet been adopted.

Means of correction and reformation, far superior to imprisonment, have been sought, and to a considerable extent found, by an increased resort to FINES, WARNINGS, and CONDITIONAL LIBERTY. And, above all, a marked diminution of serious crimes has been obtained by the important PREVENTIVE AGENCIES of extended EDUCATION, with the establishment of REFORMATORY and INDUSTRIAL SCHOOLS, and by efforts to promote TEMPERANCE, THRIFT, KINDNESS TO ANIMALS, SANITATION and RELIGION. The needs of the POOR have been more considered, and a broader spirit of CHARITY and HUMANITY has been diffused amongst the British people, as a whole, characterising the PULPIT, the PRESS, and the PLATFORM, and influencing the general feeling and action of the community.

THE COLONIES AND INDIA.

Similar causes have produced similar effects, though not in so satisfactory a degree, in the British Colonies and in India. The AUSTRALIAN COLONIES and NEW ZEALAND have taken the lead in this progress, although much remains to be accomplished there. In certain matters, especially the care of NEGLECTED YOUTH, some of these Colonies have outstripped the Mother Country. NEW ZEALAND has preceded Great Britain in an interesting and successful attempt to substitute pecuniary RESTITUTION for Imprisonment, at least amongst the Maori population. In INDIA, a remarkable PENAL CODE has greatly aided judicial procedure. And at length, in the last decade of the century, long needed reforms in the Indian Prisons have received a decided impulse. Sir J. W. Tyler, and other prison officials, have also initiated efforts for the aid of DISCHARGED PRISONERS in that country. In the ANDAMAN ISLANDS an interesting experiment in convict colonisation has been made, with some success. INDIA, in particular, has long possessed a body of most efficient and conscientious public servants and administrators.

CANADA, which has made wonderful advances in material prosperity, has been somewhat slow, until latterly, in the movement for the better Treatment and Prevention of Crime. But some progress has now been made. An active PRISON SOCIETY has been established at Toronto, and the ONTARIO PRISON COMMISSION of 1891 (like the QUEENSLAND, Australia, COMMISSION of 1887) was a model, as to its modes of operation and its Report. And in efforts to promote TEMPERANCE, Canada is perhaps unsurpassed in the world.

In the SOUTH AFRICAN COLONIES (the CAPE, NATAL, etc.) and in the WEST INDIES, the PRESS seems to be in advance of the Executive, in regard to an interest in Penal Reform. Many of the Prisons there afford scope for much improvement.

THE UNITED STATES.

The century has witnessed the abolition of the great curse of American SLAVERY, by the awful CIVIL WAR. That conflict, however, has further been overruled for good, by a closer union of North and South, and by a wonderful energising and re-organisation of the Southern States.

Whilst the Common (or County) Jails of the United States are still a century behind European Prisons, generally, and whilst American penal treatment is often so indulgent, as to place a premium upon crime instead of honesty, yet a vast advance has been latterly made, in this great country, in regard to CHILD-SAVING and the introduction of PROGRESSIVE STAGES in Prison Discipline. Intelligent Americans contend that the arduous process, adopted in some of the chief prisons, of compelling a prisoner to "work himself out" of detention, by complying with strict terms of industrial, educational, and moral attainment, as a necessary preliminary to conditional liberation, under the Indeterminate Sentence System, acts as a useful deterrent, as well as a successfully reformatory influence. Massachusetts and other States have well pioneered the PROBATION SYSTEM, both for juvenile and adult minor offenders. The PLACING OUT of dependent and neglected children, in carefully selected and inspected Homes, has been very successfully adopted, by Michigan and some other States. During the century, America has gone from a cruel extreme of absolute isolation in prisons, to the opposite, but still cruel, extreme of promiscuous association, in most jails at least. The wise or middle course of the SEPARATE SYSTEM, under requisite conditions of industry, instruction, and judicious visitation, is now the chief desideratum in most of the penal establishments of the United States. The imprisonment of INNOCENT WITNESSES of crime is still, also, a stain on the United States penal legislation.

But, on the whole, the United States have made great progress, in the last quarter of the century, owing mainly to the operation of PRISON SOCIETIES, the action of the BOARDS of STATE CHARITIES, and the discussions at Philanthropic CONGRESSES.

BELGIUM AND HOLLAND.

For many years, these two countries were pioneers in Penal Treatment, and both of them have, for long periods, been able safely to dispense with the PUNISHMENT OF DEATH. In particular, they have exemplified the benefits of a wisely conditioned system of CELLULAR IMPRISONMENT. Holland, however, has placed limitations on its extent, which Belgium might suitably imitate. But both countries have admirably succeeded in preventing the "SEPARATE" from becoming the "SOLITARY" system, whilst obviating the corrupting association of criminals with each other. Both countries have also made interesting and long-continued experiments in placing beggars and vagabonds upon INDUSTRIAL COLONIES, as at Veenhuizen, Merxplas, etc. In this matter, Belgium has been the more successful of the two. She has also been a pioneer in INDUSTRIAL ARBITRATION.

The treatment of PAUPERISM, in Holland, by a vigilant encouragement of *self-help*, is in advance of most nations of the world. The Belgian BÉGUINAGES, and the GHEEL

Cottage System for the insane, are peculiarly suggestive institutions.

Sweden, Norway, Denmark, and Finland.

The influence of one intelligent monarch, King Oscar I., of Sweden, has given an abiding impetus to Penal Reform, and especially to the Separate System, in the three Scandinavian nations, and also in Finland. The Stockholm Prison Congress afforded to many visitors very interesting proofs of this. The Scandinavian Union of Prison Officers and the Danish *Prison Magazine* have been effective helps to prison administration in these countries. The "Sloyd" mode of mechanical instruction, the "Gothenburg" License System, and the admirable Agricultural Schools of Denmark are each very honourable to the Norsk people and their Governments.

France.

This great country has long taken special interest in Penal Reform. To a Frenchman, Voltaire (together with Beccaria, the Italian), is mainly due the high honour of causing the general abolition of the Torture in Europe. During this century, France has abolished the Galleys for her convicts. French philanthropists have taken a prominent position in Prison Literature and discipline. During the last quarter of the century, France has extended the Separate System in her prisons with diligence. A Frenchman, M. Bertillon, has invented the best mode of identifying criminals ever adopted. The chief States of the world have copied it from France, with much advantage. The French Government and people organised and welcomed the International Prison Congress of 1895 with remarkable ability and hospitality. The French Prison Society, with its very influential membership and its monthly *Bulletin*, has conferred great benefit, not only upon France, but upon Europe in general. (It was highly grati-

fying to some readers in England, to observe the announce-
ment, in the **Paris** *Moniteur Universel*, of June 13, 1877,
that "The labours and example of the English HOWARD
ASSOCIATION have caused the establishment of a similar
Society in France, the "*Société des Prisons*," of which Senator
Berenger, M. Charles Lucas, M. F. Desportes, and others
were the Founders.)

During the Nineteenth Century, a vastly beneficent
increase of SMALL FREEHOLDS has taken place in France, so
that there are now more than eight million proprietors of
houses and lands; the small proprietors being owners of
one-third of the productive portions of that country.

The experiences of France, in regard to TRANSPORTATION
to Cayenne and New Caledonia, have not been favourable.
She would do well to abandon that system. But she has
been one of the chief pioneers in the introduction of
CONDITIONAL LIBERATION, as a useful substitute for Imprisonment. And recently she has made laudable efforts
to promote KINDNESS TO ANIMALS.

If France can secure popular BIBLICAL EDUCATION for
her youth in general, she will immensely increase her
national power and happiness.

GERMANY.

Germany, like France, has with advantage introduced
CONDITIONAL LIBERTY, by means of Suspended Sentences.
Germany also has occupied an honourable position in the
early development of ORPHANAGES, REFORMATORIES, and
other CHILD-SAVING INSTITUTIONS. Her Home and
Foreign MISSIONS, her noble KAISERSWERTH for training
DEACONESSES, and her intelligent appreciation of the merits
of the SEPARATE SYSTEM of Prison Discipline, together with
her elaborately organised UNIVERSITIES and SCHOOLS, have
given her a high position amongst the nations, in these
departments of progress. In efforts to diminish VAGRANCY,
the numerous "LABOUR COLONIES" of Germany have

attracted world-wide attention. The hundreds of "HER-
BERGEN," or respectable Cheap Lodgings, have rendered aid
to honest seekers after employment.   Most interesting is
the wonderful group of philanthropic institutions, established of late years, by BARON BODELSCHWINGH, at WIL-
HELMSDORF, near Bielefeld, in West Prussia.   In MUSIC,
POETRY, and ART, Germany has made many advances. The
manly tribes of early Germany set an example to the world
in CHASTITY and practical homage to FEMALE HONOUR.
But has modern Germany upheld that noble standard ?
Germany has excelled in PENOLOGICAL LITERATURE, and in
the training and selection of a fine body of PRISON OFFICERS,
from the highest to the lowest.   Her social advancement
might have been still greater, but for excessive MILITARISM.

AUSTRIA AND HUNGARY.

This great Empire has made successful efforts to develop
a GRADUATED SYSTEM of Prison Discipline, together with
much industrial occupation of convicts, especially in
agriculture and public works in the open.   The reformation
and training of criminal and neglected YOUTH have also
had much practical attention there.

ITALY.

Italy, under POPE CLEMENT XI., anticipated modern
Prison Reform by more than a century. In later years
she has made some further progress, but has been heavily
handicapped by her enormously disproportionate expenditure on her Army and Navy, which has immensely
impeded efforts to reduce Pauperism and Crime. Italy
also has unwisely fostered the association of criminals
in prison. Her JURISTS occupy a prominent position in
Europe ; her scholars have written elaborate works on Crime
and the theory of Criminal Treatment ; but MILITARISM has
materially interfered with wise practice and with Education.
Yet true PHILANTHROPY has found admirable exemplars

in that country. But the Italians (like the people in most Roman Catholic countries) are still very cruel to animals, especially to horses and dogs.

RUSSIA AND SIBERIA.

The vast Empire of Russia and Siberia had long lingered in the rear of Civilisation. But in the last quarter of the century, RAILROADS have been energetically pushed forward, and with their development have come other features of progress. Siberian Transportation has been greatly restricted. New and better Prisons are being built. An active Administrative Department, for prisons, has been established and placed under able leadership. Some of the finest PHILANTHROPISTS in the world are Russians. And with more Constitutional Freedom, and more scope for Legal Justice, in place of Arbitrary Punishment, both Nihilism and Conspiracy may be eradicated. Russia is shaking herself from the slumber of centuries. She still honours the memory of JOHN HOWARD, who died in the Crimea. And she gave a cordial reception to the INTERNATIONAL PRISON CONGRESS of 1890.

SPAIN AND PORTUGAL.

Spain and Portugal have peoples capable of great things, but religious bigotry has long impeded their national advancement. Spain has not yet recovered from the expulsion of the highly civilised MOORS, and the annihilation of its Protestantism, by the INQUISITION, centuries ago. Neither American nor Indian conquests have assisted to raise her much, since. She has, however, of late, made some hopeful efforts at Penal Reform, of a local and limited nature. Portugal has abolished CAPITAL PUNISHMENT and is improving her Prison Discipline by degrees.

SWITZERLAND.

This little country has latterly been honoured by the

labours and writings of some of her citizens who have
taken a very creditable position in Penology and in practical efforts to diminish Pauperism, Crime, and Ignorance.
Switzerland has the most democratic constitution in Europe,
by its " REFERENDUM." It offers its cities as centres for
philanthropic and scientific Congresses. And it manages
to secure effective National Defence, with the absence of
that burden of most nations—a great standing army. The
Swiss are unsurpassed in their arrangements for the aid of
DISCHARGED PRISONERS, and they excel also in the care of
JUVENILE OFFENDERS and neglected YOUTH.

JAPAN.

Of the three large Continents of ASIA, AFRICA, and
SOUTH AMERICA, in reference to Penal Reform (and in many
other matters also), it may almost be said that it is " *Japan
first*, and all the rest nowhere." For of all the great social
and national revolutions of the Nineteenth Century, the
change which has taken place in Japan is one of the most
marvellous. She has sent hundreds of her most intelligent
people to study and report on European and American
Institutions, and amongst other matters has adopted the
chief Western improvements in Prisons. Scarcely any
country in the world has a more completely organised
Prison System than Japan. In 1895, her Government
published an elaborate series of illustrations, depicting
almost every feature of ordinary European prison life, as
being now adopted in Japan, even including cellular
carriages for conveying prisoners. Japan also has an ably
edited JOURNAL OF PRISON DISCIPLINE; and it may be here
mentioned that its conductors translated into Japanese, for
its columns, the first edition of " Penological and Preventive
Principles." Japan sends very intelligent Delegates to the
International Prison Congresses.

OTHER COUNTRIES.

Turkey, Morocco, and other Mahometan countries have scarcely made any progress in Penal Reform during the century, but still retain the savagery of Mediæval nations. Under ISLAM, both women and prisoners will probably continue to be in a condition of almost hopeless degra. dation so long as that system lasts. MOROCCO indeed, down to the last decade of the century, has retained the barbarous punishments of blinding, of rolling to death in spiked casks, and of causing the permanent shrinkage of limbs, by gashes filled with salt. EGYPTIAN PRISONS were horrible dens, until recently reformed by British admini- strators. CHINA retains the cruel punishments of slow starvation, the wooden collar, and wholesale executions by gradually cutting off small pieces of the body. The SOUTH AMERICAN REPUBLICS, except perhaps CHILI, have made some advances in prison administration.

Doubtless, as Railways and Steam communication are developed in these regions of the world, both Penal Reform and other features of modern Civilisation will become collateral features of such changed conditions. The outlook throughout the world is, for the most part, hopeful.

INDEX.

PENOLOGICAL AND PREVENTIVE PRINCIPLES.

PERSONAL OPINIONS OF THE FIRST EDITION.

PROFESSOR FRANCIS WAYLAND,
Dean of Faculty, of Yale College, U.S.A., and State Commissioner of Prisons.

"*I do not know any work containing so many sensible and pertinent suggestions in regard to most important penological problems.* It is a mine of information on all questions which concern the TREATMENT AND PREVENTION OF CRIME.

"*Your work must be an indispensable handbook for all Penologists, in all civilised countries.*"

THE LATE CHIEF ADMINISTRATOR OF THE PRISONS OF BELGIUM (M. GAUTIER DE RASSE).

"I cannot tell you with what pleasure I have read your remarkable book, and have observed, at every step, the agreement between your opinions and mine, on the greater proportion of the questions of which you have treated in an incontestably superior manner. You have comprehensively surveyed and discussed the subjects of VAGABONDAGE, ALCOHOLISM, PROSTITUTION, NEGLECTED YOUTH, the ruin of FAMILY LIFE, and the chief CAUSES OF CRIME, and you clearly point out the means of controlling these evils. You have heartily recognised and appreciated the efforts of BELGIUM in the promotion of SEPARATE IMPRISONMENT. I entirely agree with the views which you have expressed in regard to the importance of the services and duties of the POLICE."

THE EMPRESS FREDERICK, OF GERMANY.

"COUNT SECKENDORFF has been laying this book before HER MAJESTY the EMPRESS FREDERICK, who has graciously expressed the wish to keep it. HER MAJESTY commands COUNT SECKENDORFF to say that she is reading it with great interest. COUNT SECKENDORFF is desired to thank MR. TALLACK very much for this book."

THE KING OF SWEDEN (OSCAR II.).

The KING'S SECRETARY writes:—"I am desired to express HIS MAJESTY's best thanks for ' Penological and Preventive Principles.'"

THE ROYAL LIBRARIAN (WINDSOR CASTLE).

"I have much pleasure in adding your work to the Royal Library."

THE LATE EARL OF DERBY.

" Full of interesting matter."

THE NEW YORK PRISON ASSOCIATION.

MR. WILLIAM M. F. ROUND, Secretary of this Association, and also Joint Secretary of the National Prison Association of the United States, writes :—"Permit me, on behalf of the Executive Committee of this Association, to thank you for the admirable and valuable book, received for our Library. *It is a long time since we received anything so valuable.*"

I I

General Brinkerhoff (President of the National Prison Association of the United States).

" I have read your book with great interest. and consider it one of the ablest and soundest contributions to penological literature which has ever appeared."

Mr William P. Letchworth (President of the New York State Board of Charities).

" Of the many books I have read, relating to Penology, I have found nothing in which I have been more deeply interested than in your work, entitled ' Penological and Preventive Principles.' It is full of instruction, and abounds in profitable suggestion. I wish a copy could be placed in the hands of every one in America, interested in the subject of Penology."

The late Ex-President Rutherford B. Hayes, U.S.A.

" Your work on Prisons and Crime strikes me as a valuable contribution to this interesting topic."

Right Hon. W. E. Gladstone.

" A work the importance of which I at once recognise."

The late Lord-Justice Bramwell.

" I entirely agree with your remarks as to Indiscriminate Charity. As to Sentences, nothing gave me so much anxiety and doubt. The subject is most difficult."

Professor Max Müller (Oxford University).

" Your valuable volume."

The Governor of Sing-Sing Prison, New York (Mr. A. A. Brush).

" I appreciate the book very much indeed. *The general information contained therein is just what I wanted.*"

The late Archbishop Ullathorne (Birmingham).

" I am extremely glad that you have dwelt upon the importance of a Christian Education, which cannot be too often inculcated, especially with relation to the Moral Condition of the people. Unhappily, so many political leaders are blind on this all-important question."

Dr. Aschrott (Berlin).

This German Judge, and influential Penologist, writes :—" On the whole, *it is one of the best books that has ever been written, on this interesting subject.* I shall do my best to make it known in Germany."

From a Large Prison.

" It is already added to the catalogue of the Officers' Library ; and from the numerous applications already made for it, I have no doubt it will be extensively read."

Rev. Dr. James Martineau.

" I thank you sincerely for the gift of such a guide to right judgment, and stimulus to the conscience, on problems of duty too apt to slip out of the notice of the private citizen."

THE CHAPLAIN OF PENNSYLVANIA EASTERN STATE PRISON.

"I have had the pleasure of directing the attention of His Excellency the Governor of Pennsylvania to this work."

SIR CHARLES HALL, Q.C., M.P., RECORDER OF LONDON.

Acknowledging copies of this book and of the Howard Association Annual Report:—"I have read them both with great interest, and I heartily congratulate the Association upon their efforts, which in many cases, *e.g.*, the calling attention to the First Offenders' Act, have had such successful results."

DR. LAMMASCH, PROFESSOR OF CRIMINAL LAW, VIENNA.

"I have drawn a great deal of most valuable information out of it. In an article in the *Gerichtsaal*, of Stuttgart, I drew public attention, in Germany and Austria, to this admirable work."

THE PRESS.

This book has been very favourably noticed by the Press at home and abroad.

THE "REFORMATORY AND REFUGE JOURNAL" (LONDON) remarks:—

"Few people have more carefully studied the various topics dealt with in this work, than the Secretary of the Howard Association. He does not, however, confine himself to his own deductions, but very frankly draws upon the experience and learning of others; and quotations are freely given of the opinions of nearly every student of Penology, of any eminence, at home and abroad. In not a few instances, antagonistic opinions are quoted, and the author does not venture to 'decide where doctors disagree,' but endeavours to make manifest, through the mist of differences, both of opinion and practice, 'a preponderance of experience in certain directions.' As a book of reference, the work is doubtless more valuable than it would have been, if the author had only called into his service such experts as would endorse his own views."

WERTHEIMER, LEA & Co., Printers, Circus Place, London Wall.

9 781330 067055